Four Paths
to Jerusalem

ALSO BY HUNT JANIN

*Fort Bridger, Wyoming: Trading Post for
Indians, Mountain Men and Westward Migrants*
(McFarland, 2001)

The India-China Opium Trade in the Nineteenth Century
(McFarland, 1999)

Four Paths to Jerusalem

Jewish, Christian, Muslim, and Secular Pilgrimages, 1000 BCE to 2001 CE

by HUNT JANIN

McFarland & Company, Inc., Publishers

Jefferson, North Carolina, and London

The present work is a reprint of the illustrated case bound edition of Four Paths to Jerusalem: Jewish, Christian, Muslim, and Secular Pilgrimages, 1000 BCE to 2001 CE, *first published in 2002 by McFarland.*

LIBRARY OF CONGRESS CATALOGUING-IN-PUBLICATION DATA

Janin, Hunt, 1940–
    Four paths to Jerusalem : Jewish, Christian, Muslim, and secular
pilgrimages, 1000 BCE to 2001 CE / by Hunt Janin.
        p. cm.
    Includes bibliographical references and index.

    ISBN 0-7864-2730-2 (softcover : 50# alkaline paper) ∞

    1. Jerusalem—History.   2. Jewish pilgrims and pilgrimages—
Jerusalem.   3. Christian pilgrims and pilgrimages—Jerusalem.
4. Muslim pilgrims and pilgrimages—Jerusalem.   I. Title.
DS109.9.J38   2006
291.3'5'09569442—dc21   2002000157

British Library cataloguing data are available

On the cover (clockwise): A Palestinian in the Old City; Roman Catholic priests in a side-chapel of the Church of the Holy Sepulcher; the Dome of the Rock; and a Jew at the Western Wall *(all photographs by the author)*

Manufactured in the United States of America

McFarland & Company, Inc., Publishers
  Box 611, Jefferson, North Carolina 28640
  www.mcfarlandpub.com

To the Rev. Craig Eder (born 1919).

He puts others first.

Contents

List of Maps	viii
Preface	ix
Introduction	1

   I. Ghostly and Other Pilgrims — 9

  II. A Primer on the Importance of Jerusalem — 19

 III. The Old City — 36

 IV. Beginnings of the Jerusalem Pilgrimage: The First and Second Temples (c. 1000 BCE–63 BCE) — 42

  V. Pilgrims Under Roman and Byzantine Rule (63 BCE–638 CE) — 50

 VI. The Early Islamic Period: Christian and Muslim Pilgrimages (638–1095) — 69

 VII. "A Pilgrimage in Arms": The First Crusade and Its Aftermath (1095–1187) — 86

VIII. More Crusades and More Pilgrims: The Ayyubid and Mamluk Dynasties (1187–1517) — 110

 IX. Pilgrimages Under Ottoman Rule (1517–1917) — 148

  X. Pilgrimages During the British Mandate and Under the Israelis (1917–2001) — 187

 XI. A Summing-Up: "Unity in Diversity" and the Symbolism of the Journey — 202

Selected Chronology — 207

Appendix I. Selected List of Accounts Cited, in Chronological Order — 215

Appendix II. The Destruction of the Herodian Temple: An Account by Flavius Josephus, 70 CE — 217

Appendix III. The Travels of St. Willibald, 720–726   219

Appendix IV. List of the Presents Brought Home from Jerusalem
             by Nompar de Caumont, 1420   221

Appendix V. Instructions for Christian Pilgrims, c. 1484   223

Appendix VI. Balfour and the Zionists   225

Appendix VII. Reports by Albright Fellows, 1990–2000   227

Notes   229

Selected Bibliography   249

Index   259

List of Maps

Israel today (CIA World Factbook 2000)   2

Circular map of the world, thirteenth century (The British Library)   17

Jerusalem: the Old City (Eklectica Graphic Design)   37

Mini-map from Bernhard von Breydenbach's map of Jerusalem, 1486
     (Courtesy of the Osher Map Library, University of Southern Maine)   138

Medieval "T in O" map (Eklectica Graphic Design)   171

Preface

Four Paths to Jerusalem is written for the general reader—that is, for someone with no special knowledge of this tangled subject. Its goals are clarity and simplicity, not academic hairsplitting. At the same time, however, it tries to fill a scholarly gap.

A staggering amount has been written about pilgrimages in general and about Christian pilgrimages in particular. However, computer trawls through the extensive holdings of the British Library in London suggest that no other book has so far been published, at least in English or in French, which (1) focuses exclusively on and gives equal weight to Jewish, Christian, Muslim and secular pilgrimages to Jerusalem over the last 3,000 years and (2) relies heavily on contemporary accounts. To the best of my knowledge, then, this book is unique.

I owe thanks to many people. These include Petronella van Gorkom; Brother James Koester of the Society of St. John the Evangelist; Nanda Harvey Purcell; Dr. Rupert Chapman and Felicity Cobbing, both of the Palestine Exploration Fund; and Michele Janin. The Rev. Craig Eder shared with me his experiences as a pilgrim in the Holy Land, England, Ireland and Scotland. These ladies and gentlemen read parts of this book and gave me trenchant editorial and substantive suggestions.

If, despite the efforts of these people and others, factual errors remain in the book, they are my fault alone.

Hunt Janin
St. Urcisse, France
January 2002

I was glad when they said to me:
"Let us go to the house of the Lord!"
At last our feet are standing
Within your gates, O Jerusalem!

Psalm 122: 1–2

Introduction

The book you have in your hands is an overview—more accurately, a *chronicle*—of pilgrimages to Jerusalem over the last 3,000 years. It is drawn from more than 165 contemporary accounts of travels to that ancient city known in English as Jerusalem, in Hebrew as *Yerushalayim* and in Arabic as *al-Quds* ("The Holy"). Sacred to three world faiths, Jerusalem has been a major pilgrim destination for more than three millennia. Its pull remains very strong today. During the 1990s, for example, an average of nearly 2,000,000 "tourist-pilgrims" visited Israel each year.[1] This rose to a total of 2,670,000 visitors in 2000.[2]

The millennial year 2000, highlighted by the pilgrimage of Pope John Paul II, was expected to draw more than 3,000,000 pilgrims to the Holy City. That, however, did not happen. The lethal brew of religion and politics which is so characteristic of Jerusalem flared up again that autumn. On 28 September 2000, Ariel Sharon, a right-wing politician who was later elected Prime Minister of Israel, led a delegation of his supporters, escorted by more than 1,000 Israeli police officers, to a sacred center known to Jews as the Temple Mount and to Muslims as the Haram al-Sharif, i.e., the "Noble Sanctuary."[3] (The terms Temple Mount and Haram al-Sharif will be used interchangeably in this book.)

Then–Prime Minister Ehud Barak did not prohibit this visit because he believed it was only a political ploy by Sharon to influence the Israeli electorate. Sharon himself, however, said that his visit was designed to demonstrate Israeli sovereignty over this hotly contested site. Events the next day proved that the visit had been highly provocative. On 29 September 2000, a large number of unarmed Palestinian demonstrators threw stones at Israeli police near of the Western (Wailing) Wall of the Old City. The police replied by firing rubber-coated bullets and live ammunition at these young men, killing four of them and wounding about 200 others. Fourteen Israeli policemen were injured.

This confrontation proved to be the catalyst for a broadly-based Palestinian uprising known as the *Al-Aqsa intifada*, that is, an uprising which began at the Al-Aqsa Mosque on the Haram al-Sharif. The *intifada* was essentially a protest by Palestinians against Israeli hegemony and especially against Israel's policy of establishing permanent Jewish settlements in the West Bank and in the Gaza Strip. These are former Arab territories which Israel has occupied since the 1967 war. The Israelis claim them as their biblical birthright. The Palestinians, for their part, claim them as the basis of a future Palestinian state.

1

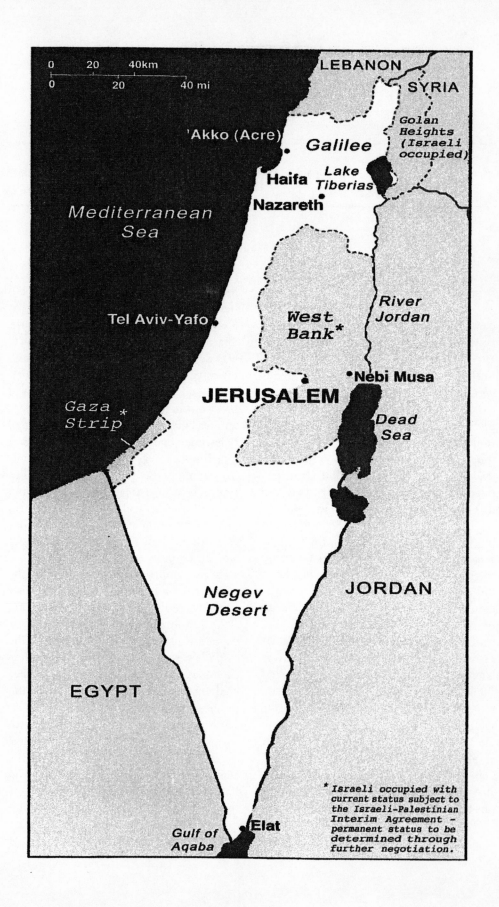

When this book was finished (January 2002), the conflict still continued. More than 1,000 people, three-quarters of them Palestinians, had been killed. Many other people had been wounded.

The effect of the *intifada* on pilgrimage was predictable: fearing for their own safety, people stayed away from the Holy Land. According to the mayor of Bethlehem, only 400 pilgrims came to Bethlehem to celebrate Christmas Eve 2000—a sharp contrast to the 10,000 people who had been there the previous year.[4] Jews living abroad stayed away, too, canceling or postponing trips to Israel. This prompted the Israeli transportation minister to criticize as "disgraceful" the behavior of Jews "who for all these years have talked about the unity of the Jewish people over mounds of bagel and lox."[5]

The *intifada* thus drove home the fact that Jerusalem remains one of the most intractable religious and political problems of modern times. Both Israelis and Palestinians reach deep into their interlocked histories to support their claims. Both want to control key holy places. Both have an unshakeable attachment to the Holy City as their legitimate capital. Both insist on the "right of return" for their people.[6] Despite the best efforts of the United States and other interested countries, it has so far proved impossible to reconcile their antithetical demands. All that seems certain is that Jerusalem will continue to be a flashpoint for the foreseeable future.

Secular pilgrims

The description "secular pilgrim" may seem to be a contradiction in terms but it is in fact a legitimate concept.[7] Secular pilgrims are men and women who travel to Jerusalem not for religious reasons but to pursue their own academic, literary, historical, scientific, political, military, artistic or other interests. Of course, many secular pilgrims hold religious beliefs, too, but these are not the main reason for their journey to Jerusalem. The American humorist Mark Twain is a good case in point. He was at least nominally a Christian but the reason he visited the Holy City in 1867 was to gather material for what would become an extraordinarily popular travel book, *The Innocents Abroad* (1869).

Jerusalem is not a sacred center for secular pilgrims as it is for the faithful, but it can be equally important in other ways. The famous British surveyor Claude Reignier Conder gave a clear explanation of why the Palestine Exploration Fund—a classically secular institution—was set up in London in 1865. It was the result, he said, of a conviction

> forced upon the minds of a very large number of scholars, travellers, and persons interested in science and sacred history, that the state of our knowledge of Palestine was very far from what it ought to be; and that, to make it as complete as possible, individual effort must give way to such scientific exploration as can only be obtained by organised expeditions conducted by specially-trained and qualified explorers.[8]

Secular motives are visible in many other fields as well. During World War I, British Prime Minister Lloyd George hoped that a dramatic victory in the Middle East would divert public attention from the endless carnage of trench warfare

Opposite: Israel borders the Mediterranean Sea, between Egypt and Lebanon, and is slightly smaller than the American state of New Jersey. Its population is about 5,900,000, of whom 80 percent are Jewish. (CIA World Factbook 2000.)

Wearing bullet-proof vests and carrying collapsible 9 mm submachine guns, these Israeli security guards were standing duty on the Christian Via Dolorosa ("Way of Sorrows") in the southern part of the Muslim Quarter on Easter Day, 2001. (Photograph by the author.)

The Dome of the Rock overlooks the Western (Wailing) Wall. (Photograph by the author.)

in France. He therefore told his military staff that as a Christmas present for the British people he wanted the liberation of Jerusalem, which he called "the most famous city in the world."[9] As a result, General Allenby captured the Holy City in November 1917. To show his great respect for it, however, he entered it like a pilgrim, on foot rather than on horseback.

Secular pilgrims have even made their way to the Holy City simply to pursue *gambling* interests. Some members of the aristocratic Hellfire Club, which was founded in Dublin in 1735 and which by its own admission was dedicated to gambling, whoring and profanity, walked all the way to Jerusalem (after first crossing the Irish Sea and the English channel by ship) simply to play handball against Judaism's most sacred relic, the 65-yard long Western (Wailing) Wall, in order to win a £15,000 bet.[10]

Relying on contemporary accounts

Four Paths to Jerusalem makes a special point of letting the Jerusalem pilgrims speak for themselves. This is the reason for the unusual number of long, direct quotes in this book. It would have been easy enough to paraphrase them but in their original, if translated, form they convey the flavor of their times much better than any modern paraphrase possibly can. To keep the text as lively as possible, these quotes are not burdened with scholarly commentaries. They are all taken from published sources, which can be consulted for further information should the reader desire it. To help the reader place these works in historical context, the authors or titles of 165 of these contemporary accounts are listed in chronological order in Appendix I.

There is a tradeoff inherent in relying

so heavily on these first-hand accounts. They do impart a refreshing "I-was-there" quality to the text, but they do not explain the ups and downs of Jerusalem's political economy, i.e., why the city was thriving at one point but depressed at another. Unfortunately, limitations of space make it impossible to go into this kind of detail. The reader who is interested in the reasons for the ever-changing fortunes of the city should consult some of the sources listed below.

Sources

It is one of the ironies of history that although only a small percentage of pilgrims left any written record of their travels, there have been so many pilgrims over so many years that in the end an immense amount has been written about Jerusalem. Long before the modern period—between the years 333 and 1500, for example— Christian pilgrims wrote more than 550 accounts of their journeys.[11] Not surprisingly, these sources were produced in many different languages. For the Middle Ages alone, primary sources exist in eight or nine languages, and secondary sources are available in at least six additional languages.

It is evident that no one today can master so many different works. The great bibliographic and linguistic diversity of sources on Jerusalem thus has one important consequence: modern writers must be very selective in choosing between and citing from a nearly endless variety of sources. If the reader's favorite source or personality has been overlooked, this need for selectivity is probably the reason.

As mentioned earlier, *Four Paths to Jerusalem* is a *chronicle* of Jerusalem pilgrimages, not a history of them. In other words, it presents a continuous, relatively straightforward account of events arranged in order of time. Unlike a history, it does not try to ferret out, or to impose, a thematic order which purports to prove what these events really "mean." The reader of this book must be the ultimate judge of what the Jerusalem pilgrimage means.

Those who want a thematic survey of Jerusalem's history could well begin with a source used extensively here: *The History of Jerusalem* (1997), an excellent, wide-ranging account by Karen Armstrong, a former Roman Catholic nun. Simon Coleman and John Elsner's *Pilgrimage Past and Present* (1995) gives good summaries of sacred travel in all the major religions of the world. The *Encyclopaedia Britannica Online* and the powerful Internet search engine www.google.com are both exceptionally useful reference tools for names, dates, places and sometimes for texts as well.

Readers with an academic bent may be interested in three recent compilations: *Jerusalem: The Holy City in the Eyes of Chroniclers, Visitors, Pilgrims, and Prophets from the Days of Abraham to the Beginnings of Modern Times*, edited by F.E. Peters (1985); *City of the Great King: Jerusalem from David to the Present*, edited by Nitza Rosovsky (1996); and *Jerusalem: Its Sanctity and Centrality to Judaism, Christianity, and Islam* (1999), edited by Lee I. Levine.

Some of the best primary sources on Christian pilgrimages are contained in the 14 volumes translated by the Palestine Pilgrims' Text Society between 1887 and 1897. John Wilkinson's *Jerusalem Pilgrims Before the Crusades* (1977) is equally valuable. Danielle Régnier-Bohler's *Croisades et Pèlerinages: Récits, Chroniques et Voyages en Terre Sainte, XIIe–XVIe Siècle* (1997) is excellent, too.

Jewish and Muslim pilgrimages to Jerusalem in early times are less well documented, at least in English and French. Fortunately, there are some exceptions. The most accessible early Jewish sources are the Hebrew Scriptures themselves—the books of the Old Testament of the Bible, which represent the sacred teachings of the ancient Israelites. For reasons discussed in Chapter II, however, these scriptures must be used with caution. Other Jewish sources are the works of Flavius Josephus, a Jewish priest, scholar, soldier, historian and traitor who was born in Jerusalem in 37/38 CE and who died in Rome in 100. Elkan Nathan Adler's *Jewish Travellers in the Middle Ages: 19 Firsthand Accounts* (1987) is extremely useful as well.

Excellent sources for Muslim pilgrimages to Jerusalem and Muslim religious activities within the city itself are Amikam Elad's *Medieval Jerusalem and Islamic Worship* (1995) and Francesco Gabrieli's *Arab Historians of the Crusades* (1993). Another helpful work is Amin Maalouf's 1983 compilation, *Les croisades vues par les Arabes* (*The Crusades as seen by the Arabs*).

Keeping the historical record and religious sensitivities in sight

More than 3,000 years of history are involved here. To keep the historical record clearly in sight, seven of the eleven chapters will begin with a brief historical overview of the major developments of their era. Subheadings have been used extensively here. A relevant date will usually be given after the name of an important event or a memorable person mentioned in the subheading.

If the reader is to understand why Jerusalem has been so important to so many people for so long, some familiarity with Judaism, Christianity, Islam and with certain secular issues is critically important. For this reason, Chapter II risks offering some comments on the importance of Jerusalem to these three major religions and to secular interests as well. The

word "risk" is used advisedly here because religion has always been such a sensitive issue in the Holy Land that it will surely be impossible to please all readers.

Religious sensitivities there are always ready to erupt. Even what might appear to be purely secular undertakings frequently get caught up in Jerusalem's lethal brew of religion and politics. Archeology is perhaps the best case in point. Excavations are invariably seen as threatening the integrity of long-buried ruins sacred to one, two or three world religions. In 1996, for example, Israeli prime minister Benjamin Netanyahu authorized the opening of a tunnel along the deeply buried base of the Haram al–Sharif. This was done without prior consultation with the Muslims, who therefore saw it as an unjustified assertion of Israeli sovereignty over East Jerusalem. Passions ran so high that in the ensuing "Tunnel War" riots, 62 Palestinians and 14 Israelis were killed.[12]

Dates

Dates are given here as BCE (Before the Common Era) or as CE (Common Era), the Common Era referring to the years since the birth of Christ. To avoid repetition, after the first CE date is cited, only numbers will be used in most cases for later dates, e.g., "The Muslim Caliph Omar I conquered Jerusalem in 638."

Sometimes, due to differences between the Jewish, Christian and Muslim calendars, it is difficult to date certain events with great precision. For example, the destruction of the First Temple is variously given as 587 BCE and as 586 BCE. When different dates are given, both will be cited here, separated by an oblique, e.g., "In 538/537 BCE the Persian King Cyrus the Great gave the Jews permission to return to Jerusalem and rebuild the Temple."

Place-names

National boundaries have changed so much and so frequently over the last 3,000 years that to simplify matters this book will usually refer to countries as they exist today. For example, the *bedouin* were camel-mounted nomadic Arabs who attacked unescorted pilgrims bound for Jerusalem. Rather than explaining that some of the *bedouin* came out of the Hejaz and that this region is the northwestern coast of what is now Saudi Arabia, the reference would simply be to "*bedouin* from Saudi Arabia."

Appendices, endnotes and a summing-up

Seven appendices and a selected chronology at the end of this book highlight matters which are relevant but too detailed to be discussed in the text. The text will stand alone, but readers are encouraged to consult the endnotes. These have been used freely here, not only for attribution, but also to elaborate on historically relevant points that might break up the flow of the text proper.

Despite Palestinian uprisings or other disturbances, pilgrimages to Jerusalem are certain to continue. The pilgrims of the future, whether religious or secular, will have much in common with today's pilgrims and with those of the distant past. They, too, will come from many different countries and for many different reasons. Their experiences, however, no matter how varied, are likely to fall under two broad themes. The first theme is the "unity in diversity" of the Jerusalem pilgrimage; the second is the symbolism of the journey itself. Both of them will be discussed in the last chapter of the book, which attempts a summing-up of three millennia of the Jerusalem pilgrimage.

I

Ghostly and Other Pilgrims

In many regions of the world, pilgrimage is still popular today but it is not as familiar a part of the Western cultural landscape as it once was. Some readers may know relatively little about this very human activity, which is more complicated and more extensive than it might appear at first glance. For this reason, it is important for us to begin by pulling together a number of disparate items to set the stage for the chapters to come. These items are:

- the definition of "pilgrim"
- the problem of belief
- pilgrimage as a long-running human activity
- the pilgrims in Chaucer's *Canterbury Tales*
- reasons for the popularity of pilgrimage
- Jerusalem as a sacred center
- returning home
- critics of pilgrimage

Pilgrim defined

A pilgrim is a man or a woman who makes a journey, sometimes a long and difficult journey, to a sacred place. There are many and frequently overlapping reasons for pilgrimages: to seek spiritual perfection, to ask for supernatural help in some enterprise, to express devotion, to perform an act of penance,[13] to give thanks, to search for secular knowledge or simply to have a good time.

Two British tour leaders who have led or participated in more than 30 Christian pilgrim tours to the Holy Land say that a pilgrimage typically has three components: (1) it can be a pleasant holiday, (2) traveling with like-minded people is a major source of enjoyment, and (3) it can lead to a spiritual reawakening and reaffirmation of faith.[14] Perhaps we can run their first two points together and repeat that, historically, one of the best reasons to go on a pilgrimage has been to see new places and meet new people.

This "enjoyment factor" must not be overlooked. Of the many contemporary examples that could be cited to prove it, let us take only two. First, in the twelfth century, Maurice of Sully, Bishop of Paris, wondered aloud whether pilgrimages were of any spiritual use whatsoever if those who undertook them "left their villages but not their vices behind."[15] Second, when the Lollard priest William Thorpe appeared before the Archbishop of Canterbury in 1407 on a charge of heresy, Thorpe was eloquent in his denunciation of pilgrimages:

> Also, Sir, I know well, that when divers men and women will go thus [on pilgrimage] after their own wills, and

finding out one pilgrimage, they will ordain with them before[hand] to have with them both men and women that can well sing wanton songs; and some other pilgrims will have with them bagpipes; so that every town that they come through, what with the noise of their singing and the sound of their piping … they make more noise than if the King came there away, with all his clarions and other minstrels. And if these men and women be a month out in their pilgrimage, many of them shall be, a half year later, great janglers [idle, noisy people], tale-tellers, and liars.[16]

Nevertheless, what most pilgrims (excluding secular visitors, who will be discussed later) have in common is some degree of genuine religious belief. Indeed, since the end of the fifth century, many Christian pilgrims, consciously or not, have sided with St. Augustine. In his magisterial work *The City of God*, written between 413 CE and 426 CE, Augustine divided mankind into two camps. There are those, he said, who are merely the citizens of "Babylon," the *civitas terrena* or earthly city, which is the symbol of self-love and carnal desire.

In contrast, there are also the more enlightened, spiritually alert men and women who do not chase after the vanities of this world but who yearn instead for "the heavenly city" above, that is, the otherworldly Jerusalem—the *civitas Dei*, or City of God.[17] But despite the yearnings of this latter group for consummation with the divine, the City of God can never be attained in this world. It follows that, according to Augustine, everyone who seeks the City of God must therefore become a perpetual *peregrinus* ("pilgrim") committed to a ceaseless *peregrinatio* (literally "going abroad," i.e., going off on a pilgrimage).[18]

Although the English words "pilgrim" and "pilgrimage" are accurate trans-lations of their Latin originals, they fail to capture *the sense of exile* or of *being a stranger* which is strongly implicit in Augustine's conviction that mankind is separated from God. (Indeed, *peregrinus* was a technical term in Roman law. A *peregrinus* was a resident alien, i.e., a stranger, a person without friends, kinsmen or patrons.[19]) To end this estrangement from God, Augustine believed that men and women must cut their ties to worldly matters and should focus instead on attaining the City of God. In theological terms, this quest was feasible because it was thought that a strong, mutual attraction existed between God and man. Augustine assured his readers that the City of God was *actively seeking them*:

> The Heavenly City, while on its earthly pilgrimage, calls forth its citizens from every nation and assembles a multilingual band of pilgrims; not caring about any diversity in the customs, laws and institutions whereby they severally make provision for the achievement and maintenance of earthly peace.[20]

It remained an article of faith well into the Middle Ages that all human beings are called to their heavenly origin. As the German Dominican mystic Meister Eckehart put it in a memorable phrase, *earth cannot escape the sky*.[21]

The concept of a pilgrim as an exile and a stranger has struck a responsive chord in many people. In 1630, for example, William Bradford, governor of the English Puritans who founded the colony of Plymouth, Massachusetts, said of his colleagues: "They knew they were but pilgrimes, & looked not much on those [earthly] things; but lift up their eyes to ye heavens, their dearest cuntrie."[22] The seventeenth century English author John Bunyan made this same point, too. His famous religious allegory, *The Pilgrim's Progress*, which at one time rivaled the

Bible in popularity, was a guidebook for a spiritual pilgrimage to Jerusalem. Bunyan explicitly tells his reader:

This Book will make a Travailer [traveler] of thee,
If by its Counsel thou will ruled be;
It will direct thee to the Holy Land,
If thou wilt its Directions understand.[23]

In Part I of *Pilgrim's Progress*, written in 1678, Bunyan's protagonist, a "poor burdened sinner" aptly named Christian, makes his way with great difficulty from the City of Destruction to the heavenly city of Mount Zion (one of Jerusalem's many names[24]) so that he may be saved "from the Wrath to come." In Part II, written in 1684, Christian's wife, his son and his companions manage to join him in Mount Zion. In a poem which later became a favorite hymn and is still sung today, one of Christian's companions, Mr. Valiant-for-Truth, sums up Bunyan's vision of life as a ceaseless spiritual pilgrimage:

He who would valiant be
'Gainst all disaster,
Let him in constancy
Follow the Master.
There's no discouragement
Shall make him once relent
His first avowed intent
To be a pilgrim....

Since, Lord, thou dost defend
Us with thy Spirit,
We know we at the end
Shall life inherit.
Then fancies flee away!
I'll fear not what men say,
I'll labor night and day
To be a pilgrim.[25]

The problem of belief

It is important for us to keep in mind here that, historically speaking, widespread atheism is a recent phenomenon. Atheism was very rare in the ancient and medieval world, where nearly everyone took it for granted that a divine reality existed and had to be honored. While in the past many people may have had private doubts about the existence of God, they did not set them down on paper. It is not until the eighteenth century that we find one of the first Europeans to do so: a French country priest named Jean Meslier, who died in 1729 and who left a memoir testifying to his atheism.[26] At that date this was a very dangerous stand to take publicly, however, as witnessed by the fact that 20 years later the French philosopher Denis Diderot was jailed for publishing *A Letter to the Blind for the Use of Those Who See*, which put forward a full-blown atheism.[27]

Thus we must never forget that in the past—and certainly in traditional societies today—the average person has, as least publicly, always been a believer. The American historian Barbara Tuchman used this fact to stress how different the medieval Christian world was from our own. The main barrier to our understanding the Middle Ages, she said, is

the Christian religion as it then was: the matrix and law of medieval life, omnipresent, indeed compulsory. Its insistent principle that the life of the spirit and of the afterworld was superior to the here and now, to material life on earth, is one that the modern world does not share.... The rupture of this principle and its replacement by belief in the worth of the individual and of an active life not necessarily focused on God is, in fact, what created the modern world....[28]

Our own secular age is in this fundamental respect quite different from anything in the past and quite different from traditional societies today. One token of

Christianity was the focal point of medieval life. These sculptures adorn a pillar in the Cathedral of St. Caprais in Agen, southwestern France. Since most people in the Middle Ages were illiterate, they were taught about Biblical events by sermons and by graphic representations. French pilgrims returning to Agen from Jerusalem brought back with them stories of kings and nobles they had seen or heard about in the Holy Land. Sculptors later turned these stories into enduring works of art to instruct the faithful. (Photograph courtesy Bernard Shaw.)

this change is that the word "ghostly" was commonly used in English, beginning in about 900, to mean "sacred activities" or "sacred people." In Old English, *gast* (the source of our own word "ghost") meant "spirit" or "soul." The *Oxford English Dictionary* defines "a ghostly day" as a day set apart for worship. Many contemporary examples of "ghostly" could be cited.

The fourteenth century English pilgrim Margery Kempe, who suffered from uncontrollable "boystous" crying spells because of the intensity of her religious feelings, said that while most people found her affliction extremely annoying, "other ghostly men loved her and favored her the more."[29] Another example is Walter Hilton, the greatest English mystic of the fourteenth century, who wrote *The Ladder* (or *Scale*) *of Perfection* for a nun who lived alone in her cell. Hilton hailed this recluse as his "ghostly sister in Jesus Christ" and defined the genuine pilgrim as being a "ghostly pilgrim":

> Right as a true pilgrim going to Jerusalem, leaveth behind him his house and land, wife and child, and maketh himself poor and bare from all that he hath, that he may go lightly without letting: right so, if thou wilt be a ghostly pilgrim, thou shalt make thyself naked from all that thou wouldst be at Jerusalem, and at none other place but there.[30]

We shall follow this ancient usage in much of this book by looking primarily at *the ghostly pilgrim*, that is, at the pilgrim whose motivation for making a journey to a holy place is primarily spiritual, rather than being purely secular or a longing to see new places.

Pilgrimage: a long-running human activity

It is certain that in prehistoric times people traveled to distant sites which for one reason or another struck them as being particularly sacred—perhaps to a miraculous spring, a mountain, a cave or even to a tree. At these cultic centers, they believed, deities revealed themselves, oracles spoke, miracles occurred and holy men and women could be revered. Sacrifices—agricultural products or livestock—could be offered to the gods as tokens of homage and thanksgiving.[31] Ever since these long-lost beginnings of pilgrimage, it has been a universal and highly popular human activity. Within historic times the tracks of the ghostly pilgrim are always visible.

The ancient Syrians, for example, visited holy places, usually temples. In Sophocles' play *Oedipus Tyrannus*, King Laios is on a pilgrimage when he is met and killed by his own son, Oedipus.[32] Celtic pilgrims known as *gyrovagi* were "wanderers for God" and traveled more or less at random.[33] Hindus from all over India still go to Varanasi, Allahabad or other holy sites along the course of the Ganges River to worship or to die, seeking salvation there by a last immersion in or a last sip of the redeeming waters of the river. In 1995, in fact, an estimated 12,000,000 Hindus visited Varanasi. This was the greatest gathering of pilgrims in recorded history.

In 2001, more than 7,000,000 Hindus, led by 200,000 ash-smeared *sadhus* (ascetic holy men), bathed in the Ganges near Allahabad on the first of four "royal bathing days" during the Kumbh Mela festival.[34] Other Hindus make the long trek from India to Pashupatinath (near Kathmandu, Nepal), where the holy Bagmati river flows. The site of Pashupatinath itself dates from 500 BCE and its temple buildings date from 200 CE. In going there, the Hindus are following the teachings of the Indian epic *Mahabharata*, which recommends that pilgrimages should be made to places known for the extraordinary power of their earth and the efficacy of their healing waters.[35]

Tibetan traders wintering in Nepal still prostrate themselves before the great *stupas* (Buddhist temples) of Swayambhunath and Bodhanath. Pilgrims have a wide choice of holy sites in Nepal because there are no fewer than 3,000 Buddhist and Hindu temples and religious monuments in the Kathmandu valley alone.[36] Buddhists also pay their respects at Bodhgaya in northern India, where the Buddha attained enlightenment, and at other shrines commemorating his life.[37] In the eighteenth century, the king of Siam (Thailand) and his extensive entourage used 120 ornately carved rowing barges to convey them up the Chaophraya river, once a year, to the temple of Phra Phutthabat, where they revered the Buddha's Footprint.[38]

Each year, more than 2,000,000 Muslims from all over the world flock to Mecca in Saudi Arabia. Jews, Christians, and Muslims make their way to Jerusalem. Christians also visit a host of other sacred places in Europe. Rome and Santiago de Compostela (in the northwestern corner of Spain) have historically been the two most important pilgrim destinations after Jerusalem itself.[39] Marian pilgrimages (to places associated with Mary, the mother of Jesus) have also drawn large numbers of the faithful to sites in Italy, Switzerland, Portugal and France. Each year between 3,000,000 and 5,000,000 pilgrims come to a miraculous spring in Lourdes, France, where the Virgin Mary is believed to have appeared to a 14-year-old girl in 1858. Pilgrimages are still important parts of life in Latin America and in other regions of the world.

Chaucer and The Canterbury Tales

Pilgrimage has often featured in literature, too. The best account of it ever written is *The Canterbury Tales*, begun around 1386–1387 by the English poet Geoffrey Chaucer but never finished. Since nothing like *The Canterbury Tales* exists for the Jerusalem pilgrimage, we will use Chaucer to get an idea of the different kinds of men and women who made long journeys to holy centers. (We will see from *The Canterbury Tales* that pilgrimage could be lighthearted and jolly as well as penitential and burdensome.)

In the General Prologue to *The Canterbury Tales*, Chaucer introduces us to the idea of pilgrimage with these memorable lines:

Whan that April with his showres soote
The drought of March hath perced to
    the roote....
Than longen folk to goon on pilgrim-
    ages,
And palmeres for to seeken straunge
    strondes,
To fern halwes, kouth in sundry londes;
And specially, from every shires ende
Of Engelond, to Canterbury they wende,
The holy blissful martyr for to seeke,
That hem hath holpen whan that they
    were seke.[40]

An informal translation of this Middle English would be:

As soon as spring comes, people are eager to set off on pilgrimages. Experi-

enced pilgrims [known as "palmers" because of the palm branches, broken off in Jericho, which they carried as proof of having been to the Holy Land] long to seek out the distant shrines they know of in foreign countries. And especially, from the far corners of every county in England, pilgrims went to Canterbury, to the shrine of St. Thomas Becket, because he had helped them when they were sick.

The popularity of medieval pilgrimages is clear from the surprisingly wide variety of people who went on them. Although Chaucer himself never made the pilgrimage to Canterbury, he uses poetic license and tells us that when he was staying at the Tabard (a London inn near the River Thames) and was getting ready to depart on a pilgrimage to Canterbury,

At night was come into that hostelrye
Well nine and twenty of a compaignye
Of sundry folk, by aventure y-falle
In fellawship, and pilgrims were they alle
That toward Canterbury wolden ride.[41]

Pilgrimage was an exceptionally useful literary device for Chaucer because it allowed him to group together and tell the tales of members of many different layers of fourteenth-century English society. His pilgrims included a knight, a squire, a peasant farmer (the yeoman), a prioress, a nun, a monk, a friar, a merchant, an Oxford student, a high-ranking legal official, an important landowner, a dealer in small goods, a carpenter, a weaver, a dyer, a rug-maker, a cook, a ship's captain, a medical doctor, a bawdy housewife (the five-times married Wife of Bath, who had made the pilgrimage to Jerusalem three times and had visited many of the great European pilgrimage sites as well),[42] a parish priest, a common laborer (the plowman), a miller, a purchasing agent for a law school, a farm manager, a police officer, and a minor religious official who sold indulgences to pardon sins (the pardoner).

Why has pilgrimage always been so popular?

The continuing popularity of *The Canterbury Tales* raises the question of why so many people have been so interested in pilgrimages for so long. There are two answers to this. The first is that pilgrimage has something for everyone. On an elementary level, it may be physically challenging but in many other ways it can be both enjoyable and instructive.

Let us use a few of Chaucer's pilgrims as examples. The Wife of Bath is on the lookout for a new husband, in case she has to replace her present spouse (her fifth). She tells us this explicitly:

> Of five husbands scoleying I am [I have
> studied five husbands like a scholar] –
> Welcome the sixte whan that ever he
> shall!
> For sith I wol not keep me chaste in all
> [entirely],
> Whan mine husband is fro the world
> y-gon
> Some Christian man shall wedde me
> anon.[43]

The pardoner is far from being an ascetic. "I wol not do no labour with mine handes," he assures us, "Nay, I wol drinke licour of the vine/And have a jolly wench in every town!"[44] What about Chaucer's plowman? Given the relatively static nature of medieval society, this is probably the first time he has ever left his native village—probably, in fact, it will be his only chance to travel and see something of the wider world. Such wanderlust applied to Jerusalem, too, as well as to Canterbury. Barbara Tuchman believed, in fact, that "most often, it was neither piety or sin, but *pure love of travel*, that carried the generations of English pilgrims to Palestine."[45]

For their part, Chaucer's miller and the other businessmen will certainly be interested in the intricate commercial arrangements which permitted cities like Canterbury, Jerusalem and Mecca to feed, lodge and otherwise accommodate large numbers of pilgrims.[46] The pardoner hopes to find a ready market in Canterbury for the indulgences he sells. A noble soldier—Chaucer's "veray, parfait gentil knight"—would remember his own travels and achievements during the Crusades, which, as we will see, contemporary writers described as "pilgrimages in arms."

The second answer to the question of why pilgrimage has attracted so many people is a more weighty one. The fundamental pull of pilgrimage is not its amorous, travel or scholarly qualities but its *ghostly* dimension. Chaucer's parish priest draws a parallel between the worldly pilgrimage to Canterbury that he and his colleagues are embarked on and the higher pilgrimage toward the heavenly Jerusalem itself. The latter he describes as "the parfait glorious pilgrimage / That highte Jerusalem Celestial."[47] Many other cases could be cited, too. For example, in 1531 an English friar and printer with the wonderful name of Wynkn de Worde printed a book on pilgrimage, in which he called the attention of the faithful to "Ye heuenly Ierusalem [*sic*] to the whiche we journey."[48]

Jerusalem as a sacred center

Pilgrimage's ghostly dimension is of singular importance and has attracted many modern scholars. One of the best known was the historian of comparative religion Mircea Eliade, who studied sacred geography, particularly what he called "the sacred center." A sacred center can

variously be a special tree (or, by extension, the Christian cross), a mountain, a
palace, a temple or a tomb. It is the point
where the three cosmic regions—traditionally defined as heaven, earth and
hell—come together. As such, it can be a
source of great spiritual power. Martin
Robinson, a modern student of pilgrimages, tells us that

> The holy place is seen as a physical lo-
> cation where the membrane between
> this world and a reality beyond is espe-
> cially thin, where a transcendent reality
> impinges on the immanent. The hope-
> ful traveller seeks to meet with the holy
> as a means of bringing meaning to his
> life.[49]

The concept of the sacred center is
not, of course, confined to any one religion but is an idea common to most faiths.
This is what Eliade concluded from his
cross-cultural studies:

> The center, then, is pre-eminently the
> zone of the sacred, the zone of absolute
> reality. Similarly, all other symbols of
> absolute reality (trees of life and im-
> mortality, Fountain of Youth, etc.) are
> also situated at a center. The road lead-
> ing to the center is a "difficult road" …
> pilgrimage to sacred places (Mecca,
> Hardwar, Jerusalem) … is arduous,
> fraught with perils, because it is, in fact,
> a rite of the passage from the profane to
> the sacred, from the ephemeral and il-
> lusory to reality and eternity, from
> death to life, from man to the divinity.
> Attaining this center is equivalent to a
> consecration, an initiation; yesterday's
> profane and illusory existence gives
> place to a life that is real, enduring, and
> effective.[50]

Jews, Christians and Muslims have
been drawn to Jerusalem precisely because
they believe it to be a sacred center—"the
touching point between the divine and the

earthly, the place where heaven and earth
meet."[51]

Returning home

The ghostly benefits imparted to believers by making a pilgrimage to a sacred
center have never been confined to those
earned at the center itself. A more subtle
goal of pilgrimage has always been to
equip the pilgrim so that he or she can see
the world with newly opened eyes
after getting back home again. The poet
T.S. Eliot put this with great elegance
and clarity. In his poem "Journey of the
Magi," he made the point that the net result of all our travels is simply to return to our starting-place and, for the first
time, truly to understand where we came
from.[52]

This implies not only a greater
ghostly awareness but also a greater awareness of daily life as well. In her essay on
"The Pastons and Chaucer,"[53] set at Caister Castle on the southeastern coast of
England, the British writer Virginia Woolf
tells us that in the fifteenth century pilgrims flocked to Bromholm Priory, not far
from Caister Castle, to see what they believed was a fragment of the True Cross of
Jerusalem—the cross on which Christ was
crucified. This profound experience, says
Woolf,

> sent them away again with eyes opened
> and limbs straightened. But some of
> them with their newly-opened eyes saw
> a sight which shocked them—the grave
> of John Paston in Bromholm Priory
> without a tombstone. The news spread
> over the countryside. The Pastons had
> fallen; they that had been so powerful
> could no longer afford a stone to put
> above John Paston's head.[54]

Pilgrimage, then, is designed to help
returning travelers to understand not only

Jerusalem is at the center of this ***mappe mundi*** (map of the world), which appeared in a thirteenth century English psalter. The Holy City's position shows that it is the sacred center of the world. At the top of the picture, Christ symbolically reigns over the whole world. (The British Library.)

their sacred past but also their workaday present.

Critics of pilgrimage

One sign of the enormous popular appeal of pilgrimage is that, in the West, at least, it has never lacked critics who implicitly or explicitly condemned it. We learn, for example, that St. Hilarion (c. 291–371), a native Palestinian monk and mystic who founded Christian monasticism in the Holy Land, spent just one day of his life in Jerusalem. He made this concession only grudgingly because he did not want to leave the impression that one who lived so close to the holy places appeared to despise them. St. Hilarion believed that he would be close to God no matter where he was on this earth. He therefore refused "to confine God within prescribed limits," i.e., to Jerusalem itself, and so took his leave from Palestine in 329.[55]

In about 380 St. Gregory of Nyssa, an influential writer on mysticism and asceticism, visited Jerusalem and disliked the fashionable, style-conscious pilgrims he found there. He pointed out sternly that "when the Lord invites the blest to their inheritance in the kingdom of Heaven, He does not include a pilgrimage to Jerusalem amongst their good deeds."[56] Nor did Gregory, never a man to mince words, have a favorable opinion of Jerusalem itself:

If God's grace were more plentiful in the Jerusalem neighbourhood than elsewhere, then its inhabitants would not make sin so much the fashion. But as it is, there is no sort of filthy conduct they do not practice—cheating, adultery, theft, idolatry, poisoning, quarrelling and murder are commonplace. ... Then what proof have you, in a place which allows things like that to go on, of the abundance of divine grace?[57]

St. Boniface (d. 754) did not want women to set out on pilgrimages because, he claimed, many of them died on the way, while others fell into prostitution. A ninth century figure, Theodulph of Orléans (d. 821), argued that the way to heaven was through good works, not pilgrimage. A twelfth century writer, Honorius of Autun (France), thought that money spent on pilgrimages would be better used for works of charity. An Italian of the Middle Ages, Pietro Azario, gave this stern advice to husbands:

O how dangerous it is to lead attractive, nay beautiful young women (in whom levity and lust are inherent) into foreign parts in quest of indulgences, particularly inexperienced wives.... For indulgences and pilgrimages are more suitable to the old than to the young; for a ship standing in the harbour, which has never been to foreign ports, does not sense the danger of shipwreck.[58]

The Protestant Reformers of the sixteenth century were even more condemning, but we shall save their views for a later chapter. It is now time to look at the importance of Jerusalem to ghostly and secular pilgrims alike.

II

A Primer on the Importance of Jerusalem

What is it about Jerusalem that makes it such an important pilgrimage destination? The answer to this question constitutes the warp and woof of three major monotheistic religions of the world and of some secular beliefs as well. At least a passing familiarity with these patterns of thought is essential if we are to understand the Jerusalem pilgrimage. Towards this end, a highly simplified primer may be helpful here.

The importance of Jerusalem to Jews

Judaism is a complex religion and an all-embracing way of life originally developed by the ancient Hebrews in what was later known as Palestine or Israel. The Old Testament says that there is one transcendent God, traditionally referred to as Yahweh[59] who has revealed himself to certain leaders. These included the patriarchs (Abraham, Isaac, Jacob and Jacob's 12 sons) and the divinely inspired spokesmen known as prophets. Jacob was also called "Israel," hence "Israelite" and "Israel."

The Old Testament remains an important source for information on the earliest days of Jerusalem, but there is considerable uncertainty about the Bible's historical accuracy here. There are four reasons for this uncertainty.

The first and most important is that efforts to establish the historicity of the Old Testament are probably misplaced. Ancient biblical narratives are what one modern British scholar, Jonathan Tubb, has aptly called "literary constructs." This means, he explains, that

> they relate to the history of Israel *as part of the literary heritage of the people*, and, in a sense, whether they have any genuine historical value or not becomes irrelevant, and the rationale that seeks to establish their historicity becomes tenuous. It is perfectly true that stories of this sort may be, and often are, based on historical fact, but equally they are often not, or are so only in part.[60]

The second reason is that there is an appreciable gap between Biblical accounts and what the archeological record tells us. For example, there is no archeological evidence for the conquest of Jerusalem by anyone named David or Solomon. In fact, from a secular point of view David and Solomon have much more in common with such folkloric figures as Beowulf and King Arthur than with a historically verifiable person such as King Herod. The "real"—that is to say, the *independently verifiable*—history of Israel does not begin until around the time of the divided monarchy (roughly 922 BCE–586 BCE), when we have corroborating records from Assyrian and Babylonian sources.

A third reason for uncertainty is that the Jews did not start writing their own history until well after David allegedly captured Jerusalem in about 1000 BCE. Conceivably, they may not even have begun setting it down until the late sixth century BCE. There was thus a considerable lag between the historical events themselves and the recording of them—more than enough time, to be sure, for hearsay, elaboration, personal motivation and simple errors to corrupt an oral tradition.

A final reason for uncertainty is that Biblical authors invariably placed their versions of long-past events into a theological and political—not a historical—framework. From a secular point of view, many the details they present are no more than religious legends. What is certain, however, is that these authors themselves had no doubt that Yahweh was playing a direct, pivotal role in the life of his people. Yahweh had singled out the Jews as his chosen people and the land of Israel as his chosen land. This special relationship between Yahweh and the Jews was (and still is) known as the *Covenant*.

In return for singling them out, Yahweh required from his people their obedience to a body of teachings known as the Torah. The Torah is the entirety of the divine revelation to the Jewish people. It refers here to the first five books of the Old Testament, which are also called the Pentateuch or the Law. Such obedience, however, proved to be very difficult for the Jews to sustain over time. As a result, divinely inspired prophets repeatedly had to remind the Jews of their obligations to Yahweh and of the calamities that would befall them if they did not mend their ways. Despite their self-confessed religious shortcomings, however, the Jews always hoped for and expected the eventual appearance of a *Messiah* ("the anointed one"), who would redeem them.[61]

The Jews had very strong emotional and cultural attachments to Jerusalem. A Jewish custom dictated that when a householder was whitewashing the walls of a room, he was to leave one corner unpainted so that whenever he entered the room he would be reminded that nothing can be perfect until Jerusalem is rebuilt in all its ancient glory.[62] The city was also extremely important to Jews in eschatological terms. (Eschatology is a branch of theology concerned with the final events in the history of the world or of mankind.) Jerusalem was treasured because it was believed to be the final destination for the Jewish people at the coming of the Messiah at the End of Days, i.e., at the end of time. The appeal of this city-centered Jewish eschatology was so great that, as we shall see, it was later embraced by Christians and Muslims, who modified it to fit the tenets of their own faiths.

The central point of Jewish religious life and pilgrimage was the Temple in Jerusalem. Hebrew tradition holds that the rock on which the city is founded reaches deep into the "subterranean waters" which symbolize the chaos (or hell) which existed before the creation of the world. The Temple of Jerusalem, the prime destination for Jewish pilgrims and whose Western Wall still plays a major role in Judaism, was thought to be located precisely above this very spot. Although built solidly upon the earth, the Temple itself was symbolically aiming at heaven, so each pilgrim who went there was aiming at heaven, too.[63]

The Jewish general and historian Flavius Josephus explained the traditional symbolism of the Temple as a sacred center.

The three parts of the sanctuary, he said, corresponded to the three cosmic regions. The courtyard represented the sea itself (chaos or hell). The Holy Place (a sacred part of the Temple) stood for the earth. The Holy of Holies, known as the *Devir*, was the most sacred spot of all—the inner sanctum where the Ark of the Covenant was once kept. The main purpose of this inner sanctum was to remind the faithful of heaven.[64]

The Ark of the Covenant

The Ark was an ornate, gold-plated, acacia-wood chest about 4½ feet long and 2½ feet wide. It was carried on poles which passed through four rings attached to its sides. Two gilded carvings of cherubim (the highest rank of angels) were fixed to the ends of the Ark to guard the invisible Divine Presence, known as the *Shekhina*, which inhabited the Ark.[65] The chest itself held only two stone tablets, but their importance cannot be overemphasized. The Jews believed that God himself had given these tablets, on which the Torah was engraved, to the prophet Moses, the first great leader of the Israelites, at Mount Sinai.[66]

According to the Bible, the Ark was carried by the ancient Jews during their wanderings in the wilderness after their escape from bondage in Egypt. It may have figured in the three great pilgrimage festivals of Judaism as well. During the turbulent years of early Jewish history, however, the Ark disappeared. Its fate is unknown but some hope it still lies hidden in an unexplored niche deep in the labyrinth of tunnels underlying the Temple Mount. In 1982 Chief Rabbi Goren made an abortive attempt to tunnel under the Temple Mount in hopes of finding the Ark. The excavations, carried out by workers from the Israeli Religious Affairs Ministry, were halted when Muslim protestors blocked the project.[67]

Successive Temples

Thanks to the presence of the Ark, the Holy of Holies in the Temple became a sacred center. This fact is stressed by the Mishnah, a collection of the oral traditions of Jewish law which was compiled about 200 CE and which forms the first part of the Talmud. (The Talmud is an authoritative set of religious books that includes the Mishnah, the Gemara and certain auxiliary materials. In Jewish tradition the Talmud holds a place second only to the Old Testament.) The Mishnah says: "There are ten degrees of holiness. The Land of Israel is holier than any other land [and] the Holy of Holies is still more holy, for none may enter therein save only the High Priest on the Day of Atonement at the time of the [Temple] service."[68]

Over the years there have been three Temples. The First Temple was destroyed by the Babylonians in 587/586 BCE. The Second Temple was built by the Jews in 516/515 BCE but was later plundered, desecrated and left in ruins. Beginning in 19/20 BCE, King Herod the Great built an entirely new temple on the ruins of the Second Temple. This was in fact the third temple to stand on the Mount but since Herod took pains to assure that religious ceremonies continued unabated during the construction program, the new building was officially considered to be merely a refurbishment of the Second Temple. To keep the facts straight, however, it will be referred to here as the Herodian Temple.

The Herodian Temple was in turn entirely destroyed by the Romans in 70 CE. It has never been rebuilt. The only fragment that has survived is the Western Wall. Thus, ever since 70, the Western Wall has been the vital, emotionally-charged focal

The Western Wall is the most sacred Jewish site in the world. It was not part of the Temple it-self but helped support the Temple Mount. The massive stones of the lower section were put in place by Herod in about 20 BCE. Later Muslim renovators could not handle such heavy stones and used lighter blocks on the upper section. (Photograph by the author.)

An ultra–Orthodox Jew praying at the Western Wall. (Photograph by the author.)

the winter rains and the beginning of the spring planting season. More importantly, it was used later to commemorate the Exodus, the Israelites' escape from Egypt.[69] For thousands of years, Jews celebrating the Passover feast (*seder*) promised themselves that they would celebrate it "next year in Jerusalem"—a phrase still used today even when *seder* is held in Jerusalem itself. *Pesah* played a pivotal role in the last days of the life of Jesus. The New Testament records that

> Now the Passover of the Jews was near, and many went up from the country to Jerusalem to purify themselves ... the chief priests and the Pharisees had given orders that any who knew where Jesus was should let them know, so that they might arrest him.... Now before the festival of the Passover, Jesus knew that his hour had come to depart from the world and go to the Father.[70]

point for Jewish prayers and pilgrimage. Young, battle-hardened Israeli paratroopers wept unashamedly when they recaptured the Western Wall from the Jordanians during the 1967 war.

Jewish pilgrim festivals

The three annual pilgrim festivals, still celebrated in Israel today, were originally agricultural celebrations but soon became religious ceremonies centering on the Temple. They constitute the earliest examples of mass pilgrimages to Jerusalem: all adult Jewish males were required to appear at the Temple for them.

The first pilgrim festival was *Pesah* (Passover or the Feast of Unleavened Bread), which was held in March or April. It marked the barley harvest, the end of

The second pilgrim festival was *Shavuot* (the Feast of Weeks or First-Fruits, also called Pentecost), which came seven weeks after *Pesah* and was held in May/June. It initially celebrated the wheat harvest: "First-Fruits" was a special cereal offering consisting of two breads made from the new wheat crop. *Shavuot* was later used to commemorate the revelation of the Torah at Mount Sinai.

The third and final pilgrim festival was *Sukkot* (the Feast of Booths or Tabernacles), a September/October harvest festival which recalled the "booths" or "tabernacles" made from branches of olive, myrtle, palm and other leafy trees, which provided temporary shelters for the Jews after they escaped from Egypt. According to Flavius Josephus, chronicler of the Jewish wars against Rome, *Sukkot* was "the greatest and holiest feast of the Jews."[71]

One unmistakable sign of the importance of Jerusalem to the Jews is that the Midrash, a written version of the oral law which was produced in the centuries following the destruction of the Temple by the Romans in 70 CE, gives the city no fewer than 70 poetic names. These include: Peace, Heights, Rest, Beautiful, Beloved, Fortress, Joy, Garden of God, City of Doves, Faithful City, City of Righteousness, Valley of Vision, Doorway of the World's Peoples, and Eden.[72]

The importance of Jerusalem to Christians

The largest of the world's religions with about 2,000,000,000 believers, Christianity offers both a complex monotheistic theology and a world-wide culture which focuses on the life, teachings and death of Jesus of Nazareth, a Jewish teacher, healer and prophet who is considered by believers to have been the Christ (*christos*, the Greek word for Messiah.) Jesus was born in Judea (Israel or Palestine) between about 7 and 4 BCE. The faithful believe that his birth was divine: God was his father and the Virgin Mary was his mother.

Jesus' religious abilities first surfaced at the age of 12. As the New Testament tells us,

> Now every year his parents went to Jerusalem for the festival of the Passover [*Pesah*]. And when he was twelve years old, they went up as usual for the festival. When the festival was ended and they started to return, the boy Jesus stayed behind in Jerusalem, but his parents did not know it.... [After looking for him for three days in Jerusalem] they found him in the Temple, sitting among the teachers, listening to them and asking them questions.[73]

In about 29 or 30 CE Jesus made the annual pilgrimage to Jerusalem for *Pesah* and was crucified there, on a hillock called Golgotha (also known as the Mount of Calvary), for being a rebel against Rome.[74] According to believers, he rose from the dead three days later.

The basic texts for Christianity are the 27 books of the New Testament of the Bible, but the Old Testament is invoked frequently, too. Although divided by sharp doctrinal and historical differences into Eastern Orthodox, Roman Catholic, Protestant, and other smaller denominations, most Christians consider Jesus to have been divine. Christians also believe that his suffering, death, and resurrection constituted an atonement for the sins of mankind. As a result of his self-sacrifice, they say, the broken relationship between human beings and God has been restored.

Christians feel that studying Jesus' teachings—for example, the Sermon on the Mount (Matthew 5–7)—and using them as a guide for their own behavior will put them on the path toward salvation, that is, toward a heavenly life after death. Thoroughly evil and unrepentant behavior, on the other hand, has been traditionally thought to lead to the endless punishments of hell. Jesus himself is considered to be one of the three co-equal members of a divine Trinity, the other members being God the Father, and God the Holy Spirit or Holy Ghost. Mary, the virgin mother of Jesus, is venerated by many Christians, too.

Jerusalem has been the most important center for Christian pilgrimage because it is revered as the site of Jesus' suffering, death and resurrection. Unlike Judaism, which required the faithful to make the pilgrimage to Jerusalem, and unlike Islam, which mandates the pilgrimage to Mecca, Christianity has treated pilgrimage as a meritorious but purely voluntary effort, usually undertaken on individual initiative.

The Holy City has been important to Christians in eschatological terms as well. It has been thought of as the setting for the Day of Last Judgment, i.e., the end of time. Moreover, as early as the time of the apostle Paul (d. c. 67), the real Jerusalem had evolved into the concept of a "heavenly Jerusalem" or "Zion," that is to say, heaven itself. Some early Christians believed that a heavenly Jerusalem would physically descend from the clouds and that God would establish a divine kingdom on earth there.[75]

Since the fourth century, the Holy Sepulcher in Jerusalem (the tomb in which tradition says that Jesus was buried) has been of enormous importance to believers. Constantine the Great was the first to build a church upon this spot (in about 336). Since then, the Church of the Holy Sepulcher, which remains the most important single sanctuary in Christian culture, has been repeatedly destroyed, rebuilt and remodeled.

Six separate Christian denominations now have custodians there and hold daily or weekly religious services. These denominations are the Latins (Roman Catholics), Greek Orthodox, Armenian Orthodox, Syrian Orthodox (Jacobites), Ethiopians and Copts. Their respective rights were first fixed by an Ottoman edict of 1757, known as the Status Quo agreements, and were spelled out in greater detail by the British in 1922.[76] Ironically, however, since none of these Christian groups trust each other, the key to the holiest church in Christendom is held by a local Muslim family, which has been its custodian since the seventeenth century.

The importance of Jerusalem to Muslims

Islam is a monotheistic religion and a total way of life with more than 700,000,000 adherents all over the world.[77] In Arabic, "Islam" means "submission," that is, submission to the will of God (Allah). Those

Looking much like a Biblical prophet, this priest or monk, probably a member of the Latin Patriarchate, rests in the April sunshine in front of the Church of the Holy Sepulcher after Easter services. (Photograph by the author.)

who believe in Islam are known as Muslims.

This religion is based on the life and teachings of the Prophet Muhammad, who was born in Mecca in about 571. His parents died when he was young, so he was raised by his grandfather, who was a guardian of the Ka'bah, a holy stone building which was a center of the Arabs' worship of *jinn* (spirits). Muhammad himself was poor but at about the age of about 25 he married a rich widow 15 years his senior. He developed strong religious inclinations. From the age of about 40, he would retreat to a cave outside Mecca to pray and meditate on ways to improve what he saw as the shortcomings of religious life in Saudi Arabia's tribal society. Tradition says that it was in this cave that

On Easter Day 2001, pilgrims wait in line to enter the Holy Sepulcher. First they go into a little anteroom (the Chapel of the Angel), which the faithful believe contains the stone the angel sat on when he announced Christ's resurrection. The tomb chamber itself is very small, holding only four people at a time, so the line moves slowly. (Photograph by the author.)

Pilgrims kneel to kiss the Stone of Unction (or Stone of Anointing), a limestone slab located immediately inside the entrance to the Church of the Holy Sepulcher. This rock is variously believed to mark the spot where Christ was taken down from the cross or where he was anointed before being buried.

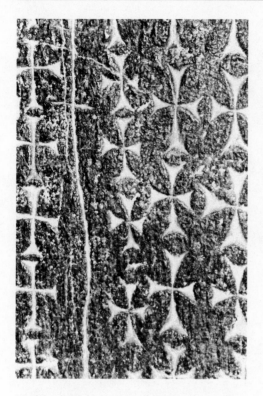

Medieval pilgrims carved these crosses into the walls of the stairway leading into the Chapel of St. Helena in the Church of the Holy Sepulcher. (Photograph by the author.)

the archangel Gabriel first revealed to him the word of God.

By about 613 Muhammad was preaching about what had been revealed to him. Writing down what he said, his followers gradually compiled a holy book known as the Koran or Qu'ran (literally, "Recitation"), which they believed had been given to Muhammad by God via the angel Gabriel. This holy book plays the same central role in Islam as the Old Testament does in Judaism and the New Testament does in Christianity. It is cherished by the faithful as a divinely inspired, never-failing source of religious instruction and literary excellence. A later compilation of the sayings and traditions surrounding Muhammad, known as the *hadith*, is frequently cited by Muslims, too. The *hadith* (literally, "report" or "record")

are collected traditions about the *sunna* of Muhammad, i.e., the specific actions and sayings of the Prophet.

Because Muhammad's radical new teachings threatened the traditional *jinn* worship at the Ka'bah in Mecca and would thus harm Mecca's economy, he was not popular there. To escape persecution, in 622 he and some of his followers fled to Medina, a neighboring city; this migration, known as the Hegira, marks the starting point of the Muslim calendar. After Muhammad died in 632, his followers began to define more formally what it meant to be a Moslem. They identified five key responsibilities for members of the faith.

Known as the "Five Pillars of Islam" and still valid today, these are: (1) a declaration of faith ("There is no god but God; Muhammad is the Messenger of God"); (2) daily prayers, said five times a day; (3) paying a special religious tax; (4) fasting during Ramadan, the ninth month of Islam's lunar calendar; and (5) making the pilgrimage to Mecca (a rite known as the *hajj*), which every Muslim is required to do at least once in his or her lifetime if they can afford it. Pilgrimage to Mecca is thus extremely important to Islam—today more than 2,000,000 Muslims make the *hajj* each year. Jerusalem is important to Muslims, too. As we shall see, it is the third most important pilgrimage site, after Mecca and Medina (the latter is the site of Muhammad's tomb).

Muhammad's night flight and ascension to heaven

After the Muslims conquered Jerusalem in 638, the city gradually became known to them as *Al-Quds* ("The Holy") or as *al-Quds-al-sharifa* ("the noble holy one")[78] because two important events were associated with it. The first event was

Like many other shrines in the Church of the Holy Sepulcher, this glittery Greek Orthodox altar is usually quite crowded. Underneath the altar is a silver-mounted hole where the faithful believe the cross of Christ stood. (Photograph by the author.)

Muhammad's miraculous Night Journey (*Isra'*) from Mecca. The Koran states in Sura (chapter) 17.1:

> Glory be to Him, who carried his
>   servant by night
> from the Holy Mosque (*al-masjid
>   al-haram*) to the Further
> Mosque (*al-masjid al-aqsa*)
> the precincts of which We have
>   blessed,
> That We might show him some of
>   Our signs.
> He is the All-hearing, the All-seeing.[79]

Many Muslims believe that the servant of God referred to in this Sura was Muhammad and that the Holy Mosque was in Mecca. The Further Mosque was at one time thought to be heaven. It was therefore held at first that Sura 17.1 referred to Muhammad's ascension into heaven (an event known as *Mi'raj*), which

also originated in Mecca. By the end of the eighth century, however, Jerusalem, not heaven, was considered to be the Further Mosque.

Later on, to resolve any uncertainty, *Isra'* was defined as the Night Journey itself and Jerusalem as the point from which Muhammad ascended into heaven. A modern scholar, R. H. Zwi Werblowsky, has summed up this solution less reverently but perhaps more clearly: "There are no direct flights from Mecca to heaven; you have to make a stopover in Jerusalem."[80] In any case, Muhammad's spiritual journey is still celebrated throughout the Islamic world on the 27th day of the seventh month of the Muslim calendar.[81]

Jerusalem's key role in the *Isra'* and *Mi'raj* has inspired a great number of devotional writings known as *fada'il* ("excellencies" or "virtues").[82] These reflect the fact that the city lies in the very heart of

Muslim eschatology. One of the gates of the great shrine known as Dome of the Rock, for example, is named after Israfil, the angel of death. Muslims expect that the Day of Judgment will take place at the Dome of the Rock, where the Scales of Judgment will be hung. The Blessed will leave via the Gate of Mercy; the Damned will be sent elsewhere. On the slope of the Mount of Olives, the remainder of mankind will be summoned for Judgment, as indicated by the name of another gate—the Gate of the Place of Judgment.[83]

Another important event associated with Jerusalem was that, as tradition has it, after Muhammad was carried at night from Mecca to Jerusalem by Buraq (a mythical white winged steed, part-donkey and part-mule, with a woman's head) he entered heaven itself, accompanied by the archangel Gabriel. As Muhammad and Gabriel approached the throne of God, they met a number of religious leaders, including

Having knelt and kissed the silver-mounted hole where Christ's cross is believed to have stood, this pilgrim is rising and turning to leave. (Photograph by the author.)

Moses and Jesus. After visiting hell, Muhammad came to within "two bow-lengths" of the presence of God[84] and was ordered to recite the ritual prayer 50 times a day. Moses, however, thought this would be too heavy a burden for believers and suggested that Muhammad ask God for a lesser figure instead. Muhammad did so and the obligation to pray was reduced to only five times a day.

Muslims do not believe that Muhammad himself was divine. They revere him, however, as a divinely inspired transmitter of God's messages to humanity. Jerusalem itself is so important to Muslims that it bears what is called the "triple honorary name":

First of the two directions of prayer
Second of the two sanctuaries
Third after the two places of worship."[85]

Roman Catholic clergy celebrate mass at the Holy Sepulcher on Easter morning, 2001. (Photograph by the author.)

This traditional formulation is succinct and poetic but not very clear, so an explanation is needed here. The first part of the city's honorary name ("First of the two directions of prayer") refers to the fact that, in the earliest days of Islam, the faithful faced Jerusalem, not the Ka'bah in Mecca, when they prayed.[86] The next part of the honorary name ("Second of the two sanctuaries") means that Mecca is now considered senior to Jerusalem and therefore take precedence over it in terms of holiness. The last part of the honorary name ("Third after the two places of worship") means that after Muhammad's tomb in Medina had become a pilgrimage destination, too, Jerusalem itself was relegated to third place, i.e., after Mecca and Medina.

For Muslims, the holiest site in Jerusalem is the Haram al-Sharif ("the Noble Sanctuary"), which contains the Dome of the Rock, completed in 691/692, and the Aqsa Mosque, dating from 715. Muslims consider Jerusalem to be "the Blessed Land" and hold it in such high esteem that an Islamic litany gives it eight formal attributes:

• The place to which the Prophet Abraham migrated from Iraq
• The Holy Land
• The land of the Night Journey and the Ascension into heaven
• The land to which Muslims first turned when praying
• The land of steadfastness and sacred struggle for God's cause
• The land of promise
• The center of the future Islamic Caliphate, a political structure to be governed by a successor of Muhammad
• The place where believers will be raised from the dead and assembled on the Day of Judgment.[87]

The Dome of the Rock seen through a narrow archway in the Old City. (Photograph by the author.)

The gray-domed Aqsa Mosque is located on the Temple Mount to the far left of the golden Dome of the Rock. (Photograph by the author.)

The importance of Jerusalem to secular pilgrims

If the religious importance of Jerusalem is obvious, its secular importance may be less well known and is worth outlining here. The story begins when, after the intense religiosity of the Middle Ages, the Renaissance ushered in a new age of rationalism in Europe. These new patterns of thought slowly eroded the unquestioning acceptance of sacred space and marked the beginnings of secular visits to Jerusalem. The Holy City's complex, colorful and turbulent history gradually became a powerful magnet tugging at scholars, archeologists, military officers, cartographers, tourists, writers, photographers and artists.

Before Jerusalem could become a popular destination for secular pilgrims, however, it first had to be demystified. This process was begun by the greatest scholar of the northern Renaissance, Desiderius Erasmus (1469–1536), a Dutch humanist and philologist who laid the foundations for modern historical-critical (that is, non-devotional) studies of the Holy Land. Erasmus specifically mocked the vanities of pilgrims, whom he describes as being "all covered with cockle shells [emblems of the pilgrimage to Santiago de Compostela in Spain], laden on every side with images of lead and tynne [emblems of other pilgrimages]."[88] There were many other critics, too. In 1559 the Protestant reformer John Calvin derided pilgrimage as being a form of "counterfeit worship."[89] In *Paradise Lost*, begun between 1655 and 1658, the English poet John Milton dismissed pilgrims simply as misguided people "that strayed to farr to seek/ In Golgotha him dead, who lives in Heav'n."[90]

Economic and intellectual developments in Europe combined to increase scholarly and scientific interest to the Holy

Land. As rationalism began to clear away some of the religious mists in Europe, it sent its own pilgrims to Jerusalem in the seventeenth and eighteenth centuries. Among them were the chaplain of the English Levant[91] Company in Syria, Henry Maundrell (1697); one of the fathers of modern Middle Eastern studies, Richard Pococke (1743); the Swedish botanist Frederick Hasselquist (1749–1752); and the French surveyor Constantin Volney (1784).

Later, the Industrial Revolution generated new wealth in Western Europe and encouraged radically new modes of production, travel and thought. Positivist philosophy replaced traditional theology and metaphysics with an empirically based theory of knowledge. Comparative studies of religion suggested that religious truth was relative rather than absolute. Darwinism taught that natural selection, not God, was responsible for the origin and evolution of the species.

Secular travel to Jerusalem did not become commonplace, however, until the nineteenth century. In the late 1830s, steam had begun to replace sail in the Mediterranean, making transport to the Holy Land safer and more reliable. Palestine soon became a stop on the "Grand Tour" that was a mandatory part of every well-bred young man's education. The celebrated Scottish artist David Roberts visited Jerusalem in 1839 and captivated British viewers with his remarkable scenes of daily life in the Middle East.

Controversial religious, ethnic and political issues swirled around Jerusalem and brought new waves of travelers. In 1841 the American scholar Edward Robinson published *Biblical Researches in Palestine*, an empirical, pathfinding venture into what would be called "Biblical archeology"—the search for archeological evidence about sites mentioned in the Bible.[92] This search was important to scholars because, previously, the only information about Biblical sites had come from impressionistic pilgrim accounts, many of which will be cited later.

Thanks to the Crimean War, the Haram itself was opened up to non–Muslims in 1855 for the first time in hundreds of years and Western visitors flocked to this holy center. In 1862 Moses Hess, the intellectual father of Zionism (a doctrine calling for the establishment of a separate Jewish state in the Holy Land), published the Zionist classic, *Rome and Jerusalem.* And in 1865 the British founded the Palestine Exploration Fund—which, remarkably, is still going strong in London today—to promote secular studies of the region.

One of the results of the great nineteenth century surge of interest in the Holy Land was an extraordinary outpouring of first-hand travel accounts. It has been estimated that between the years 333 and 1878 a total of about 3,515 such works were written by travelers-turned-author. However, more than half of these books—that is, about 2,000 of them, or 56 percent—were written in the 40 years between 1838 and 1878.[93] Early photographers also flocked to Jerusalem between 1850 and 1880 to capture permanent images of the holy sites. Sergeant James McDonald, for example, who accompanied the British Royal Engineers on their 1864 and 1880 surveys of Jerusalem and the Sinai, took hundreds of photos.[94]

Later on, secular events in the twentieth century continued to stimulate secular interest in Jerusalem. In November 1917 the British issued the Balfour Declaration, which called for the establishment in Palestine of a "national home" for the Jewish people. Shortly thereafter, a British army led by General Sir Edmund Allenby entered Jerusalem peacefully as World War I brought Ottoman rule to an end. Subsequently, however, irreconcilable hostility between the Arabs and the Jews led to the founding of the independent state of Israel (1948) and to the Israeli capture of Jerusalem itself during the Six-Day War (1967). It seems likely that secular, as well as religious, pilgrimages to Jerusalem will continue to increase during the age of mass travel in the early twenty-first century.

III

The Old City

Jerusalem is located on the Judean watershed about 2,600 feet above sea level and on the geographical borderline between the Mediterranean basin to the west and the Jordanian desert to the east. Held by the Israelis since the 1967 war, Jerusalem now covers an area of about 42 square miles and consists of two parts: East Jerusalem, which contains the lovely Old City and will be our focus here, and West Jerusalem, the modern and less attractive "New City," which dates from about 1850 and has grown tremendously since 1967. Because the Old City lies at the heart of our story, unless otherwise stated all references to Jerusalem in this book will to be to it.

The Old City is built on two limestone ridges which run north-south and which are cut by narrow valleys, some of which have been filled in over the millennia by huge amounts of rubble—the remains of earlier Jerusalems. Archeologists have found that, even near the ridgelines of these valleys, the earliest structures of the city can lie buried beneath 30 feet of debris. According to the most recent (1998) census, 32,488 people now live in the Old City, which consists of four distinct quarters: Muslim, Christian, Jewish and Armenian. Roughly 70 percent of the inhabitants are Muslims, 20 percent are Christians, 8.5 percent are Jews, and 1.5 percent are members of other ethnic communities. The Old City, girdled round by mellow stone walls, covers about 215 acres. The walls themselves, which have been destroyed and rebuilt over the centuries, now measure about two and one-half miles in circumference and are pierced by seven gates.

I made a secular pilgrimage to the Old City at Easter 2001. A visit during this season reveals the rich diversity of Christian churches there. These include: (1) the Orthodox churches (Greek and Russian), (2) the Oriental Orthodox churches (Armenian, Syrian, Coptic and Ethiopian), (3) the Catholic churches (Latin, Greek, Maronite, Syrian, Armenian and Chaldean), (4) and the Protestant churches (Anglican, Lutheran, Scottish Presbyterian, Baptist, Pentecostal and Evangelical). Easter services in Jerusalem were held that year in Latin, Arabic, German, French, Finnish, Dutch, Spanish, English, Armenian and Syriac.[95]

Do not go into the Old City through the Jaffa Gate. This entrance is always noisy and crowded because it is the main entry point for tourists, cars, taxis, trucks and buses. Even worse, it forces the traveler to run a gauntlet of insistent "guides" in order to reach the labyrinthine maze of *souqs* (markets) and alleys which form the heart of the Old City. It is much better to enter through the Damascus Gate. This is the main passageway for Muslim resi-

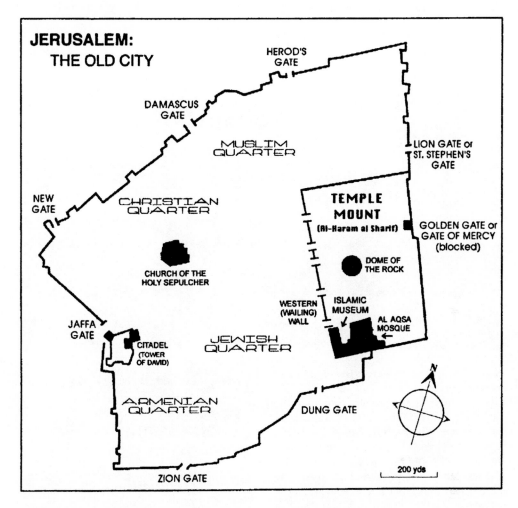

JERUSALEM:
THE OLD CITY

HEROD'S GATE

DAMASCUS GATE

MUSLIM QUARTER

LION GATE or ST. STEPHEN'S GATE

NEW GATE

CHRISTIAN QUARTER

TEMPLE MOUNT
(Al-Haram al Sharif)

GOLDEN GATE or GATE OF MERCY (blocked)

DOME OF THE ROCK

CHURCH OF THE HOLY SEPULCHER

WESTERN (WAILING) WALL

ISLAMIC MUSEUM

AL AQSA MOSQUE

JAFFA GATE

CITADEL (TOWER OF DAVID)

JEWISH QUARTER

ARMENIAN QUARTER

DUNG GATE

N

ZION GATE

200 yds

Four major holy sites, sacred to three world religions, are all located in the Old City. On the Temple Mount, the Dome of the Rock and Al-Aqsa Mosque are revered by the Muslims. The Western (Wailing) Wall of the Temple Mount is sacred to the Jews. The Church of the Holy Sepulcher is a center of Christian devotion. (Eklectica Graphic Design.)

dents. It leads the intrepid visitor into exceptionally colorful open air markets and mellow neighborhoods built of golden stone.

Visually, however, the most impressive structure in the Old City is a huge masonry platform covering about 36 acres. It has several names. In Arabic, it is known as the Haram al-Sharif ("the Noble Sanctuary") or Bait al-Maqdis ("the Holy House"). In Hebrew it is called Har ha-Moriyya ("Mount Moriah"), Har ha-Bayit ("the Temple Mount") or Beth

ha-Maqdas ("the Holy House"). To avoid any confusion, we will refer to it in this book either as the Temple Mount or as the Haram.

By whatever name we choose, this platform is of enormous importance to Jews and Muslims alike. It was the site of the long-destroyed Temples and still contains the Western Wall, sacred to Judaism. It also holds two of the great sites that are centers of Islamic piety: the Dome of the Rock and the Aqsa Mosque. Today it constitutes the fault line between Judaism and

Above: The Damascus Gate is the biggest and most elaborate of the seven gates of the Old City. Dating from the reign of Suleiman the Magnificent early in the sixteenth century, it was designed to be easily defended. By aiming through the arrow slits, soldiers stationed inside the wall could rain arrows down on attackers. Moreover, immediately inside the main gate the entrance angles sharply to the left. Attackers would not only have had to break through the heavy wooden doors of the gate (now no longer in place) but would then have had to fight their way through a narrow corridor to get into the Old City itself. *Right:* Arrow slits in the Old City's walls near the Jaffa Gate. (Both photographs by the author.)

Islam. Christians, for their part, flock to the Church of the Holy Sepulcher, which is located in the Old City about 400 yards to the west of the Temple Mount.

The Old City is renowned for the colorful religious, cultural, linguistic and visual diversity that 3,000 years of turbulent history have crammed into such a small area. What must be remembered about this venerable city is that it has had more than its fair share of natural and man-made problems. There has never been enough arable land in the region or enough fresh water. Severe earthquakes have repeatedly toppled mosques and

At 8:30 A.M. the Muslim market (*souq*) is still relatively uncrowded. Later in the day it will be choked with pedestrians, vendors, shoppers and barrow boys (young men maneuvering narrow wheelbarrows laden with fruits, vegetables or consumer goods). (Photograph by the author.)

Secluded passageways of the Old City early in the morning. (Photographs by the author.)

churches. Heat, dust, droughts and plagues have been common. And when Jerusalem has changed hands, as has happened more than 20 times, its inhabitants have run the risks of being massacred, enslaved, forced to emigrate or being reduced to abject poverty. It is for these reasons that the Talmud laments:

> Ten measures of beauty gave God to the world: nine to Jerusalem and one to the remainder.
>
> Ten measures of sorrow gave God to the world: nine to Jerusalem and one to the remainder.[96]

It is possible that more blood has been shed for Jerusalem than for any other city on the face of the earth. If a historian from Mars had to make only two statements about Jerusalem, the first would probably be: *This is a place where human beings like to pray.* The second, however, would have to be: *This is a place where human beings like to fight.* To this we might well add a corollary: Jerusalem is also *a place where people like to argue.* As Yehuda al-Harizi, a Jewish pilgrim who came to Jerusalem in 1217, put it,

> we would be very happy here were it not for the tedious internal problems of the various communities and the spirit of discord which reigns among them, to the point that one could well name this place "the rock of dissentions."[97]

An Israeli newspaper columnist summed up the situation very well during the failed Israeli-Palestinian peace negotiations of the millennial year 2000:

> There is something about Jerusalem that addles the brain. When the subject

is Jerusalem, pragmatism is replaced by anxiety and rational interests are replaced by slogans. It is as if some "force majeur" has decided that Jerusalem must remain a city that defies all solutions.[98]

The columnist was right. Despite the 54 years that have lapsed since Israel's independence in 1948, there is still no international agreement today on who should exercise sovereignty over Jerusalem. Both Israelis and Palestinians claim it as their rightful capital. Passions run so high on this issue that it is unlikely to be resolved anytime soon. Perhaps the best that can be hoped for is that all parties concerned will tacitly adopt a Jewish legal concept known in the Talmud as *teiku.*

This needs a word of explanation. During the *seder*, the annual family dinner at *Pesah* (Passover), one of the five ceremonial cups of wine is left untouched in honor of the prophet Elijah. This is "Elijah's cup." Jewish tradition holds that Elijah will arrive one day at the *seder* as an unknown guest. He is considered to be the "Forerunner of the Messiah": when Elijah appears, the Messiah can be expected not long thereafter.

Teiku—an Aramaic word which means "unresolved" or "let it stand"— refers to a custom established by Talmudic scholars. Whenever they could not resolve an exceptionally difficult legal or theological issue, they would simply defer any decision on it *until the coming of Elijah.* He would resolve all controversial questions connected with the Torah. Seen in a good-humored light, the final status of Jerusalem is certainly *teiku.*

IV

Beginnings of the Jerusalem Pilgrimage: The First and Second Temples (c. 1000 BCE–63 BCE)

The prehistory of Jerusalem dates from roughly 3200 BCE. According to the Bible, David captured Jerusalem in about 1000 BCE and made it the capital of his combined kingdom of Israel and Judah. Subsequently, Israel was crushed by the Assyrians in 722/721 BCE and Judah was conquered by the Babylonians in 587/586 BCE. After this latter defeat the Jews were exiled to Babylon. King Cyrus of Persia conquered Babylon and in 538/537 BCE allowed the Jews to return to Jerusalem. Following the death of the Greek Emperor Alexander the Great, who in 333/332 BCE had defeated the Persians, Jerusalem was ruled first by Ptolemaic Egypt (after c. 301 BCE) and then by the Seleucid Syrians (from 198 BCE). In 168 BCE the Jews revolted against Hellenistic culture (a blend of Greek and Middle Eastern elements) and enjoyed a brief period of independence. This ended when the Roman general Pompey seized Jerusalem in 63 BCE.

The earliest days of the city

The prehistory of Jerusalem is vague and subject to revision by scholars. Judging from the potsherds and flints that have been unearthed by archeologists, the city goes back to about 3200 BCE, although it has not been inhabited continuously ever since that time.[99] The earliest mention of Jerusalem itself dates from about 1850–1810 BCE, when an Egyptian pharaoh, Sesostris III, listed "*Urushalimmu*" in one of the Execration Texts[100] as being among the enemies of Egypt. The origins of the word "Jerusalem" remain unclear but some scholars believe that "*Urushalimmu*" probably means "Shalim has founded"—Shalim (or Shalem) being a Middle Eastern deity who was manifest in the evening star.

The next mention of Jerusalem is found about 500 years later in Egypt's Amarna Letters (roughly 1350 BCE), which identify Jerusalem's leader of the time as a minor hereditary ruler who was subject to Egypt and who was called "Abdi-Khipa." Khipa was a goddess worshipped in Anatolia, Turkey. Abdi-Khipa was at war with marauding nomadic or refugee bands of an ill-defined group of people known as "Hapiru." Given the similarity of this word to the later term "Hebrew," it was formerly thought that the Hebrews must have originated from these shadowy Hapiru. Scholars now believe, however, that since Hapirus are mentioned in many ancient texts, this was probably a general term for "homeless persons" and does not imply a specific ethnic, cultural or religious identity. It is quite possible, therefore, that while some Hebrews were Hapirus, not all of the Hapirus were Hebrews.

Due to the political stability and relative prosperity imposed by Egyptian overlordship of the area, Jerusalem experienced a surge of building activity in the fourteenth and thirteenth centuries BCE. Archeologists have unearthed the remains of massive terracing, suggesting that a strong citadel was constructed above a permanent water source, the spring Gihon. Burial caves dating from this era also point to a pattern of well-established human settlement.

The Old Testament sets Israel's beginnings at about 1200 BCE. The earliest Biblical mention of Jerusalem itself is thought to be Genesis 14:18–19, which tells us that King Melchizedek of Salem (i.e., Jerusalem), a "priest of God Most High," blessed the patriarch Abraham. This encounter took place, according to Genesis 14:17, at "the Valley of Shavah (that is, the King's Valley)." Jewish tradition holds that this valley is where the spring of Ain Rogel—about 1500 yards south of what is now the Temple Mount—is located. Another early reference to Jerusalem can be found in Joshua 10:1, 3, 5, which mentions King Adoni-Zedek of Jerusalem, who together with four other kings was eventually defeated by the Israelites, perhaps in the late thirteenth century BCE.

It is clear from corroborating non–Biblical sources, however, that by the thirteenth century BCE the Israelites were not a major force in the land. They stood no chance against Egypt, the superpower of the time. In an inscribed stele (a stone slab monument) dating from 1207 BCE, the Egyptian pharaoh Merneptah claimed that thanks to his successful military campaigns, "Israel is laid waste, his seed is not."

Early shrines

Local pilgrimages to nearby cultic shrines must have been a familiar feature of early Israelite life because worship was not centralized in Jerusalem until the reign of Josiah (c. 640–609 BCE). Since Ain Rogel was a cultic center associated with the coronation of Jerusalem's kings, it is possible that it was also an early center for local pilgrimage, although there is no hard evidence to support this theory. At first Yahweh was revered at rudimentary altars of earth or uncut stone but he was certainly not the only god of the time.[101] Some of the Hebrews worshipped Baal, a storm god venerated along the coast of Syria. Others were devotees of the female figurines, known as Astarte plaques, that have been found at archeological sites. Alternatively, they may have prayed to idols cast of precious metal.

There may have been early precedents for visiting Jerusalem for religious reasons but in the end it was a military-political issue that was responsible for the beginnings of the Jerusalem pilgrimage itself. In their earliest days the Israelites were facing formidable enemies, including the Philistines, a coastal people armed with iron swords that held their edge much better than the obsolete bronze blades used by the Israelites. According to the Bible, the poorly armed, loosely organized, semi-nomadic Israelite tribes soon saw that if they were to survive they needed a more centralized and more disciplined form of government to improve their military capabilities.

Their solution was to have a king, ideally a man who was also a proven warrior. The first Israelite king, put on the throne in about 1020 BCE, was Saul. He had proved his military ability by defeating a hostile tribe known as the Ammonites. Saul, however, ruled the country from his home town, which was about three miles north of Jerusalem. It was only under the second king—David—that Jerusalem itself became permanently established as the religious and political center of Israelite life.

David (c. 1000 BCE)

The Bible tells us that David began his career at the court of Saul, where his raids against the Philistines made him so popular that Saul plotted to kill him. David, however, escaped to the desert frontier of Judah and became a leader of other refugees and outlaws there. He proved to be a political and military genius, first winning the support of Judean elders and later, in about 1000 BCE, capturing Jerusalem itself.

The city was at that time the stronghold of the Jebusites, another tribe of the region.[102] The Jebusites had boasted that their high, walled city was so impregnable that "even the blind and the lame" could defend it.[103] But David assembled his own forces around the base of the city and called for volunteers for a death-or-glory mission. The details of this expedition are unclear but may have involved sending a good climber up a narrow vertical fissure in the rocks, used as a water shaft, to set upon the Jebusites from an unexpected quarter. David promised that "Whoever

attacks the Jebusites first shall be chief and commander." One bold young man stepped forward. This was "Joab, son of Zeruiah." He led the assault on Jerusalem and, inspired by his valor, the Israelites carried the day. Joab was promoted to chief and subsequently "David resided in the stronghold; therefore it was called the city of David."[104]

David's most creative decision was to adopt as his own the Jebusite policy of ruling Jerusalem *both as king and as high priest.* This centralization of political and religious power in the person of the king was such a good idea that under the Israelites it lasted for more than 400 years. In a similar stroke of genius, David also brought to Jerusalem the Ark of the Covenant, which had accompanied the Israelites in their wanderings and was believed to be the dwelling place of Yahweh. He did this for two reasons: to consolidate his new position as the sole mediator between Yahweh and the Israelites, and to emphasize the primacy of his new capital, "the city of David."[105] As a result, Jerusalem soon became known as "the Holy City," a title it has retained for more than 3,000 years.

Here we should remember that the Israelites never thought of David or his successors as being divine. But thanks to their mediating role between God and man, these kings were honored as the forerunners of the expected Messiah. This explains why New Testament writers were so keen to show that Jesus was a descendent of David. The gospel of Matthew, for example, opens with the lines, "An account of the genealogy of Jesus the Messiah, the son of David, the son of Abraham" and then goes on to trace this genealogy over 42 generations.[106]

In the gospel of Luke, an angel appears to Mary and tells her that her son Jesus "will be great, and will be called the Son of the Most High, and the Lord God

This model shows what the City of David may have looked like before the First Temple was built. (The Tower of David Museum of the History of Jerusalem.)

will give to him the throne of his ancestor David."[107] And after Jesus' death and resurrection, the apostle Peter, preaching in Jerusalem, explains to his listeners that God had sworn an oath to David to put one of David's descendants on the throne. Peter says that David himself had predicted the resurrection of the Messiah, foreseeing the appearance of a man who, though killed, "was not abandoned to Hades, nor did his flesh experience corruption."[108]

The First Temple

Because the ancient Israelites followed a nomadic lifestyle and were surrounded by enemies, they believed, according to the Bible, that the best housing for the Ark of the Convenant was a tent, not a permanent building. David, however, wanted to build a magnificent temple in Jerusalem to solidify the political and religious gains he had made there. Towards this end, he acquired a Jebusite threshing floor, which was already revered as a holy center because a plague had been stopped there. This threshing floor was also conveniently situated in a commanding position atop Mount Moriah (later called the Temple Mount), the place where the Israelites believed Abraham had bound his son Isaac and had been ready to sacrifice him to Yahweh.

The First Temple, however, was built not by David but by his son Solomon. The Bible, our only source of information on this undertaking, reports that prodigious labor and precious materials were invested in the project, which was finally finished in 957 BCE.[109] Cedar and cypress logs were cut in Lebanon, lashed together and rafted down the coast to Palestine. Staggering if greatly exaggerated numbers of Israelites were conscripted by Solomon to work on the Temple. It is said that 30,000 men were sent in shifts to Lebanon to cut wood. An additional 70,000 laborers and 80,000 stonecutters worked in Palestine itself, directed by 3,300 supervisors.

Since the First Temple was to be the permanent home of Yahweh, no expense was spared on it. The inner sanction and its altar were both overlaid with gold and were protected by golden chains. Two big cherubim carved out of olivewood kept watch over the Ark of the Covenant, which was located in the *Devir*, the Holy of Holies. What was called the "molten sea"—a huge bronze bowl of water, used both for ritual ablutions and to recall the formless watery world which existed at the beginning of time[110]—rested on the statues of 12 oxen. This enormous bowl was said to have held enough water for 2,000 ritual ablutions.

Early Jewish pilgrimages

With the First Temple in place, there was at last a central focal point for Jewish worship. There is no record of when pilgrimages to Jerusalem began after the Davidic conquest but it is clear they increased significantly after the Babylonian Exile.[111] By then the Jews already had a long tradition of pilgrimage. In the thirteenth century BCE Moses had stressed the importance of traveling to some as-yet-undefined sacred space to worship Yahweh. At Mount Sinai, Moses instructed his followers:

> Three times a year all your males shall appear before the Lord your God at a place he will choose [i.e., Jerusalem]: at the festival of unleavened bread [*Pesah*], at the festival of weeks [*Shavuot*], and at the festival of booths [*Sukkot*]. They shall not appear before the Lord empty-handed: all shall give as much as they are able, according to the

blessing of the Lord your God that he has given you.[112]

After David moved the Ark of the Covenant to Jerusalem, the city gradually became the major setting for these three great pilgrim festivals.[113] During his reign (c. 640–609), King Josiah abolished all the rival sanctuaries and established the First Temple as the only legitimate place of sacrifice.[114] By the seventh century BCE, Jerusalem had become a thriving center with an area of about 120 acres and about 10,000 inhabitants. Much of its wealth came from trade: wine, olive oil, perfumes, dates, figs and grain.[115] No quantitative estimates are available but it is reasonable to suppose that a fair number of pilgrims came to the First Temple. If so, they too would have contributed materially to Jerusalem's economic prosperity.

Yet in the long history of Jerusalem, change—often violent change—has been the order of the day. The First Temple was looted by the Babylonians, first in 604 BCE and then again in 597 BCE. Finally, in 587/586, Nebuchadnezzar, king of Babylon, destroyed it entirely. A contemporary account reveals the profound impact the destruction of the First Temple had on the Israelites:

> How lonely sits the city
> that once was full of people!
> How like a widow she has become,
> she that was great among the nations!…
> She weeps bitterly in the night,
> with tears on her cheeks;
> among all her lovers
> she has no one to comfort her…
> Jerusalem remembers,
> in the days of her affliction and wan-
> dering,
> all the precious things
> that were hers in days of old.[116]

Not only was the Temple destroyed, but all the Jewish leaders and skilled workers were deported to Babylon, an event known as the Babylonian Exile.[117] The Jews remained there from somewhere between 48 and 70 years but never ceased to bewail the loss of Jerusalem. The painful lament of their psalmist is still moving today:

> By the rivers of Babylon—
> there we sat down and there we wept
> when we remembered Zion.
> On the willows there we hung up our
> harps.
> For there our captors asked us for
> songs,
> and our tormentors asked for mirth,
> saying,
> "Sing us one of the songs of Zion!"
> How could we sing the Lord's song in a
> foreign land?
> If I forget you, O Jerusalem
> let my right hand wither!
> Let my tongue cling to the roof of my
> mouth
> If I do not remember you,
> if I do not set Jerusalem
> above my highest joy![118]

At least once in their lifetimes, some of the most prosperous and most pious Jews may have managed to leave Babylon to visit the ruins of the Temple but this was too difficult and too expensive a journey to be undertaken every year. Instead, the eventual return to Jerusalem was projected into the distant future as the major goal of the Jewish people of the Diaspora. ("Diaspora" means "dispersion" in Greek and refers to the Jews living "in exile" outside Palestine.)

The Jews believed that, when finally achieved, the return to Jerusalem would more than compensate for the long separation from their homeland. In the meantime, they vowed, it was essential to keep the memory of Jerusalem alive and clear in the minds of the faithful, especially the younger generation. It is for this reason that the prophet Isaiah promises:

> For Zion's sake I will not keep silent, and for Jerusalem's sake I will not rest, until her vindication shines out like the dawn, and her salvation like a burning torch. The nations shall see your vindication, and all the kings your glory.[119]

There were still many Jews left in the kingdom of Israel, however, and some of them made a point of visiting the ruins of the Temple twice a year. The prophet Jeremiah describes how "eighty men arrived from Shechem and Shiloh and Samaria, with their beards shaved and their bodies gashed [these were traditional signs of mourning], bringing grain offering and incense to present at the Temple of the Lord."[120] Thus, even in its ruinous state, the First Temple still remained a lodestone for pilgrims.

The Second Temple

In 538/537 BCE the Babylonians were defeated by Cyrus the Great, the young king of Persia, and the next year he gave the Jews permission to return to Jerusalem and rebuild the Temple. This event marks the end of the Babylonian Exile. Many of the Jews hurried back to Jerusalem, where in 520 BCE they laid down the foundations for the Second Temple on the site of the First Temple.

The Second Temple seems to have been a less impressive structure than its predecessor, however. It drew mixed reviews when it was finally completed in 516/515 BCE. The prophet Ezra tells us that although young Jews loved it and registered their pleasure with shouts of joy, many of the elderly people who had known the First Temple in all its glory—the priests, the members of a group of priestly functionaries known as the Levites, and the old men and women—"wept with a loud voice" when they saw the new Temple.[121]

Despite its apparent shortcomings, however, the Second Temple immediately became the goal of pilgrimage because it was now the sacred center of Judaism. "The Land of Israel," says the Midrash, "is situated in the center of the world, and Jerusalem is in the center of the Land of Israel, and the Holy Temple is in the center of Jerusalem."[122] A Jewish scholar of that era, Rabbi ben Gurion, assured his readers that the Rock of Jerusalem, on which the Temple was built, was none other than "the Foundation Stone of the Earth, which is to say the Earth's umbilicus [navel], because it is from there that the entire earth unfurled."[123]

The Bible makes a similar point: "Thus says the Lord God: This is Jerusalem; I have set her in the center of the nations, with countries all around her."[124] There was a further sign to the faithful that Jerusalem was truly the center of the earth. On the day of the summer solstice, it was said that the sun at noon cast no shadow on the Fountain of Jacob, which Jewish tradition considered to be a kind of cosmic pillar.[125]

The Midrash gives us this idealized picture of early Jewish pilgrimages:

> In the early morning, the official in charge says: "Arise! We will go up to Zion, to the house of our God!" From the neighbourhood [the pilgrims] bring figs and grapes, dried figs and raisins from further afield. The cattle go before them, their horns adorned with gold, and wreathes of olive on their heads. Flutes play before them, until they come close to Jerusalem. When they draw close to Jerusalem, they send messengers ahead and send their first-fruits in garlands. The dignitaries and treasurers come out of the city to meet them, according to the rank of the new arrivals.[126]

Great crowds of pilgrims turned out for the three major festivals at the Second Temple. Reaching for dramatic effect, some ancient authors claimed that a total of 2,000,000 to 3,000,000 pilgrims went there. Modern scholars, however, think that 150,000 visitors is a more reasonable estimate. Since Jerusalem's permanent population at the time was only about 30,000, the pilgrimages would have multiplied it six-fold.[127] Regardless of the exact numbers involved, the pilgrims were in a joyous mood. People from the same town or village traveled to Jerusalem festivals together, enjoying at the same time both the excitement of travel and the pleasures of a communal holiday.

Visits must have ceased entirely in 167 BCE, however, when Antiochus IV Epiphanes, the Seleucid king of the Hellenistic Syrian kingdom, captured Jerusalem and began to impose Greek culture on the Jews. "Epiphanes" means "God Manifest" but because of Antiochus' mental instability he was known behind his back as "Antiochus Epimanes," i.e., "Antiochus the Mad." He made it a capital offense to worship Yahweh or perform other Jewish rites.[128] He especially infuriated the Jews by desecrating the Second Temple, where he set up an altar to Zeus and sacrificed a pig on it. This was a mortal insult which the Jews bewailed, in a memorable phrase, as "the abomination of desolation."[129]

It was said that Antiochus also offered sacrifices at the feet of an idol made in his own likeness. These ill-considered actions were seen by the Jews as frontal assaults on their religion. They sparked the first Jewish revolt, which was led by a charismatic leader named Judas Maccabeus. (An indication of this man's sturdy character is that Maccabeus means "hammer-head.") The revolt succeeded and in 164 BCE Judas Maccabeus was able to tear down the altar of Zeus and to reconsecrate the Temple. This was such an important event that Jews still celebrate it today in the annual festival of Hanukkah ("Dedication").

Thus purified, the Second Temple remained supremely important to the Jews as the sacred center of their cultural and religious life. This was true not only for the Jews living in Israel itself but also for the 5,000,000 Jews of the Diaspora, large numbers of whom came to the Temple to offer sacrifices.

Aristeas (second century BCE)

One of these pilgrims was a Hellenistic Jew named Aristeas. Writing near the middle of second century BCE, he recorded his favorable impressions about the great strength, skill and silence demonstrated by the Temple priests. He watched how they quickly and efficiently slaughtered the large number of animals brought to the Temple for sacrifice. Aristeas tells us that the priests displayed "surpassing bodily strength" as they tossed the heavy carcasses about. "So great is the silence everywhere," he added, "that one would suppose there was no one in the place, although the priests number seven hundred and [the pilgrims and local worshipers] who bring the victims to the Temple are many; but everything is done with awe and reverence for its great sanctity."[130]

The end of the Temple

Many other Jewish pilgrims followed in Aristeas' footsteps but the Temple itself would not last forever. As we shall see in the next chapter, although entirely rebuilt by King Herod, it was later reduced to ruins by the Romans and has not been rebuilt to this day.

V

Pilgrims Under Roman and Byzantine Rule (63 BCE–638 CE)

The Romans came to power in Palestine in 63 BCE. King Herod ruled the region on their behalf from 37 BCE to 4 CE and rebuilt the Temple. The ministry of Jesus of Nazareth extended from about 20 to 33. In 66 the Jews revolted again against the Romans, a failed uprising that led to the destruction of Jerusalem, including the Temple, in 70. Jerusalem was replaced by a new city known as Aelia Capitolina, built by the Emperor Hadrian. Another Jewish rebellion in 132 was also suppressed. In 323–324 the Emperor Constantine won control of the eastern half of the Roman Empire, which became known as the Byzantine Empire and which included Jerusalem. Christianity was the official religion. The Church of the Holy Sepulcher, built by Constantine in 334–336, became the holiest site in Christendom. The Persians conquered Jerusalem in 614. The Emperor Heraclius restored Byzantine rule and became the master of Jerusalem in 629 but was in turn defeated by the Muslims in 638.

Roman intervention

Jerusalem grew into a metropolitan city under the Hasmonean dynasty, whose rule began in 164 BCE, but it was always easy for the Israelites to slide back into political instability. In 63 BCE, one of the Jewish factions that was trying to seize power decided to ask the Romans for help. As a result, the Romans intervened militarily, conquering Jerusalem and capturing the Second Temple. According to Josephus, they killed thousands of people in the process. Pompey, commander of Roman forces in the East, had the effrontery to desecrate the Holy of Holies by daring to look inside it—something that, according to pious Jews, no human being in the world but the High Priest had the right to do, and only on one day of the year, Yom Kippur, the Day of Atonement.

The Herodian Temple (19/20 BCE)

By 19/20 BCE, the Second Temple was such in poor condition that Herod the Great, king of Judea, decided to rebuild it entirely. There were two reasons for his decision. First, a magnificent new public building would reflect and increase his own political power. Second, Herod hoped that such a big capital investment would pay off in terms of greatly increased pilgrimages, especially by the large numbers of Jews in the Diaspora. This made financial sense because the economic impact of pilgrimages was immense. In fact, they constituted the annual "harvest" for the inhabitants of Jerusalem, whose service industries were almost entirely dependent on them.[131]

Herod proceeded to dismantle the old Temple and put up a glorious edifice in its place. He made sure, however, that sacrifices still continued in the old Temple during the construction process. This permitted him to claim that he was merely restoring the Second Temple. In fact, however, what he actually built was the third Temple. It was a great success. The new Herodian Temple was the centerpiece of

the city and was an impressive structure. The Temple Mount itself was expanded to the north, west and south, increasing its dimensions to about 525 yards long by 306

During the later days of the Herodian Temple, this street (top) was paved with flagstones, edged by curbstones and lined by shops catering to the pilgrim trade. It ran for about half a mile along the edge of the Western Wall (as shown in the photo above). (Photographs by the author.)

Urban Simulation Team

ISRAEL ANTIQUITIES AUTHORITY

Opened in Jerusalem in April 2001, the Ethan and Miriam Davidson Exhibition and Virtual Reconstruction Center is located in the Umayyad Palace complex near the Dung Gate. Using the latest archeological data, it offers visitors a unique virtual-interactive tour of the Temple Mount, as evidence suggests it was before destruction by the Romans in 70 CE. Visitors can also watch a high-definition digital video film starring an Israeli actor who reconstructs the experience of an actual pilgrimage to the Herodian Temple. (Ethan and Miriam Davidson Exhibition and Virtual Reconstruction Center.)

yards wide. Its inner courts and its sanctuary formed a rectangle about 190 yards long and 120 yards wide, with the Holy of Holies located in the most protected and most inaccessible place.[132]

Herod also built three magnificent towers to strengthen the city's fortifications. The first he named Phasael, after his brother. This tower has now been restored and houses the Museum of the History of Jerusalem, which is well worth visiting. The second tower he called Hippicus, after a good friend of that name. The third tower was known as Miriam, after Herod's wife. Moreover, Herod also built a gigantic 35-acre platform (the Temple Mount) which surrounded the Temple. This whole project—Temple and platform together—

took about 80 years and required the combined skills of some 18,000 craftsmen. They did their work well: the Temple Mount was so strongly constructed that its massive western wall survived the total destruction of the Temple by the Romans in 70 CE. Ever since then, this last remaining fragment of the Herodian Temple has been revered by the Jews as the Western Wall.

Jews came to the Herodian Temple in very large numbers for the three great pilgrim festivals—*Pesah, Shavuot,* and *Sukkot.* There were two reasons for Jerusalem's prosperity during the Hasmonean and Roman periods. The first was the income and trade generated by the pilgrimages themselves. The second reason was the "half-shekel due," which was a tax levied on every Jewish male, including the Jews of the Diaspora, above the age of thirteen. This tax was used for the upkeep of the Temple. Because pilgrims had to convert their own currencies into the half-shekel coin, money changers set up tables on the Temple Mount. The New Testament relates that Jesus overturned some of these tables, accusing the money changers of dishonesty and usury.[133]

Pilgrim festivals drew very large numbers of Jews from Palestine itself and from the lands of the Diaspora. An area outside the Temple Mount was prepared for the use of these pilgrims. Gateways and staircases were built. Streets and plazas were paved. A sewage system and ritual baths (miqva'ot) were installed. In numerous shops along the streets, pilgrims could change money, buy animals for sacrifice and find food and drink for their stay in Jerusalem. Because by the first century CE these pilgrim festivals were well-documented, it is worth looking at them in some detail.[134]

Pesah (Passover or the Feast of Unleavened Bread)

This was the major pilgrim festival and drew from 300,000 to 500,000 visitors, most of whom brought their own tents and camped outside the city. As mentioned earlier, Pesah commemorates the Exodus from Egypt. According to the Old Testament, God wanted his chosen people, the Jews, to return to Israel but they could not do so as long as they were held in servitude by the Pharaoh. The Bible says that to compel the Pharaoh to let his people go, God killed the first-born child in every Egyptian home and the first-born of all the cattle as well. Jewish homes were passed over because, on Moses' orders, the Jews had smeared the blood of sacrificial lambs on the lintels and doorposts of their homes.[135]

Initially, the celebrations of Passover and Unleavened Bread were two separate festivals but gradually merged into one. The Jews could celebrate Pesah only in Jerusalem and only after they had been ritually purified.[136] Philo of Alexandria, a Greek-speaking Jewish philosopher, made a Pesah visit to Jerusalem in 40. Like all other pilgrims in a ritually impure state, he had to undergo a seven-day purification process before being allowed to enter the Herodian Temple.

Once admitted to the Temple itself, worshippers sang or recited the Hallel ("Praise" in Hebrew). This consisted of Psalms 113–118, which express faith in and gratitude for the national and personal salvation provided by God. As an essential part of Pesah, each group of ten pilgrims brought to the Temple one lamb for sacrifice. Given the estimated attendance of 300,000 to 500,000 pilgrims, over a period of hours between 30,000 and 50,000 lambs were slaughtered. Their blood was caught in basins and tossed against the base of the altar. The pilgrims took the carcasses back to their homes or tents, roasted them on skewers and ate the lambs that night, accompanied by unleavened bread and bitter herbs.

Pesah was a time for instructing children about Jewish traditions. The unleavened bread and bitter herbs taught them about the difficulties of their ancestors' lives as slaves in Egypt. To demonstrate the breathless haste in which the Jews left Egypt, the head of the family was directed by the Old Testament to come to the Pesah meal fully prepared for travel. "This is how you shall eat it," commands Exodus 12:11: "your loins girded, your sandals on your feet, your staff in your hand; and you shall eat it hurriedly." Pesah is still used today in Jewish homes to pass on this tradition from one generation to another. The youngest son is enjoined to put a ritual question to his father: "Why is this night different from other nights?" The father gives him this ritual answer:

> A wandering Aramean was my ances-
> tor; he went down into Egypt and lived
> there as an alien.... The Lord brought
> us out of Egypt with a mighty hand and
> an outstretched arm, with a terrifying
> display of power, and with signs and
> wonders; and he brought us into the
> place and gave us this land [Israel], a
> land flowing with milk and honey.[137]

Although *Pesah* was a religious festival, it could have political overtones as well. Because it celebrated the liberation of the Jews from foreign bondage, it lent itself admirably to demonstrations against Roman rule. Josephus tells us that in 4 CE a riot broke out in Jerusalem when Jews protested the execution by the Romans of two teachers who had encouraged their students to remove the legionary eagle (the symbol of a Roman legion) that had been mounted over the entrance to the Herodian Temple. The Romans sent in troops and about 3,000 Jews were killed.[138]

In another *Pesah* incident related by Josephus, a cohort of Roman soldiers (500 to 1,000 men) was standing guard from a rooftop overlooking the Temple complex. One of them "stooped in an indecent attitude, so as to turn his backside to the Jews, and made a noise in keeping with his posture."[139] The Jewish pilgrims resented this insult and began to throw stones at the Romans. The result was much the same as before: the Romans called in more troops, who killed large numbers of Jews.

Shavuot (Feast of Weeks or First-Fruits, also called Pentecost)

Shavuot was the smallest of the three pilgrim festivals but still attracted a large number of Jews. We noted earlier that it was originally an agricultural commemoration. It was celebrated 50 days or seven weeks after *Pesah* and involved an offering of the new wheat crop known as "first-fruits." The instructions from the Old Testament were clear enough:

> When you have come into the land that
> the Lord your God is giving you as an
> inheritance to possess, and you possess
> it, and settle in it, you shall take some
> of the first of all the fruit of the ground
> ... and you shall put it in a basket and
> go to the place that the Lord your God
> will choose as a dwelling for his name
> [the Temple].[140]

Shavuot also gave the Jews the opportunity to thank God for choosing them as his people and for revealing the Torah to them on Mount Sinai. Political struggles entered into this festival, too. Josephus recounts that after the death of King Herod in 4 BCE, fighting broke out in Jerusalem between Jews and Romans when the Roman procurator (the senior financial officer) wanted to seize some of Herod's treasure, which the Jews felt by rights belonged to them. The net result was a large loss of life on both sides.[141]

Sukkot (the Feast of Booths, also known as the Feast of Tabernacles)

Sukkot was second to *Pesah* in terms of the number of pilgrims who attended it. Coming five days after the Day of Atonement, *Sukkot* marked both the harvest season and the Exodus from Egypt. The Old Testament instructed the faithful:

when you have gathered in the produce of the land, you shall keep the festival of the Lord…. On the first day you shall take the fruit of majestic trees, branches of palm trees, boughs of leafy trees, and willows of the brook…. You shall live in booths [or tabernacles] for seven days; all that are citizens of Israel shall live in booths, so that your generations may know that I made the people of Israel live in booths when I brought them out of the land of Egypt: I am the Lord your God.[142]

Sukkot was a very happy occasion. Josephus says it was always "observed with special care."[143] We can imagine how much fun Jewish children must have had gathering branches, helping their parents build the booths and then camping out in them. For its part, the Mishnah seems to invite us to join the *Sukkot* celebrations at night:

Men of piety and good works used to dance before [the priests of the Temple] with burning torches in their hands, singing songs and praises. And countless Levites [played] on harps, lyres, cymbals and trumpets and instruments of music, on the fifteen steps [of the Temple] leading down from the Court of the Israelites to the Court of the Women…; upon them the Levites used to stand with instruments of music and make melody.[144]

In the midst of all this joy, however, the presence of large crowds of pilgrims made riots an ever-present possibility. The indefatigable Josephus reports that when the Jewish priest Alexander Jannaeus was serving at the altar, worshippers began to throw citrons at him. (Citrons are lemon-like fruit with a thick rind.) Adding insult to injury, the pilgrims also shouted that Jannaeus was not eligible to serve as a priest. His parents had been slaves, they howled, and he himself may have been a bastard. Enraged and fearing that the disturbances might get out of hand, Jannaeus called in the Roman troops, who promptly killed large numbers of Jews.[145]

So many people came to Jerusalem for the pilgrim festivals that a few deranged individuals were invariably among them. According to Josephus, it was at *Sukkot* that a Jew named Jeshua (i.e., "Jesus"—but not Jesus of Nazareth) stood in the Temple and suddenly bellowed out: "A voice from the east, a voice from the west, a voice from the four winds; a voice against Jerusalem and the sanctuary, a voice against bridegrooms and brides, a voice against the whole people."

He was promptly arrested and scourged (whipped) by the Romans for this seditious outcry but he could not be silenced. He did not beg for mercy or shed any tears when struck, but even when his flesh hung in tatters he repeated, every time he was whipped, "Woe to Jerusalem!" Finally realizing they had a maniac on their hands, the Romans released him. For more than seven years thereafter Jeshua continued to cry out "Woe to Jerusalem!" or "Woe again to the City, the people, and the Sanctuary!" at all the pilgrim festivals, until he was finally killed by a stone thrown by a Roman siege engine, probably during a riot.[146]

"Scenes of genial cheerfulness"

Several sources testify to the popularity of Jewish pilgrimage to Jerusalem during the first century CE. Writing in 40 CE, Philo of Alexandria stressed that the pilgrimage offered both sacred and profane (that is to say, worldly) attractions:

And we have the surest proof of this in what actually happens. Countless multitudes from countless cities come, some over land, others over sea, from east and west and north and south at every feast. They take the Temple for their port as a general haven from the bustle and great turmoil of life, and there they seek to find calm weather, and, released from the cares whose yoke has been heavy upon them from their earliest years, to enjoy a brief breathing-space in scenes of genial cheerfulness. Thus filled with comfortable hopes they devote their leisure, as is their bounded duty, to holiness and the honouring of God. Friendships are formed between those who hitherto knew not each other, and the sacrifices and libations are the occasion of reciprocity of feeling and constitute the surest pledge that all are of one mind.[147]

The destruction of the Herodian Temple (70)

On the political front, instability again reared its head. Beginning in the year 60, the quality of the Roman officials ruling Jerusalem began to decline. One governor took bribes from Jewish bandits; his successor, Gessius Florus (64–66), not only did the same thing but—even worse—he also took money from the treasury of the Herodian Temple. This last step was such an affront to the Jews that it sparked severe rioting between the Jews and the Roman cohorts, which Florus tried to quell by calling in more Roman troops.[148]

His strategy was initially unsuccessful (in one battle the Jews are said to have killed more than 5,000 Roman soldiers) but at this time the Jews were also quarrelling and fighting with each other. Even if they had been united, however, there was no way they could have defeated the might of imperial Rome. Their doom was sealed in 70, when the emperor Vespasian put his son Titus in charge of suppressing the Jewish insurgency. Despite a heroic defense of the Temple by a radical group of Jews known as the Zealots, who preferred

suicide to surrender, under Titus' leadership the Romans captured the Temple and razed it completely. (See Appendix II for Flavius Josephus' eyewitness account of this event.) When Titus' troops were finished with their bloody work, all that remained of the Herodian Temple was one wall of the Holy of Holies—the Western Wall.

The loss of the Temple raised a thorny problem for the three great pilgrim festivals. As we have seen, all adult Jewish males were required to come to the Temple for these celebrations. According to the traditional Jewish worldview underlying the festivals, God had chosen Mount Zion (the Temple Mount) to be his home. Pessimists claimed that since the Temple was not only the house of God but also God's house, its total destruction meant that God had abandoned his house—and presumably his people as well.[149] A basic question remained unanswered: how could there be Temple pilgrimages without a Temple?

Three solutions gradually emerged over the years and proved the pessimists wrong. The first solution was made possible by the Romans themselves. By the middle of the third century they had given the Jews permission to return to Jerusalem and climb Mount Scopus or the Mount of Olives to mourn the Temple from afar. At some later point they were also allowed to enter the ruins of the Temple itself on the *Tisha be-Av*, the ninth day of the Jewish month of Av, which was (and still is) the traditional day of mourning for the destruction of the First and Second Temples. The Temple had become so important to Judaism that, even after this building had ceased to exist, pilgrimage to Jerusalem gradually resumed without any halakhic basis, that is, without any foundation in traditional ritual law.[150]

This is what a contemporary document, found in a storehouse known as the

Cairo Geniza[151], advised Jewish pilgrims to do:

> If you are worthy to go up to Jerusalem, when you look at the city from Mount Scopus [you should do the following]. If you are riding on a donkey, step down; if you are on foot, take off your sandals, then rending your garments say: "This sanctuary was destroyed".... When you arrive in the city, continue to rend your garments for the Temple and the people and the house of Israel. Then pray saying "May the Lord our God be exalted" and "Let us worship at his footstool.... We give you thanks, O Lord our God, that you have given us life, brought us to this point, and made us worthy to enter your house"... Then return and circle all the gates of the city and go round all its corners, make a circuit and count its towers.[152]

The second solution to the pilgrimage-without-a-Temple problem was the synagogue. This word comes from a Greek word meaning "to bring together." A synagogue is simultaneously a "house of prayer," a "house of assembly," and a "house of study." The earliest synagogues may have appeared after the First Temple was destroyed in 587/586 BCE. Their successors played an even larger role in Jewish religious life after the destruction of the Herodian Temple—not only in Palestine but also in the lands of the Diaspora. Morning, afternoon, and evening services were held at the synagogue, with special ceremonies on the Sabbath and on religious festivals. The synagogue did not have to be an impressive building: in about 1034, the synagogue in Jerusalem was only an underground structure known as "the Cave."[153]

The third solution for the loss of the Temple was the home itself. The best example here is *Pesah*. This a seven-day festival which traditionally begins with an evening service at the synagogue and then is highlighted by an elaborate ritually-prescribed meal (*seder*) at home. Some Jews spend the whole night of *Shavuot* at home, studying the Torah. *Sukkot* lasts for seven days, during which many Jews take their meals in a "booth" but still live at home, where a citron and a branch of a palm tree, tied with branches of myrtle and willow, are waved as symbols of rejoicing.

The second Jewish revolt (c. 132)

By 130 the Roman emperor Hadrian decided to replace Jerusalem, which except for the garrison of the Tenth Legion now lay in complete ruins, with a new city. This would be a new Roman colony named Aelia Capitolina—in honor of Hadrian's family (Aelius) and the deities of the Capitoline Triad (Jupiter, Juno and Minerva). Hadrian also decided to build a temple to Jupiter on Mount Zion, the site of the First, Second and Herodian Temples. The next year he outlawed some key Jewish practices: circumcision, teaching the Torah and public gatherings. Hadrian's plans and edicts infuriated the Jews, who launched the Second Jewish Revolt under the leadership of a formidable Jewish solider named Simon Bar Koseba.

Despite some initial successes, Bar Koseba's guerrillas were doomed because Hadrian sent one of Rome's best generals to put down the rebellion. Bar Koseba himself was killed in 135, after a scorched-earth campaign by the Romans in which they were said to have captured 50 Jewish forts, destroyed 985 villages, and killed 580,000 Jewish soldiers.[154] Jerusalem itself was razed by the Romans and was rebuilt as Aelia Capitolina, with the temple to Jupiter proudly crowning the Temple Mount. The Jews themselves were forbidden to live in or enter the city at all.

The beginnings of Christian pilgrimage

Unlike Judaism and Islam, Christianity has never made pilgrimage a mandatory undertaking for the faithful. Instead, it has always been a voluntary and sometimes solitary enterprise that never lacked critics. Perhaps it is not surprising, then, that the first recorded Christian pilgrimage to Jerusalem did not take place until 170, some 140 years after the death of Christ, when Melito, the bishop of Sardis (Turkey), visited the Holy City.

Melito (170)

Melito was not at all interested in Jerusalem itself. One reason was that the city was in his time an insignificant Roman colony, Aelia Capitolina. Another reason was much more important to him. In theological terms, the earthly Jerusalem, he said, was "worthless now because of the [heavenly] Jerusalem above."[155] The upshot was that Melito made his pilgrimage to pursue *scholarly* rather than devotional interests. He wanted to establish an accurate canon (an authoritative list) of the books of the Old Testament by going to the Holy Land himself and personally studying the sites "where these things [the Biblical events] were preached and done."[156] He is now remembered, among other things, for coining the phrase "Old Testament" to distinguish these earlier books of the Bible from the much later works of the Christian Gospel writers.

The legacy of St. Paul

The early Christians continued to focus on spiritual pilgrimages to the heavenly Jerusalem. The apostle Paul (died c. 67) had not been in favor of earthly pilgrimages because he believed they were irrelevant. In his opinion, it was *the believers themselves* who now constituted the new temple of Jerusalem. Paul wrote to his followers:

So you are no longer strangers and aliens, but you are citizens with the saints and also members of the household of God, built upon the foundation of the apostles and prophets, with Christ Jesus himself as the cornerstone. In him the whole structure is joined together and grows into a holy temple in the Lord; in whom you also are built together spiritually into a dwelling place for God.[157]

In another letter to the faithful, Paul assured them that it was spiritual travel, not physical travel, which would bring them to the heavenly Jerusalem:

Therefore, since we are surrounded by so great a cloud of witnesses ... let us run with perseverance the race that is set before us.... [Y]ou have come [symbolically] to Mount Zion and to the city of the living God, the heavenly Jerusalem, and to innumerable angels in festal gathering, and to the assembly of the firstborn, who are enrolled in heaven, and to God the judge of all, and to the sprits of the righteous made perfect, and to Jesus, the mediator of a new covenant....[158]

Origen (230–235)

Paul's teachings were important to Origen, the greatest theologian and Biblical scholar of the early Christian church. Origen taught in Palestine from about 230 to 235 and attracted many students. Echoing Paul, he called attention to the importance of spiritual rather than physical pilgrimages:

Understand, then, if you can, what the pilgrimages of the soul are in which it laments with groaning and grief that it has been on [earthly] pilgrimage for so long. We understand these pilgrimages only dully and darkly so long as the pilgrimage lasts. But when the soul has returned to its rest, that is, to the fatherland in paradise, it will be taught more truly and will understand more truly what the meaning of its pilgrimage was.[159]

Constantine the Great (325/326)

One man—the Emperor Constantine—was single-handedly responsible for changing the way Christians saw the earthly Jerusalem. According to Bishop Eusebius of Caesarea (see below), on the afternoon of a decisive battle at the Milvian bridge near Rome in 312, Constantine "saw with his own eyes the trophy of a cross of light in the heavens, above the sun."[160] The cross bore an inscription: *In hoc signo vinces* ("In this sign thou shalt conquer").

This vision so impressed Constantine that the next year he decreed that Christianity would be one of the official religions of the far-flung Byzantine empire, although for political reasons he continued to support pilgrimages to pagan shrines for at least 14 years thereafter. He never made a pilgrimage to the Holy Land himself but in 325/326 he did the next best thing: he sent his mother, Queen Helena, on an official political-religious pilgrimage which would have enormous consequences.

Helena's visit was an unqualified success. Indeed, it was a triumph. As legend has it, in Jerusalem the Queen discovered not only the tomb of Christ but also, nearby, the True Cross and Golgotha, the site of Christ's crucifixion. These finds were readily accepted because the tomb of Christ was thought to be very close to the place where he was crucified. John 19:41–42, for example, says that

> there was a garden in the place where he was crucified, and in the garden there was a new tomb in which no one had ever been laid. And so, because it was the Jewish Day of Preparation, and the tomb was nearby, they laid Jesus there.

The discovery of Golgotha seemed believable, too, because this word means "the place of the skull" and referred to the top of a buried block of limestone that protruded from the soil like a skullcap.

It was on this sacred spot that from 334 to 336 Constantine built the Church of the Holy Sepulcher. It had two main components. The first was the Basilica of Constantine (also called the Martyrium, or "place of witness"), marking the site of the crucifixion. The second was a rotunda approximately 131 feet in diameter, known as the Anastasis ("Resurrection"), over the tomb itself.[161] With its spacious courts and subsidiary buildings, the Church of the Holy Sepulcher was by far the largest edifice in Jerusalem.

We know something about the earliest days of this church and the services held there thanks to two pilgrim accounts, one written by the Bordeaux Pilgrim in 333 and the other by the Spanish nun Egeria in 384. Their travels are described below. What is most important, however, is that the structure that Constantine put in place has survived to our own day. Even though frequently modified or rebuilt, the Church of the Holy Sepulcher has remained the sacred center of Christendom and the destination of uncounted millions of pilgrims for more than 1,665 years.

Jewish pilgrimage continues, too

Under Byzantine rule, Jewish pilgrims from Palestine and from Antioch, Alexandria and other cites of the Middle East were allowed periodically to pray at the Western Wall. No matter how long they remained in exile, the Jews never lost hope of returning to Jerusalem. A fourth century inscription in Hebrew, carved on a stone set in the Herodian wall of the Old City, cites the prophet Isaiah and assures the faithful, "And when ye see this your heart shall rejoice, and your bones shall flourish like a herb."[162]

The Bordeaux Pilgrim (333)

The precursor of the multitudes of pilgrims who would flock to the Holy Land in the fourth century was a solitary, anonymous man from Bordeaux known to scholars simply as "the Bordeaux Pilgrim." We have no information on him as a person. A reasonable guess, however, is that since in the fourth century Bordeaux was a flourishing city, port and educational center, the Bordeaux Pilgrim was a pious, educated, prosperous and (judging from his laconic style of writing) a taciturn man. In any case, he was the first person to leave a detailed itinerary of his travels, entirely by land, to and from the Holy Land.

The Bordeaux Pilgrim reached Jerusalem in 333 after a long, difficult journey.[163] He traveled about 20 miles a day, spent about 328 days on the road, and stayed in the Holy Land for about 95 days.[164] Like many of his successors, he saw the Holy Land entirely in terms of its sacred rather than its "real" geography. The Bible was, he believed, the best guide for a walking tour. A typical entry in his itinerary reads:

Twenty-eight miles from there [Sychar, a famous well] on the left of the road to Jerusalem is the village called Bethar, and a mile from there is the place where Jacob slept on his way from Mesopotamia, and the almond-tree is there, and he saw a vision, and an angel wrestled with him.[165]

Once in Jerusalem, the Bordeaux Pilgrim does not display the slightest elation about his success in reaching his destination, nor does he engage in any theological speculation. He makes no effort to list the holy places in any order of importance but limits himself to a dry and (for him) strictly factual account of what he sees. He tells us, for example, that amid the ruins of the Herodian Temple there stands

a vault where Solomon used to torture demons, and the corner of a very lofty tower.... Below the pinnacle of the tower are very many chambers where Solomon had his palace.... And in the sanctuary itself, where the Temple stood which Solomon built, there is marble in front of the altar which has on it the blood of Zacharias [an early Christian martyr]—you would think it had only been shed today. All around you can see the marks of the hobnails of the soldiers who killed him, as plainly as if they had been pressed into wax. Two statues of Hadrian stand there, and, not far from them, a pierced stone [the outcropping of rock later enclosed within the Muslim Dome of the Rock] which the Jews come and anoint each year. They mourn and rend their garments, and then depart.[166]

After leaving Jerusalem, the Bordeaux Pilgrim visited Bethlehem, where Christ was born (Constantine had built a basilica there, too), Terebinthus and Hebron. He offers only sparse accounts of these towns. The rest of his manuscript consists simply of lists of staging posts and the distances between them. No further information about holy places is provided.[167]

Eusebius (d. 340)

The new official status of Christianity in the Byzantine Empire and the presence of such a magnificent church in Jerusalem itself necessitated a "clarification" of Paul's and Origen's doctrine about pilgrimage. A new party line was accordingly put forward by one of the Church Fathers, the Biblical scholar Eusebius (d. 340), a native of and later the bishop of the coastal Palestinian city of Caesarea. He began to see the religious value of foreigners' visiting the Holy City:

> So on the monument of salvation itself [i.e., the Church of the Holy Sepulcher] was the new Jerusalem built, over against the one so famous of old.... Opposite [the old Jerusalem] the emperor [Constantine] reared, with rich and lavish expenditure, the trophy of the Saviour's victory over death. Perhaps this was that strange and new Jerusalem, proclaimed in the oracles of the prophets, to which long passages prophesying by the aid of the Divine spirit make countless allusions in song.[168]

With the seemingly antithetical concepts of the heavenly and the earthly Jerusalem thus forced into a marriage of convenience by Eusebius, the stage was set for the beginnings of mass Christian pilgrimage.

Rufinus and Melania (379)

The influx of pilgrims increased markedly after Theodosius I, a devout Spanish Christian, became emperor in 379. That same year, two pilgrims from the West—Rufinus, a Roman priest, writer and translator of Greek theological works into Latin, and Melania the Elder, a Spanish noblewoman—founded a hostel in Jerusalem on the Mount of Olives. This institution, apparently the first of its kind, performed two important functions for pilgrims: it provided food and shelter, and it served as a refuge for men and women who wished to enter into a quiet life of prayer and penitence in the Holy City. Rufinus and Melania had a good idea of what pilgrims needed and how to provide it. They succeeded so well, in fact, that ascetic St. Jerome (see below) would later criticize them for living too lavishly.[169]

Gregory of Nyssa (380)

A noted theologian, scholar and mystic, Gregory was consecrated bishop of Nyssa, a small city in Turkey, in about 372. As will be remembered from the citations used earlier in this book, this outspoken man was not in favor of pilgrimages to Jerusalem, which he visited from about 380 to 383.[170] The long journey to Palestine, he believed, offered too many temptations. En route, women pilgrims might become sexually involved with their male companions because, he said,

> it is impossible for a woman to accomplish so long a journey without a conductor; on account of her natural weakness she has to be put upon her horse and then to be lifted down again; she has to be supported in difficult situations.... Whether she leans on the help of a stranger, or on that of a servant she fails to keep the law of correct conduct....[171]

Once in Jerusalem, the notoriously loose morals of the local inhabitants offered other temptations as well. The city was packed "with the whole variety of people you find in such centers, prostitutes, actors, and clowns."[172] Gregory argued that pilgrimage to Jerusalem "is found to inflict on those who have begun to lead a stricter life a moral mischief" and that it was absurd to imagine "the Holy Spirit is in abundance in Jerusalem but unable to travel as far as us [i.e., to our native places].[173] Still, Jerusalem made a noticeable impact on even this nay-sayer: after all, Gregory admitted, the Holy City was special because it had "received the footprints of Life itself."[174]

Egeria (c. 381)

Towards the end of the fourth century, an independently wealthy Spanish nun probably named Egeria (other possible names are Aetheria, Etheria or Eucheria) wrote for her colleagues back in Spain an account of her travels in the Middle East. This work is now damaged and incomplete but is still valuable because it gives us a vivid description of the daily and annual Christian celebrations in Jerusalem. It also appears to be the earliest usage of a phrase that differentiated Christian pilgrims from all other travelers. These pilgrims were consciously traveling with the Bible as their guidebook. They were travelling, as they put it, *juxta scripturas*, that is, "accompanied by" or "joined to" the Bible.[175]

A modern scholar has remarked that "In part Egeria's journey was a grand adventure, a sightseeing tour of biblical history, the breathless journey of one of the idle rich."[176] In about 381 she and several companions left Constantinople (modern-day Istanbul) on an extended tour of the Middle East. Their only guidebook was the Bible. Whenever they came to a sacred site, they would simply look it up in the Bible and read the holy words "on the very spot."[177] For example, when she came to Salem, she remembered that it was near

here that John the Baptist had baptized people. So she asked the priest who was serving as a guide whether the site was far away. "There it is," said the priest, "two hundred yards away. If you like we can walk over there."[178]

When she first got to Jerusalem, Egeria found it full of monks and nuns who had made the long pilgrimage from Mesopotamia, Syria or Egypt to be present at the annual festival commemorating both Constantine's founding of the Church of the Holy Sepulcher and Queen Helena's discovery of the True Cross. Egeria was enthralled by the daily liturgical life of the city:

> Loving sisters [she writes to the nuns in the convent back home], since I know you are eager to know about the services they have in the holy places, I shall tell you about them. All the doors of the Anastasis are opened before cock-crow each day, and the monks and virgins ... come in, and also some lay men and women.... From that hour to daybreak, hymns are sung and psalms and antiphons sung in response. And after each hymn a prayer is offered.... [On Sunday] the people assemble in the Great Church built by Constantine on Golgotha behind the Cross ... any presbyter who is seated there may preach, if he so wishes, and when they have finished, the bishop preaches.... Because of all this preaching it is a long time before [the worshippers] are dismissed from the church, which takes place not before ten or even eleven o'clock.[179]

Egeria was also captivated by the sensual quality of the Christian churches in Jerusalem. They blazed with lamps and were redolent with the smell of incense. "All you can see," she reports, are

> gold and jewels and silk; the hangings are entirely silk with gold stripes, the

curtains the same, and everything they use for the services at the festival is made of gold and jewels. You simply cannot imagine the number, and the sheer weight of the candles and the tapers and the lamps and everything else they use for the services.[180]

Egeria's account also shows that by the time of her visit a well-established system of guides and lodgings for pilgrims was already in place. The Holy City held such scenic and religious attractions and made such a strong impression on her that she stayed there for three years.

St. Jerome and Paula (385)

St. Jerome, a Biblical translator and monastic leader, was the most learned of the Fathers of the Christian church. His Latin version of the Bible, known as the Vulgate, used the non-classical Latin spoken by common people and was for many centuries the authoritative Biblical text of the Roman Catholic Church. Jerome's influence on subsequent Christian pilgrimages to the Holy Land was enormous. Later writers, for example, were quick to draw on his works and on his translation of Eusebius.[181]

Between 382 and 385 Jerome served as secretary to Pope Damasus but his preaching in support of the ascetic life and his corrections of Biblical texts proved to be too controversial. In 385 he angrily left Rome. That same year, together with Paula, a widowed Roman noblewoman, and her daughter Eustochium, Jerome embarked on an extensive pilgrimage to Palestine and Egypt. At first he and Paula stayed at the hostel built by Rufinus and Melania, but Jerome soon got enmeshed in a theological quarrel with Melania and thereafter publicly criticized the hostel's comforts, worldly atmosphere and its close ties with the Byzantine court. Given his strong feel-

ings, it is not surprising that in 386 Jerome moved to Bethlehem, where in 389 he and Paula opened a less-ornate hostel, with a monastery for men and a convent for women.

What is more important for us, however, is the extraordinary impact the holy places had on Paula and, by extension, on other pilgrims as well. Jerome says of Paula:

> With a zeal and courage unbelievable in a woman she forgot her sex and her physical weakness, and longed to make there [in Jerusalem], amongst those thousands of monks, a dwelling for herself.... And she might have done so, if she had not been summoned away by a still greater longing for the holy places [e.g., Bethlehem]....[182]

What follows here appears to be the first authoritative account of a Christian pilgrim giving the freest possible rein to his or her emotions. The Proconsul of Palestine, an important official who knew Paula's family in Rome, had prepared luxurious accommodations for her in Jerusalem but she chose to live in a humble cell instead. Moreover, in the Church of the Holy Sepulcher,

> She fell down and worshipped before the Cross as though she saw the Lord hanging on it. On entering the Tomb of the Resurrection, she kissed the stone which the angel had removed from the sepulcher door, then like a thirsty man who had waited long and at last comes to water, she faithfully kissed the very place where the Lord had lain. Her tears and lamentations were known all over Jerusalem: the Lord is her witness, to whom she prayed.[183]

And at Bethlehem, Jerome tells us,

> She solemnly declared in my own hearing that, with the eye of faith, she saw a

child wrapped in swaddling clothes, weeping in the Lord's manger, the Magi worshipping, the star shining above, the Virgin mother, the attentive foster-father; and the shepherds coming by night to see [the new-born Jesus]....[184]

One of Jerome's correspondents, the Latin poet Paulinus of Nola (Italy), gave the reason for these and later emotional outpourings by pilgrims, especially for their surprisingly tactile quality. "The principal motive which draws people to Jerusalem," he wrote, "is the desire to see *and touch* the places where Christ was present in the body."[185] This same point was made by St. Cyril, the bishop of Jerusalem, who was among the first to encourage the belief that this "holy city" should be a pilgrimage center for all Christians. "Others merely hear [about Christ]," he said, "but we see *and touch*."[186]

Touching, however, was not essential for a transcendental experience. The mere sight of Jerusalem was enough to send some pilgrims into raptures. For example, a sixth century account of the life of a Spanish pilgrim known as Peter the Iberian tells us what happened when some Christian pilgrims saw the Holy City for the first time:

> When they had reached the outskirts of the holy city of Jerusalem which they loved, they saw from a high place five stades [a little over half a mile] away the lofty roof of the Holy Church of the Resurrection, shining like the morning sun, and cried aloud: "See that is Sion, the city of our deliverance!" They fell down upon their faces, and from there onwards they crept upon their knees, frequently kissing the soil with their lips and eyes, until they were within the holy walls and had embraced the sacred Cross on Golgotha.[187]

Pelagius (c. 412)

Pelagius was an English monk and theologian who was not so much a pilgrim *per se* as a refugee from religious persecution. He is remembered today as the father of Pelagianism, a heretical teaching that rejected the Christian doctrine of original sin. Pelagianism argued that sin was a matter of personal choice, not an unavoidable inheritance from Adam, the first man.[188] If this was in fact the case, it followed that men and women could achieve salvation entirely through their own efforts to avoid sin, i.e., by becoming ascetics. The heresy of Pelagianism lay in the logical conclusion of this point of view: there was thus no need either for Jesus' own atonement on the cross or for the elaborate hierarchy of the church itself.

Not surprisingly, Pelagius soon found himself in trouble with religious conservatives. After the Visigoths conquered Rome in 410, he fled to North Africa, where he got into further theological struggles with St. Augustine. Presumably seeking a more tranquil life, Pelagius then made his way to Jerusalem in about 412. Here he was again accused of heresy. At first he managed to escape censure but in 416 he responded to attacks from Augustine and Jerome by publishing a controversial document entitled "On Free Will." But this only added fuel to the theological fire. Pelagius' work was condemned and he was excommunicated by Pope Innocent I in 417.

He then wrote a "Brief Statement of Faith," which persuaded the next pope, Zosimus, to clear him. The conservatives did not give up, however, and eventually carried the day. Pelagius was condemned again in 418. By then he was about 64 years old and is thought to have died in Jerusalem shortly thereafter.

Eucherius (c. 414)

By the fifth century, descriptions of Jerusalem were becoming more detailed. Thanks to the monks who were emigrating from Egypt to settle in the Judean wilderness, the city became a new center of monastic Christianity. Eucherius, bishop of Lyons in France, was inspired by a traveler who had been to Jerusalem and has left us a good description of the Holy City. This was written at some point between 414 and 449:

> Jerusalem, they say, is naturally lofty, so that you must ascend to it from all sides; it rises by a long but gentle slope. The site of the city is almost circular in shape, enclosed by a lengthy wall, which now includes Mount Sion, though this was once outside. It is on the south and overlooks the city like a citadel. The greater part of the city lies on the flat top of a hill which is lower than this mount. Mount Sion on its northern slope is set aside for the dwellings of priests and monks, and its summit, which is level, is covered by monks' cells surrounding a church.... The Temple, which was situated in the lower city near the eastern wall, was once a world's wonder, but of its ruins there stands today only the pinnacle of one wall [the Western Wall], and the rest are destroyed down to their foundations.... Round Jerusalem the country has a rough, hilly appearance, and the Mount of Olives is to be seen on the east at about a mile's distance.[189]

Empress Eudokia (438)

By this time there were already about 200 monasteries and hospices in or near Jerusalem which welcomed pilgrims.[190] The increasing Christianization of Jerusalem, however, did not manifest itself in any greater tolerance toward the Jews. In 438 the Empress Eudokia, wife of Theodosius II, made an official pilgrimage to the Holy City.[191] She had previously given the Jews the right to pray on the Temple Mount, not only on the Ninth of Av but on other holy days as well. Eudokia's generous edict encouraged the Jews to hope that their redemption might at last be near at hand. As a result, Palestinian Jews invited their Diaspora brethren to come to Jerusalem to celebrate the pilgrim festival of *Sukkot*, which that year coincided with the Empress' visit.

Thus on the first day of *Sukkot*, large numbers of Jews began to gather on the Temple Mount. A Syrian monk named Bar Sauma had come to Jerusalem, too. He had long advocated using violence to keep the Jews in their place, i.e., under Christian control. On this occasion, he ordered the monks who were under his leadership to stone the Jews clustered together on the Temple platform. This his men proceeded to do. Many Jews were killed by the hail of rocks, while many others were crushed to death in Jerusalem's narrow streets by the panic-stricken, fleeing survivors.

Although the Jews managed to capture 18 of Bar Sauma's men, Jerusalem was in such an uproar that Eudokia feared that his followers would burn her alive if she sentenced the prisoners. She felt she had no choice but to give in. The outcome was that the dead Jews were officially found to have died of natural causes. This ruling was clearly a victory for Bar Sauma. In Jerusalem his herald proclaimed, "The cross has triumphed!" and Bar Sauma himself celebrated a mass on Mount Sion.

Eudokia returned to Constantinople but soon got into a row with Pulcheria, the emperor's sister, and was exiled to Jerusalem in 444 as the new ruler of Palestine. There she embarked on an extensive building program. Her generosity was legendary.[192] A contemporary observer reported that she built "a great number of churches, and monasteries for the poor and aged more than I can count."[193] In Jerusalem itself she built the church of St. Stephen and a residence for the patriarch. She had a palace for herself constructed on one corner of the Temple Mount. She may also have enlarged Jerusalem by extending the city's walls. She donated a huge copper cross weighing 6,000 pounds, which was to be installed at the top of the Mount of Olives. Finally, she endowed monasteries in the Judean desert.

Eudokia never flinched from controversy. In the 450s she took sides in a virulent, long-running theological-political dispute over Monophysitism, a heretical doctrine that focused on the two natures of Jesus—both human and divine.[194] Ultimately, the Monophysites lost. Riots broke out in Jerusalem when Eudokia appointed a Monophysite priest to be the new bishop. After the emperor Theodosius II died in 457, however, Eudokia sought counsel from an Orthodox monastic leader. His teachings made such a strong impression on her that she changed her mind and entirely abandoned the Monophysite cause. She herself died in Jerusalem in 460.

The Breviarius (c. 530)

The growing importance of Jerusalem as a center for Christian pilgrims resulted in more documents being written about it. (The Jews also continued writing about the Holy Land. Both the Jerusalem or Palestinian Talmud and the Babylonian Talmud, written between the third the sixth centuries, identified many holy sites.) One of the Christian works was a c. 530 handbook known as the *Breviarius de Hierosolyma* (*Jerusalem Breviary*), which identified the holiest relics in the city.[195]

At the basilica of Constantine, for example, the anonymous writer of this guide assured believers that there they would find not only the True Cross but also the spear which pierced Jesus' side as he hung on the cross; the plate on which the severed head of John the Baptist was carried; and the horn which was used to anoint David as king. This same church, the *Breviarius* asserted, was also the site of the creation of Adam and of Abraham's proposed sacrifice of his son, Isaac.

The Sion basilica, continued the *Breviarius*, displayed the Crown of Thorns placed on Jesus' head; the column to which Jesus was tied when he was whipped and which still bore the marks of his hands where he clutched it in agony; and some of the rocks used to stone St. Stephen to death. Other holy sites included the house of Pontius Pilate, who handed Jesus over to the Jews for crucifixion. The faithful could also visit the site of the Temple built by Solomon but, warned the *Breviarius*, "there is nothing left there apart from a single cave." This desolate site had one redeeming feature, however—"the pinnacle of the Temple on which Satan tempted Our Lord Jesus Christ."[196]

The pilgrim Theodosius (c. 530)

All that is known about this Western traveler is that he came to Jerusalem in about 530 and left us an unfinished document entitled *On the Topography of the Holy Land*. Theodosius apparently compiled this work from earlier written sources and probably intended to edit and polish it before it was reproduced.[197] Although poorly organized in its present form, the *Topography* is still valuable because it lists the large number of places in the Holy Land to which pilgrimages were made. More tangibly, it also gave the faithful a detailed picture of the physical trail allegedly left in Jerusalem by Jesus. According to Theodosius,

The column which was in the House of Caiaphas, at which the Lord Christ was scourged, is now in Holy Sion. This pillar by the Lord's command followed him. And you can see the way He clung to it when He was being scourged as if the marks were in wax. His arms, hands and fingers clove to it, as it shows even today. Also He made on it the impression of His whole face, chin, nose and eyes as if it had been wax.[198]

The Piacenza Pilgrim (c. 570)

An account written in about 570 by an anonymous pilgrim from Piacenza (Italy) is said to be by far the most vivid and unselfconscious description of Christian pilgrimage before the Crusades, which began in 1095.[199] It gives us a good insight into the profound emotional impact the True Cross made on susceptible pilgrims:

> In the courtyard of the basilica [in the Church of the Holy Sepulcher] is a small room where they keep the Wood of the Cross. We venerated it with a kiss.... At the moment when the Cross is brought out of this small room for veneration, and arrives in the court to be venerated, a star appears in the sky, and comes over the place where lay the Cross. It stops overhead whilst [the pilgrims] are venerating the Cross, and they offer oil to be blessed in little flasks. When the mouth of one of these flasks touches the Wood of the Cross, the oil instantly bubbles over, and unless it is closed very quickly it all spills out. When the Cross is put back into its place, the star also vanishes, and appears no more once the Cross has been put away.[200]

Pilgrim souvenirs (c. 604)

There was considerable Christian pilgrim traffic to Jerusalem in the early Middle Ages. As they still do today, most pilgrims came home clutching souvenirs from "the God-trodden land."[201] Known in the past as "blessings," these souvenirs included dried flowers from the garden of Gethsemane, stones or dirt from Golgotha, pinches of dust from places Christ had walked and tiny fragments of the True Cross. Ship owners even filled jars with "holy water" from the River Jordan and sprinkled it on their ships before they set sail. One very popular item for pilgrims was a round metal flask decorated with Biblical scenes. This was filled with oil from the lamps which burned at the Church of the Holy Sepulcher or at other shrines. One such flask, depicting the Ascension of Christ, was brought to Rome during the reign of Gregory the Great (590–604) and is now in the treasury of an Italian cathedral.[202]

The Persian conquest (614) and the Byzantine reconquest (630)

While Christian pilgrims were savoring the experience of being in the Holy City, the Byzantine empire itself was fraying at the edges. Its decline encouraged the Persians to attack. In 614 they invaded Palestine, captured Jerusalem after a three-week siege and slaughtered 66,555 of its inhabitants, including women and children (an estimate we should read only as meaning "a great many").

Two accounts of this catastrophe survive: one by a monk known as Strategius and the other by an Armenian named Sebeos.[203] Both agree that the Persians set the city on fire and burned down or desecrated many churches. Strategius tells us that the Persians "pulled down the glorious altars, trod venerable crosses underfoot and— filthy wretches!—spat at the life-giving icons."[204] The Persians also carted off all the gold and silver found in the church treasuries and divided Jerusalem's sur- vivors into two groups. The skilled work- ers were rounded up for later deportation to Persia, while the rest were detained within the city itself. As all this was going on, some of the remaining churches were assaulted and burned by Jerusalem's Jews.

Remarkably enough, when word of this attack reached Chosroes II, the Per- sian king, he pardoned the captives, or- dered that Jerusalem be rebuilt and ex- pelled the Jews. As the Persians pulled out of Jerusalem, they left Modestus, the Abbot of St. Theodosius, in charge of re- construction. Funded by the Patriarch of Egypt, the work went so well that in a let- ter to the head of the Armenian Church, written not long after 617, Modestus could report that many of the churches had been restored and that the annual pilgrimage from Armenia had resumed.[205]

Byzantium, however, did not give up. The emperor Heraclius continued the struggle against Persia until about 628, when both nations, by then thoroughly ex- hausted, made peace. Heraclius was able to enter Jerusalem in triumph in 630, bring- ing with him the True Cross, which the Persians had seized 16 years before. The

Christians were ecstatic because they were once again masters of the city. They had long memories and had never forgotten the tactile qualities of their holy places. In about 633, for example, the Orthodox monk Sophronius, then Patriarch of Jerusalem, wrote a poem about the tomb of Christ. It read in part:

> O light-giving Tomb, thou art the ocean stream of eternal life and the true river of Lethe.[206] I would lie at full length and kiss that stone, the sacred center of the world.... Hail to thee, Zion, splendid sun of the world, for whom I long and groan by day and by night.[207]

The end of the Christian era (638)

As we shall see in the next chapter, in 638—only a few years after the Byzantines had recaptured Jerusalem—it passed into Muslim hands. Except for short interludes during the Crusades, it was to remain an Islamic city until World War I, when the Turks abandoned it in 1917 to a British army led by General Allenby.

VI

The Early Islamic Period: Christian and Muslim Pilgrimages (638–1095)

The Muslims conquered Jerusalem in 638. In 691/692, determined to create a structure that would outshine the Christians' Church of the Holy Sepulcher, Caliph Abd al-Malik of the Umayyad Dynasty built, at the center of the Temple Mount, the magnificent Dome of the Rock. The Western Wall, sacred to the Jews, was incorporated into the wall surrounding the Dome. On the southern edge of the Temple Mount, a handsome if less glorious mosque (Al-Aqsa Mosque) was completed in 715. These two structures are still Islam's holiest sites in Jerusalem. The Umayyads were succeeded by the Abbasids. In Europe, the beginnings (in 1095) of the First Crusade heralded the temporary eclipse of Muslim rule in the Holy Land.

The expansion of Islam

Muhammad died in 632. By that time almost all of what is now Saudi Arabia was in Muslim hands. The stage was set for the international expansion of Islam. Muhammad's successor, Abu Bakr, first crushed rebellious Saudi tribesmen and then, in 633, turned his energies to the conquest of Persia, Syria and Iraq. He and later Muslim leaders were so successful that within 100 years after Muhammad's death, Islam was master of a vast empire stretching from Spain to India. A modern European scholar has concluded that "In the whole history of the world there has been nothing comparable, in the universal and immediate nature of its consequences, with the expansion of Islam in the 7th century."[208] This expansion was so unexpected and so remarkable that it worth asking how it happened. There seem to be at least four reasons[209]:

- Perhaps most importantly, Muslims believed that God had ordered them to spread Islam throughout the whole world by means of the *jihad*. This Arabic word is often translated as "holy war" but "holy struggle" is a better translation because *non-violent* means of persuasion, i.e., preaching and good works, are also legitimate ways of propagating Islam.
- Saudi Arabia was so hot, so dry and so barren a land that the *bedouin* were virtually forced to become raiders and con-

querors in order to survive. In 1480 a German pilgrim, the Dominican monk Felix Fabri (discussed below) described them as "a naked, miserable, bestial, wandering people, who alone can dwell in the desert which is uninhabitable to all others, and conquer all men alike, even the king himself, the most puissant sultan of Egypt."[210] The hardships of *bedouin* life were so great that once these tribesmen were unified under Islam and became a cohesive military force, expansion abroad held out great attractions to them.

• Foreign wars were a good way to sop up the excess energies of Saudi warriors, who might otherwise have been tempted to fight among themselves.

• Finally, there was a power vacuum in the region. Neighboring regimes, e.g., Persia and Byzantium, were exhausted by their own struggles. This made it impossible for them to defeat a militant Islam.

Caliph 'Umar (638)

Whatever the reasons for their vigorous expansion, in 638 a Muslim army under the leadership of Caliph 'Umar captured Jerusalem. According to Muslim tradition, as soon as 'Umar entered the Holy City, he ordered that the Haram be cleared of the heaps of rubbish that had filled it during the Byzantine period. The city had surrendered peacefully, so there was no slaughter. There were no forced conversions to Islam, either.

The Muslims respected Jews and Christians alike as "People of the Book" (*Ahl al-Kitab*), that is, as members of faiths also based on divine revelations, such as the Torah and the New Testament. True, Jews and Christians did have to pay special taxes but they were permitted to practice their religions and live their lives in peace. Tradition has it that this is what 'Umar

promised his new subjects, who became "protected minorities" (*ahl al-dhimma*):

> In the Name of God the Merciful and Lord of Mercy. From 'Umar ... to the citizens of Aelia [Jerusalem], They shall have security for their lives, their children, their goods, and their churches, which shall neither be pulled down or occupied.[211]

Arculf (c. 680)

'Umar also built the first mosque in Jerusalem, a modest structure which was described by Arculf (or Arculfus), a French bishop who made a pilgrimage to the Holy Land in about 680 and stayed there nine months. Little is known about Arculf himself. When returning from Jerusalem, however, he was shipwrecked on the west coast of Scotland.

After many adventures, he visited the learned Adomnan (or Adamnan), the ninth abbot of a monastery on the nearby island of Iona, who wrote down Arculf's experiences. The Venerable Bede, father of English history, helped propagate Adomnan's work, so this account received what was for the time a wide circulation.[212] Even today it makes interesting reading, so it is easy to understand why in the seventh century it stimulated Christian interest in the pilgrimage to Jerusalem.

This is how Adomnan described Jerusalem to Bede:

> For those entering the city of Jerusalem from the northern side, the lay-out of the streets makes the Church of Constantinople the first of the Holy Places to be visited. This was erected by the Emperor Constantine in a magnificent regal style, for this is where his mother Helena discovered the Cross of our Lord. To the west, the church of Golgotha comes into view, where can be seen the rock on which once stood the

Cross, with the Body of our Lord nailed to it: it now supports an enormous silver cross, over which hangs a great bronze wheel bearing lamps.... To the west of this stands the Church of the *Anastasis*, which is the church of the Lord's Resurrection.... The exterior is completely covered with marble to the top of the roof, which is adorned with gold and bears a great golden cross.[213]

Referring to the crowds that came together in Jerusalem for the enthusiastic buying and selling associated with the pilgrim festival of *Sukkot*, Arculf reported that each year "an immense number of different nations are used to meet in Jerusalem for the purpose of commerce, and the streets are so clogged with the dung of camels, horses, mules and oxen, that they become almost impassable."[214]

Arculf mentioned 'Umar's mosque only in passing:

near the wall on the east [of Jerusalem], in that famous place where once stood the magnificent Temple, the Saracens have now built an oblong house of prayer, which they pieced together with upright planks and large beams over some ruined remains. This they attend, and it is said that this building can hold three thousand people.[215]

He devotes much more space to a description of Constantine's Church of the Holy Sepulcher. For Adomnan's benefit, he even drew a floor plan of it on a wax tablet. "This is a very large church," Arculf told Adomnan,

made entirely of stone, and built in a remarkable round plan.... The church rests on twelve columns of remarkable size.... In the centre of this round space enclosed by this church there is a small building hewn from a single rock.... Its whole exterior is covered with choice marble, and the roof is decorated on the

outside with gold, and supports a large gold cross. This small building contains the Lord's Sepulchre, which has been cut into the rock on the north side.[216]

When Arculf arrived in Jerusalem, he found that the local Christians were always ready to show credulous visitors a large number of spurious relics and holy sites associated with Jesus' life. On display, for example, was the silver cup which Jesus used when he ate with his disciples after his resurrection. Pilgrims could also see the lance which a Roman soldier had used during the crucifixion to pierce Jesus' side; the cloth, now vested with supernatural powers, that had been placed over Jesus' head when he was buried; and the very footprints of Jesus himself, miraculously embedded in the rock from which he had ascended to heaven.

Jewish pilgrimage continues

The journey to Jerusalem was a hazardous one but Diaspora Jews continued to make pilgrimages there even during the early years of Muslim control.[217] The major attraction for Jewish pilgrims was Hoshanah Rabah, the seventh day of *Sukkot*, when a procession wound its way through the city up to the Mount of Olives. This was supposed to be a happy occasion but a dominant sect, the Rabbanites, who represented rabbinical Judaism, used *Sukkot* to show their disapproval of Jewish separatists known as the Karaites.

The Karaites had set themselves in direct opposition to rabbinical Judaism by rejecting the orally based Talmud as a source of divine guidance. They relied instead on the Torah. Thus, according to Ibn Daud, an Arab observer reporting on conditions in the ninth century,

When the Jews used to celebrate at the Festival of Tabernacles on the Mount of Olives, [the rabbinical congregations] would encamp on the mountain in groups and greet each other warmly.... The heretics would encamp before them like little flocks of goats. Then the rabbis would take out a scroll from the Torah and pronounce a ban on the heretics right in their faces, while the latter remained silent like dumb dogs.[218]

New centers for Islamic pilgrims: the Dome of the Rock and the Aqsa Mosque

In 691/692 the tenth Caliph, 'Abd al-Malik, completed the Dome of the Rock (*Qubbat al-Sakhra*), a magnificent structure which incorporated part of the Western Wall, the last remnant of the First Temple of the Jews. The Dome of the Rock has been called "the first Muslim masterpiece"[219] and is the crowning jewel of the Haram al-Sharif (the Temple Mount). A description of the Dome of the Rock given by Kay Prag, a modern archaeologist, cannot easily be improved upon. This mosque is built, she says,

in Byzantine-Syrian architectural style, with innovations marking it as one of the first great buildings of Islamic architecture. It is a shrine of gem-like beauty, once shining with the rich colours of gold and polychrome glass mosaic both inside and out.[220]

Thanks to a personal donation from King Hussein of Jordan, the roof of the Dome was completely renovated in 1994. The new roof is made of copper sheets coated with a fine layer of nickel and an outer layer of gold leaf. With its newly-guilded exterior, the Dome has recovered all of the beauty and glory it lost in 1954 when it was restored with large plates of anodized aluminum.

The Dome's religious significance to Muslims is even more important than its esthetic qualities. It is the third holiest place in Islam, after the Ka'bah in Mecca and Muhammad's tomb in Medina, and is revered as the site of Muhammad's miraculous Night Journey. The Holy Rock, located in the middle of the Dome of the Rock, measures about 57 feet by 42 feet and projects about 5 feet above the present paving.

The Jews considered this rock to be the center of the world, lying above a bottomless pit. It was the spot where they believed the Ark of the Covenant first stood and under which it had been hidden when the First Temple was destroyed in 587/586 BCE. Subsequently, the Muslims elaborated on this sacred geography. They have defined the rock as being the center of the world; as being supported on a palm tree watered by the river of Paradise; as the place where the spirits of the dead await the Day of Judgment; and as the site where, on that last day, the Ka'bah will come from Mecca and where God's throne will be erected.[221] Popular legend had it that when Muhammad prayed in the Dome of the Rock, the rock itself began to rise up out of the ground in tribute to the Prophet's holiness. Muhammad restrained it with his hand, however, and the rock still remains frozen in midair, half-in and half-out of the ground.[222]

Muslims visited this shrine as part of the great annual pilgrimage to Mecca. The Dome of the Rock held up to 3,000 worshippers and was said to have cost the staggering sum of seven years' revenue from the province of Egypt, which had been piled up in gold in the adjacent Dome of the Chain while construction was going on. No expense was spared in maintaining the Dome of the Rock, either. It was cleaned with water suffused with the scent of roses, musk and saffron. Light was provided by hanging lamps burning fragrant oils. Incense and the smoke from fires fed with aromatic woods slowly drifted heavenwards.[223]

If the Dome of the Rock was the sacred center of Muslim pilgrimage, the Aqsa Mosque (*al-Masjid al-Aqsa al-Mubarak*, "the Furthermost Blessed Mosque") was where the masses of faithful came to pray. This great mosque was completed in 715, possibly at or near the spot where Caliph 'Umar had built the first mosque in Jerusalem, and in its present form can hold up to 5,000 worshippers.[224] After the Crusaders conquered Jerusalem in 1099, the Aqsa Mosque became their own headquarters and, later, the headquarters of the Knights Templar, a military-religious order which will be discussed in Chapter VII.

Beginnings of the great age of Christian pilgrimage

Many early Christian pilgrims are thought to have come to Jerusalem from Byzantium, Egypt and Iraq but few records of them survive. What we have instead are numerous and often very detailed accounts of travels by Latin pilgrims, i.e., men and women from Western Europe.[225]

St. Willibald (723) and other visitors

One of the most famous of these travelers was St. Willibald of Wessex, the first Anglo-Saxon pilgrim to visit the Holy Land. (See Appendix III for an account of his travels from 720 to 726.) He spent several years there and visited Jerusalem four times, beginning in 723, being deeply moved by his surroundings. "What spot was there which had witnessed the Lord's miracles," he wrote, "on which Willibald, the man of God, did not imprint his kisses?"[226]

Other notable pilgrims of this era included Bishop Madelveus of Verdun (c. 750), who brought many relics of the saints to his native France; St. Elia of Castrogiovanni (c. 850), an Italian who had been captured at sea and been made a slave; Frotmund (858), a French aristocrat who took three years to get to Jerusalem; and another Frenchman, Bernard the Monk (c. 858), who sailed from the port of Tarente (now known as Tarento) in southern Italy, where he watched ten ships loading a total of 15,000 Christian prisoners to be sold as slaves in North Africa.[227]

Charlemagne the Great (c. 800)

By the beginning of the ninth century, the Christian pilgrimage to Jerusalem was solidly established. An anonymous document, the *Memorandum on the Houses of God and Monasteries in the Holy City*, was produced in about 800 as a briefing paper for the Holy Roman Emperor Charlemagne. It shows that the Christian holy places of Jerusalem were staffed with non–Palestinian monks and nuns, many of whom had come long distances (from Europe, for example) to live piously in Jerusalem and to help the pilgrims who came there.[228]

Charlemagne never visited Jerusalem himself but this inconvenient fact did not deter contemporary chroniclers. In about 1000, for example, the monk Benedict of St. Andrew claimed that

Then [Charlemagne] came to the Most Holy Sepulchre of our Lord and Saviour Jesus Christ (also the place of the Resurrection), adorned the holy place with gold and gems, and also placed on it an immense gold banner. Amongst all the holy places he specially adorned the Manger of the Lord and his Sepulchre, for King Aaron [a phonetic rendering of the name of al-Harun al-Rashid, the Ayyubid caliph in Baghdad] granted him permission to do as he wished. And what garments and spices, and wealth of eastern treasures he gave Charles [Charlemagne]![229]

A similar spurious account was a French *chanson de geste* ("song of deeds") entitled the *Pèlerinage de Charlemagne* ("*Charlemagne's Pilgrimage*"). The facts of the matter are that Charlemagne had only indirect contact with the Holy City. Monks from Jerusalem attended his inauguration in 800 and Charlemagne exchanged gifts with Caliph al-Harun al-Rashid. A monk named Einhard, who traveled with Charlemagne's entourage, reported that the Emperor's relations with the caliph were so friendly that

> this prince preferred his favor to that of all the kings and potentates of the earth, and considered that to him alone marks of honor and munificence were due. Accordingly, when the ambassadors sent by Charles to visit the most holy sepulcher and place of resurrection of our Lord and Savior presented themselves before him with gifts, and made known their master's wishes, he not only granted what was asked, but gave possession of that holy and blessed spot. When they returned, he dispatched his ambassadors with them, and sent magnificent gifts, besides stuffs, perfumes, and other rich products of the Eastern lands. A few years before this, Charles had asked him for an elephant, and he sent the only one he had.[230]

The caliph allowed Charlemagne to build two pilgrim hospices in the Holy Land, as well as a church, a library and an estate containing vineyards, fields and gardens. Later Christian writers even claimed that al-Harun al-Rashid was so impressed by their Emperor that he wanted to give him the Holy Land in its entirety.[231] False as the assertion was, it formed the basis for the belief, prevalent in Crusader times and even later on, that Jerusalem really belonged to Christianity and not to Islam. If so, it followed that the Christians had every right to "liberate" the Holy City from Muslim control.

The great age of Christian pilgrimage

A number of factors combined to make the millennial tenth century a high point of Christian pilgrimage. In part, this reflected the great economic and demographic expansion of Western Europe that was going on at this time. Lands were reclaimed, harvests doubled, cities grew and international commerce increased. There was a great spiritual expansion as well. Probably writing in the 1030s but drawing his inspiration from the year 1000, the French monk Glaber tells us that around this time,

> Men, especially in Italy and Gaul [France], began to construct churches.... It was as if the whole world were shaking itself free, shrugging off the burden of the past and cladding itself everywhere with a white mantle of churches.[232]

Other developments were at play here, too. Passage by sea became safer when Muslim pirates were driven from their bases in southern Italy, southern France and the eastern Mediterranean. Travel by land became safer as well when Hungary was converted to Christianity by King Stephen. It was said of Stephen that "he made the way very safe for all and thus allowed by his benevolence a countless multitude both of noble and common people to start for Jerusalem."[233] The Muslim rulers of Palestine began to welcome pilgrims as a good source of income.[234]

Pilgrimage got a much-needed administrative boost when in the tenth century the Benedictine abbey of Cluny in east-central France became an organizing center for Latin pilgrims bound for Jerusalem.[235] The documentary trail of the ghostly pilgrim now becomes much clearer, chiefly left by Christian but also to some extent by Muslim travelers. Finally, the approach of the millennial year 1000 exerted a strong eschatological pull on Christian pilgrims, who believed that this year might be the last one, marking the end of time.

Some Christian and Muslim pilgrims

On the Christian side of the ledger,[236] we can note that Countess Adelinda of Swabia (southwestern Germany) made a pilgrimage to Jerusalem in about 900 after her three sons had been killed in battle. In 970 King Henry II's grandmother, Judith, led a large party of noble ladies to Jerusalem. Hidda, the mother of the bishop of Cologne, was there at the same time. The theological tug-of-war between the heavenly and the earthly Jerusalem still had not been resolved. So although Conrad (d. 976), the bishop of Constance in southern Germany, visited Jerusalem three times, his biographer takes pains to assure us that his patron

> braved the perils of the sea three times in order to see Jerusalem the same number of times, even if this was the earthly city, for he attached importance to seeing the promised land in a physical sense, the place where the prefigurations of the patriarchs and prophets' oracles made it possible to see the God-man in a spiritual way.[237]

Gontier, the abbot of a monastery in western France, visited the Holy City in 988. He was followed in 990 by Adalpert, the bishop of the Slavs, and in 992 by

Adso, the head of a monastery in eastern France, who died aboard ship.

Darani and the Muslim holy women (c. 826)

There are fewer entries for this period on the Muslim side of the ledger. One of the best of these reports dates from about 826 and gives us a long, tantalizing, evocative glimpse of Islamic holy women in the Jerusalem pilgrimage. This verbatim account, sourced to a Muslim ascetic known as Darani, has been lightly edited:

> One day while I [Darani] was making my way toward Jerusalem, I saw a woman dressed in a robe of heavy cloth and wearing a wool scarf around her head. She was sitting on the path, bent over, her head between her knees and she was crying. I came up to her and said, "What is it that makes you cry, young lady?" She replied, "How can I not be in tears, having met Him?" I asked her, "Who is it that you long for?" She answered, "Does a lover long for anything other than meeting the Beloved?" I asked her, "Who, then, is your Beloved?" She replied, "He who knows the Invisible." I asked, "What does one have to do to love this person?" She told me, "If you succeed in purifying your soul from all its defects and if your spirit mounts to the heavenly kingdom, you will know how to love the Beloved." I asked her, "What do such lovers look like?" She responded, "Their bodies are thin, their complexions distorted, their eyes full of tears, their hearts beat strongly and their souls are split open. However, the very thought of their Beloved fills their speech with ease and abundance." I asked her, "Where did you get the wisdom with which you express yourself?" She joked, "It is not something that comes with age!" I asked, "How did you achieve it?" She replied, "By purity of affection and

by good behavior." Then, after reciting some verses about love, she rose and while I watched her leave, she slipped away between two mountains.[238]

In the same era there are other accounts of Muslim holy women, too. Some of them refer to Rabi'a al-Adawiyah (c. 717–801), who has been accorded first place in the list of Islamic saints. By injecting the element of "disinterested love"—that is, a pure love of God that did not depend either on the believer's hope of heaven or fear of hell—she is credited with changing Muslim asceticism into mysticism. Rabi'a set a standard for others to follow. Her life was marked by penitence, patience, gratitude, holy fear, voluntary poverty and utter dependence upon God. She left her native Iraq to live, meditate and die in Jerusalem.[239]

Another report of an Islamic holy woman comes from an Egyptian mystic, Dhu al-Nun. During a pilgrimage to Mecca in about 859, he met a female mystic named Fatima de Nishapur, who had left her native Iraq to become one of the "neighbors of God" (*mujawir*) in Mecca. Dhu al-Nun became her disciple and the two of them set off together for Syria, where both Muslim and Christian ascetics lived in caves. Fatima de Nishapur, however, died en route in Jerusalem. Her last instruction to her pupil was: "Persist in sincerity, and fight against carnal desires by doing good works."[240]

Ibn al-Faqih (903)

In about 903 the Persian geographer Ibn al-Faqih was struck by the magnificence of the Haram al-Sharif, which by then was not only the site of the Dome of the Rock and the Aqsa Mosque but of several smaller sanctuaries, too. This whole complex was tended by 140 slaves and lit by 1,600 lamps. Sixteen chests held fine copies of the Koran. There were five pulpits for preachers and three special areas reserved for women. Al-Faqih also identified the features of the Haram that had been important to Jews and Christians, and which were now important to Muslims for different reasons, e.g., because of Muhammad's miraculous Night Journey.

Ibn 'Abd Rabbih (c. 913)

Ibn 'Abd Rabbih was a Spanish Muslim scholar who made important contributions to the first encyclopedia written in Arabic. He visited Jerusalem about a decade after Ibn al-Faqih's visit and recognized its importance as a sacred center. He recorded in about 913 that one of the stone slabs in floor of the Dome of the Rock was believed to lie directly over one of the entrances to Paradise.

Al-Muqaddesi (985)

In 985, another Muslim geographer, al-Muqaddesi, surnamed "the Jerusalemite," published a *Description of the Muslim Empire* as a result of his own travels. He decided that life was so agreeable in Jerusalem, the city itself must be close to Paradise.[241] He found the markets well-stocked with local produce (oil, cheese, cotton and fruits). This abundance reflected the importance of the pilgrim trade because the city itself was something of an economic backwater.

Al-Muqaddesi noted that many Muslims came to Jerusalem either to study or to teach. Others, especially North Africans, used the city as a base from which to start their *ihram* for the pilgrimage to Mecca.[242] (*Ihram* is a state of ritual purity which a Muslim must enter to perform either the major pilgrimage, the *hajj*, or the "minor pilgrimage," the *'umrah*. The *'umrah* is undertaken by Muslims whenever they enter Mecca.)

Even from this devout Muslim's point of view, however, the Holy City was not perfect. There were some Jews and too many Christians living in Jerusalem, he wrote, and far too many Christian pilgrims from distant lands. The calendar year was dotted with Christian celebrations. Although he noted that the Haram al-Sharif was one of the biggest structures in the Muslim world and that the Muslim call to prayer could be heard everywhere, he concluded that Jerusalem was not at that time a major intellectual center for Islam. "The Mosque is empty," al-Muqaddesi complained, "there are no scholars, no savants, no disputations, and no instruction."[243]

The Holy Fire

Arab chroniclers report that by about the year 1000, hordes of Christian pilgrims, many of them from Byzantium, were descending on Jerusalem for the Easter season.[244] Emperors, generals and senior officials brought with them money, richly woven carpets, and silver and gold ornaments. These would be carried in religious processions and then donated to the Church of the Holy Sepulcher. According to these Arab chroniclers, however, this same church deserved to be roundly criticized for deceiving the faithful through the "miracle" of the Holy Fire.

Many of the more naïve Christian pilgrims believed that at Easter a holy light miraculously descended from heaven and lit the candles of the church. This Holy Fire (or Flame) was first mentioned in 867, but many educated Christians and virtually all Jews and Muslims remained unconvinced. The mad Caliph Hakim ordered the destruction of the Church of the Holy Sepulcher in 1009, as well as the tomb

of Christ, in large part because he was convinced the Holy Fire was an impious fraud.[245]

Abbot Daniel (1006)

One of the earliest accounts of the Holy Fire comes from the Russian abbot Daniel, who made a pilgrimage to the Holy Land in 1006–1007. This is what he has to say:

At the moment of the sixth hour of the day [Holy Saturday], everyone assembles in front of the Church of the Holy Resurrection; foreigners and natives, people from all countries, from Babylon, from Egypt, and from every part of the world, come together in countless numbers; the crowd fills the open space round the church and round the place of the Crucifixion. The crush is terrible, and the turmoil so great that many persons are suffocated in the dense crowd of people who stand, unlighted tapers in hand, waiting for the opening of the church doors.... The faithful shed torrents of tears; even he who has a heart of stone cannot refrain from weeping; each one ... thinks of his sins, and says secretly to himself, "Will my sins prevent the descent of the Holy Light?" ... It was at this moment [the ninth hour] that the Holy Light suddenly illuminated the Holy Sepulchre, shining with an awe-inspiring and splendid brightness. The bishop ... entered with the taper of Prince Baldwin so as to light it first at the Holy Light.... We lighted our tapers from those of the Prince, and so passed on the flame to everyone in the church. The Holy Light is no ordinary flame, for it burns in a marvellous way with indescribable brightness, and a ruddy colour like that of cinnabar.... Man can experience no joy like that which every Christian feels at the moment when he sees the Holy Light of God.[246]

Jerusalem as an alternative to Mecca

We noted earlier that Muslims are required by their faith to make at least one pilgrimage to Mecca if they can afford it. By the eleventh century, Jerusalem had emerged as an alternative destination for pilgrims who for one reason or another could not go to Mecca. This substitution was possible because the sanctity of Jerusalem rested on solid doctrinal foundations. An especially famous *hadith* attributed to Muhammad himself makes this clear:

> The saddles of the camels shall not be fastened [for setting out on pilgrimage] except for three mosques: the Haram mosque [in Mecca], my mosque [in Medina], and al-Aqsa Mosque [in Jerusalem].[247]

Jerusalem held such a strong symbolic attraction for Muslims that it became the site of a mini-pilgrimage known as the *ziyara* (a pious visit or pious journey), so named to distinguish it from the mandatory pilgrimage to Mecca. The *ziyara* could be undertaken at any time, but in practice it was usually made as part of the required pilgrimage to Mecca.[248] Another well-known *hadith* confirms the holiness of Jerusalem:

> The Prophet said: "Mecca is the city Allah exalted or sanctified, created and surrounded by angels a thousand years before creating anything else on earth. Then He joined it with Medina and united Medina to Jerusalem, and only a thousand years later created the [rest of the world] in a single act."[249]

Thus, on the same night when Muslim pilgrims were standing in vigil on a plain near Mecca, their counterparts in Palestine congregated at the Haram platform and the Aqsa Mosque in Jerusalem.

On the last day of the *hajj*, these Muslims would sacrifice animals on the Haram, just as they would have done in Mecca. Moreover, after making the *hajj*, some devout Muslims would then make a *ziyara* to Jerusalem. There they wore the white robes prescribed for the *hajj* and would keep themselves in a state of ritual purity.[250]

Richard of St. Vannes (c. 1026)

In 1026 the abbot of the French monastery of Grace Dieu was Richard of St. Vannes. Weighed down by the cares of his office, and recalling that certain people who had gone to Jerusalem had died a happy death there, Richard resolved to make a pilgrimage to the Holy City. He did not die but instead experienced a dramatic reaffirmation of his faith. In this process, his biographer tells us, Richard

> faithfully toured all the places of the Nativity, Passing and Resurrection, and when he was not feasting on them with his eyes, he browsed upon them in his mind, for at the most delectable sight of the wonders of God, which he had so longed and prepared for in his desirous mind, he was filled with an unspeakable joy and gladness. Oh, what was his love towards God! What the exaltation of his contrite and humbled spirit!... Everywhere that he prayed, he soaked the ground in tears, the cry of his heart rose up to the Lord, his body sank down, his spirit rose aloft. He spent the night continually in vigils, he wore down his body with fasts, never without tears, never without prayers, his whole being exulted in the Lord....[251]

Fulk III Nerra (1040)

Not all pilgrims were angels. Fulk III Nerra ("Nerra" means "the Blade") was count of Anjou and one of the most powerful French nobles of the eleventh century. Intelligent, violent, cruel, charismatic and a master castle-builder, he never hesitated to burn and pillage any monastery which lay in his path. His depredations were so notorious that he was nicknamed "le Noir" ("the Black") by his enemies. His own confessor, appalled by what Fulk confided to him, strongly recommended that, as an act of penance, Fulk should make the pilgrimage to Jerusalem. Perhaps calculating that his sins were so numerous and so heinous that one pilgrimage to the Holy City would not be enough, Fulk made no less than three pilgrimages there. He also visited Rome and founded two abbeys in France.

A contemporary account of one of Fulk's pilgrimages to Jerusalem proves that he was an unusually resourceful man. When he and his fellow pilgrims tried to enter the Church of the Holy Sepulcher, the Muslim guards there, seeing that he was an important personage, told him he could not enter the church unless he would urinate on it and on the True Cross. Fulk unwillingly agreed to these conditions and at once sought out

> a ram's bladder, and had it thoroughly cleaned and scoured and filled with the best white wine and placed it between his thighs; taking off his shoes he approached the Sepulchre and poured the wine over it, and so he was able to enter freely with his companions and pray, shedding many tears.... He gave great gifts to the poor there and in return those who guarded the Sepulchre gave him a piece of the Holy Cross.[252]

Fulk died in 1040, not long after returning from his last Jerusalem pilgrimage.

Rodolfus Glaber (1044)

At the same time as Muslim pilgrimages to Jerusalem were increasing, Christian pilgrimages from Western Europe were on the rise, too. In 1044, Rodolfus (or Rodulf or Raoul) Glaber, a Cluniac monk, finished writing *The Five Books of the Histories*, which chronicled the doings of the Capetian kings of France and of their great vassals.[253] Glaber notes that a major reason for the increase in pilgrimages was the opening up an overland route through Hungary at the end of the tenth century, following that country's conversion to Christianity.[254] Here is what he says about the Jerusalem pilgrimage:

> At this time [c. 1000] an innumerable multitude of people from the whole world, greater than any man before could have hoped to see, began to travel to the Sepulchre of the Saviour at Jerusalem. First to go were the petty people, then those of middling estate, and next the powerful, kings, counts, marquesses, and bishops; finally, and this was something that had never happened before, numerous women, noble and poor, undertook the journey.... Moreover, some of those [who] were then most concerned in these matters, being consulted by many concerning the signification of this concourse to Jerusalem, greater than any past age had ever heard of, answered with some caution that it portended no other than the advent of that reprobate Antichrist, whose coming at the [end] of this world is prophesied in Holy Scripture.[255]

Glaber adds that many pilgrims wanted to die in Jerusalem rather than return to their native land. He cites the case of one Lethbaud, a pilgrim from Burgundy. Upon reaching the Mount of Olives, this devout man threw himself on the ground in the shape of a cross and prayed that he be permitted to die in the holy city. Lethbaud then went back to the pilgrim hostel for lunch. His companions sat down to eat but he declined, saying that he was very tired and wished to take a nap. Suddenly he cried out in his sleep: "Glory be to thee, O God! Glory be to thee, O God!" Hearing this, his companions urged him to get up and eat, but he again declined, telling them he did not feel well.

In the evening, Lethbaud "asked for and received the viaticum of the life-giving Eucharist, sweetly bade all farewell, and died." Glaber draws a moral from this incident which serves to remind us, yet again, that not all pilgrims traveled for ghostly reasons: "Truly he [Lethbaud] was free from that vanity which inspires so many to undertake the journey simply to gain the prestige of having been to Jerusalem."[256]

Glaber also reports an interesting incident involving the Holy Fire, which was witnessed by Ulric, the bishop of Orléans. Ulric was part of the crowd awaiting the appearance of the Holy Fire, when

> a Saracen, truly an impudent jester, one of the crowd of that race which gathers and mixes with the Christians, cried out in the manner of the Christians when the fire is first seen: "Alios Kyrie Eleison" ["Holy Lord, have mercy on us"]. Then, laughing aloud mockingly he reached out and snatched a candle from the hand of one of the Christians and made to flee. But he was seized by a demon who much troubled him [i.e., he had a seizure of some sort]. The Christian followed him and took back his candle. The fellow at once died in agony in the hands of the other Saracens. This event terrified all the Saracens alike, but brought joy and exaltation to the Christians.[257]

As if all this were not enough, continues Glaber, the Holy Fire appeared "at this very moment" in one of the seven lamps hanging in the Church of the Holy Sepulcher. Bishop Ulric bought the lamp and its oil for one pound of gold and brought it back to his own see, "where it provided many benefits for the sick."[258]

At the end of his account of the pilgrimage, Glaber, who was a conscientious and thoughtful man, raised the question of "what was meant by so many people, in numbers unheard-of in earlier ages, going to Jerusalem." The answer, he decided, lay in eschatology. This great influx of people might herald the appearance of the Antichrist, a demonic figure who was expected to appear at the end of the world. However, even if the Antichrist did emerge, Glaber assured his readers, believers need have no fear: "the pious labours of the faithful will be then rewarded and paid for by the Just Judge."[259]

Abu Mu'in Nasir (1047)

Muslim pilgrims first came to Jerusalem to pray at its sacred places in the 660s but few records of these early visits have survived.[260] By that time, however, Jerusalem was already a center for Muslim ascetics and mystics, so its holiness was well-established. Some Muslim pilgrims came to fulfill personal vows. Anyone who could not afford to go to Jerusalem could instead send olive oil to be burned in the lamps of the main mosque there.[261] Foreign Muslims sometimes came to Jerusalem just before the season of the *hajj* to prepare themselves spiritually before the long journey to Mecca. For example, a Persian traveler, Abu Mu'in Nasir, who visited Jerusalem in 1047, noted that

> The men of Syria, and of the neighbouring parts, call the Holy City by the name of Kuds (the Holy); and the people of these provinces, if they are unable to make the pilgrimage to Mecca, will go up at the appointed season to Jerusalem, and there perform their rites,

and upon the feast day slay the sacrifice, as it is customary to do in Mecca on the same day. There are years when as many as twenty thousand people will be present at Jerusalem during the first days of the pilgrimage month.... From all the countries of the Greeks, too, and from other lands, the Christians and the Jews come up to Jerusalem in great numbers in order to make their visitation to the Church of the Resurrection and the synagogue that is there.[262]

Ibn al-Murajja (first half of the eleventh century)

The first step-by-step guidebook for Muslim pilgrims in Jerusalem dates from the first half of the eleventh century and reflects the growing popularity of the city for Islamic travelers. It was written by Ibn al-Murajja, who recommended more than 20 places as sites for prayers or invocations. These included the Dome of the Rock; the Dome of the Chain; the Dome of the Ascension to Heaven; the Dome of the Prophet; the Gate of Mercy; the Place of Prayer of Zechariah; Solomon's Chair; the Aqsa Mosque; the Place of Prayer of Mary, also known as the Cradle of Jesus; the rock where the Angel Gabriel used his finger as a drill to make a hole to tether Muhammad's mount, the mythical steed Buraq; the Mount of Olives; and the Place of Prayer of David.[263] Murajja probably also collected and edited prayers which were appropriate for use at these holy places. Taken all in all, his account of the pilgrimage to Jerusalem was so useful that it was copied extensively by later Muslim writers. These scholars gradually raised the number of Islamic holy places within the Old City to 59.[264]

Naser-e Khosraw (1047)

In 1046 a Persian poet, theologian and civil servant named Naser-e Khosraw set off on a pilgrimage to Mecca which he later expanded into a seven-year journey throughout the Middle East. He reached Jerusalem in 1047 after a year of nearly continuous travel and in his *Book of Travels* gave a detailed account of what he found there. Khosraw was less swayed by popular superstitions than many other pilgrims.

He reports, for example, that at Jerusalem's Valley of Gehenna (a name derived from *jahannam*, an Arabic word for hell) "the common people say that anyone who goes to the edge of the valley can hear the voices of the people in hell" but candidly admits to his readers: "I went there but heard nothing."[265] He was a relatively objective observer and confirms that Syrian and other Muslims—more than 20,000 of them in some years—flocked to Jerusalem if they could not afford to make the *hajj* to Mecca. They were not alone: Christians and Jews went there, too, to visit the churches and synagogues. Hospices or other accommodations welcomed all these pilgrims.

The Jerusalem of Khosraw's time must have been a pleasant place to live. It was, he says,

a large city, there being some twenty thousand men there when I saw it. The bazaars are nice, the buildings tall, and the ground paved with stone.... They have built many buildings around [the Spring of Siloam], and it waters the gardens. They say that whoever washes in that water will be cured of chronic illness.... Jerusalem has a fine, heavily endowed hospital. People are given potions and draughts, and the physicians who are there draw their salaries from the endowment [rather than charging the patients themselves].[266]

This general prosperity almost seemed a reflection of Jerusalem's holiness. Large numbers of Muslim men and women made the pilgrimage to be "neighbors of God," remaining in the Holy City for months or even years.[267] Khosraw remarked that

> Passing out of the mosque you come out onto a large, expansive, and flat plain called Sahera. They say this is where the Resurrection will take place, where all men will be gathered together. For this reason many people have come there from all over the world and taken up residence in order to die in that city. When God's appointed time comes, they will already be in the stipulated place…. [Jerusalem] is the third most holy place of God, and it is well known among those learned in religion that [one] prayer made in Jerusalem is worth twenty-five thousand ordinary prayers. Every prayer said in Medina is worth fifty thousand, and every prayer said in Mekka is worth one hundred thousand.[268]

Khosraw devotes many pages to a careful, very detailed description of the Haram al-Sharif, the Dome of the Rock and the Aqsa Mosque. He was especially struck by the beauty of the Dome of the Rock, which was adorned with patterns of colored tiles and with the titles of the sultan of Egypt. "When the sun strikes this," he reports, "the rays play so that the mind of the beholder is absolutely stunned."[269] The Aqsa Mosque and the Prophet's Gate were equally impressive. One of the mosque's gates was clad with "such beautifully ornate brass that one would think it was made of gold burnished with silver"; for its part, the Prophet's Gate was built of stones "so enormous that the mind of man cannot comprehend how human strength could have moved them."[270]

Earl Sweyn (1053)

An excellent example of a rogue forced into pilgrimage for the sake of penance is Earl Sweyn, a notorious sinner.[271] One of his earliest offenses was to seduce Edviga, Abbess of Leominster. Declared an outlaw for this offense, he fled to Denmark but broke the law there, too. As soon as he returned to England, he became involved in a land dispute with his cousin, Earl Beorn, and murdered Beorn when the two men met under a flag of truce. Proclaimed a *nithing* (a man without honor in Saxon society), Sweyn continued to cause so much trouble that in 1053 his family pressured him into leaving England on a pilgrimage to Jerusalem, where he would be out of sight and could earn much-needed indulgences by praying at one of the 99 holy places in the city.

In this manner, by simultaneously putting himself beyond the reach of Christian law and by reducing the time he might have to spend in purgatory (a kind of halfway house between heaven and hell), Sweyn set a pattern for the Jerusalem pilgrim that would become popular later on, especially during the Crusades. Barbara Tuchman found that "This system proved so attractive to transgressors that cutthroats and misfits aplenty mingled with the pious, the adventurous, and the purely curious amid the pilgrim multitudes."[272] As for Sweyn himself, he spared his family any further embarrassment by dying at Constantinople in about 1055 on his way back home from Jerusalem.

Jewish aliya *and pilgrimage*

For Diaspora Jews there was a close relationship between *aliya* and pilgrimage. Literally, *aliya* means "going up to." This term initially referred to pilgrimages to Jerusalem but later came to mean the decision to settle permanently in the land of Israel. During the period under discussion here, it was usually political and economic hardship, not religious zeal, that triggered *aliya*.

Israel ben Sahlun (1059)

The copyist (scribe) Israel ben Sahlun, for example, faced so many financial problems in his native Cairo that he promised God he would immigrate to Jerusalem if God would only help him resolve his difficulties. To escape his debtors, he "went up to" Jerusalem in 1051 and seems to have stayed there for the rest of his life. This is evident from a letter he wrote in 1059, in which he admitted that he was afraid to return to Cairo because of the heavy taxes he still owed there.[273]

Jews from such distant locations as southern Italy, Babylon, Syria and North Africa continued to visit Jerusalem whenever it was safe to do so. Many pilgrims came to the Mount of Olives during the Jewish month of Tishri, near the time of the great festival of *Sukkot*. Life in Jerusalem, however, was not easy for the Jews of this time. In the first place, it was dangerous to get there. Travel by sea was to risk storms and shipwreck; travel by land (that is, when the poorly maintained roads were passable) was to risk thieves, roaming bands of lawless men and warring armies.

Secondly, neither the economic prospects in the city itself nor the winter weather were good. One man wrote to his son-in-law in Egypt, earnestly begging him to come home and "eat onions in Jerusalem rather than chicken in Egypt."[274] And in 1059 Israel ben Sahlun confided to a friend:

I arrived yesterday in Jerusalem, my dear Sir, in sound health, after terrible suffering and after having been caught by snow on the way.... I am, Sir, in need of chickens and I intend to go down to Ramla [a town on the coastal plain southeast of Tel Aviv] but I do not know how long I will remain, as the city is beset by terrible rain and snow, the rain having continued now for four days.[275]

Despite these dangers and difficulties, however, Jewish *aliya* and pilgrimage continued year after year in the early Islamic period, reflecting the deep attachment that Diaspora Jews always felt for Jerusalem. An interesting historical footnote is that, ironically, a Muslim blessing for pilgrims was used to welcome home the Jews who had completed their travels: "May the exalted God graciously accept your pilgrimage."[276]

The great German pilgrimage (1064/1065)

Western Europe's growing enthusiasm for the pilgrimage to Jerusalem is reflected in several accounts, which differ only in minor details, of a mass German pilgrimage of 1064/1065. This great undertaking was by far the most important pilgrimage of its day, involving huge numbers of people—estimates range from 7,000 to 12,000 men and women. It was a precursor of the First Crusade and was famous in its own time. A German chronicler, who wanted to make sure posterity knew about it, tells us that

An almost incredible multitude set out for Jerusalem this year to worship at the sepulcher of the Lord. So many people took part in the pilgrimage and so much has been said about it that, lest its omission seem serious, we should briefly summarize here what transpired.[277]

Rather using this German account, however, we will look instead at the report of an Englishman named Ingulphus.

Ingulphus (1064/1065)

One of the participants in the great German pilgrimage was Ingulphus, secretary of the Earl of Normandy (France). Other dignitaries included the Archbishop of Mainz and the bishops of Utrecht and Ratisbon. This pilgrimage, led by Gunther, bishop of Bamberg, is worth examining at some length because the atrocities it suffered served to inflame Christian opinion in Europe and helped set the stage for the First Crusade.

Ingulphus begins by telling us that although he had an excellent job supervising the Earl's court, he was still possessed of such "a youthful heat and lusty [cheerful] humour" that he was getting bored. Fortunately, just at this time "There went a report throughout all Normandy, that divers archbishops of the Empire, and secular princes were desirous for their soul's health, and for devotion sake, to go on pilgrimage to Jerusalem."[278] With the Earl's blessing, Ingulphus and 29 other "gentlemen and clerks" of the court rode to Germany and joined the Archbishop's sumptuous entourage.

The pilgrims stopped at Constantinople to pay their respects to the Emperor Alexius and to visit the great church of Santa Sophia. Continuing their eastward journey, in Latakia (Syria) they met, according to another account, many pilgrims returning from Jerusalem, who brought this dismaying news:

> The returning parties told of the deaths of an uncounted number of their companions. They also shouted about and displayed their own recent and still bloody wounds. They bore witness

publicly that no one could pass along that route because the whole land was occupied by a most ferocious tribe of Arabs who thirsted for human blood.[279]

The German pilgrims decided to press on regardless of the danger and soon came to the coastal city of Tripoli (Syria). Here the Muslim commander of the city stopped them and demanded "an infinite sum of money," threatening to have them slaughtered if they did not give it to him. Fortunately for the pilgrims, a violent storm broke out just at this time, bringing thunder, lightning and high waves. The tempest lasted until noon of the next day. The Syrians were so frightened that they "shouted to each other that the Christian God was fighting for his people and was going to cast the city into the abyss [the sea]." The commander finally gave the Christians permission to leave and, we are told, "at once the disturbance of the sea was calmed."[280]

When the German pilgrims were only two days' journey from Jerusalem and were near Ramla, they were suddenly attacked by *bedouin*,

> who leaped at them like famished wolves on long-awaited prey. They slaughtered the first pilgrims pitiably, tearing them to pieces.... Bishop William of Utrecht, badly wounded and stripped of his clothes, was left lying on the ground with many others to die a miserable death.... [the pilgrims lost] their horses and mules and everything that the animals were carrying. The enemy divided these things among themselves and soon hastened to destroy the owners of the wealth. The pilgrims, on the other hand, decided to take up arms and with weapons in hand they courageously fought back.[281]

According to a sensational account by a contemporary English historian, Florence of Worcester, the thieves believed that most of the rich pilgrims were carrying gold coins. This was a reasonable guess since many of them openly displayed their wealth. The thieves further believed that the pilgrims had swallowed the gold coins when they saw they would be captured. As a result, Florence claims, the *bedouin* pinned many pilgrims to the ground in the shape of a cross and cut them open to look for the swallowed gold.[282]

The rape of a nun was reported, too. Another account of the German pilgrimage claims that on this expedition there was

> a certain noble abbess, fair of form and devout of mind, who had abandoned the care of the sisters entrusted to her and against all the advice of wiser heads had subjected herself to the dangers of this pilgrimage. She was captured by the pagans, and in the sight of everybody, raped by the shameless ones for so long that at last, to the disgrace of all Christians, she breathed her last.[283]

The desperate pilgrims were saved from more widespread slaughter only by the timely intervention of the Fatimid governor of Ramla, who sent troops to arrest the *bedouin*. According to one chronicler, the governor did this not as a work of charity but only because he thought that if the pilgrims perished "as a result of such wretched slaughter, nobody would thereafter cross that territory on pilgrimage and he and his people would suffer considerable loss in consequence."[284] Even so, only 2,000 of the 7,000 pilgrims are said to have

survived this and other ordeals—an assertion that would later be cited by the Crusaders as yet another reason to "liberate" Jerusalem from Muslim control.[285]

Ingulphus gives no gory details of this encounter with the thieves, saying only that "after we had been robbed of infinite sums of money, and had lost many of our people, hardly escaping with extreme danger of our lives, at length we joyfully entered into the most wished city of Jerusalem," where he and his companions were moved to tears by the sight of the Church of the Holy Sepulcher.[286] Leaving Jerusalem, however, proved nearly as difficult as getting to it. Ingulphus complained that "the thievish Arabians lurking upon every way" would not allow them to leave the city. Nevertheless, he and his colleagues somehow managed to get to the port of Jaffa [now Tel Aviv–Yafo]. There they arranged their passage back to Europe on an Italian ship that had come from Genoa to trade with the Holy Land.

After visiting Rome, the participants of the great German pilgrimage split up. The prelates went to Germany, while Ingulphus and his colleagues headed back to France. For them, this adventure had been anything but a resounding success. He confesses that:

> At so at length, of thirty horsemen which went out of Normandy fat, lusty, and frolic, we returned thither scarce twenty poor pilgrims of us, being all footmen, and consumed with leanness to the bare bones.[287]

VII

"A Pilgrimage in Arms": The First Crusade and Its Aftermath (1095–1187)

The First Crusade was preached (proclaimed) in France in 1095. From the Christian point of view, this "pilgrimage in arms" was an unqualified if bloody success: the Crusaders captured Jerusalem in 1099 and made it the capital of a new feudal state, the Kingdom of Jerusalem. With the Holy City now in Christian hands, Christian pilgrimages increased dramatically. Because French was the common language of the Crusaders, "Franks," i.e., Frenchmen, came to be used as a generic term for all Westerners. Latin became the language of prayer. The Church of the Holy Sepulcher was rebuilt in stone in a heavy Romanesque style. The Temple Mount became the headquarters of the Knights Templar, an order of monastic knights who protected the pilgrims. Another monastic order, the Knights Hospitaler, provided medical care for them. In 1187, however, Jerusalem returned to Muslim control when it was captured by Saladin, founder of the Ayyubid Dynasty.

Pilgrims with swords

One of the most remarkable episodes in the long history of Christian pilgrimage to Jerusalem was the sudden change in its very nature in 1095. It ceased to be a peaceful undertaking and became instead what the Crusaders themselves called "a pilgrimage in arms," that is, a series of military campaigns designed to wrest the Holy Land from "heathen" control.

Although to modern eyes there is a major difference between a peaceful pilgrimage to Jerusalem and a military conquest of the Holy Land, this was not how European Christians saw the matter.[288] To them, these were two different aspects of the same reality. They saw no contradiction in waging war to gain possession of their most important religious site. In fact, the thirteenth century Benedictine monk Matthew Paris, one of Europe's most outstanding medieval chroniclers, often used the word *peregrinatio* (pilgrimage) to describe a Crusade.

"To take the cross" meant to go off on a Crusade. The word "Crusader"—*croisé* in French, meaning "marked with the cross"—comes from the cross of red material sewn to the shoulders of the soldiers' white surcoats. Some men were so eager to take the cross that they even branded or cut a cross on their own bodies. One account

In death, the Crusader nobility was depicted with legs crossed. This life-size brass at St. Mary's Church at Chartham, Kent, is one of the finest and oldest military brasses in the United Kingdom. Sir Robert probably fought in the Seventh Crusade (1244) at the age of about 29. Later, for his gallantry at the siege of the Scottish castle of Caerlaverock in 1300, he was created banneret by Edward I. (A banneret was a knight privileged to fly a square banner, as distinct from the tapering flag of a simple knight.) (Photograph by the author, taken of a brass rubbing made by Bernard and Lea Shaw.)

tells us: "with a sharpe knyfe he share [cut], A crosse upon his shoulder bare."[289]

At the time of the First Crusade, the word *croisé* was only rarely used in official documents. Instead, contemporary designations emphasized the pilgrimage aspect. The First Crusade was officially termed the "pilgrimage," the "expedition to Jerusalem," the "path to Jerusalem," the "road to the Holy Sepulcher" or the "road to the Lord." Those who took part in the Crusades were known as "the people of the Lord" or as *Hierosolymitani* ("the Jerusalemites"). This latter word was also used to designate the unarmed pilgrims who had made their way to the Holy City before the Crusades.[290]

The details of how and why the First Crusade came about are complicated and are still the subject of scholarly debate. The broad outlines, however, are clear enough. They deserve our attention because of the lasting damage the First Crusade did to Christian-Muslim relations. Fundamentalist Islam's distrust of the West today may have its roots in the First Crusade.

Reasons for the First Crusade

The First Crusade came about for two reasons. The first was the increasing difficulty—frequently amounting to the impossibility—of European Christians making the long journey to Jerusalem. The second reason was the growing threat posed to the Byzantine Empire by victorious Turkish armies. The relative weights which should be given to each of these factors is still a matter of scholarly debate, so in the interest of brevity we will treat them here as having roughly equal weight.[291]

Pilgrimage to Jerusalem was very popular in Europe during the eleventh century and continued at high levels until its last decades. Then, however, pilgrims found that the roads to the Holy Land were becoming more and more dangerous because of military and political instability. Turks and Egyptians fought each other in Palestine. An armed escort was needed to cross Turkey, where localized battles raged and where hostile officials made life difficult for pilgrims. The Syrians were no longer friendly. Outside the biggest towns, outlaws roamed virtually unchecked. Rapacious nobles extracted transit fees or taxes from the pilgrims, who had no choice but to pay up or abandon their quest. Lurid accounts of Muslim atrocities in or near Palestine circulated widely in Europe and lost nothing in the retelling.

By the mid–1090s, conditions had deteriorated even further. The roads leading to the Holy Land were now said to be closed entirely; it was thought to be impossible for pilgrims to reach Jerusalem at all. No wonder, then, that as a noted British historian of the Crusades has summarized the state of affairs, "The pilgrims that succeeded in overcoming all the difficulties returned to the West weary and impoverished, with a dreadful tale to tell."[292]

Recovering from their ordeal once they were safely back home again, these travelers found a receptive audience for their stories of how the Muslims had willfully closed the Holy Land to Christian pilgrims. Regaining this sacred center by force—that is, by waging a "holy war" against Islam—was an idea that fell on fertile ground. In fact, Spain had already been a testing ground for this concept because an affront to pilgrimage had occurred there, too.[293]

In 997 a Muslim commander in Spain (most of which the Muslims had conquered more than 200 years before), burned the city of Santiago de Compostela, the third holiest destination for Christian pilgrims (after Jerusalem and Rome). European Christians were able to enlist the support of the influential abbey of Cluny, which had long been a protector of pilgrims both in Palestine and in Spain, in a campaign against the Muslims. Later, when the king of Aragon was murdered by a Muslim, Pope Alexander II promised a plenary (full) indulgence for all those who would participate in a holy war against the infidels in Spain. Before he preached the First Crusade in 1095, Pope Urban II had recommended that pilgrims who were thinking about going to Jerusalem should instead donate money to help rebuild the Spanish towns destroyed in the battles between Christians and Muslims.

The idea of a holy war to restore Jerusalem to Christian control drew support not only from a Papal desire to help pilgrims in the Holy Land but also from strategic concerns. The Seljuq Turks were threatening the heartland of the Byzantine empire. Jerusalem surrendered to them in 1073. In 1084 they seized the city of Antioch (south-central Turkey), which for more than a century had served the Byzantines as a frontier fort commanding the roads across northwestern Syria. Although by 1094 the power of the Turks seemed to be waning a bit, the Byzantine emperor, Alexius I Comnenus, still found it necessary to ask Pope Urban II for military help. This was the equivalent of asking Europe as a whole to send him knights, archers and foot-soldiers.

Alexius I may have thought that only a token force—say, a few detachments of Norman mercenaries—would be provided by the Europeans but that this would be enough to tip the military balance in his favor. Probably to the emperor's astonishment, however, Pope Urban II seized on his request to launch the first of the eight mass movements now collectively known as the Crusades. These would last for 200 years and would involve millions of men, women and children in many different theaters of war.

Preaching the First Crusade (1095)

Initially, during the Council of Piacenza (Italy) in March 1095, Pope Urban II had only called for a campaign to help Byzantium, but his aims soon became more ambitious. In August 1095 he sent letters to the bishops of France and to other prelates asking them to meet him at Clermont in south-central France. In October 1095 Urban dedicated the great church at the abbey of Cluny, where he must have talked to men who had firsthand knowledge of the difficulties facing travelers to Palestine. He was almost certainly told that the roads to Palestine were blocked and that the Holy Land itself was virtually closed to pilgrims.[294] Perhaps it was as a result of these conversations at Cluny that Urban decided to stress the necessity of recapturing the Holy Land itself.

When he addressed the Council of Clermont in November 1095 he urgently called on Christians to take up arms to recover the Holy Sepulcher. The task of the Crusaders would be to conquer the earthly Jerusalem so that they could participate in the heavenly Jerusalem to come. Ironically, despite the great historical importance of this speech, no reliable account of it exists. There are five versions of what Urban said.[295] Four of these were contemporary; the fifth was written many years later. They all differ in detail, probably because each of them reflects what their authors, with the benefit of hindsight, felt the Pope should have said. By piecing them together today, however, we can see that Urban probably made five key points:[296]

1. Jerusalem was in the hands of the infidels. Christian pilgrims were running enormous risks and were experiencing great suffering in their efforts to reach the Holy City. A "holy pilgrimage" was needed to right these wrongs. Robert the Monk, writing 25 years after Urban's speech, claimed that Urban had said:

Whoever, therefore, shall determine upon this holy pilgrimage and shall make his vow to God to that effect and shall offer himself to Him as a living sacrifice, holy, acceptable unto God, shall wear the sign of the cross of the Lord on his forehead or on his breast. When, truly having fulfilled his vow, he wishes to return, let him place the cross on his back between his shoulders. Such, indeed, by this twofold action will fulfill the precept of the Lord, as he commands it in the Gospel, "He that taketh not his cross and followeth after me, is not worthy of me."[297]

2. For their part, the Eastern (Byzantine) Christians urgently needed the military support of the West to halt the Turkish advance.

3. Western Christians therefore had to put aside their own destructive civil wars and must go—rich and poor alike, and as soon as possible—to the aid of their beleaguered co-religionists in the East.

4. There was no contradiction between the Christian ideal of brotherly love and the medieval ideal of knightly combat. The Pope drew a clear parallel between monks and knights. Monks were *milites Christi* ("knights of Christ") who fought against evil with spiritual weapons. By extension, the Crusaders became *milites Christi* who fought with temporal weapons. At Clermont the Pope reportedly ordered: "*Nunc fiant [Christi] milites, qui dudum exstiterunt raptores*" ("Now let those become knights of Christ who had previously been but robbers").[298]

5. While the Crusaders were away from home, their worldly goods would be under the protection of the Roman Catholic Church. Anyone who died in battle would be absolved of all his sins; those who survived could consider themselves as true friends of God and as heirs to the heavenly Jerusalem.

Regardless of the exact words he used, Urban's message met with a decisive, enthusiastic, overwhelming response. The crowd listening to him roared out ecstatically, "*Deus le volt!*" ("God wills it!"). Then, in a move choreographed in advance, Adhemar de Monteil, bishop of Le Puy (France), who had already made the pilgrimage to Jerusalem, knelt before the Pope and offered himself as the first volunteer. Urban later made him the leader of the whole expedition.

How many Europeans were directly or indirectly involved in the First Crusade is still a matter of scholarly argument but a reasonable guess is a total of about 100,000 people. Not all of these actually left home. It is estimated, however, that in 1097 at least 60,000 men and women, including 6,000 to 7,000 knights, had congregated at Nicaea (about 70 miles southeast of Constantinople) en route to Jerusalem.[299]

Peter the Hermit and the People's Crusade (c. 1096)

The popular appeal of Urban's call to arms was such that its most effective spokesmen were not bishops of the church, who formally promulgated from their pulpits the Pope's policy of a holy war, but itinerant preachers who were acting on their own behalf. The most colorful and most famous of these men was an older monk who wore the cape of a hermit and was therefore known as Peter the Hermit. Although barefoot and dressed in filthy clothes, this charismatic figure was a great orator and exerted a strange, hypnotic power over people. Guibert of Nogent, a Frenchman who knew Peter personally, reported that

I saw him empty cities and towns by the success of his preaching. He was the center of such a crowd, and was so loaded with presents and had such a reputation for holiness, that I do not remember hearing of any person who received similar honors. He was very generous in sharing what people gave him. He made honest women of prostitutes by arranging their marriages and in each case he gave the bride a present. With a remarkable authority, he established peace and tranquility everywhere. Whatever he said or did, it always seemed like something divine.[300]

Peter began preaching the First Crusade not long after the Council of Clermont. He was motivated chiefly by religious zeal but may also have held a personal grudge against the Turks, who may have treated him badly when he made (or tried to make) a pilgrimage to Jerusalem in about 1093. Whatever his real motivations, as a firebrand for the First Crusade Peter was remarkably successful in his new calling, attracting large crowds of followers as he traveled through France, Germany and Italy.

Few of the peasants who joined his ragtag army, however, could make a clear distinction between the earthly Jerusalem Peter was leading them to and the heavenly Jerusalem they hoped to inherit. Many believed that in addition to helping them escape from the crushing problems they were facing at home (these included poverty, overpopulation, floods, pestilence, drought and famine), Peter would lead them to a new Jerusalem flowing with the proverbial milk and honey. This was the heavenly Jerusalem, where their physical tribulations would be at an end and where their spiritual salvation would be assured.

This heady combination of economics and eschatology made Peter's appeal so great that about 20,000 men, women and children joined the untrained ranks of what came to be called the People's or

This illustration from a medieval manuscript shows Peter the Hermit ordering a group of knights to attack Jerusalem. (Bibliothèque nationale de France, Paris.)

Peasants' Crusade. Peter's followers included some knights and infantrymen but this was not a real army in any sense of the word. A good percentage of the people were unarmed or only lightly armed: militarily, they were quite ineffective. The People's Crusade was essentially a pilgrimage escorted by a few professional soldiers. Not surprisingly, many of these innocents came to grief. In the process many Central European civilians lost their lives, too.

In 1096 Peter led his Crusaders into the Balkans en route to Jerusalem. Anna Comnena, daughter of the Byzantine Emperor, did not associate these people with the European mercenaries her father was hoping the Pope would send him to beat back the Muslims. This is how she described Peter's followers:

Full of enthusiasm and ardour they thronged every highway, and with these warriors came a host of civilians, out-numbering the sand of the seashore or the stars of heaven, carrying palms [symbols of the Jerusalem pilgrimage] and bearing crosses on their shoulders. There were women and children, too, who had left their own countries. Like tributaries joining a river from all directions they streamed toward us in full force.[301]

In Hungary, during a riot sparked by a dispute over the sale of a pair of shoes, Peter's men killed 4,000 Hungarians.[302] Later, along the road to Sofia, Bulgarian troops routed his forces, killing many of them, enslaving some of the survivors and even capturing the chest holding all the money Peter had collected for this journey.

Subsequently, near Nicaea, while Peter himself was absent (he had gone back to Constantinople to ask the emperor for more help), a well-timed Turkish ambush dealt a fatal blow to the People's Crusade. The horses of Peter's knights were killed or wounded by showers of arrows. As the horses fell or reared up in pain, the Turks attacked, driving the cavalry, now un-horsed, upon the infantry, which in turn fled in panic back to Peter's camp. Some of his people managed to escape but the Turks did not take many captives—usually only the young boys and girls whose appearance pleased them. Many of these were sold into slavery.[303]

Peter survived the debacle of the People's Crusade and with his reputation somehow intact he went on to play a modest role in the First Crusade itself. He preached a sermon on the Mount of Olives just before the Crusaders launched their successful attack on Jerusalem in 1099. He then conducted processions in the Holy City shortly after the Crusaders had massacred most of its inhabitants. Returning to Europe in 1100, Peter founded an Augustinian monastery at Neufmoustier (Belgium) and served as its prior until his death there five years later.

The siege of Jerusalem (1099)

The failure of the People's Crusade proved that more than simple faith would be needed to retake the Holy Land: careful military preparation and well-honed fighting skills were essential, too. Four Crusading armies were slowly organized and eventually set out for Jerusalem in response to Pope Urban's call. The first three of these armies were led, respectively, by Raymond IV, Count of Toulouse and Marquis of Provence; Godfrey, Duke of Lower Lorraine; and Bohemond I, Prince of Antioch. The fourth army was led by a triumvirate consisting of Robert, Duke of Normandy; his brother-in-law Stephen, Count of Blois; and his cousin Robert II, Count of Flanders. Taken together, these forces constituted what has been called "the Crusade of the Lords."[304] Excluding

Peter's own rabble, a total of perhaps as many as 80,000 people (including many camp followers and non-combatants) began moving toward Jerusalem between the summer of 1096 and the spring of 1097.[305]

These armies followed well-established pilgrim routes to Jerusalem. First, it was necessary to get to Constantinople. To do this, three options were available[306]:

1. Travel overland to Bari in southern Italy. This port had been cleared of Arab pirates in 871, so safe passage from there across the Adriatic Sea could easily be arranged. Travelers would then follow the Via Egnatia, an old Roman road, to Constantinople.
2. Take what was called the "Bavarian Road" through central Europe. This route crossed southern Germany and Hungary and was now open because of the conversion of Hungary to Christianity.
3. Go south through Croatia to the Albanian coast and join up with the Via Egnatia there.

From Constantinople to Jerusalem there was only one major road—a former Roman highway stretching east to Antioch. From that point, both pilgrims and First Crusaders made their way down the Syrian and Palestinian coasts, via Latakia, Tripoli, Caesarea and Ramla, finally reaching the Holy City itself. Progress was very slow, however, and it was not until June 1099 that the Crusaders finally reached the hilltop called *Montjoie* ("mountain of joy") by countless earlier pilgrims. From there, directly to the south, they could see Jerusalem looming up before them.

This ancient city, one of the great fortresses of the medieval era, was strongly defended by the Fatimids and was well-provisioned. Time was on the side of the defenders because they knew that a Muslim army would eventually come from

Egypt to relieve them. The Crusaders, on the other hand, faced acute shortages of water and food, aggravated by dust, dry winds, heat and the absence of any shade. They knew they could not afford to get bogged down in a long siege.

Crusader leaders therefore went to the Mount of Olives (immediately southeast of the Old City) to seek divine guidance. An old hermit who lived there urged them to attack the city immediately. This they did but were easily beaten off by the defenders because they lacked the necessary equipment—mangonels (missile-throwing machines) and scaling ladders. There was not enough timber near rocky, treeless Jerusalem to build such devices, so the Crusaders arranged for camels and Muslim captives to carry logs and planks long distances from the forests around Samaria. Two moveable siege towers (tall wooden structures armed with catapults and mounted on wheels) were built, as well as mangonels and ladders.

At last, in mid–July 1099, everything was ready. The Crusaders now numbered about 1,200 knights and 12,000 infantry, as well as many pilgrims, women and children. Arnulf, chaplain to Robert, Duke of Normandy, preached to the Crusaders. Pointing to the Holy City shimmering before them in the summer heat, he told them:

> Here you see the cause of all our labors. This [earthly] Jerusalem is the reflection of the heavenly Jerusalem. This city has the form to which we aspire.... If you consider long and aright, you will know that this Jerusalem you see, which you face, prefigures and represents the heavenly city.[307]

As an act of penance, the Crusaders fasted and walked barefoot around the walls of Jerusalem. Despite showers of stones and "liquid fire"[308] from the Muslims inside the city, the Crusaders managed to wheel the two siege towers up against the walls of Jerusalem. At noon, 14 July 1099, the Crusaders succeeded in bridging the gap between the wall and the top of one of the towers by using a wooden walkway. In a death-or-glory charge, knights stormed over this walkway. Scaling ladders were brought up for the other troops. By early afternoon the Holy City was in the hands of the Crusaders.

In return for surrendering and for giving the victorious Crusaders a large amount of treasure, the Muslim commander and his bodyguards were spared and were escorted out of the city to safety. Most of the Muslims and the Jews in the city, however, were slaughtered. Some Christian reports say the Crusaders killed 30,000 people; others say that it was only 10,000. Ibn al-Athir (1160–1233), the chief Arab historian of the later Crusades, reports that in this sack of Jerusalem

> The population was put to the sword by the Franks, who pillaged the area for a week.... In the Masjid [Mosque] al-Aqsa the Franks slaughtered more than 70,000 people, among them a large number of Imams [religious leaders] and Muslim scholars, devout and ascetic men who had left their homelands to live lives of pious seclusion in the Holy Place. The Franks stripped the Dome of the Rock of more than forty silver candelabra, each of them weighing 3,600 drams [about 14 pounds], and a great silver lamp weighing fifty-four Syrian pounds, as well as a hundred and fifty smaller silver candelabra and more than twenty gold ones, and a great deal more booty.[309]

A French chaplain and chronicler of the First Crusade, Fulcher de Chartres, recorded that the Crusaders killed all the Saracens and the Turks they found: "They killed everyone," he wrote, "whether male or female."[310] Another French eye-witness, Raymond of Aguilers, commented with evident satisfaction that

Piles of heads, hands, and feet were to be seen.... If I tell the truth it will exceed your powers of belief. So let it suffice to say this much, at least, that in the Temple and the Porch of Solomon, men rode in blood up to their knees and bridle reins. Indeed, it was a just and splendid judgment of God that this place should be filled with the blood of unbelievers since it had suffered so long from their blasphemies.[311]

A contemporary but anonymous historian remembered that the Christian pilgrims had been just as bloodthirsty as the Crusader knights:

Entering Jerusalem, our pilgrims chased and massacred the Saracens all the way to the Temple of Solomon, where the most furious combat of the entire day took place, to the extent that the whole Temple ran with Saracen blood. Finally, after having thrashed the pagans, our men captured in the Temple a great number of men and women, whom they either killed or left alive, as they pleased.... Our Crusader knights soon ran through the city, seizing gold, silver, horses, mules and pillaging the houses, which were abundantly stocked with riches.[312]

The Crusaders showed no mercy, either, to the Jews of Jerusalem, who were murdered because they were believed to have sided with the Muslims. When the Jews took refuge in their chief synagogue, the Crusaders set it on fire; none of the Jews within it survived. Afterwards, the Crusaders halfheartedly tried to clean up the carnage they had caused, but without much success. Five months later, corpses were still lying around unburied. At that time, Fulcher de Chartres was appalled by the smell. "Oh, what a stench there was," he complained, "around the walls of the city, both within and without, from the rotting bodies of the Saracens slain by our-

selves at the time of the capture of the city, lying wherever they had been hunted down.[313]

Evaluating the First Crusade

Once the fighting was over, most of the Crusaders went back home to Europe, leaving behind only a shell of their army.[314] From the point of view of Christian pilgrims, the First Crusade had been such a dramatic, unqualified success that it must have had heavenly support. Their own piety had been rewarded. The infidels had been put to the edge of the sword. Pilgrims could now hope to make their way to the Holy Sepulcher and other sacred sites of Jerusalem in greater safety. Pilgrimage therefore boomed as thousands of pilgrims sailed from Europe each spring on "the April voyage," crossing the Mediterranean en route to the Holy Land.[315]

The legacy of the First Crusade has proved to be long-lasting. The words "crusade" and "crusader" still evoke a positive response in the West. A current dictionary definition of a crusade, for example, is "a remedial [and therefore commendable] exercise undertaken with zeal and enthusiasm." President Eisenhower chose the title *Crusade in Europe* for his memoirs of World War II. At a more trivial level, the American comic strip character Batman is known as "the Caped Crusader" because of his relentless war against crime.

The other side of the coin is that the traditional Western view of the Crusades as a protracted shoot-out between "the good guys" (Crusaders) and "the bad guys" (Muslims) has by now been completely discredited. Sir Steven Runciman's definitive three-volume *History of the Crusades*, published between 1951 and 1954, remains the standard work on the subject and it is worth repeating his conclusion here:

High [Crusading] ideals were besmirched by cruelty and greed, enterprise and endurance by a blind and narrow self-righteousness; and the Holy War itself was nothing more than a long act of intolerance in the name of God.[316]

To this we can only add that the Crusaders' aggressiveness and fanaticism, typified by the slaughter they made in Jerusalem in 1099, poisoned relations between Muslims and Christians for many centuries to come.

Abu Hamid al-Ghazali (c. 1096)

Here we must backtrack a bit to mention that before Jerusalem fell to the Crusaders in 1099 it had attracted not only Muslim pilgrims but also Muslim scholars. The most memorable of these learned men was al-Ghazali, considered today to have been the greatest Muslim scholar of all time.[317] His knowledge of Islam was so deep that his contemporaries referred to him deferentially as "Proof of Islam."

Al-Ghazali was teaching in Baghdad when he underwent a spiritual crisis. He left his post there in 1095 and traveled to Jerusalem, where he began his magisterial work, *The Revivification of the Sciences of Religion*. This synthesis of rationalism, mysticism and legal orthodoxy not only revitalized Islamic theology but also left its mark (through Latin translations) on Jewish and Christian scholasticism. While he was in the Holy City, al-Ghazali, at the insistence of his students, also wrote *The Jerusalem Tract*, a concise summary of the Muslim creed.

Fulcher de Chartres (1101)

We have already mentioned this French chaplain and chronicler, who went to Jerusalem with the First Crusade and spent the rest of his life there. His *Gesta Francorum Jerusalem Expugnantium* (*The Deeds of the Franks Who Attacked Jerusalem*) remains a reliable account of that campaign. In 1101 he also reported on the Holy Fire:

> …the long-expected light had appeared in one of the lamps of the Holy Sepulchre, and those nearest it could see its ruddy colour; on hearing this [the Patriarch of Jerusalem] at once quickened his steps, and opening the door of the Sepulchre with the key he held in his hand, he at once saw the long-desired light shining in the lamp … [he] lighted a taper and came out to show everyone the Holy Light, upon which those who were present, with joy in their hearts and tears in their eyes, cried out, "Kyrie Eleison" ["Lord, have mercy"].[318]

Saewulf (1101)

Christian pilgrims began to come to Jerusalem in large numbers once it was in Crusader hands. This flow amounted to as many as 10,000 men and women each year.[319] Some came from such distant places as Scandinavia, Russia and Portugal. Many decided to remain in the Holy City permanently. One of the first of these post–Crusade pilgrims was a prosperous English merchant named Saewulf, who has left us an exceptionally vivid account of the hazards pilgrims faced when making their way to Jerusalem.

Like many other Western European pilgrims, Saewulf began his voyage at the southern Italian port of Monopoli in 1101.[320] It was, he says an inauspicious beginning: "If God's mercy had not protected us, we should all have been drowned. That day, when were a long way from the port out at sea, our ship suffered some damage through the force of the waves."

The ship managed to return to Monopoli for repairs and later set sail from the nearby port of Brindisi.

After 13 weeks of hard travel, Saewulf and his fellow pilgrims at last neared the coast of Palestine. One day at dawn they anchored off Jaffa. The port was very congested because many other ships carrying pilgrims and cargo were already moored there. The captain of Saewulf's ship decided to remain at anchor overnight, rather than trying to land his passengers immediately. But by a stroke of good luck a business acquaintance of Saewulf (possibly a shoreside merchant who came out to the ship) advised him, "Sir, go ashore today, in case tonight or tomorrow morning a storm comes up, and tomorrow you are not able to land!" Acting on this good advice, Saewulf and his companions immediately hired a small boat and set out for shore. A storm was already coming up and the sea was rough, but the party landed safely at Jaffa. Once in the town itself, writes Saewulf, "Defeated and worn out by long labours, we ate and drank, and then retired to rest."

The storm picked up strength overnight, however, and by the next morning all the ships in the anchorage were in mortal danger. Hearing shouts and cries in the streets, Saewulf and others ran down to the shore to see what was happening. There they witnessed a terrible sight:

> When we were there, we saw the storm, with the height of its waves equal to the hills. We noticed innumerable human bodies of both sexes who had been drowned lying miserably on the shore. We saw too the remains of ships floating nearby. No sound could be heard apart from the noise of the sea, and the sinking ships, for it drowned the shouts of the people and the sound of the crowds.[321]

The ship that Saewulf had come on was for the moment still safe but it, too, was doomed:

> Our own ship, which was very large and strong, and up till now had contained much corn [wheat] and other cargo, and bore pilgrims coming and returning, was still in the deep water, held by anchors and ropes. But how it was tossed by the waves! Now was the hour of disaster, and how many of its cargoes were thrown overboard!... It was not long before the anchors gave way, through the violent waves of the current. The ropes broke, and any ships which were released from the fury of the waves were bound not to escape. For one moment they were lifted up, and the next they were down in the deep, so that gradually they drew in from the deep water to be dashed against the rocks. There they broke up, sadly going from one side to the other and being ground to bits by the storm.[322]

When Saewulf's ship broke up, all hope for its passengers and crew vanished, too. Some pilgrims and sailors clung to the ship's masts and yards; others, terror-stricken, drowned before Saewulf's eyes. Trying desperately to stay afloat, men and women thrown into the sea hung on to wooden parts of the ship but they were either battered to pieces by the waves or were swept out into deep water. Only a few strong swimmers managed to get to shore safely. The upshot was, as Saewulf sadly reports, that of 30 big ships, all laden with pilgrims and cargo, only seven remained intact. More than 1,000 men and women perished in this storm. If Saewulf had not gone ashore early, he would almost certainly have been one of them.

But there were perils on land as well. The journey from Jaffa to Jerusalem took two days along a difficult mountain road. "It was very dangerous, too," Saewulf recounts, because the Saracens, who are continually plotting an ambush against Christians, were hiding in the caves of the hills and among rocky caverns. They were awake day and night, always keeping a look-out for someone to attack, whether because he had not enough people with him, or because he was fatigued enough to leave a space between himself and his party.... Anyone who has taken that road can see how many human bodies there are in the road and next to the road, and there are countless corpses which have been torn up by wild beasts.... So in that road not only poor and weak people have dangers to flee, but also the rich and strong. Many are killed by the Saracens and many of heat and thirst—many through lack of drink and many from drinking too much.[323]

Saewulf's luck held, however, and he and his companions reached Jerusalem without further incident. There he visited the holy sites, which he described in careful detail, drawing freely from the Venerable Bede's accounts. Saewulf then journeyed to many of the other holy centers of Palestine before finally returning to Jaffa to take a ship back to Europe. Since pirates were a real menace, his own ship, accompanied by two other pilgrim ships, hugged the coastline, rather than risking a voyage across the open Mediterranean. Nevertheless, the little convoy still had a close call.

Off the northern coast of Palestine, a fleet of 25 Muslim ships suddenly hove into sight. Their mission was to transport Lebanese troops to fight on the Muslim side during the struggle against the Christian King of Jerusalem, but they were also ready to snap up any lightly armed Christian ship they might come across at sea. Faced with this grave threat, the two pilgrim ships accompanying Saewulf's vessel quickly sheered off, abandoning Saewulf's ship, and made for the port of Caesarea.

Saewulf's vessel, being heavier and slower under oars, could not follow them.

Saewulf tells us what happened next:

...all round our ship the Saracens sailed, staying about a bow-shot away, and rejoicing at such a prize. But our men were prepared to die for Christ. They took up arms, and when they were armed they defended the ship like a castle. There were almost two hundred men defending our dromund [a small medieval galley]. After about an hour, when he had taken counsel, the prince [of the Muslims] sent one of his sailors up the mast of his ship, which was very large, to learn what he could of our action. When he learned from him of the strength of our defenses, he raised his sails and went out to sea. So that day the Lord made us escape from our enemies. But later on three of our people's ships were arrested, and the Saracens were made rich by their spoils.[324]

Early guidebooks (1099–1103)

The upsurge of interest in pilgrimage which occurred after the First Crusade resulted in the appearance of three guidebooks in Latin. These documents, which broke no new ground, date from 1099 to 1103[325]:

• The first work, known as the *First Guide*, was made part of an early record of the Crusaders' assault on the Holy Land. It drew on the Bordeaux Pilgrim's account, which was by then almost 800 years old.
• The second guidebook, known from one of its first words as *Qualiter*, was signed by an anonymous pilgrim, who testified in it, "I am a witness" to what it contained. This work is linked to a history written by Archbishop Baudry of Dol (France) and may have been used at the same time as the *First Guide*.
• The latest of the three was *The Ottobon-*

ian Guide, so named because it is preserved in a collection of manuscripts at the Vatican Library known as the *Codex Ottobonianus latinus*. Unlike its predecessors, this guide covered only Jerusalem.

Scandinavian pilgrimages to the Holy Land (1103)

At first the Vikings ruthlessly pillaged the rich lands of the West but by the latter half of the ninth century they had become settlers rather than pirates.[326] In their new sedentary mode of life, they were quick to adopt the technologies and cultural values of the more advanced societies they had previously put to the sword. Chief among these values was Christianity. Thus in 991 the Norwegian king Olaf I Tryggvason led a Viking expedition to England simply in order to be baptized there. Upon his return to Norway four years later, with the zeal of a convert he spread his new faith along the coast of Norway—using friendly persuasion where possible and force when necessary.

Christianity gradually replaced the worship of the old Nordic gods. In its battle-cry, the *Olafs Saga* does not evoke Thor, but Christ: "*Fram! fram! cristmenn, crossmenn, konungsmenn!*" ("Forward! forward! champions of Christ, of the Cross, and of the king!"). The attractions of the Jerusalem pilgrimage soon became evident to the descendants of the Vikings. The *Knytlinga Saga*, which recounts the history of the Danish kings, tells what prompted Eirik the Good to set out for the Holy City in about 1103:

> I [the saga itself] describe how the
>   king
> bold in conflict, to cure
> his soul's scars, from the north
> set out with his soldiers:

> he prepared himself for Paradise,
> and went to explore
> the peace of Jerusalem,
> to make his life pure.[327]

Despite his efforts and good intentions, Eirik never reached Jerusalem, dying in Cyprus of a fever. His queen, Bodhild, however, did manage to get to Palestine safely with the rest of the Danish company. But not long thereafter she, too, died.

The most detailed accounts of the Norse pilgrimages are the adventures of Sigurd, one of the two sons of the Norwegian king Magnus Barefoot. Known as *Jorsalafarer* ("Jerusalem-farer") and described as "a very handsome youth," Sigurd was chosen at the age of 19 to lead a naval expedition to the Holy Land. With a fleet of 55 to 60 ships, he reached Jaffa at some point after the First Crusaders' capture of Jerusalem but while Muslim-Christian skirmishes were still going on.

When he arrived off Jaffa, an Egyptian fleet was attacking the city of Acre (now Akko, Israel). Taken aback by the sudden appearance of the Viking armada, the Egyptians retreated, which permitted Sigurd to enter the city without a fight. Baldwin, king of Jerusalem, welcomed him warmly and escorted him to the holy places of Jerusalem. Following a local custom, Sigurd swam across the River Jordan and recorded his feat by tying a knot in the brushwood on the other side. Later, he gave naval support to Baldwin at the siege of Sidon before leaving Palestine in 1110 and sailing back to Norway.

Jarl (Earl) Rognvald of Orkney was the last of the early Northern leaders to visit the Holy Land. The *Orkneyinga Saga* recounts how the Jarl set out in 15 ships in 1151, accompanied by four poets and a high-ranking interpreter, Bishop William of Paris. After visiting the holy places, Rognvald and a companion named Sigmund Fishhook swam across the Jordan, too, and tied knots in the brushwood before sailing for Constantinople and then going overland toward Orkney.

The Knights Hospitaler (1113)

Even before the First Crusade, a hospital had been established in Jerusalem by Italian merchants from Amalfi to care for Western pilgrims. Its first administrator was a monk named Gerard. As the number of pilgrims increased, their medical needs increased as well. In 1113 Pope Paschal II therefore established the Hospital of St. John of Jerusalem as an independent order, staffed by priests as the chief officers and by lay "hospitalers" (both male and female) to care for the pilgrims. Under the leadership of Raymond du Puy, who succeeded Gerard in 1120, this nursing order became increasingly militarized, reaching its strongest point in 1130–1136. It built the great fortress of Krak des Chevaliers (Castle of the Knights) in Syria, near the northern border of Lebanon, in 1142 and held it until 1271, when it was captured by the Mamluk sultan Baybars I. The two concentric towered walls of the Krak des Chevaliers still stand today, separated by a wide but empty moat. In its heyday the fort was manned by up to 2,000 soldiers.

The Hospitalers became very rich. Contemporary writers were critical of the lavish way in which the Order spent money. In about 1150, for example, the Patriarch of Jerusalem complained that the Hospitalers were erecting buildings "at the very door of the Holy Resurrection" which were "much more costly and lofty than the church itself."[328] A German pilgrim, John of Würzburg, who visited the hospital in about 1170 and saw 2,000 people being cared for there, remarked that "The house feeds so many ... outside and within, and it gives so large an amount of alms to poor

people ... that certainly the total of expenses can in no way be counted."[329]

The Knights Templar (c. 1118)

After the First Crusaders finished sacking Jerusalem in 1099, most of them went home. About 3,000 Franks stayed behind, however. This included some 300 knights and 1,000 foot-soldiers—a small force, to be sure, but enough to prevent the Muslims from reoccupying the Holy City and enough to provide a semblance of law and order near the city itself. In this latter undertaking, the knights were responding to a summons from the Patriarch of Jerusalem, who was trying to help the pilgrims.

Guillaume de Tyr (William of Tyre), author of the great thirteenth century work *Historia rerum in partibus transmarinis gestarum* (*History of Deeds Done Beyond the Sea*), says that the Patriarch of Jerusalem had urged the knights "to work with all their force and for the remission of their sins to protect the roads and paths, and dedicate themselves to defending the pilgrims against the attacks or ambushes of thieves and marauders."[330] The end result was that a handful of French knights—somewhere between eight and 14 men, led by Hugues de Payens—decided to form the core of a religious-military organization which became formally known as the "Poor Knights of Christ and of the Temple of Solomon."

In about 1118 these knights and their colleagues offered their services to Baldwin II, king of the Kingdom of Jerusalem, as a police force to protect unarmed pilgrims from the *bedouin* and other assailants who frequented the roads of Palestine. Pleased by this generous offer, Baldwin gave the knights part of the former Aqsa Mosque, which the Crusaders had renamed the Lord's Temple and which now rivaled the Church of the Holy Sepulcher as a sacred center for Christians. As a result, the new order became informally known as the Knights Templar, or simply as the Templars.

Although there is some uncertainty about the date of 1118 mentioned above, scholars agree that this order received papal recognition and an official rule of life at the Council of Troyes in Champagne (France) in 1128. The Templars were the dominant military force in the Holy Land and their headquarters in Jerusalem reflected this fact. Theodoric, a German monk, was visibly impressed:

> the area is full of houses, dwellings and outbuildings for every kind of purpose, and it is full of walking-places, lawns, council chambers, porches, consistories and supplies of water in splendid cisterns. Below it is equally full of washrooms, stores, grain rooms, stores for wood and other kinds of domestic stores. On the other side of the palace, that is on the west, the Templars have built a new house, whose height, length and breadth, and all its cellars and refectories, staircase and roof, are far beyond the custom of the land. Indeed, its roof is so high that, if I were to mention how high it is, those who listen would hardly believe me.[331]

Taking monastic vows of poverty, chastity and obedience, the Templars followed the ascetic rule of life laid down by St. Bernard of Clairvaux.[332] This order and its brother orders were lay orders: because priests were forbidden to shed blood, few of the members were priests. The Templars were organized into a strict military hierarchy consisting of four groups: knights, sergeants, chaplains and servants. Most of the fighting men were not knights but sergeants, who were skilled at arms but were more numerous and more lightly equipped than the heavily armed, expen-

sively mounted knights. At the head of the order itself was a Grand Master. Each "temple" (a local branch of the order) was led by a commander who owed obedience to the Grand Master.

Like the First Crusaders, the Templars adopted as their own uniform a white surcoat highlighted by a red cross. The Templars were a well-honed combat order and there was no shortage of fighting to be done. Ten years after they had received papal recognition, there was still so little law and order in parts of the Holy Land that mercenaries had to be hired to help protect the pilgrims. In recognition of their own prowess, however, in 1139 the Templars were placed directly under the Pope's control, rather than remaining under the Patriarch of Jerusalem.

By deviating for a moment from our usual chronological approach in this book, we can briefly trace the rise and fall of the Templars and the progress of the Hospitalers. One consequence of being under Papal authority was that the Templars were now no longer accountable to any bishop in whose see (jurisdiction) they owned property. As a result, they widened the scope of their activities considerably and soon became the defenders of every sizeable town in the Holy Land. At their peak the Templars could field about 20,000 knights.

Their wealth increased dramatically, too, as kings and nobles donated lands and castles to the order. Soon the Templars held properties not only in the Holy Land but also throughout Western Europe and the lands around the Mediterranean. Their firm discipline, highly centralized organization and military strength enabled them to collect, store and ship gold and silver bullion between Europe and the Holy Land, making them in effect the bankers of both kings and pilgrims.

The Templars had long been bitter rivals of the Hospitalers. By the late thirteenth century proposals were being made that these two fractious orders should be combined into one. After Acre, the last Crusader stronghold in the Holy Land, was recaptured by the Muslims in 1291, a Western military presence was no longer possible there. Moreover, the Templars' immense wealth now seemed to be available for the taking. As a result, in 1303/1304 the Templars were charged—probably falsely—with blasphemies and homosexuality.[333]

These offenses were said to have occurred during their secret rites of initiation. Ostensibly appalled by their misdeeds, in 1307 King Philip IV of France had every Templar in France arrested and seized all their property. Confessions were wrung by torture from the captured Templars. These false statements prompted Pope Clement V to order the arrest of Templars in every European country. Soon the rout of the order was complete. The Templars' properties were later transferred to the Hospitalers or were appropriated by the state. Many Templars were jailed or killed. The last Grand Master, Jacques de Molay, was burned at the stake.

Usama ibn Munqidh (c. 1140)

Cultural clashes between Christians and Muslims were inevitable. In about 1140, for example, a distinguished Syrian gentleman, Usama ibn Munqidh, came to Jerusalem. Ambitious and cosmopolitan, he was a writer, a diplomat and an unscrupulous politician accused of secretly arranging assassinations to further his own ends. Because of his friendship with the Templars, his Muslim colleagues in Damascus treated him as an expert on all questions concerning the inscrutable Franks. One experience he had in Jerusalem was so remarkable that it must have confirmed his co-religionists' belief that all the Franks

were savages. Let Usama ibn Munqidh tell the tale:

This is an example of Frankish barbarism, God damn them! When I was in Jerusalem I used to go to the Masjid al-Aqsa, beside which is a small oratory which the Franks have made into a church. Whenever I went into the mosque, which was in the hands of Templars who were friends of mine, they would put the little oratory at my disposal, so that I could say my prayers there. One day I had gone in, said the *Allah akhbar* ["God is great"—the beginning of the Muslim sequence of prayers] and risen to begin my prayers, when a Frank threw himself on me from behind, lifted me up and turned me so that I was facing the east. "That is the way to pray!," he said. Some Templars at once intervened, seized the man and took him out of my way, while I resumed my prayer. But the moment they stopped watching him he seized me again and forced me to face east, repeating that this was the way to pray. Again the Templars intervened and took him away. They apologized to me and said: "He is a foreigner who has just arrived today from his homeland in the north, and he has never seen anyone pray facing any other direction than east." [Many medieval Christians faced east when they prayed.] "I have finished my prayers," I said, and left, stupefied by the fanatic who had been so perturbed and upset to see someone pray facing the *qibla* [toward Mecca]![334]

Yet as an intelligent, well-traveled man Usama ibn Munqidh was broad-minded enough to recognize that even the Franks were capable of learning better manners once they saw them being practiced by Muslim dignitaries. "Among the Franks," he explains to his readers, "we see some who have settled down among us and who have cultivated the society of Muslims. These Franks are much superior to those who have come only recently to the territories they occupy."[335]

Judah ha-Levi (d. 1141)

We can now take up the story of the Jewish poet Judah ha-Levi, who died in 1141 and whose writings did so much to solidify the sanctity of Jerusalem in the hearts and minds of the Jews of the Diaspora. He is best remembered for a famous collection of "Zionide" poems celebrating Jerusalem (a work known as *Diwan*) and for a book in which he outlined a philosophy of Judaism. His poems stressed the vital importance of Jerusalem to the Jewish people. This is one of them:

> Beautiful heights, joy of the world, city of a great king. For you my soul yearns from the lands of the west. My pity collects and is roused when I remember the past. Your story in exile, and your Temple destroyed.... I shall cherish your stones and kiss them. And your earth will be sweeter than honey to my taste.[336]

Ha-Levi was born in Tudela (Spain) in about 1073 and spent much of his life in Toledo, where we worked as a physician—one of the few professions open to Jews in Christian surroundings—and as a poet. Finally concluding in his late 60s that the position of Jews in medieval Spain was hopeless, he decided to spend the rest of his life in Jerusalem. After careful preparations, he left Spain in 1140, en route by sea to Egypt, with the intention then taking the land route to Palestine. In one of his poems he discussed his own travels and his premonition of dying in the Holy Land:

> Thine is my soul, Oh Lord! in hope or dread:
> To Thee alone I gratefully bow the head.

> A weary pilgrim I delight in Thee,
> Throughout my wanderings, thankfully.
> ...No love but God's is great
> Thy holy Gates in joy approached, I wait
> For death: My heart to Thee I sanctify
> Upon Thine altar, love to testify.[337]

Ha-Levi was warmly received by his co-religionists in Alexandria and Cairo but for unknown reasons he delayed his trip to Jerusalem. Death overtook him in Egypt in 1141 but his fame did not die there. As late as the mid-nineteenth century, legend had it that ha-Levi had been approaching the city walls of Jerusalem itself when an Arab horseman, thundering out through one of the Holy City's gates, rode him down in the dust. As ha-Levi lay dying, he is said to have recited one of his best-known poems: "Zion, shall not I seek thee."[338] Moses Hess, one of the founders of Zionism in the nineteenth century, paid this tribute to ha-Levi: "Actuated by longing for the land of his dreams, he grasped the pilgrim's staff, only to find a grave for himself in his beloved land."[339]

Before his death, ha-Levi built up a carefully reasoned argument explaining why Jerusalem was the sacred center of the Jews.[340] He began by asserting that the land of Israel was the most favored land in the world. As such, it was especially suited for prophecy: Jewish prophets had long had visions of angels and of the "Glory" of the Lord. Drawing on these prophetic utterances, ha-Levi compiled what was in effect a theological geography. He claimed that the land of Israel was the center of the world; that Jerusalem lay at the center of Israel; and that the Temple was the center of Jerusalem.

The Temple was supremely important, he believed, because it was the very gateway to heaven—the place where the heavens and the earth were joined together. Ha-Levi thought that our own world was built along the lines of a super-natural prototype. Thus there was both a heavenly Jerusalem and a heavenly Temple, whose parallels in this world were the earthly Jerusalem and the earthly Temple.

This Jerusalem-centric line of thought led ha-Levi to conclude that the Jews of the Diaspora must move to Israel. To illustrate this point, he used the analogy of a vineyard. He said that if a fine-quality vine seedling (i.e., the Jewish people) was planted in alien soil (the lands of the Diaspora), this seedling could not flourish. It was only when the seedling was planted in appropriate soil (i.e., in Israel) that its true excellence would be revealed. By the same token, alien seedlings (Islam and Christianity) planted in Israeli soil could not flourish. Only, in fact,

> when the Jews dwell in their own land do they reach their full splendor, and only then does the land display its true attributes. As long as Moslems and Christians dwell in the land of Israel, it remains barren. In desolation and ruin it awaits its sons and daughters, and thus demonstrates that, as the chosen land, it is destined only for the chosen people. Recognition that actually going to live in the land of Israel is [thus] one of the primary commands that the Jew is obliged to fulfil....[341]

Ha-Levi's own decision near the end of his life to move to Jerusalem reflected this deeply held conviction.

The Second Crusade (1145)

In 1144 the Seljuq Turks seized from the Crusaders the city of Edessa, a strategic outpost of the Byzantine Empire located in southeastern Turkey. In the process they are said to have slaughtered 15,000 Christians, including the Archbishop of the city and many of his priests, and destroyed Christian churches and monasteries as well.[342] This defeat deeply shocked the West and prompted Pope Eugenius III to call for a Second Crusade to protect Christians in the Holy Land.

This enterprise was, at least at the outset, better organized than the First Crusade because the Pope himself took charge of the enterprise. In 1145, for the first time a formal Crusade bull (an official papal letter or document) was issued, with provisions protecting Crusaders' families and properties at home. St. Bernard of Clairvaux, the most gifted orator of his time, exhorted the faithful, assuring them that the Second Crusade "was not a plan made by man, but [was] coming from heaven and proceeding from the heart of divine love."[343]

Once again, there was no shortage of volunteers to save Christians in or near the Holy Land. It was said that whenever Bernard preached, "mothers hid their sons and wives hid their husbands." Bernard himself boasted:

> I spoke; and at once the Crusades have multiplied to infinity. Villages and towns are now deserted. You will scarcely find one man for every seven women. Everywhere you see widows whose husbands are still alive.[344]

The response to this new Crusade was overwhelming. Two of the greatest kings of Europe—the German emperor Conrad III and the French king Louis VII—each provided an army. These German and French forces were accompanied by a veritable flood of pilgrims, eager to profit both from the military protection afforded by the knights and from the plenary indulgence promised by the Pope to all who took part in the Second Crusade. As usual, by their own choice these pilgrims traveled toward the Holy Land unarmed—a fact which the expedition's historian, Eudes de Deuil, deplored because he could see how useful the pilgrims would be in battle had they been willing to carry bows and arrows and swords.[345]

The two armies, totaling about 50,000 men, met in Jerusalem in 1148 to join forces. They then laid siege to Damascus, the nearest seat of Muslim power. Remarkably, however, they gave up after a very short siege of only five days. The reasons for their timidity are still unclear but it appears this was a prudent decision. Damascus was ably defended by Nureddin, king of Damascus and Aleppo, who had already called for and was awaiting reinforcements from Aleppo. The Muslims would be able to take advantage of physical obstacles (hedges, orchards and canals) around Damascus to harass the Crusaders and slow their progress. Moreover, in contrast to the First Crusade, the Byzantine Emperor did not commit any of his troops and the leaders of the Second Crusade fell prey themselves to petty disagreements and bad planning.

Whatever the reasons for lifting the siege so early, the end result, of course, was that the German and French armies failed to take Damascus. The Arab chronicler Ibn al-Qalanisi was an eyewitness to this abortive campaign. He recorded that the Crusaders retreated "in miserable confusion and disorder," harassed by Muslim archers to such an extent that the road was choked with "innumerable corpses of men and their splendid mounts," which stank so powerfully in the summer heat that "the birds almost fell out of the sky."[346] The Second Crusade thus ended in abject failure.

Rabbi Benjamin of Tudela (1160)

This far-ranging Jewish traveler was on the road for 13 years, beginning in 1160 and ending in 1173.[347] Journeying both for commercial reasons and to learn more about the conditions of Jews in Europe and Asia, he began his wanderings in his native Spain. He first made his way to Jerusalem via Italy, Greece, Byzantium and Syria. Afterwards, he also seems to have visited Iraq, Egypt, Assyria, Persia and was apparently the first European to reach the western borders of China. After a Latin translation of Rabbi Benjamin's Hebrew itinerary appeared in 1575, his travels became better known.

Twelfth century Jerusalem was, Benjamin tells us, "a small city strongly fortified with three walls. It contains a numerous population, composed of Jacobites, Armenians, Greeks, Georgians, Franks, and of people of all tongues."[348] Although after the Crusader conquest in 1099, no Muslims or Jews were officially permitted to live in Jerusalem, Rabbi Benjamin found that 200 Jews were living "in one corner of the city, under the tower of David," where they were engaged in the dyeing trade. He took careful note of the activities of the Templars and Hospitalers, recording that

> There are in Jerusalem two hospitals, which support four hundred knights, and afford shelter to the sick; these are provided with everything they may want, both during life and in death; the second [the first hospital is not discussed] is called the hospital of Solomon, being the palace originally built by King Solomon. This hospital also harbours and furnishes four hundred knights, who are ever ready to wage war, over and above those knights who arrive from the country of the Franks and other parts of Christendom. These generally have taken a vow upon themselves to stay for a year or two, and they remain until the period of their vow is expired. The large place of worship, called Sepulchre, and containing the sepulchre of that man [Rabbi Benjamin apparently cannot bring himself to write the name of Jesus], is visited by all pilgrims.[349]

Even in Rabbi Benjamin's day, stories abounded about Jerusalem's hidden treasures. A pious Jewish ascetic named Abraham el-Constantini, described by Rabbi Benjamin as "one of the mourners of the downfall of Jerusalem," said that fifteen years before the Rabbi's visit, a team of workmen had been sent to Mount Sion (believed to be the site of the sepulcher of David and his successors) to rebuild a church which was in poor repair. Two of these men were good friends and one day treated each other to a special lunch. Their supervisor criticized them for spending so much time eating, but they promised him that in the days ahead they would continue to work when the other laborers stopped for lunch.

True to their word, one day during the lunch-break they kept on working and smashed apart a huge stone that concealed the mouth of a cave. As Abraham told Rabbi Benjamin,

> they agreed to enter it in search of treasure, and they proceeded until they reached a large hall, supported by pillars of marble, encrusted with gold and silver, and before which stood a table, with a golden sceptre and crown. This was the sepulchre of David, king of Israel, to the left of which they saw that of Solomon in a similar state, and so on the sepulchres of all the kings of Juda, who were buried there. They further saw chests locked up, the contents of which nobody knew....[350]

This was wealth beyond their wildest dreams. Divine intervention, however, was said to have thwarted their plans for untold riches. As soon as they tried to enter the cave, "a blast of wind like a storm issued forth from the mouth of the cavern so strong that it threw them down almost lifeless to the ground." They lay there motionless until evening, when "another wind rushed forth, from which they heard a voice like that of a man calling aloud, 'Get up, and go forth from this place.'"[351] Terrified, they ran away and told their story to the Patriarch of Jerusalem, who consulted Abraham and was informed that the men had stumbled across the sepulchers of David and other early kings.

The next morning, the men were ordered to go back to work but "they were found stretched on their beds and still full of fear; they declared that they would not attempt to go again into the cave, as it was not God's will to discover it to any one." As a result, the Patriarch ordered the entrance to the cave be walled up "so as to hide it effectually [sic] until the present day."[352]

John of Würzburg (c. 1170)

This pilgrim remarked on the extent of the Hospitalers' activities in Jerusalem when he visited the city in about 1170. All that is known about him is that he was a priest from Würzburg, Germany. He, too, was recorded by the wide variety of pilgrims who had made their way to Jerusalem. There were, he says,

> Greeks, Bulgarians, Latins, Germans, Hungarians, Scots, Navarrese, Bretons, English, Franks, Ruthenians, Bohemians, Georgians, Armenians, Jacobites, Syrians, Nestorians, Indians, Egyptians, Copts, Capheturici, Maronites, and many others, [of] whom it would take too long to tell.[353]

John of Würzburg is also a good source on the sacred spaces of Jerusalem, notably the dramatic crevice in the rock which was located deep within the Church of the Holy Sepulcher. In medieval times, it was believed that this rock constituted the very center of the earth and had split apart when Jesus was crucified directly over it. John of Würzburg watched other pilgrims cast offerings into the opening in the rock. He later explained to his readers how this sacred geography symbolically brought together three major themes: Jesus Christ; the center of the earth; and Adam, the first man. John explained this as follows:

> As our lord was dying on the cross, the veil of the temple was rent from the top to the bottom and the rock in which the cross was fixed was split through the midst, in the place where it was touched by his blood; through which rent the blood flowed to the lower parts wherein Adam is said to have been buried, and who was thus baptized in the blood of Christ. It is said to be in commemoration of this that a skull is always represented in paintings at the foot of the Cross.[354]

Theodoric (c. 1171)

In the meantime, the ceremony of the Holy Fire never changed very much. In about 1171, a German pilgrim named Theodoric (or Theoderich), who would later become bishop of Würzburg, reported that

> It is customary in the Church of the Holy Sepulchre, both in the church itself and in all the other churches in the city, at daybreak on the morning of Easter Even [the day before Easter], to put out the earthly lights, and to await the coming of light from heaven; for the reception of which one of the silver lamps, seven of which hang there, is prepared. Then all the clergy and people stand waiting with great and anxious expectation.... The fire is wont to appear at certain hours and in certain places.... However, on the day when our humble selves, with the other pilgrims, were awaiting the sacred fire, immediately after the ninth hour that sacred fire came; whereupon, behold,

with ringing of church-bells, the service of the Mass was said throughout the whole city.... As soon as the holy fire arrives, it is customary to present it to the Temple of the Lord before anyone, except the Patriarch, has lighted his candle at it.[355]

The Muslims did not, of course, share the Christians' awe of the Holy Fire: they believed it was simply a farce. The dramatic appearance of the flame, they maintained, was due to human rather than divine intervention. It was either caused by lighting oil-soaked threads or by igniting an iron wire covered with thick oil. Gradually, the skeptics carried the day, until by the end of the nineteenth century the Holy Fire was no longer revered as a miracle by most non–Russian pilgrims. It still has a ceremonial value in Jerusalem, but one devoid of miraculous qualities. During the Easter season in 2001, for example, the Holy Fire was celebrated on Holy Saturday by the Greek Catholic Patriarchate and by the Armenian, Coptic, Greek, Russian and Syrian Orthodox churches.[356]

'Ali al-Hawari (1173)

This Arab traveler compiled an elaborate description of Muslim pilgrimage sites, including Jerusalem, which he visited in 1173.[357] For him, the Dome of the Rock was by far the city's most important feature. This was where Muhammad had ascended into heaven and where the Prophet's footprint could still be seen on the Rock itself. After a careful description of the Dome of the Rock, al-Hawari discussed the Aqsa Mosque and other Muslim and Christian holy monuments, including the Church of the Holy Sepulcher.

Although he admired the architecture of this church, he disparagingly referred to the building as *Qumama* (dung heap) rather than *Qiyama* (resurrection). He was referring, he explained, to that fact that before the Muslims conquered Jerusalem in 638, this site was where the Christians dumped Jerusalem's excrement and rubbish, where the hands of thieves were cut off and where criminals were crucified. Al-Hawari tells us that he lived in Jerusalem long enough to understand what caused the Holy Fire to appear, but gives no details of this controversial practice. Al-Hawari promised his readers that, in a separate work, he would describe Jerusalem's monuments more fully. If he ever undertook this project, however, nothing of it has survived.

Rabbi Petachia of Ratisbon (1175)

After living in Prague for some time, Rabbi Petachia, a German, traveled in the Middle East for ten years—from 1175 to 1185. He found there was only one Jew in Jerusalem—a dyer, who was also a Rabbi and who had to pay a heavy tax to the king in order to stay there. Rabbi Petachia reports a bit of local folklore about one of the gates of the Holy City:

> At Jerusalem there is a gate: its name is Gate of Mercy. The gate is piled up with stone and lime. No Jew is permitted to go there, and still less a Gentile. One day the Gentiles wished to remove the rubbish and open the gate, but the whole land of Israel shook and there was a tumult in the city until they abstained. There is a tradition that the Divine glory [the *Shekhina*] had gone into exile through this gate and through it would return.[358]

Rabbi Jacob ha Cohen (c. 1180)

Rabbi Jacob ha Cohen was a European Jewish pilgrim who visited Palestine not long before it was recaptured by the Muslims in 1187. He left only a short account of his journey and had nothing new to say about Jerusalem itself. He did, however, witness a miraculous or at least an unexplained sight: "At sunrise ... a portent appeared on Mount Carmel like a wheel four cubits high, and it went back. I write of what I saw with my own eyes."[359] Like Rabbi Benjamin of Tudela, Rabbi Jacob did not want to refer to Jesus by name; he mentions at the end of his account only that he stopped at the tomb of "that man."

Saladin's conquest of Jerusalem (1187)

The Second Crusaders' failure to capture Damascus marked the beginning of military setbacks which would ultimately end in 1291 with the Muslims' capture of Acre, the last Crusader stronghold in the Holy Land. In the aftermath of the Second Crusade, the Muslims were fortunate to have as one of their leaders a celebrated hero known as Saladin, whose name in Arabic means "Righteousness of the Faith." Saladin rose to became the sultan of Egypt, Syria, Yemen, and Palestine. He founded the Ayyubid dynasty. Thanks his ability to use both diplomacy and military force as circumstances required, he was able to unify disunited Muslims and inspire them with his own vision of *jihad* ("holy struggle").

The high point of his career came in 1187, when he trapped and decimated an army of Crusaders at Hattin in northern Palestine. Three months later he attacked Jerusalem itself. Its Christian defenders saw how strong Saladin's forces were and how busily they were tunneling under the city's walls. The Christians knew that even the most imposing city wall could be brought down by digging a wood-braced tunnel under it, filling the tunnel with highly-inflammable material and then setting it on fire. When the wood braces burned, the tunnel—and the section of the city walls above it—would collapse. The defenders therefore told Saladin they would surrender if he would let them leave the city in safety. According to Ibn al-Athir, a Muslim historian who was an eye-witness to the scene, Saladin replied that "We shall deal with you just as you dealt with the population of Jerusalem when you took it in 1099, with murder and enslavement and other such savageries!"[360]

Faced with this rejection, the defenders then threatened Saladin with a fight to the last man. They told him:

> if we see that death is inevitable, then by God we shall kill our children and our wives, burn our possessions, so as not to leave you with a *dinar* or a *drachma* or a single man or woman to enslave. When this is done, we shall pull down the Sanctuary [Dome] of the Rock and the Masjid [Mosque] al-Aqsa and other sacred places, slaughtering the Muslim prisoners we hold—5,000 of them—and killing every horse and animal we possess. Then we shall come out to fight you like men fighting for their lives, when each man, before he falls dead, kills his equals; we shall die with honour, or win a noble victory![361]

Saladin saw that the Christians made these threats seriously and decided to let them surrender. For the first time in 88 years, Jerusalem was again in Muslim hands. Saladin kept his word: unlike the First Crusaders, he pointedly refrained from slaughtering the inhabitants of the Holy City. True, the great gilt cross was stripped from the Dome of the Rock and some Christian churches were turned into stables or granaries, but Saladin did not harm the Church of the Holy Sepulcher itself.

Imad ad-Din al-Isfahani, a scholar and rhetorician who served as Saladin's secretary, explained why. Al-Isfahani tells us that some of Saladin's advisers had strongly urged him to tear down this holy monument:

> When its buildings are destroyed [said the advisers] and it is razed to the ground, and its sepulchre opened and destroyed, and its fires spent and extinguished, and its traces rubbed out and removed, and its soil ploughed up, and the Church scattered far and wide, then the people will cease to visit it, and the longings of those destined to damnation will no longer turn to seeing it, whereas if it is left standing the pilgrimage will go on without end.[362]

Fortunately for posterity, however, Saladin's less fanatical counselors urged a more prudent course of action. They argued that, on the contrary,

> Demolishing and destroying [the Church of the Holy Sepulcher] would serve no purpose, nor would it prevent the infidels from visiting it or prevent their having access to it. For it is not the building as it appears to the eyes but the home of the Cross and the Sepulchre that is the object of worship. The various Christian races will still be making pilgrimages here even if the earth had been dug up and thrown into the sky. And when [Caliph] 'Umar, the prince of the believers, conquered Jerusalem in the early days of Islam, he confirmed to the Christians the possession of the place, and did not order them to demolish the building.[363]

Saladin found the moderates' argument persuasive. Instead of demolishing, he rebuilt. He had the Templars' latrines removed from the Aqsa Mosque and had it readied for Friday prayers. Christian pictures and statues were stripped from the Dome of the Rock. Its Koranic inscriptions were brought to light again. Saladin himself worked side by side with his laborers, personally cleansing the courts of the Haram with rose water. He also founded a convent and a law school in what had been, respectively, a Christian convent and the residence of the Patriarch. Thousands of Muslim pilgrims flocked to Jerusalem now that it was again safe to do so. Magnanimously, Saladin permitted both Christians and Jews not only to visit the Holy City but to live there, too.

VIII

More Crusades and More Pilgrims: The Ayyubid and Mamluk Dynasties (1187–1517)

This long (330-year) turbulent era was highlighted by seven Crusades and a large number of pilgrimages. After capturing Jerusalem in 1187, the Ayyubid ruler Saladin rebuilt the city's fortifications. In 1219, however, his nephew, who succeeded him, pulled down the outer walls, fearing the Crusaders would recapture the city and use it again as a stronghold. The Khwarizmian Turks sacked Jerusalem in 1244. In 1260 the Mamluk sultan Baybars I conquered Palestine and became the new ruler of Jerusalem. He began an intensive building program, particularly around the Temple Mount, setting up hostels and charitable institutions. In 1291 the Crusaders lost the city of Acre, their last stronghold in the Levant. This defeat spelled the end of Christian influence in Palestine. Between 1351 and 1353 the Black Death (bubonic plague) killed many people in Jerusalem. The city entered an era of economic and political stagnation. Mamluk rule gradually decayed and in 1517 the Ottoman Turks came to power.

The Third Crusade (1187)

The fall of Jerusalem genuinely shocked Western Europe. Pope Urban III, it was said, died of a heart attack soon after hearing the news. His successor, Gregory VIII, lost no time issuing a bull for a Third Crusade, calling on the faithful to wrest the Holy Land from Muslim control. The Western response was, once again, encouraging.

William II of Sicily sent a fleet. The Holy Roman emperor Frederick Barbarossa set out in 1189 with the largest Crusader army thus far assembled but he drowned en route the next year, probably suffering a heart attack while trying to ford a river in southern Turkey. Philip II Augustus of France and Richard I the Lionhearted joined the Crusade as well. This undertaking, however, was not a success, either from the Christian or from the Muslim point of view. Richard captured Acre and several other cities but never reached Jerusalem itself. Saladin, on the other hand, could not drive him out of the Holy Land. In the end, exhausted by their struggles, both sides saw the merits of a peaceful settlement.

Negotiations went on for a whole year. Baha ad-Din Ibn Shaddad, a member of Saladin's staff and a reliable chronicler of the Third Crusade, stresses the importance Jerusalem held for Richard and Saladin alike. In a letter to Saladin, Richard warned him: "Jerusalem is for us an object of worship that we could not give up even if there were only one of us left." Saladin replied just as sternly:

> Jerusalem is ours as much as yours; indeed, it is even more sacred to us than it is to you, for it is the place from which our Prophet accomplished his nocturnal journey and the place where our community will gather [on the day of Judgment]. Do not imagine that we can renounce it or vacillate on this point.[364]

Nevertheless, in 1192 Saladin and Richard signed a peace treaty which guaranteed, among other things, that the Crusaders would continue to hold Acre and a thin strip along the Palestinian coast. Moreover, during the three-year life of the treaty, Christian pilgrims would have free access to the holy sites of Jerusalem.

Canon Richard (c. 1192)

Canon Richard of London, one of the first English pilgrims to go to Jerusalem under the terms of this treaty, found that the visit still had dangers:

> Those who were mounted went quickly on ahead, the more freely to kiss the tomb of the Lord in fulfillment of their vows.... Afterwards we went to the church on Mount Sion on whose left side is the place where the Blessed Mother of God departed this world to the Father. After we had bathed that place with tearful kisses we went on to see the most holy table at which Christ

deigned to sup. Quickly kissing this, we departed in a group without delay. It was not safe to enter there except in groups because of the treachery of that profane people. If the Turks find pilgrims wandering around, three here, four there, they drag them off into the inside of the crypts and strangle them.[365]

The Teutonic Knights (1198)

Never as rich, as powerful or as colorful in the Holy Land as the Templars or the Hospitalers, the order of the Teutonic Knights was formally established in 1198, after a prior existence as a German hospital in Acre. It was led by knights and was staffed by middle class priests and by noblewomen, who served as nursing sisters. Most of its members were Germans and most of the property it owned was located in Germany as well. Thus this order did not play a major role in the Holy Land itself.

Perhaps for this reason, early in the thirteenth century the Teutonic Knights decided to expand the scope of their activities and began to colonize deserted lands in Hungary on behalf of King Andrew of Hungary. They soon became so rich and powerful, however, that King Andrew expelled the order in 1225. The Teutonic Knights then turned to subduing the "pagans" of Prussia, with such singular success that the historian of the order could record that by 1283 "all the peoples in Prussia had been attacked and exterminated so that not one was left who did not bow to the Roman Church."[366]

The Fourth Crusade (1198)

The Christians and Muslims who had actually fought in Palestine were willing enough to keep the hard-earned peace, but

Western Europeans at home still wanted to recover Jerusalem. Toward this end, in 1198 Pope Innocent III called for another Crusade. This expedition was not a great success, either. The Crusaders wanted to begin by conquering Egypt, the locus of Muslim power, and from there move on to attack Jerusalem. But in 1202, finding they were unable to pay the Venetians for all the ships needed to carry huge numbers of men, horses and equipment to Egypt, the Crusaders agreed to a major change of strategy. In return for the ships they needed, they would first help the Venetians capture Zara (Croatia).

This they did. Then they turned their sights on the rich city of Constantinople, which they seized and sacked in 1204. There the Crusaders and Venetians set up a "Latin Empire of Constantinople." Pope Innocent III, appalled by their actions, strongly reprimanded the leaders of the Crusade but events had already passed beyond his control. Acting on his own initiative, a papal legate had released the Crusaders from their vow to go to the Holy Land, thus spelling the end of a misguided adventure.

Hazards of traveling by sea (c. 1199)

A law enacted during the reign of Richard I (d. 1199) reflects some of the dangers pilgrims faced when taking ship for the Holy Land. Conditions aboard galleys and in the ports were cramped, uncomfortable and dangerous. It did not take much to provoke hotheads to reach for their knives, which all men carried to cut their food and to defend themselves. The potential for violence was so high that Richard's law provided stiff penalties for bloodshed:

He who kills a man on shipboard shall be bound to the dead body and thrown into the sea; if the man is killed on shore, the slayer shall be bound to the dead body, and buried with it. He who shall draw his knife and strike another, or who shall have blood drawn from him, to lose his hand; if he shall have only struck with the palm of his hand, without drawing blood, he shall be thrice ducked in the sea.[367]

Herbert of Patsley (1207)

According to a medieval court convened in Norfolk, England, in the autumn of 1207 a man named Herbert of Patsley hit another Englishman, Drew Chamberlain, over the head with a bow. Although the blow was so heavy that Drew's skull was broken open and his brains poured out, Herbert was "not content" with this but immediately drove his knife into Drew's heart, "so that he died."[368] Herbert was charged with homicide. Drew's kinsmen got ready for trial by battle with Herbert's kinsmen but Thomas of Ingoldisthorp, a local magnate, managed to avoid further bloodshed by mediating a settlement between the parties.

This agreement provided, among other things, that within the next 40 days Herbert would leave on a penitential pilgrimage to Jerusalem and would stay there for seven years, serving God and praying for Drew's soul. Court records do not confirm that Herbert went to Jerusalem, but this seems very likely. Under the terms of the settlement, if he returned to England before the seven years were up, he would subject to execution as a convicted murderer. Moreover, the eight local knights who stood surety for this agreement would have been honor-bound to enforce it.

Rabbi Samuel ben Samson (1210)

Jewish pilgrimage to Jerusalem experienced a revival in the early thirteenth century. In 1210-1211, for example, Rabbi Samuel ben Samson made a pilgrimage to the Holy City, probably as serving as secretary to his distinguished companion, Rabbi Jonathan ha Cohen, the most influential and wealthy French Jew of his time. "We arrived at Jerusalem by the western end of the city," Rabbi Samuel remembered, "rending our garments on beholding it, as it has been ordained we should do. It was a moment of tenderest emotion, and we wept bitterly, the great priest of Lunel [France] and I."[369]

They then visited the holy places sacred to the Jews. Rabbi Samuel recorded that

On the Sabbath day we recited the Afternoon Prayer on the spot where the uncircumcised [Christians] had time and again set up a sanctuary with idols, whose presence the place would not endure, causing them to fall down again as fast as they were set up. It was one of the ten stations visited by the divine Majesty when He came [to earth] from His dwelling-place. The Ismaelites [Muslims] venerate this spot. Only the foundations remain now in existence, but the place where the Ark stood is still to be seen.[370]

When he returned to Europe, Rabbi Samuel was carrying a letter from John de Brienne, king of Jerusalem, which may have encouraged the Jews to return to Palestine. If so, this would explain the pilgrimage to Jerusalem made by 300 rabbis from France and England in 1211.[371]

The Children's Crusade (1212)

Despite the setbacks experienced by the Second, Third, and Fourth Crusades,

Europe's commitment to recapturing Jerusalem was far from dead. It now degenerated into a mass hysteria which ruined the lives of tens of thousands of children. During the First Crusade, some destitute followers of Peter the Hermit had been known as "Tafurs" (in Arabic *tafuria* means "penniless') and had pledged their allegiance to a mythical king called Tafur. Guibert of Nogent described the Tafurs as

some of the poorest people in the crusading army ... [they] always marched barefoot, bore no arms, themselves had no money but, entirely filthy in their nakedness and want, marched in advance of all the others and lived on the roots of plants.[372]

The Tafurs believed it was the poor, not the rich, who were destined to conquer Jerusalem. They were convinced that where armed pilgrimages by sinful adults had failed, an unarmed pilgrimage by innocent children would succeed. Thus in 1212, when a French shepherd boy named Stephen claimed that Jesus, dressed as a pilgrim, had appeared to him in a vision and had given him a letter for the king of France, many local people believed him. Stephen set off to deliver the letter and a great many children followed him. Although this estimate must be greatly exaggerated, legend has it that eventually 30,000 children made their way to Marseilles with the intention of going to the Holy Land. None of them, of course, ever got there: unscrupulous merchants rounded them up and shipped them off to the slave markets of North Africa instead.

This madness was not confined to France. At about the same time, a 10-year-old boy named Nicholas preached a Children's Crusade in his native Germany and attracted 20,000 children. After crossing the Alps into Italy, these youngsters, too, failed to get to Jerusalem. Some of them remained in Italian towns of their own free will. Others were refused a free passage across the Mediterranean. A few managed to get to Rome, where Pope Innocent III released them from their Crusader vows. A good many of these children, however, also ended up in the North African slave markets.

The Fifth Crusade (1215)

But the Europeans were still not daunted. If Cairo could be captured, they reasoned, perhaps it could then be exchanged for Jerusalem. Thus in 1215 Pope Innocent III called for a Fifth Crusade, the last one directly organized by the papacy. Manned chiefly by French and Germans, it, too, was unsuccessful, even though conditions initially favored the Crusaders.

The Muslims, divided and fearful, tore down the walls of Jerusalem to make the city so indefensible that the Crusaders would not want to occupy it. Moreover, the Muslims were quite willing to surrender Jerusalem in return for peace. Nevertheless, the Crusaders decided to press ahead and to attack Cairo. They were stopped by floods on the Nile, however, and in 1221 had to settle for an indecisive eight-year truce, which did not include control of Jerusalem.

Magister Thietmar (1217)

Meanwhile, pilgrims were still coming to the Holy Land. One of them was a German Christian, Magister Thietmar. ("Magister" is an honorific that means "Master" or "Teacher.") We know nothing about him except that he had a high degree of curiosity and no small literary ability. He opens his account by telling us:

I, Thietmar, seeking pardon for my sins, armed myself with the sign of the cross

and left my home [in 1217], as a pilgrim, with my companions. I reached Acre after having run, on land and on sea, dangers which seemed to be very threatening but were in fact minimal when compared to the divine recompense I could hope for.... In writing these lines, I only wish to please God, and I reject all pride and false sense of glory, not wanting to be one of those who are looking for praise from other people.... If the reader wishes to open this book and take pleasure in it, as I do ... he will see that my book has been written without artificiality and in all simplicity, to occupy my leisure hours and to remember the places I visited in the Holy Land and the miracles which the power of God accomplished there.[373]

Thietmar had a harrowing experience as he was nearing Jerusalem:

As I was proceeding through the mountains of Judea toward Bethlehem ... I fell into a trap ... [and] was captured by Saracens and taken to Jerusalem. At that moment I thought I was dead, since the difference between my present sufferings and the fear of death or perpetual captivity seemed to me minimal. Indeed, overwhelmed by these my fears, it seemed to me that I would die at any instant. Thus it was that I was held captive for two days and one night outside the gate of the city. When there seemed no hope for me in my straitened captivity, God ... saved me in miraculous fashion. It happened in this way. I had as a companion (in prison), a noble Hungarian who knew that a number of his fellow Hungarians had obtained leave to be in Jerusalem for the purpose of study. He had them summoned. They came, recognized him, and received him in a most friendly manner. When they finally understood the reason for our imprisonment, they used their good offices and after a great deal of effort had us freed.[374]

Yehuda al-Harizi (1217)

Jewish pilgrims, too, were still coming to Jerusalem. The Spanish poet Yehuda al-Harizi was in the Holy City the same year as Magister Thietmar. Al-Harizi and his companions were saddened to see Muslim buildings standing on the site of what had once been the Jewish Temple. "What torment to see our holy courts converted into an alien temple!" he wrote. "We tried to turn our faces away from this great and majestic church now raised on the site of the ancient tabernacle where once Providence had its dwelling."[375] Still, al-Harizi expressed his appreciation that the Muslims had no objections to Jews settling in Jerusalem and letting them live peacefully there.

Castle Pilgrim (c. 1217)

The Teutonic Knights worked closely with the Templars to help pilgrims in the Holy Land. In about 1217, for example, the two orders, led by Pedro de Montaigu, the Grand Master of the Knights Templar, and aided by pilgrims from Austria and Hungary, built a huge coastal fortress at 'Atlit, a promontory jutting out into the Mediterranean between Jaffa and Haifa. They called it "Castle Pilgrim" to acknowledge the help they had received from the pilgrims.

The foundations of this stronghold, the largest and most strongly fortified Christian castle ever built in the Holy Land, lay beneath sea level. This made it impossible for attackers to undermine its walls by using the well-proven medieval tactic of digging a tunnel underneath them. (The roof of the tunnel would be propped up with wooden beams. The tunnel was then packed with inflammable material and set on fire. The tunnel would collapse when the beams burned through,

bringing down the wall above it.) Surrounded on three sides by water, Castle Pilgrim was manned by 300 Templars. It had a deep moat and a strong double wall on its landward side. Inside the castle were three big halls and a Templar church with a rotunda. One contemporary German chronicler, Oliver of Paderborn, reported that this fortification was stocked with enough food and supplies to support 4,000 fighting men.

Another first-hand observer, the German Dominican monk Burchard of Mount Sion (see below), reported that Castle Pilgrim had "walls and ramparts and barbicans [towers] so strong and castellated [studded with battlements], that the whole world should not be able to conquer it."[376] Protected by the sea and by walls up to 18 feet thick, Castle Pilgrim was a familiar sight and an imposing landmark for travelers bound for Jerusalem. It was mentioned frequently in pilgrimage accounts.[377] Sir John Mandeville (see below) said that from Acre "you may go to the city of Gerare [Caesarea], and so to the Castle of Pilgrims, and then to Jaffa, and so to Jerusalem."[378]

In the end, however, the size and fame of Castle Pilgrim could not save it. It may have been impervious to direct assault but when Acre fell to the Muslims in 1291, the Templars abandoned all their castles along the coast and pulled out of the Holy Land entirely. The Muslims then systematically destroyed these fortifications, including Castle Pilgrim. It faded from history until its ruins were finally excavated in the 1930s.

The Sixth Crusade (1228)

In Europe, the dream of regaining Jerusalem had never faded. A fleet carrying a Sixth Crusade sailed from Italy in 1227, ostensibly led by Frederick II of Germany.

But Frederick himself had been so slow setting out that Pope Gregory IX had ex-communicated him. Finally arriving in Cyprus in 1228, Frederick found that many people refused to support him because of the excommunication. With the support of the Teutonic Knights, however, he managed to win Jerusalem by diplomacy alone, signing a 10-year peace treaty with Egypt in 1229.[379]

A month after the treaty was signed, Frederick made a visit to Jerusalem and was struck by the beauty of the Dome of the Rock and the Aqsa Mosque. He was keenly aware of Muslim sensitivities, too. According to an Arab chronicler, when he saw that a European priest, who was car-rying a Bible in one hand, wanted to enter the mosque, Frederick exploded in anger. "Who brought you to this place?" he shouted. Then, addressing other nearby Christians, he roared, "By God, if any one of you dares to enter the mosque without permission, I will gouge out his eyes!"[380]

Under the terms of the treaty, the Crusaders were given most of Jerusalem, all of Bethlehem and a corridor to the sea. The Muslims, for their part, kept the Dome of the Rock and the Aqsa Mosque. Although Frederick's excommunication was canceled in 1230, the treaty itself was highly unpopular with Muslims and Christians alike. One Muslim writer re-corded that "The new disaster [the loss of Jerusalem] inflicted on us has broken our hearts. Our pilgrims can no longer go to Jerusalem. The verses of the Koran will no longer be recited in its schools. How great is the shame of the Muslim leaders re-sponsible for this!"[381]

Rabbi Jacob (1238)

Known as the "messenger" of Rabbi Jachiel of Paris, Rabbi Jacob visited Pales-tine and Iraq from 1238 to 1244—not to carry messages but to collect funds for the rabbinical college of Paris. Rabbi Jacob wrote a detailed account for Jewish pil-grims and began it with a moving invoca-tion:

> These are the journeyings of the chil-dren of Israel who wish to go to con-template and pray at the graves of the patriarchs, the righteous and the saints of the Holy Land, and to our holy and glorious Temple wherein our fathers prayed in Jerusalem. May it be rebuilt, and established in our days.[382]

He instructed Jewish pilgrims to make one rent in their garments when they first saw Jerusalem and another rent at the site of the Temple. At the Temple Mount, they were to pray in the direction of the former Temple. Rabbi Jacob marveled at the Dome of the Rock:

> Round the *Eben Shethiah* [the founda-tion stone or rock of the Temple], the Ishmaelite[383] Kings have built a very beautiful building for a house of prayer and erected on the top a very fine cupola. The building is on the site of the Holy of Holies and the Sanctuary, and in front of the Mosque towards the Altar is a structure of pillars and the cupola is at the top of these pillars and it would seem that this place was the outer Altar which was in the Court of Israel. The Moslems gather there on their holy day in crowds and dance around it in procession as the Israelites used to do on the seventh day of the [pilgrim] festivals, if we may compare holy things with profane.[384]

Jacques de Vitry (1239)

Consecrated bishop of Acre in 1216 and elected Patriarch of Jerusalem in 1239, this French priest was the greatest preacher of his time. He pioneered the use of sermon-stories known as *exempla* because, as he candidly explained, "It is necessary to employ a great many proverbs, historical stories and anecdotes, especially when the audience is tired and begins to get sleepy."[385]

De Vitry was a firm believer in penitential pilgrimages. He was convinced that suffering was an inescapable and, in fact, a necessary part of them. He taught that since a pilgrim had sinned with all his limbs, he must make reparation with all of them, too. This meant, in practice, that "exhaustion and sore feet were to be his only delight."[386]

Not surprisingly, de Vitry was especially keen on armed pilgrimages, i.e., Crusades. He first preached a Crusade against French heretics and personally led a large army of Crusaders at the siege of Toulouse (France). After preaching another expedition against the Muslims, he played a prominent role in the Fifth Crusade. In the sermons he addressed to pilgrims, he usually made two points. The first was that the journey to a holy place was a metaphor for man's life on earth. The second was that it was the Church's responsibility to equip each pilgrim for this journey by means of sermons and sacraments so that he would not be deflected from the path of salvation.[387]

Thanks to his long experience in the Holy Land, de Vitry knew all about the perils facing hapless pilgrims. It is worth quoting at some length what he told prospective travelers:

I have heard how certain abominable traitors, having received payment to furnish the pilgrims with victuals even to the port [of their destination], have stocked their ships with but little meat [food in general], and then, after a few days' journey, have starved their pilgrims to death and cast them ashore on an island, or (most cruel of all) have sold them as manservants or maidservants to the Saracens. I have known certain sailors bound for the city of Acre who had hired a ship from a man on condition that, if it perished on the sea, they should be bound to pay naught. When therefore they were within a short distance of the haven [port], without the knowledge of those pilgrims and merchants who were on board, they pierced the hold and entered into a boat while the ship was sinking. All the passengers were drowned; and the sailors, having laden their boat with the money and goods of the pilgrims, put on feigned faces of sadness when they drew near the shore. Therefore, having drowned the pilgrims and carried away their wealth, they paid not the hire of the ship, saying that they were not bound thereunto unless the vessel should come safe and sound to haven.[388]

The Khwarizmian Turks come to power (1244)

Near the middle of the thirteenth century, civil conflict broke out in Jerusalem and Cyprus, setting the stage for another Muslim conquest of Jerusalem. This time the victors were the Khwarizmian Turks from Iraq, who sacked the city in 1244 and reportedly killed 7,000 Christians in the process.[389] Al-Makrisi, a Muslim chronicler, tells us that these Turks were

a people whose lives were passed in war and plunder. When they had despoiled all the country near to Damascus they advanced to Jerusalem, took it by storm, and put all the Christians to the sword. The women and girls, having suffered every insult from a brutal disorderly soldiery, were loaded with chains. They destroyed the Church of the Holy Sepulchre; and when they found nothing among the living, to glut their rage, they opened the tombs of the

Christians, took out the bodies, and burnt them.[390]

A contemporary Christian account, written in 1244 by the Grand Master of the Hospitalers, confirmed the slaughter:

> ... the blood of those of the faith, with sorrow I say it, ran down the sides of the mountain like water. Young men and virgins [the Turks] hurried off with them into captivity, and retired into the Holy City, where they cut the throats, as of sheep doomed to the slaughter, of the nuns, and aged and infirm men.... In the said battle, then, the power of the Christians was crushed, and the number of slain in both armies was incomputable. The masters of the Templars and Hospitalers were slain as also the masters of other orders, with their brethren and followers. Walter, count of Brienne, and the lord Philip de Montfort, and those who fought under the patriarch [of Jerusalem], were cut to pieces; of the Templars only eighteen escaped, and sixteen of the Hospitalers, who were afterwards sorry that they had saved themselves.[391]

The Seventh Crusade (1244)

In 1244 the king of France, Louis IX, decided to take up the cross and reconquer Jerusalem. With the backing of Pope Innocent IV, he launched a Seventh Crusade, initially aiming (again) at Cairo. Like most of its predecessors, this enterprise failed, too. The French chronicler Jean, lord of Joinville, took the cross at the same time and was a member of this expedition. Although he admired Louis IX as a person, he was later to criticize the king's unworldliness and the lack of discipline and confusion among the Crusaders themselves.

With 100 ships carrying somewhere between 15,000 and 35,000 Seventh Cru-

saders, Louis IX landed in Egypt in 1249. Although he managed to capture the port of Damietta and the castle of al-Mansurah, floods on the Nile, an outbreak of plague and a shortage of food prevented him from getting to Cairo itself. He was forced to retreat. In the process, the king himself, his barons and his tattered army were captured by the Egyptians in 1250, who held them until a high ransom had been paid for their release.

Matthew Paris (d. 1259)

We have already mentioned this thirteenth century monk, who was one of the best chroniclers of medieval life. He lived and worked at the Benedictine monastery of St. Albans (north of London), where he died in 1259. Matthew explains that many English and French nobles had to sell their estates to get the money needed to set off on the Crusades:

> Robert de Montalt, one of the higher ranking English barons, having taken the cross, made over his share of the woods and other revenues at Coventry to the prior and convent of that place in ... return for a large sum of money, so that he could procure necessities for the journey; he also sold a good deal and [disposed of] much else. Other nobles, both on this and the other side of the sea [the English Channel], did the same. Besides this same Robert a great many of the English nobility took the sign of the cross at this time, to assist and follow the king of the French in the cause of the cross.[392]

Despite their enthusiasm for another crusade, however, these nobles were well aware of its subtle legal and bureaucratic dangers. They became very cautious. Matthew tells us: "Innumerable, too, were those who, fearing the traps of the Roman curia, would neither publicly take the sign of the cross nor wear it on their shoulders, but secretly and firmly vowed and proposed to go to the Holy Land devoutly and in strength."[393]

Pilgrimages under Sultan Baybars (1263)

In 1260 the Mamluk sultan Baybars defeated an invading Mongol army in Galilee and thus became the undisputed ruler of Palestine. His headquarters were in Cairo but he visited Jerusalem in 1263. At that time, to make sure that the crowds of Christian pilgrims who came to the Holy City to celebrate Easter understood that they were there only on Muslim sufferance, Baybars set up two new Islamic sanctuaries nearby.

One was Nebi Musa, near Jericho, and marked the burial site of Moses. (Nebi Musa was also the name of an annual Christian pilgrimage and religious festival commemorating Moses.) The other sanctuary, in Ramla, honored the Arab prophet Salih. Baybars' plan, which apparently worked well, was that Muslim pilgrims heading for Jericho would first meet in Jerusalem, confirming by their presence their ownership of the Holy City. This would put Christian pilgrims on their good behavior.[394]

Built near Jericho in 1263 by the Mamluk sultan Baybars, Nebi Musa marks the supposed tomb of the prophet Moses. As such, it was a sacred center both for Muslim and Christian pilgrims. This shrine is located about 30 miles east of Jerusalem. It is now, alas, in a semi-ruinous state. (Illustration from the author's collection.)

Rabbi Moses ben Nachman (1267)

Jewish pilgrimages to Jerusalem during *Sukkot* were increasing in this era. In 1267 Rabbi Moses ben Nachman, better known to history as Nachmanides, was exiled from Spain and came to Jerusalem. He found that the Holy City was in bad shape. It had been abandoned by many of its former inhabitants because the protective walls had never been repaired. There were only 2,000 people living there, of whom 300 were Christians. Nachmanides was presumably more interested in two Jewish dyers and their families, the only Jewish inhabitants of the city.[395] Undismayed by the ruinous condition of Jerusalem, Nachmanides founded the Ramban Synagogue, which became the center of Jewish life in the Holy City and attracted many pilgrims and students from abroad.

Nachmanides himself left Jerusalem after about one month and settled in Acre, but his affection for the Holy City never flagged. In 1267 he wrote to his son:

> What shall I say of this land? Great is its desolation. The more holy the place, the greater the desolation. Jerusalem is the most desolate of all.... Men flock from Damascus, Aleppo, and from all parts of Jerusalem to behold the Place of the Sanctuary [Temple], and to mourn over it. May you, my son and your brothers, and the whole of our family, see the salvation of Jerusalem.... He who merits to see Jerusalem in her ruins will merit to see her rebuilt and repaired when the Divine Presence returns to her.[396]

The Eighth Crusade (1270)

Jerusalem was still in Muslim hands. This inevitably led to calls for another Crusade. Despite his setbacks in the Seventh Crusade and a lack of popular support for any new expedition, Louis IX assumed the leadership of the Eighth Crusade, too. He and his forces sailed from southern France in 1270, en route this time not to Egypt but to Tunisia. The reasoning behind the decision to go to Tunis is murky but seems to have involved the political aspirations of the king of Sicily, Charles of Anjou, who was the brother of Louis IX.

Whatever the reasons for going to Tunis, it turned out to be a serious mistake. Many Crusaders died there of disease, including Louis IX himself, his son John Tristan and the papal legate Raoul Grosparmi. Louis' dying words are said to have been: "Jerusalem, Jerusalem."[397] Charles of Anjou, arriving belatedly, managed to evacuate the remainder of the army. Taken all in all, however, the Tunis crusade, the last of the eight "numbered"[398] Crusades, was an abject failure.

Burchard of Mount Sion (1280)

Not all of the Christian pilgrims who came to Jerusalem were saints: many of them were sinners. Burchard of Mount Sion, the Dominican monk from Germany, made a pilgrimage to Jerusalem in about 1280. He liked the Muslims, whom he described as "very hospitable, courteous and kindly" but he was scathing in his condemnation of his fellow Christians, who

> tread the holy places with polluted feet.... To tell the truth, our own people, the Latins, are worse than all the other people of the land.... Whenever someone was a malefactor, such as a robber, a thief, or an adulterer, he used to cross the sea, either as a penitent, or else because he feared for his skin and therefore did not dare to stay in his own country; and so they came thither from all parts, such as Germany, Italy, France, England, Spain, Hungary and

other parts of the world. And while they change the sky above them they do not change their minds. Once being here, after they have spent what they had brought with them, they have to acquire new [funds] and so, they return to their "vomit," doing the worse of the worst....[399]

These same scoundrels also put themselves forward as guides for law-abiding but gullible pilgrims. The upshot was, Burchard tells us, that the "pilgrims who do not know how to take care of themselves, trust their hosts [guides] and lose their goods and their honour."[400]

The fall of Acre (1291)

The repeated failures of the later Crusades proved that the Christians' days of glory in the Holy Land had come to an end. Baybars' successors completed what a modern writer has called "the liquidation of the Crusaders."[401] The Muslims conquered Tripoli in 1289; Acre, the last Crusader stronghold on the mainland, fell in 1291. The Arab scholar Abu I-Fida was present at both battles and describes the fall of Acre in these words:

Within the city was a number of well-fortified towers, and some Franks shut themselves inside and defended them. The Muslims killed vast numbers of people and gathered immense booty. The Sultan forced all those in the towers to surrender, and they submitted to the last man, and to the last man were decapitated outside the city walls. At the Sultan's command the city was razed to the ground.... With these conquests the whole of Palestine was now in Muslim hands, a result that no one would have dared to hope for or to desire. Thus the whole of Syria and the coastal zones were purified of the Franks, who had once been on the point

of conquering Egypt and subduing Damascus and other cities. Praise be to God![402]

After the fall of Acre, the Crusaders surrendered or abandoned all their remaining fortresses, including Castle Pilgrim, by the end of 1291. For more than 600 years the Holy Land would remain under Muslim rule. The Christians would not come back to power again until 1917, when the Ottoman Turks surrendered Jerusalem to a British general, Sir Edmund Allenby, toward the end of World War I.

William of Boldensele (1334)

In the early 1330s a German monk named William of Boldensele left his monastery without permission. A French cardinal imposed a penitential pilgrimage on him and also required him to submit a report on his travels. The result was a *Treatise on the State of the Holy Land*, which covered William's journey of 1334–1335.

Like so many other devout pilgrims, he was quite taken by Jerusalem itself:

It is the capital of the Promised Land. The air there is good and pure.... The temple of Our Lord is located in this city ... [it is] round, large and covered with lead. It is made of dressed and polished stone, surrounded by a great courtyard, paved with white marble, and is held in high esteem by the Saracens, who greatly revere this spot. They take off their shoes before entering it, kneel down and kiss the pavement. They will not let any Christian enter, saying that a place as holy as the house of God must not be polluted or contaminated by Jews or Christians, whom they consider to be infidel dogs.[403]

Among the many other places he visited was Mount Sion. Conscious, perhaps,

This painting hangs in the Château de Versailles et de Trianon, where it bears a caption: "Guillaume de Clermont defending the city of Acre, which was attacked by 160,000 soldiers of the sultan of Egypt El-Asrad between 5 April and 29 May 1291." Although the Crusaders usually wore white surcoats marked with red crosses (red and white are the colors symbolically associated with Christ), Guillaume is wearing the opposite combination. (Louis Dominique Papety, 1845; photograph courtesy of Réunion des Musées Nationaux Agence Photographique.)

that the reason for his pilgrimage was his own failure to obey religious authority, William expressed regret that at Mount Sion only the Armenian Catholics gave allegiance to the Pope of Rome. "All the other Christians," William complained,

> are schismatics who do not obey the Holy Church. These are the Greeks, Arians, Nestorians, Jacobins, Nubians, Ethiopians, Indians, Georgians and other heretics who call themselves Christians. It would take too long to expose the errors of each of these sects, but the Decree [a compilation of canon law edited in the middle of the thirteenth century] identifies them.[404]

Isaac ben Joseph ibn Chelo (1334)

This Spanish traveler was a Kabbalist (a member of a Jewish esoteric mystical sect) who went to Jerusalem with his family in 1334. In a letter to his father and friends he describes seven routes from the Holy City to notable sights in other parts of Palestine. Playing on the opening lines of a well-known psalm, he begins his letter, "For the love of *Jerusalem* I will not keep silence. For the love of *Zion* I will not rest, although I have already written to you twice or thrice." He then goes on to describe the "seven wonders of the Holy City," which he lists as the Tower of David, Solomon's Palace, the tomb of Huldah the prophetess, the Sepulchres of the Kings, the Palace of Queen Helena, the Gate of Mercy, and the Western Wall.[405]

Isaac reported that the Jewish community in Jerusalem was numerous and prosperous. Most of the rabbis and leading men had originally come from France. Some of the Jews were artisans or merchants (dyers, tailors, shoemakers, shopkeepers). A few were doctors, calligraphers or mathematicians. The most highly educated men were the religious scholars,

"working day and night at the study of the Holy Law and of the true wisdom, which is the Kabbalah. These are maintained out of the coffers of the community, because the study of the law is their only calling."[406]

Ibn Battuta (1335)

Ibn Battuta, the greatest medieval traveler of the Arab world, covered about 75,000 miles in journeys to almost all the Muslim countries. Known as "the traveler of Islam," he loved journeying for its own sake and tried never to travel any road more than once. Because of his brilliance and academic accomplishments, he was well-received wherever he went.

Ibn Battuta gives us a good description of some of the logistics involved in visiting the Holy Land in 1335.[407] He found that pilgrims could stop at a string of way-stations between Egypt and Syria, each of which had a public watering place for animals and a small shop for travelers. Local officials checked passports, levied a poll-tax on merchants, examined their goods and "most rigorously searched" their baggage for any contraband items. Even in these tiny way-stations, bureaucracy was alive and well. Ibn Battuta found a full panoply of "officers, clerks, and notaries" whose daily revenue was "a thousand gold dinars."

Ibn Battuta adds that the road between Egypt and Palestine was "under the guarantee of the *bedouin*." This was a diplomatic way of saying that because the nomads had been bought off, travelers could take that road in safety. When Christian pilgrims finally got to Jerusalem, however, they faced additional costs there:

> At Jerusalem there is another venerated church [the Church of the Holy Sepulcher] to which the Christians go on pilgrimages. This is the church about

which they lie and are persuaded that it contains the grave of Jesus—upon whom be peace. All who come on pilgrimage to it are liable to a stipulated tax to the Muslims as well as various humiliations, which they suffer very unwillingly.[408]

It may be worth pointing out here the reason why an intelligent Muslim like Ibn Battuta was convinced that the Christians were lying when they said the Church of the Holy Sepulcher contained the grave, i.e., the body, of Jesus. According to an Islamic belief, Jesus only appeared to die on the cross. Since there was no body to bury, the grave itself must have been empty.

Niccolo of Poggibonsi (1346)

This Franciscan friar made a pilgrimage to Jerusalem in 1346 and had a frightening experience there.[409] Niccolo recounts this story not to give local color but to warn prospective pilgrims about the necessity of having enough ready cash to deal with emergencies.

When he and his colleagues were presented to the amir (prince) of Jerusalem, they told the sultan through an interpreter that they were only poor friars who carried neither gold nor silver. This reply so enraged the sultan that he had the interpreter beaten on the spot. When the punishment was finished, the interpreter told the friars: "I have been caned in your place because I said you had no money to pay. Keep in mind that you will either have to pay or be beaten to death."[410]

Niccolo tells us, "Then the amir had me searched, and in truth I could not stand straight up from fear." Asked by the amir if he had any money to pay the tribute, Niccolo replied that he had none himself but could get some that same day. The amir had Niccolo and his colleagues arrested and led off towards the prison. En route, however, Niccolo met a friend of his, a Christian from Cyprus, who brought the friars back to the amir and promised to pay what they owed. As soon as they were freed, Niccolo and the others "lost no time in paying the sultan's tribute, which was seventy-two dirhams, which in our money amounts to about four florins a head."

The Muslims also exercised strict control over the Church of the Holy Sepulcher, the main destination for Christian pilgrims. It was closely guarded and fees had to be paid to enter it. Niccolo tells us that the inner chapel containing the tomb of Jesus had three doors. Two were always kept locked. The third door was opened just long enough to admit one pilgrim, who was permitted to remain in the chapel only for the short amount of time needed to say the "Our Father" prayer three times. The pilgrim then had to leave and the door was locked behind him. By paying an extra fee, however, a pilgrim could stay there all day and all night, if he or she wished. In this case the pilgrim would have to remain locked in the chapel at night after the guards had gone home.

Ludolph of Sudheim (1346)

Ludolph was a German priest who traveled in the Middle East from 1336 to 1341, probably as chaplain to a knight who was in the service of the king of Armenia. Ludolph's wide-ranging account, *The Path to the Holy Land*, contains many items of interest.[411]

Ludolph warns his readers, for example, that, except in special circumstances, if they wish to go to the Holy Land they must first get a license from the Pope. Not only will a pilgrim who travels without a license be excommunicated but he will also have to pay tribute to the Muslims, "to the dishonor of the Church." Ludolph tells prospective pilgrims that the way to the Holy Land is studded with dangers. In the Mediterranean, travelers face storms, whirlwinds, pirates, sandbanks, sharks and monstrous fish with teeth so long and sharp they can penetrate the wooden hull of a ship. Pilgrims passing through to Egypt must also beware of the crocodile, which Ludolph describes as "very strong, very savage, very quick and the cause of great harm to people and livestock. Because of it, it is dangerous to navigate on the Nile."

Sir John Mandeville (1356)

Famous both in his own time and later as the greatest Western traveler of the Middle Ages, Sir John may not have journeyed much farther than the nearest good library. There he would have had easy access to encyclopedias and to travelers' accounts. The book attributed to him, entitled *The Travels of Sir John Mandeville*, is to modern eyes no more than an entertaining mixture of fact and fiction but it reached a very wide contemporary audience. In fact, it still makes good reading today because of the author's editorial skill and his wry sense of humor. "Of Paradise I cannot speak properly," Sir John confesses, "for I have not been there; and that I regret."[412]

By his own account, Sir John was an English knight who had traveled extensively in the Middle East and Asia (including China) between 1322 and 1356, or perhaps between 1332 and 1366. However, virtually nothing is known about him apart from what he himself tells us in the book. How far he traveled—if he traveled at all—is still an unanswered question. Still, we can hazard a guess. By the middle of the fourteenth century, any resourceful man with such a keen interest in distant lands would almost certainly have managed to get at least as far as the Holy Land, which was the destination of countless ordinary pilgrims.[413] We can therefore entertain the possibility that Mandeville did manage to get to Jerusalem. In any case, his book was a great success.

Originally written in French in 1356–1357, the *Travels* had been translated into Latin and every other major European language by 1400. This work continued to influence successive generations of travelers up to about 1600, by which time the new facts emerging from European voyages of discovery around the world had destroyed Sir John's credibility on many issues.

Roughly half of his book focuses directly or indirectly on the pilgrimage to Jerusalem. Much of what he had to say was in fact useful to pilgrims. One anonymous owner of a late fourteenth or early fifteenth century manuscript of the *Travels* (this document, known as the Cotton text, is now in the British Library) even tore out part of the Jerusalem section and may have used it himself as a guidebook. If so, this would certainly have pleased Sir John.

He makes it clear in his sonorous *Prologue* that his goal was to produce a practical handbook for travel to the Holy Land:

> Since it is so that the land beyond the sea, that is to say the Land of Promise which men call the Holy Land, among all other lands is the most worthy land and mistress over all others ... and as much as it is a long time past since there were any general passage over the sea into the Holy Land, and since men covet to hear that land spoken of, and have of that great pleasure and enjoyment, I, John Mandeville, knight, ... shall describe a part of those things that are there ... specially for those who desire and intend to visit the holy city of Jerusalem and the holy places that are thereabout ... for I have many times

In this symbolic illustration taken from a medieval manuscript, Sir John Mandeville points out to newly arrived pilgrims the way to Jerusalem. (The British Library.)

travelled and ridden over it in goodly company of lords.[414]

The *Travels* take the reader from England to Constantinople and then provide a running commentary on the sea and land routes to Jerusalem itself, as well as on the customs and beliefs of the peoples of the regions traversed. Mandeville's mastery of details, whether true or false, and his command of local color keep his book from falling into the torpor of the usual travelogue.

Pilgrims coming from Mount Sinai, for example, are told that they will have to spend no less than 13 or 14 days crossing the Sinai desert but that they will be adequately provisioned before they set out by the monks of St. Catherine's monastery. Once in the desert, they may face attacks from the lawless *bedouin*, whom Mandeville describes as formidable foes. These raiders, he warns the prospective pilgrim, are

> people of evil condition, full of all kinds of wickedness and malice. Houses they have none, only tents, which they make of skins of camels and other wild beasts they eat, and they drink water [only] when they can get it.... Nevertheless they are strong men, good fighters; and there is a great multitude of them. They do nothing else but hunt wild beasts, to catch them for their food. And they care not for their lives, and therefore do not fear the Sultan [of Egypt] nor any other prince of the world, and will fight with them if they do them any annoyance.... They have no armour to defend themselves with, only a shield and a spear. They wind a white linen cloth about their heads and necks. They are a very foul and cruel folk, and of evil nature.[415]

Once a pilgrim reaches Jerusalem, Mandeville takes him or her by the hand as a good guide should. In the chapter entitled "Of the pilgrimages in Jerusalem, and of the holy places thereabout," the *Travels* explain that

> To speak of Jerusalem: you must understand that it stands well set among the hills. There is neither river nor well, but water comes thither by conduit from Hebron.... You must understand that when men arrive in Jerusalem they make their first pilgrimage to the church where is the Sepulchre of Our Lord, which was once outside the city on the north; but is now enclosed within the town wall.... Among the

other lights there is one [the Holy Fire] which is always burning before the [Holy] Sepulchre, and every Good Friday it goes out by itself, and on Easter Day it lights again by itself at the very hour when Our Lord rose from the dead to life.[416]

Pages of generally helpful and always colorful details and snippets of folklore are then presented. It is not until Mandeville finishes with the Holy Land and begins to entertain us in the second half of his book with improbable fantasies about the Great Khan of Cathy (China) and about Prester John, the mythical Christian ruler of the East, that the *Travels* cease to have any practical value.[417]

Pilgrim equipment and documents in medieval times

Despite the Muslim occupation of the Holy Land, a pilgrimage to Jerusalem was still high on the "must do" list of medieval Christians in Western Europe. The Holy City was not, of course, the only destination for the faithful. Many went to Santiago de Compostela in Spain or to Rome instead of, or in addition to, Jerusalem. There were other if lesser pilgrimages sites in Western Europe, too.

Over the years, certain well-defined patterns of behavior had been developed and were now widely accepted. The first step was to get ready for the trip. In 1406 Richard Alkerton, an English pilgrim, described the preparatory steps:

> When the debts are thus paid and the [household] thus set in governance, the pilgrim shall array himself. And then he oweth first to make himself be marked with a cross, as men be wont to do that shall pass to the Holy Land.... Afterwards the pilgrim shall have a staff, a sclavein, and a scrip [all three are described below].[418]

This citation and other contemporary evidence show that in the Middle Ages, before embarking on the journey itself a pilgrim donned a special outfit which was often marked with a cross and resembled that of a penitent.[419] Pilgrims could be identified at first sight. The quasi-uniform for a man consisted of:

- A long iron-tipped "pilgrim's staff"—an important accessory, not only when walking over rough terrain but also useful for self-defense.
- A long, coarse, russet gown with large sleeves, known as a sclavein.
- A large, round, broad-brimmed hat to keep off sun and rain.
- A soft leather pouch, called a scrip, strapped across his back or around his waist and used to carry food, personal items and money.

Gottfried von Strassburg, one of the greatest medieval poets and the author of the courtly love epic *Tristan und Isolde*, gives this account of the pilgrims of his time (c. 1210):

> Meanwhile, as he [a traveler] sat there and lamented ... he caught sight of two old pilgrims approaching in the distance. They were of godly aspect, advanced in days and years, hairy, and bearded, as God's true children and pilgrims often are. Those wayfarers wore cloaks of linen and such other clothing as is appropriate to pilgrims, and on the outside of their clothes there were sewn-on sea-shells [symbols of the pilgrimage to Santiago de Compostela] and many other tokens from distant lands. Each bore a staff in his hand. Their head and legcovering was well-suited to their kind. These servants of God wore round their thighs linen hose trussed close to the leg and reaching down within a hand's breadth of the ankles. Feet and ankles were bare to the obstacles underfoot. They also bore

> saintly palms [symbols of the pilgrimage to Jerusalem] on their backs which showed that they were penitents. At this moment they were intoning their psalms and prayers and all the good things they knew.[420]

A medieval pilgrim would have made out a will and received a special blessing before setting out. He was instructed to put funds aside for his family to use while he was gone. Getting to Jerusalem in medieval times was never easy or cheap, so he had to carry enough money to pay his own way. Bringing large sums was frowned on, however, for both religious and practical reasons. Pilgrims were supposed to emulate the simple, austere life of Jesus himself. One medieval guidebook, probably exaggerating for effect, put forward this injunction in the most unequivocal terms:

> The pilgrim may bring with him no money at all, except perhaps to distribute it to the poor on the road. Those who sell their property before leaving must give every penny of it to the poor, for if they spend it on their own journey they are departing from the path of the Lord ... the pilgrim who dies on the road with money in his pocket is permanently excluded from the kingdom of heaven.[421]

In practice, however, pilgrims had to pay their own way to Jerusalem, so it is clear they must have brought money with them. Bringing too much money, however, was not only inherently sinful but very foolish as well.

An obvious display of wealth was an open invitation to a thief. Pilgrimages became so popular in medieval times that they attracted a large number of robbers, beggars and rogues of all kinds, as well as the saintly and the devout. This influx of undesirable elements eventually became such a problem that European pilgrims had to be able to produce, on demand, a letter from their bishop or abbot establishing their *bona fides*. In 1388 King Richard II of England even ordered that any pilgrim found in his domains without such a letter could be arrested. His edict did not solve the problem, however, and abuses continued.

William Blakeney (1412)

A good example of the life of a rogue is William Blakeney, a London shetilmaker—a worker who made shuttles, which are wooden devices used in weaving. In 1412 Blakeney was hauled before the mayor, aldermen and sheriffs of the city on the charge that although

> he was able to work for his food and raiment, he, the same William, went about, barefooted and with long hair, under the guise of sanctity, and pretended to be a hermit, saying that he was such, and that he had made pilgrimage to Jerusalem, Rome, Venice, and the city of Seville, in Spain; and under colour of such falsehood he had and received many good things from divers persons, to the defrauding, and in manifest deceit, of all the people.[422]

Blakeney confessed that for the last six years he had lived by "such lies, falsities, and deceits, so invented by him, to the defrauding of the people, under the colour of such feigned sanctity, and that he was never in the parts aforesaid." He was convicted and condemned to be "put upon the pillory for three market-days, there to remain for one hour each day, the reason for the same being there proclaimed; and he was to have, in the meantime, [a heavy] whetstone hung from his neck."[423]

Nompar de Caumont (1419)

Lord of a small fief in Gascony (southwestern France), this pilgrim left for Jerusalem in 1419 and later recorded his travels in a long work entitled *Le Voyage d'outre-mer à Jérusalem* (*The Overseas Voyage to Jerusalem*).[424] He says that he embarked on the pilgrimage not only for the sake of his own soul but also to fulfill a vow made by his father, who had died before being able to go to Jerusalem himself. Nompar was about 28 years old when he left home and was absent for more than a year. His account ends with a unique list of the expensive presents he brought back from the Holy Land for his wife and for the neighboring lords and ladies of Gascony (see Appendix IV).

The high point of Nompar's pilgrimage came at the Church of the Holy Sepulcher, where he spent the night and where the next morning he became a member of the knightly "order of the Holy Sepulcher."[425] His account of this experience is worth reading:

> Arriving in front of the church, I saw a large paved area, nearly full of Saracens. At the doorway of the Holy Sepulcher an officer and other men stood guard to make sure than no one could enter the church without first paying tribute; they let the pilgrims in one after another, counting them at the same time. Then they locked the door with big keys. I passed the whole night in front of the Holy Sepulcher ... [and] that night I confessed my sins. [After mass the next morning] a knight ... made me a member of the order of chivalry: I strapped on my sword, put on my spurs, and he struck me lightly five times with his own sword, in memory of the five wounds of Our Lord, and once again, in memory of St. George. Then the priest who said the mass, still dressed in his robes, put a naked sword into my hands; while kneeling, I swore:

"I take this sword in honor of God and of St. George, to guard and defend the Holy Church against the enemies of the faith."[426]

Nompar also gives us an extensive list of the indulgences which could be earned at various spots in the Holy Land. In Jerusalem, a devout visit to "Herod's house, where Jesus Christ was dressed in white to signify that he was mad" could earn the faithful "seven years and seven *quarantaines* of indulgences." The same amount of credit was given for going to the spot near Mount Sion where "St. John said mass for the Virgin Mary, after the death of Jesus Christ."[427] In French, a *quarantaine* means "about 40" but it is unclear what period of time—weeks or days—Nompar is referring to here. "Seven years and seven *quarantaines*," however, appears to have been the average amount of indulgences to be gained from visits to holy sites in Jerusalem.[428]

An anonymous French pilgrim (1420)

Writing in about 1420, this unidentified pilgrim tells us that national and social distinctions were carefully maintained by the friars who shepherded pilgrims around the holy places. There were three guided tours. The first of these traced the *via captivitatis*, "the way of captivity," i.e., the places where the arrest and trial of Jesus occurred. The second followed the *via Crucis*, "the way of the Cross," from the site of the trial to the Church of the Holy Sepulcher. The tour sometimes moved in the opposite direction to avoid congestion and jostling in the narrow streets of the Old City as the day wore on. The third tour was conducted inside the Church of the Holy Sepulcher.

According to our anonymous pilgrim, the friar in charge of the tours always put the French pilgrims at the head of the queue. They were lined up "two by two or three by three, as they wished, with the nobles in front." Then came the Germans and the Spanish. After them came the remaining nationalities, arranged so that no national group would mix with any other during the tours. This seems to have been done more for linguistic rather than for political reasons. Our pilgrim jokingly asked his guide whether, if a group of English pilgrims ("les Engloiz") appeared, they would be put in line, alphabetically, between the Germans ("la nacion d'Allemaigne") and the Spaniards ("celle d'Espaigne"). The guide replied that he did not know.[429]

Emmanuel Piloti (1420)

Written between 1420 and 1438 for papal and princely readers, the *Traité d'Emmanuel Piloti sur l'Égypte et les moyens de conquérir la Terre sainte* (*Emmanuel Piloti's Treatise on Egypt and on ways to conquer the Holy Land*) called for a new crusade to recapture Jerusalem. Piloti himself was an Italian who was well-qualified to write about the Middle East, having traveled there extensively and having lived in Egypt for 22 years. His manuscript is incomplete and has much more to say about Egypt than about the Holy Land, but it is relevant here because of the importance he attaches to Jerusalem.[430]

In Piloti's day, Jerusalem was ruled by the sultan of Egypt. Piloti's strategy for a new crusade was simple and straightforward:

When one wishes to confront one's enemies, it is essential to strike them directly on the head, not on the arms or legs. Because if the head remains undamaged, injuries to other parts of the body can always be healed. If the past is any guide to the future, we can say that [as a result of a new crusade] Jerusalem and the city of Acre and all the rest of Syria will be in Christian hands. But [in that case] the sultan, with the big army he would lead out of Cairo, would reconquer Jerusalem and the rest of the area held by the Christians, and he would cause a great deal of trouble for us. Therefore, my Christian lords, the Christian army must have as its [first] goal the conquest of Cairo, which is the head on which the blow must fall and which [once taken] will permit us to seize the rest of the body without further resistance.[431]

Despite Piloti's conviction that a new Crusade would surely be successful, nothing came of his plans. After eight "numbered" Crusades—the last seven of which had failed—Western Europeans had gradually realized that recapturing Jerusalem would cost them too much blood and treasure to be a sensible goal.

Bertrandon de la Brocquière (1432)

Lord of Vieux-Château in Gascony, this French pilgrim was in the service of the Duke of Burgundy. "Having formed a resolution to make a devout pilgrimage to Jerusalem," he says, "and being determined to discharge my vow, I quitted, in the month of February, 1432, the court of my most redoubted lord, who was then in Ghent."[432] He reports that indulgences for pilgrims began in Jaffa as soon as they set foot in the Holy Land. The pilgrim trade was well-established there. Bertrandon found that "interpreters and other officers of the sultan [of Egypt] instantly hasten to ascertain their numbers, to serve them as guides, and to receive, in the name of their master, the customary tribute."[433]

Bertrandon also found that while Jerusalem was still a sizeable town, it appeared to have been much bigger in the past. After visiting the holy sites, he, like many other pilgrims, wanted to cross the Sinai desert to see Mount Sinai and then continue on to Cairo. The trip to Mount Sinai was a potentially dangerous journey of more than 400 miles, so a *bedouin* escort was mandatory. Bertrandon tells his readers how to arrange this:

> For the advice of others, who like myself may wish to visit this country [Mount Sinai], I shall say that the custom is to treat with the chief interpreter of Jerusalem, who receives a tax for the sultan and one for himself, and then sends to inform the interpreter at Gaza, who in turn negotiates a passage with the Arabians of the desert. These Arabs enjoy the right of conducting pilgrims, and as they are not always under due subjection to the sultan, their camels must be used, which they let to hire at ten ducats a head.[434]

Bertrandon reports that once the chief interpreter had received an affirmative reply from Gaza, he would ask the pilgrims to come to the Church of the Holy Sepulcher, where he would write down their names and ages and describe what they looked like. A copy of this document was sent to the chief interpreter in Cairo. The Muslims claimed that this paperwork was necessary for the security of the pilgrims and to prevent the *bedouin* from holding any of them hostage, but Bertrandon was thought otherwise. "It is done likewise through mistrust," he said, "and through fear of some exchange or substitution that may make them lose the tribute money...."[435]

Elijah of Ferrara (1434)

This Jewish scholar and part of his family left Italy for Jerusalem in 1434 and suffered more than their share of misfortunes en route. First, Elijah's grandson Jacob—"one most near and dear, the desire of my eyes, the joy of my heart"—died of the plague. Then, in Egypt, his son Menahem—"the child of my old age"—fell ill and died from the same disease. Finally, his "well-beloved son Isaac" died of the plague, too, a few days after Menahem.[436] Elijah stoically endured all these losses, however, and after he had been in Jerusalem a short time was asked by the local Jews to teach at the synagogue. In addition, he served as a religious adviser not only for the city of Jerusalem but also for other cities in Egypt and Syria.

Elijah found that the Jews in Jerusalem worked as shopkeepers, carpenters, druggists, goldsmiths, shoemakers, and silk merchants. They were accepted by the Muslims and there was no communal strife. The Jews, said Elijah, "ply their trades side by side with the Ismaelites, and no jealously between them results, such I have remarked in other places."[437] He himself wanted to travel more widely. He told his brother and his remaining children:

> I will not speak to you now of the miracles and marvels constantly manifested at the tombs of the prophets and of the pious men of Galilee and beyond Jordan, as well as in other places of the country of Israel, because, with God's help, I hope to go there and see them for myself. I will make them known to you next year.[438]

Margery Kempe (d. c. 1440)

With so many Christian pilgrims on the road to Jerusalem in medieval times, it is not surprising that some of them were emotionally disturbed or at least remarkably eccentric.[439] Probably the most famous of these was the English pilgrim Margery Kempe, who died in about 1440. After dutifully bearing her husband 14 children, she set out on a string of pilgrimages to Jerusalem, Rome, Germany and Spain.

Margery was given to religious ecstasies, punctuated by uncontrollable crying spells. She was illiterate, but over a four-year period toward the end of her life she dictated to two clerks (or perhaps to one priest) a work known as *The Book of Margery Kempe.* This is worth citing here because of her unselfconscious use of language. She always referred to herself in the third person, e.g., "this creature," and made no effort to hide her emotional reactions:

> And so they [Kempe and two Dutch companions] went forth into the Holy Land till they might see Jerusalem. And when this creature saw Jerusalem, riding on an ass, she thanked God with all her heart, praying him for his mercy that like as he had brought her to see this earthly city Jerusalem, he would grant her grace to see the blissful city Jerusalem above, the city of Heaven. Our Lord Jesu Christ, answering her thought, granted her to have her desire. Then for joy that she had and the sweetness that she felt in the dalliance with Our Lord, she was in point to 'a [have] fallen off her ass, for she might not bear the sweetness and grace that God wrought in her soul. The twain pilgrims of Dutchmen went to her and kept her from falling, of which the one was a priest. And he put spices in her mouth to comfort her, weening she had been sick. And so they helped her forth to Jerusalem.[440]

William Wey (1458)

One of the original Fellows of Eton College, the famous British secondary school founded in 1440, William Wey made two pilgrimages to Jerusalem, one in 1458 and the other in 1462. It is possible he was commissioned by King Henry VI to write a guidebook to the Holy Land.[441] His account remains one of the most detailed records of fifteenth century pilgrimage and was full of practical and even life-saving advice.

Here are some excerpts. "A good provision," Wey tells us,

when a man is at Venice and purposeth, by the grace of God, to pass by sea unto Port Jaffa in the Holy Land and so to the sepulchre of our Lord Christ Jesu in Jerusalem. He must dispose him in this wise:

First, if ye go in a galley, make your covenant with the patron betimes and choose you a place in the said galley in the overest stage [i.e., on the top deck], for in the lowest under it is right smouldering hot and stinking.

Also, ye must ordain for yourself and your fellow, if ye have any, three barrels ... which holdeth ten gallons; two of these barrels shall serve for wine and the third for water. In the one barrel take red wine and keep it ever in store, and tame [open] it not if ye may till ye come homeward again without sickness cause it or any other need. For ye shall this in special note: an ye had the flux, if ye would give twenty ducats for a barrel ye shall have none after ye pass much Venice.

Also, ye must ordain you biscuit to have with you, for though ye shall be at table with your patron, notwithstanding, ye shall oftentime have need to your victuals, bread, cheese, eggs, fruit, and bacon, wine, and other, to make your collation. For sometimes ye shall have feeble bread, wine, and stinking water; many times you shall be full fain to eat of your own.

Also, take a barrel with you, closed, for a siege [toilet] for your chamber in the galley; it is full necessary that if ye be sick that ye come not in the air.

Also, when you come to divers havens, be well ware of divers fruits, for they be not according to your complexion and they gender a bloody flux: and if an Englishman have that sickness, it is a marvel and scape-it but he die thereof.

Also ... if ye go up to the place where our Lord Jesu Christ fasted forty days and forty nights, it is passing hot and right high; when ye come down again, for nothing drink no water, but rest you a little, and then eat bread and drink clean wine without water—after that great heat, water engendereth a great flux or a fever, or both; then a man may haply lose his life thereby.[442]

Louis de Rochechouart (1461)

Elected Bishop of Saintes (France) in 1460 at the age of 27, Louis set off the next year from Paris on a pilgrimage to Jerusalem.[443] His travels are recorded in a long but incomplete manuscript, *Journal de Voyage à Jérusalem* (*Journal of a Trip to Jerusalem*). One of the things he, like other pilgrims, found remarkable was the confusing array of Christian sects that were directly involved in services at the Church of the Holy Sepulcher.

He found that there were ten of them: Latins, Greeks, Armenians, Georgians, Jacobites, Nestorians, Syrians, Indians, "Christians of the Belt" [resident Christians who served as intermediaries between the pilgrims and the Muslim officials], and Maronites. Louis did not go into the doctrinal differences between these sects, however, explaining that he was too caught up in church services and visiting holy sites.

Like other pilgrims, too, he commented on the lives of the "Arabs," i.e., the *bedouin*. They became formidable enemies of the pilgrims as soon as the local Muslim government was too weak to hold them in check. "They live like wild beasts," Louis tells us,

> Instead of houses, they live in tents which they carry with them. They have no attachments and no fear. They live by rapine, camel's milk and meat, are covered with clothes during the summer [the men wore very long belted shirts reaching down to their ankles], do not drink wine of any sort, and are the enemies of the Saracens: when we were in Jerusalem, they killed 60 of them in front of the city gates. We saw the bodies carried away on stretchers.[444]

Felix Fabri (1480)

A Dominican monk, Felix Fabri of Ulm (Germany), made two pilgrimages to the Holy Land, the first in 1480 and the second in 1483. He later cheerfully set them down at great length and in painstaking detail in a book which he playfully called the *Evagatorium Fratris Felicis Fabri* (*The Wanderings of Brother Felix Fabri*).[445]
Fabri was a vivid, prolific chronicler. The *Evagatorium* as a whole runs to about 1,500 printed pages; his account of Jerusalem itself takes up 260 pages.[446] This book is one of the two best sources for what it was like to be a Christian pilgrim in the Holy Land during the fifteenth century, so we will consider it in some detail. (The other source is Canon Pietro Casola, who will be discussed later on in comparable detail.)
Like many other medieval pilgrims, Fabri came to Palestine in a Venetian galley.[447] As his ship drew near Jaffa, all the pilgrim-passengers waited for landfall with mounting excitement and expecta-

tion. Their patience was at last rewarded. As Fabri remembered the arrival:

> Soon, when the dawn began to shine, there shone forth also the land which is brighter than the sun—I mean the Holy Land, the land of Canaan, the land whose name is above every name. As soon as the watchman in the maintop beheld it, he suddenly burst out into the cry: "My lords pilgrims, rise up and come on deck; behold, the land which you long to see is in sight!"[448]

The Holy Land was still a dangerous place for pilgrims. When Fabri and his companions were about to land, they saw on the shore "a great multitude of armed men, so that the surface of the earth was covered with them."[449] The captain of Fabri's ship asked the leaders of these Muslim forces why they had come and whether it was safe "to bring unarmed pilgrims into the land with so many armed men." The Muslims explained that the *bedouin* "had come into the land out of the desert in great numbers, and plundered all they met, sparing none save those stronger than themselves." The Muslims believed that the *bedouin* "had gathered that host together because of the Christian pilgrims who were coming." The Muslims themselves had therefore "come in force that they might bring us into Jerusalem in safety."
The pilgrims, however, were not allowed to leave Jaffa until the Muslims had made an accurate tally of them. Fabri recalled that

> [Muslim officials and a scribe] so ranged themselves on either side that the pilgrims must needs pass through the midst of them; nor could two pilgrims pass through them together, but one after another. Nor would they let us pass in a continuous stream, but they laid hold of each man, looked at him narrowly, and demanded his own name

and the name of his father, both of which names the scribe wrote down in his documents.[450]

The town of Ramla was at the time the Muslim administrative center for Palestine. A Christian hospice, built by Philip, duke of Burgundy, was maintained there for pilgrims en route to or returning from Jerusalem. Fabri says that within the low, narrow door of the hospice, tired pilgrims would find "a large and beautiful court, with many chambers and vaulted rooms of various kinds, and a fountain full of good and wholesome water."[451] The chief officer of this hospice was the Father Guardian, a Franciscan priest appointed by the Pope and approved by the Muslims as the protector of all Christian pilgrims in the Holy Land.[452]

The Father Guardian warmly welcomed Fabri and the other pilgrims and handed them a set of instructions, containing 27 articles giving "the rules and method of seeing the holy places which they ought to observe while dwelling among the Saracens and infidels in the Holy Land, lest they should run into danger through ignorance."[453] These instructions provide such a good insight into the perils and pitfalls which awaited unwary pilgrims that excerpts from them are given in Appendix V.

When Fabri and his colleagues finally reached Jerusalem, they dismounted from their donkeys, bowed to the earth, and formally greeted the city with these eloquent words:

Hail Jerusalem, city of the Great King, glory and crown of the whole world, joy and delight of the believer's soul. O Jerusalem, Jerusalem, arise, lift up thine eyes round about and see all these pilgrims, thy sons, who have come together from the uttermost parts of the world, who still are coming in hosts that they may see thy brightness, and the glory of the Lord risen upon this....[454]

When they got to the Church of the Holy Sepulcher, Fabri says that he and his party "flung ourselves down in the courtyard before the door of the church, and prayed, and kissed the very earth many times." This church was such a popular destination and was so full of holy shrines that pilgrims felt they had to rush from one shrine to the next, rather than taking their time and praying devoutly at each site.

Fabri was quite astonished when two women pilgrims lay down directly in front of him and began to sob and to kiss the pavement on which he was standing. Asked why they were behaving in such an extraordinary manner, they said he was standing precisely where Jesus' body had been laid when it had been taken down from the cross. Mortified, Fabri immediately lay down too and prayed that God would forgive him for his inadvert mistake.[455]

Although Fabri managed to keep his own emotions under control, many other pilgrims could not. He saw pilgrims who were

lying powerless on the ground, forsaken by their own strength.... Others I saw who wandered hither and thither from one corner to another, beating their breasts, as though driven by an evil spirit.... Others were shaken by such violent sobs that they could not hold themselves up.... Some lay prostrate so long without motion, that they seemed as though they were dead. Above all our companions and sisters the women pilgrims shrieked as though in labour, cried aloud and wept. Some pilgrims, out of excess of devotion, lost all command of themselves, forgot how they should behave, and out of excessive zeal to please God made strange and childish gestures.[456]

Fabri was quite shocked by the unseemly behavior of the priests at the Church of the Holy Sepulcher:

The greatest struggle among the priests is to say Mass at the holy sepulchre, especially when many priests are present; for they stand outside the sepulchre and wait for the one who is celebrating [Mass] to finish, and as soon as he leaves the altar, another straightway [sic] runs up to it, and while he who has been celebrating disrobes himself, six or more priests stand round him, all struggling to obtain his sacred vestments, and when he takes off the surplice, all the six or more lay hold of it and pull at it, and use such offensive words one to another than they all but come to blows.[457]

Like many other pilgrims, Fabri was convinced that Mount Calvary (the site of Jesus' crucifixion) was of enormous importance for two reasons. It was, he believed, the actual site of Jesus' death and therefore should be revered. Equally important, however, was its allegorical or symbolic importance. Mount Calvary was held to be the sacred center of the earth— what the ancient Greeks called the *omphalos*, or navel, of this planet—and the source of all creation and redemption.[458]

Fabri understood very well that there was a contradiction here between the *sensus allegoricus* (the allegorical importance) of Mount Calvary and the *sensus literalis* (its literal, i.e., historical, importance). However, he had no trouble resolving such a conflict between theology and history. The solution was quite easy. For Fabri, there was no doubt that the *sensus allegoricus* had to prevail because it alone reflected an eternal, divine reality.

This would still be true, Fabri would have maintained, even if it could somehow be proved that the Mount Calvary visited by Jerusalem pilgrims was *not* in fact the place where Jesus had died. What mattered to most Fabri was that, in the *sensus allegoricus*, this was a sacred center. "As Christ is the central person in the

Trinity, and the mediator between God and man," Fabri summarizes his argument, "as he holds the middle position in the scheme of the Redemption of the world, even so he chose the middle point of the world and set up His cross in the same."[459]

Just as he could praise the holy sites of Jerusalem, Fabri could also criticize what he saw going on there. We have noted that for payment of an extra fee, pilgrims could spend the night in the Church of the Holy Sepulcher, locked in when the guards went home. Some clever merchants, however, arranged to be locked in, too. Fabri did not approve of their activities:

[some pilgrims] spend the whole night bargaining with traders, for to every place to which the pilgrims go when they are in the Holy Land they are accompanied by Christian traders of eastern birth, most cunning and greedy heretics, who never sleep during the time the pilgrims are in the Holy Land…. Some of the pilgrims, seeing that the time of their departure from Jerusalem was at hand, stayed awake all night bargaining and bought all kinds of things [souvenirs] … round about these merchants there was much disturbance and noise, even as in a market place…. How great a scandal it must be in the eyes of the infidels … is clear from the purity of their own mosques, wherein they will not for anything in the world allow buying or selling to go on, or any talk about the same.[460]

Fabri put a high value on the pilgrimage to Jerusalem but did not flinch from telling his readers that it was not an easy undertaking. "It requires courage and audacity to attempt this pilgrimage," he said. "That many are prompted to it by sinful and idle curiosity cannot be doubted; but to reach the holy places and return to one's home active and well is the especial gift of God." He went on to describe some of the hardships:

> No one should think visiting the holy places to be a light task; there is the intense heat of the sun, the walking from place to place, kneeling and prostration; above all there is the strain which everyone puts on himself striving with all his might to rouse himself in earnest piety and comprehension of what is shown to him in the holy places, and to devout prayer and meditation, all which cannot be done without great fatigue, because to do them fitly a man should be at rest and not walking about. To struggle after mental abstraction whilst bodily walking from place to place is exceedingly toilsome.[461]

Pilgrims also had to watch out for the *bedouin*. On three occasions, Fabri tells us, *bedouin* approached his party:

> The Arabs who at that time were spread abroad throughout many parts of the Holy Land thrice came to meet us; but seeing that we were well protected by armed defenders, they offered no violence either with stones or cold steel, but secretly joined our host by the side of the pilgrims, and tried to steal scrips [the leather pouches carried by pilgrims], clothes and the like; for they knew that we were unarmed, and therefore they ran round about us, and snatched up whatever the pilgrims let fall, or did not guard carefully. Had we not travelled with so great a force, they would have fallen upon us and beaten us with stones, sticks, and staves, as often befalls pilgrims between Jaffa and Ramle [Ramla].[462]

Rabbi Meshullam ben R. Menahem of Volterra (1481)

This Italian Rabbi went to Jerusalem in 1481 and wrote a long account of his travels. He warned his readers that when en route to the Holy City they must be sure to join a big caravan because of danger from the robbers (*bedouin*) who frequented the desert. His description of this danger is one of the most interesting and most detailed which has come down to us:

> You will always find people lying in wait on the road who are hidden in sand up to their necks, two or three days without food or drink, who put a stone in front of them, and they can see other people but the others cannot see them, and when they see a caravan smaller and weaker than their own they go out and call their fellows and ride on their horses swift as leopards, with bamboo lances topped with iron in their hands, which are very hard. They also carry a pirate's mace in their hands and bucklers [shields] made of parchment and pitch, and they ride naked with only a shirt upon them, without any trousers or shoes or spurs, and they come upon the caravans suddenly and take everything, even the clothes and horses, and sometimes kill them, but generally they rob but do not kill them, therefore it is good to be in a caravan of Turks who are all good bowmen, and the robbers fear them because they are naked and cannot shoot, and two Turks could put ten Ishmaelites to flight.[463]

When Rabbi Meshullam reached Jerusalem, he rent his garments and recited an appropriate prayer. He reported that the city's population included 10,000 Muslim households and about 250 Jewish families. Viewing the Western Wall, he commented that "The huge stones of this building are a wondrous matter, and it is difficult to believe how the strength of man could have moved them into their present position."[464] He also appreciated the good food to be had in Jerusalem but he was not pleased by local table manners. "The Moslems and also the Jews of this place are

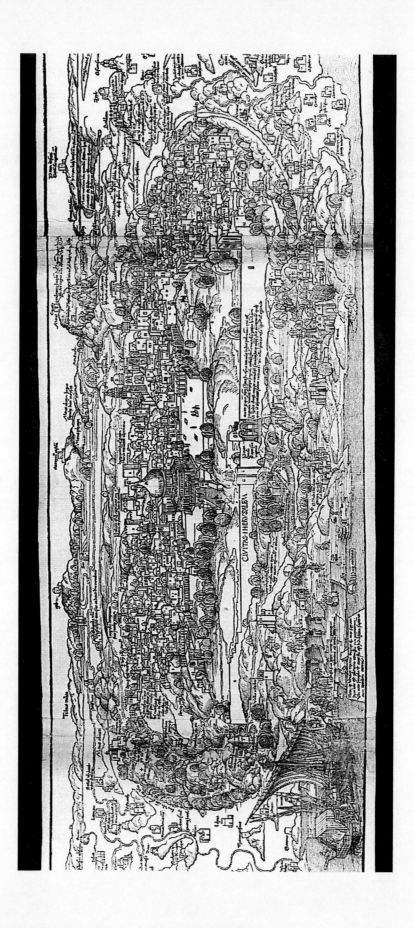

pigs at their eating," he said. "They all eat out of one vessel with their fingers, without a napkin...." He did not like Muslim marriage customs, either: "Everyone marries twenty or thirty wives as he pleases ... [the women] are all openly harlots...."[465]

Rabbi Meshullam found that the local Jews were devout. On the ninth of Av they still gathered on the Mount of Olives, from where they could see the whole Temple area, and mourned the destruction of the Temple. The Rabbi ended his description of Jerusalem on an ecumenical note that recalled the city's long history: "There are still olives on Mount Olivet, and the Moslems call the whole surroundings of Jerusalem and Mount Zion, El Kuds, that is, the holy land. May it be the will of our Father in heaven that it may be rebuilt speedily in our days. Amen."[466]

Bernhard von Breydenbach (1486)

Von Breydenbach, a German nobleman, was a deacon of Mainz Cathedral. He visited the Holy Land in 1483, accompanied by Erhard Reuwich, an accomplished Dutch artist who made on-the-spot drawings for later use as woodcut illustrations.[467] Their pilgrimage resulted in a magisterial guidebook published in 1486. Entitled *Peregrinatio in terram sanctam* (*Pilgrimage in the Holy Land*), it is not only an important text in the history of the printed word but also a book which contained a great deal of practical and moral advice for travelers.

Its best feature is a set of large, elegant fold-out maps, some of them nine pages in length, which gave prospective pilgrims accurate views of Venice, Cyprus and, most importantly, Jerusalem itself. An early copy of von Breydenbach's map of Jerusalem is now held by the Osher Map Library at the University of Southern Maine. This is the earliest printed map of the Holy Land based on contemporary eyewitness sources.[468] Inserted into the central portion of the map is an unusual close-up view of the city, oriented to the west and as seen from the Mount of Olives (facing page). This mini-map, which differs from the rest of the map both in scale and perspective.

As the Osher Map Library points out, although this map was made at a time when Jerusalem was under Islamic rule, the holy sites are marked with their Christian names. The Dome of the Rock (labeled as the *Templum Salomonis*, i.e., Solomon's Temple) is seen at the center, with the Church of the Holy Sepulchre (*Templum gloriosum Domini Sepulchri*) shown above and to the right. A hospice for pilgrims is located between the two shrines. Thanks to the first-hand observations on which they were based (rather than on vague Biblical references or on flights of fancy), these and many other holy sites are shown on this map with great accuracy. As a result, the map was extraordinarily useful to pilgrims and was widely copied.

An anonymous French pilgrim (1486)

A long but incomplete manuscript, translated into modern French only in 1979, describes the travels of an anonymous pilgrim to Jerusalem and Mount Sinai in 1486. Arriving at Jaffa after a difficult voyage aboard the galley *Contarina* along with about 200 other pilgrims, the pilgrim and his fellow travelers were forced to sleep in a grotto for two nights

Opposite: **Mini-map from Bernhard von Breydenbach's map of Jerusalem, 1486. (Osher Map Library, University of Southern Maine.)**

and had to pay a stiff price for a bit of straw to lie on. The food was horrible, especially for a Frenchman. "Then we had to dine on a sole slathered with garbage," our pilgrim complained, "and eat meat which the Muslims brought to us already cooked [that is, the meat was cold]."[469]

The accommodations were dreadful, too:

> None of us could get up during the night, even to piss, without paying off one of the debauched men who guarded us. Several pilgrims were beaten up, notably an elderly German knight, who later fainted. Through openings in the grotto, other Muslims threw big stones at us. Although the stones came close to us, no one was hurt, thank God. One rock, heavy enough to knock out a cow, fell near me.[470]

At last, the pilgrims, mounted on donkeys, were ready to set out for Ramla. First, however the muleteers demanded payment of *courtoisies*—literally "courtesies" but, in reality, bribes. When some of the pilgrims refused to pay, they were thrown to the ground and forced to proceed on foot. Our anonymous pilgrim wisely paid up, however, and was soon underway.

The going was hard. At one village, Muslim women and children threw stones at the pilgrims. After some pilgrims had been hit and knocked off their donkeys, the party as a whole was forced to flee. Moreover, for pilgrims from more northern lands it was exceptionally hot. They suffered terribly. At Ramla a German knight and another pilgrim died, "suffocated by the great heat they had been forced to endure." An abbot in the party became so ill that there was little hope that he would live; others, too, were in great danger of death. It was not until the pilgrims reached the hospice in Ramla established by the Duke of Burgundy

that they were able to rest and recuperate.

Later, when the pilgrims resumed their journey toward Jerusalem, the muleteers tried to strip them of their clothes and rob them. The anonymous pilgrim resisted courageously, however, with the result that a teamster grabbed his leg and jerked him off his donkey. He landed on a pile of stones and tells us tongue-in-cheek, "I took such a lovely dive that I could still feel it 10 days later."

When he finally reached the Holy City, our pilgrim, "joyously and praising God," kissed one of the stones in the forecourt of the Church of the Holy Sepulcher and then found lodgings with the Hospitalers. That night he had to put up with disturbances caused by rowdy Muslims, who stole wine and food from other travelers and "made such a racket that one could neither sleep nor even rest." He and the other pilgrims later spent a night in the Church of the Holy Sepulcher. He remarked on the number of Christian sects there, which he counted as nine: Franciscans, Greeks, Armenians, Georgians, Syrians, Indians, Jacobites, Nestorians, and Maronites. Finally, after visiting Bethlehem, the River Jordan and other holy sites, he left for Mount Sinai and from there returned to Europe via Cairo and Rhodes.

Rabbi Obadiah ben Abraham Yare Bertinoro (1487)

This scholarly Italian Rabbi was the leading Jew of Palestine. His commentaries on the Mishnah are still cited today. He was one of the most important Jewish travelers of the Renaissance, traveling to Jerusalem in 1487 and living there until his death three years later. He wrote three letters, which report extensively on what he experienced.

Rending his garments at the first sight of Jerusalem and again at the Temple Mount, Rabbi Obadiah found the Holy City "for the most part desolate and in ruins." The population was then about 4,000 families, of whom 70 families were those of very poor Jews, often widows, from Germany, Spain, Portugal and other countries. The Arabs did not persecute the Jews and in fact were kind to them and to other strangers. All in all, however, the caliber of the city's inhabitants was not very high. "In my opinion," commented Rabbi Obadiah,

an intelligent man versed in political science might easily raise himself to be chief of the Jews as well as of the Arabs; for among all the inhabitants there is not a wise and sensible man who knows how to deal affably with his fellow men, all are ignorant misanthropes intent only on gain....[471]

He claims that he was even forced to become an undertaker because the men of the city had "neither compassion nor pity" and refused to help carry out and bury the bodies of those who died. During one of his journeys around Jerusalem, a woman died—perhaps someone he knew. The men refused to help him lay her to rest, so Rabbi Obadiah had to ask the women to help him instead.

He was well aware of all the pilgrims in the city and remarked that some Jews were returning to Jerusalem because the Muslim authorities had reduced their taxes. He reported that

Persons of various nationalities are always to be found in Jerusalem from Christian countries, and from Babylonia and Abyssinia. The Arabs come frequently to offer up prayers at the temple, for they hold it in great veneration … every year Jews come in the Venetian galleys, and even in the pilgrim

ships, for there is really no safer and shorter way than by these ships. I wish I had known all this while I was still in those parts [i.e., in Europe], I would not then have remained so long on the journey. The galleys perform the voyage from Venice here in forty days at the most.[472]

Canon Pietro Casola (1494)[473]

Casola, an Italian priest, was an old man of 65 when he left Milan in 1494 en route to Jerusalem. He came from a noble family, spent 16 years as secretary at the Milanese Embassy in Rome and then became the senior of the cardinal's deacons in Milan. Casola traveled to the Holy City by galley from Venice, together with 63 priests of various orders plus an unstated but sizeable number of lay pilgrims. He was a keen observer of foreign cultures and had a good sense of humor. His experiences with the Muslims, however, left him with lasting prejudices.

Casola's arrival at Jaffa began inauspiciously. A young Danish pilgrim, who had fallen ill at sea after eating unripe grapes, died shortly after the galley reached Jaffa. This young man was simply "hurled on shore."[474] Next, the Muslim officials at the port refused to let the pilgrims disembark, forcing the galley to ride at anchor off the port. These officials then "pitched their tents opposite the galley, so that it appeared as if there was an army here, preparing to make war, as was the case—at least on the purses of the pilgrims."[475]

Casola's frustrations continued. "We saw the land we had come so far to enter," he complains,

and these Moorish dogs would not let us go on our way. They made difficulties, now about one thing, now about another…. However, it was necessary to tie everything up in the sack of patience, as we did not want to loosen the sack of money. Each one who goes on the voyage to the Sepulchre of our Lord has need of three sacks—a sack of patience, a sack of money and a sack of faith. The first two sacks had been used several times up to that hour; the third was still untouched.[476]

To relieve the boredom, the pilgrims were permitted to go fishing. They saw a big turtle and caught an immense shark. Casola was astounded by the shark's ferocity:

There was great difficulty in hauling it out of the water, because it defended itself boldly and resisted with force all the efforts to draw it out of the water, so that it was necessary to hold it thus tied [with strong cords] in the water until it was exhausted. The hook that caught it was so big that it took a large sheep's lung to bait it…. It was skinned. The hide was like iron…. Some of the poor pilgrims, though only a few, ate some of it. It was fearful thing to see both before and after being skinned.[477]

After ten weary days anchored off the port, the pilgrims were finally permitted to go ashore. But they still were not allowed to set out for Jerusalem itself and had to stay in Jaffa. In the meantime, the Muslims had captured ten Cypriot sailors who had hidden in a wood after being shipwrecked off Acre. The governor of Gaza told the captain of the galley that "the pilgrims must redeem [ransom] the prisoners, or that he would flay them alive before their eyes."[478] The governor demanded 1,000 ducats to release the sailors but at last settled for 150 ducats, which the pilgrims had to pay. But then, Casola tells us,

Seeing that the ground was soft, and that the Christians were compassion-

ate, those dogs brought in a Jew and a Frenchman, and the governor of Gaza threatened to flay them if we did not ransom them. The captain told him he could do as he pleased provided he let us go on our way. The Jew was well beaten, and that coward of a Frenchman denied Christ, and the *sexula* [a light cotton head shawl] was placed on his head [signifying that he had converted to Islam].[479]

A French pilgrim died and by now many of the other pilgrims were sick. Fifteen days after their arrival off Jaffa, Casola and his fellow travelers finally mounted donkeys, mules or horses for the trip to Jerusalem. Casola himself rode a mule and wisely avoided hassles later on by giving the muleteer an extra ducat as a tip. Accommodations at Ramla, the next stop, were primitive at best. Casola slept on a wooden plank which was raised from the ground by two stones. His folded mantle served as the mattress and his leather purse as his pillow. The only pleasant thing about Ramla was that there was no lack of good things to eat and drink: Casola dined with the captain of the galley.

The rest of the trip to the Holy City was not easy. It was hot and dusty. The muleteer had loaded so many sacks on Casola's mule that Casola himself could hardly move. In the evening, the teamster put his young son on the mule, too. "But the boy fell asleep," Casola remembered, "and tumbled off the mule, dragging me, the sacks and the pack-saddle to the ground, or rather on to a stone, and I hurt my arm and foot so badly that when I got back to Milan my wound were not yet healed."[480]

Finally, however, he and the other pilgrims reached the Holy City, "almost dead of heat and thirst." Most of his fellow pilgrims were quartered with the Hospitalers at Mount Sion but the Prior of Mount Sion, who was in charge of all

Christian pilgrims, had rented a house near the Church of the Holy Sepulcher. He invited Casola to stay with him. Casola was very tired and appreciated the comforts of the Prior's house. He noted, however, that he and several companions "lived like lords in the house and at the table of the captain, but the poor pilgrims fared badly [at Mount Sion], and it was all the fault of the Prior, who had little charity for the pilgrims; not a single person was satisfied with him, beginning with the captain."[481]

The pilgrims then started visiting the holy sites of Jerusalem. A small church on the Mount of Olives had a stone believed to bear the footprint of Jesus when he ascended into heaven. This stone was decked with rosaries and other objects of devotion but Casola was disappointed because the friars who were his guides offered no prayers at this site. "In these places," Casola complained,

because [the friars] are so despised by these Moorish dogs and are not otherwise venerated, it is necessary to open the third sack, called the sack of faith, otherwise the voyage would be made in vain.... I can well believe that the friars were in such a hurry to show us those places, they omitted some of the usual ceremonies.[482]

Casola, however, liked the Aqsa Mosque and the Holy City's bazaars. This is how he described the mosque:

It is a beautiful building to look at from the outside [neither Christians or Jews were permitted to enter a mosque], and strong compared with the greater part of the habitations in Jerusalem. It is wonderful to see the courts—so well paved with the whitest marble—which are built around the base of the Mosque.... I heard from the Moors that there are neither paintings nor images inside. They say that there a thousand

lamps within, which on certain occasions are all lighted at the same moment.[483]

He loved the bazaars, which have not changed much to this day:

What pleased me most was the sight of the bazaars—long, vaulted streets extending as far as the eye can reach ... cooked fowls, cooked meat, eggs and all other eatables are very cheap. I saw a long bazaar like the other, with both sides full of merchandise, and of the things the people know how to make, and this was a beautiful sight.[484]

A window in Casola's room overlooked an area where Muslims slept out in the open because of the extreme heat. He liked to watch them rise and perform their morning prayers: "In the morning when they rose they went through so many genuflexions—throwing themselves all their length straight out on the ground—that it was a marvel to see them."[485] His prejudices soon came to the surface, however. "It is great madness to talk to them about our faith," he confides to us, "because they have no rational sentiment in them. They are very impetuous and easily excited to anger, and they have no gracious or courteous impulses or actions. And I declare that they may be as great and learned as you like, but in their ways they are like dogs."[486]

Casola and the other pilgrims spent the night in the Church of the Holy Sepulcher. He was pleased that "all the time the appointed anthems were being sung, and the Litanies changed by the way." He was so moved by a sermon preached in Latin by one of the friars of Mount Sion that he declared, "If those Moorish dogs had been present, together with all the pilgrims, they would have wept."[487]

After bathing in the River Jordan and visiting Jericho, Casola returned to Jerusalem, where he learned that some of his fellow pilgrims had been arrested on suspicion of espionage. This occurred, claimed Casola, because a Jewish doctor in Jerusalem, who had been brought up in Italy and who spoke Italian fluently, told the governor of Jerusalem that

> certain of the pilgrims had refrained from going to the River Jordan in order to spy out and explore Jerusalem, and that he had heard certain of the pilgrims say that within two years the Christians would be masters of Jerusalem. Upon this accusation [the governor] caused these poor men to be chained.[488]

In fact, some of the pilgrims had stayed behind only because of the heat or illness. The Prior of Mount Sion and a Milanese prelate persuaded the governor to release the pilgrims from jail and keep them under house arrest instead. The governor, however, wanted to force the pilgrims to pay their way out of captivity. Casola grew discouraged. "We were all prisoners," he writes, "some here, some there, some in Mount Sion and some of the house of the captain, which was guarded by Moors; so that we began to weary of this pilgrimage, although it procured us great merit in the sight of God — for all the time we drew on that sack of patience."[489] At last, matters were arranged. The governor settled for 25 ducats, rather than the 1,000 ducats he had originally demanded, and all the pilgrims were released.

But then the pilgrims found that leaving the Holy Land was no easier than entering it. Casola says that "New mushrooms [obstacles] sprang up each day." The governor demanded that the pilgrims either return to him the Cypriot sailors they had ransomed earlier at Jaffa or pay him 500 ducats more. The Prior got the governor to settle for only 128 ducats. These were given to him but he initially

rejected them because they were not ducats from the Venetian Mint. He continued to harass the pilgrims, even confiscating a fine parrot one of the pilgrims had bought in Jerusalem. More money changed hands, however, and after endless negotiations the pilgrims were finally given permission leave Jerusalem for Jaffa.

At the port, their troubles were not yet at an end. When the captain boarded the galley, he found that one of the German pilgrims was dead. Before leaving Jaffa, the captain had to pay the Muslims ten ducats so they would let the pilgrims bury the German on land. At last, however,

> When the boat which had carried the body on land returned, the captain, to the great consolation of the living, decided to set sail before eating. The poor gentleman had been so maltreated by the Moors that he was in a great hurry to depart. Thus at the fourth hour of the day he ordered the anchors to be heaved, and to the praise of god and of our glorious lady [the Virgin Mary] we set sail towards the West.[490]

Mujir al-Din (c. 1496)

When the Holy Land was once again firmly under Muslim rule, Muslim writers encouraged pilgrims to go there. In about 1496 the great Arab historian Mujir al-Din, who was then chief justice of Jerusalem, called renewed attention to Jerusalem by reminding the faithful of two sayings attributed to the Prophet Muhammad himself. The first was that "Zamzam [a holy spring in Mecca] and the fountain of Siloam at Jerusalem are the springs of Paradise." The second saying eulogized the fountain of Siloam, too, but also contained a strong warning about the pitfalls of entering the Christian churches in Jerusalem:

Let anyone who has visited Jerusalem go to the Prayer Niche of David to make his prayers and bathe himself in the fountain of Siloam, since it comes from Paradise; *let him abstain from going into the churches and buying anything there*, since a sin committed at Jerusalem is the equivalent of a thousand sins, and a good work there is the equal of a thousand good works.[491]

We noted earlier that Jerusalem's role in Muslim eschatology has inspired a great number of devotional writings known as *fada'il*, which extol the "excellencies" or "virtues" of the city. Mujir al-Din was one of the culminating figures in this literary movement. His main work was a detailed two-volume narrative describing the holy places of Palestine. It flew in the face of conservative Muslim tradition, however, by elevating Jerusalem to be virtually on a par with Mecca and Medina, the two holiest cities of Islam.[492]

Religious ceremonies have a tendency to become more elaborate over time. This is what happened to the "pious journey" (*ziyara*) to Jerusalem. In the 1320s a Muslim scholar wrote a work entitled the *Book of Arousing Souls*, which gave a very detailed itinerary for visits to the Haram al-Sharif. If followed carefully, this itinerary would result in a virtual circumambulation of the Haram, much like the circumambulation of the Ka'ba in Mecca. For both theological and pragmatic reasons, however, Muslim conservatives did not want Jerusalem to displace Mecca. As a result, neither the *Book of Arousing Souls* nor Mujir al-Din's own line of reasoning ever found favor with Muslim traditionalists.

One of the sternest of these traditionalists was Ibn Taymiyya (d. 1328), who had been in the forefront of the battle to maintain Mecca's primacy. He warned devout Muslims that

In fact, there is not in the land [of Palestine] a place to circumambulate as the Ka'ba is circumambulated. Whoever believes that circumambulation of other objects is permitted is evil, just as [is] whoever believes that praying toward other than the Ka'ba is permitted.... Though [Jerusalem at one time] was the *qibla* [the direction of prayer], this part of the Koran was abrogated. So how can there be those who perceive [Jerusalem] as a place to be circumambulated as the Ka'ba is circumambulated?... In Jerusalem there is not a place one calls *truly sacred*.[493]

For him, the only "truly sacred" places were all in Saudi Arabia, not in Palestine.

Sir Richard Guildford (1506)

Sir Richard was a privy councilor to the first Tudor king, Henry VII. He left England for the Holy City in 1506, together with John Whitby, Prior of Guisborough, and with a chaplain who served as their secretary. The pilgrimage, however, was not a happy one: both Sir Richard and the Prior died in Jerusalem.

Their difficulties began in Jaffa, where they were detained aboard their ship for seven days. Once allowed on shore, they were

received by ye Mamelukes and Saracyns and put into an old cave by name and tale, and there were scryven [scribes] ever wrytying oure names man by man as we entered in the presence of the sayd Lordes and there we lay in the same grotto or cave Fridaye all day upon bare stynkynge stable grounds, as well nyght as day, right evyll intreated by ye Maures [Moors, i.e., Muslims].[494]

After this trying experience, both Guildford and Whitby felt so ill that walking to Jerusalem was out of the question.

Only the presence of muskets show that here we are looking at a nineteenth century expedition.
Otherwise, this could have been a camel caravan during the earliest days of Muslim rule in
Jerusalem. (David Roberts, 1839; illustration courtesy of Kegan Paul.)

It was only after their secretary hired
"camellys with grete dyffyculte and out-
rangyous coste" that they managed to
reach the Holy City and visit the usual
sites.[495] It was the Dome of the Rock,
which they called the Temple of Solomon,
that made the strongest impression on
them. The secretary noted that they passed
this structure frequently and that the Muslims held it in great reverence. No Christian was permitted to enter it; if he did, he
either had to renounce his faith immediately or he would be put to death.

The secretary also recorded that, inside the building, the Muslims worshiped
a rock which was enclosed by an iron rail-
ing. This rock was so holy that no Muslim
dared touch it; even so, the faithful still
made pilgrimages from great distances
to visit it. The secretary believed that in
the distant past the Jews had installed
their Ark of the Covenant on this very
spot.[496]

The rise of the secular pilgrims

It is now time to turn to one of most interesting chapters in the long history of pilgrimage to Jerusalem—the development of secular pilgrimages during Ottoman rule. Devotional pilgrimages continued, to be sure, but for the first time we can detect a widespread current of skepticism or even atheism among pilgrims going to the Holy City. Secular travelers were increasingly prone to write accounts of their pilgrimages, and there is no shortage of interesting sources here.

IX

Pilgrimages Under Ottoman Rule (1517–1917)

By the last half of the fifteenth century, the Mamluk empire was fading. The Ottoman Turks, well-organized and well-armed, seized Constantinople in 1453 and took over the tottering Christian empire of Byzantium. Jerusalem's security was threatened during these upheavals. The *bedouin* could no longer be kept in check and by the last half of the fifteenth century they were murdering travelers outside the gates of the Holy City itself. Jerusalem surrendered peacefully to the Ottomans in 1517.

The city had lost none of its importance to Islam. When the Ottoman sultan Selim I was ceremoniously presented with the keys to Jerusalem, he dismounted, prostrated himself before the gates to the city, and shouted, "Thanks be to God! I am now the possessor of the sanctuary of the first *qibla* [the direction of prayer]."[497] In Europe, the foundations for secular studies of the Holy and for secular pilgrimages to Jerusalem were laid by Desiderius Erasmus (d. 1536), the greatest scholar of the northern Renaissance.

The Ottomans were in power for 400 years (1517–1917). Under the reign of Sultan Suleiman, known as "the Magnificent," Jerusalem flourished. After his death, however, Ottoman rule entered a long period of decline. The city became an economic and cultural backwater. During the seventeenth and eighteenth centuries, although the Ottomans discriminated against the Jews in Palestine, there was still a regular flow of Jewish scholars and Jewish families between Jerusalem, Western Europe and North Africa. Christian and Muslim pilgrimages continued, too.

In 1799 Napoleon tried to conquer Palestine but was defeated near Acre by a combination of plague, the British fleet and a Muslim army. During the nineteenth and early twentieth centuries, the Holy Land made a comeback on the world's stage as Western leaders grappled with the complexities of the "Eastern Question," i.e., how to divide the spoils of the disintegrating Ottoman Empire. Pilgrimages from Europe became safer and more popular as steam began to replace sail in the Mediterranean in the late 1830s.

European rivalries over the Church of the Holy Sepulcher sparked the Crimean War of 1853–1856. Pilgrimages to Jerusalem, both religious and secular, increased significantly thereafter, in part because the Haram was now open to visitors. Monumental foreign buildings such as the Russian and the Notre Dame de France Pilgrims' Hostels changed Jerusalem's skyline. In World War I the Ottoman Turks made the fatal mistake of siding with Germany, Austria-Hungary and Bulgaria against France, England, Russia, Italy and the United States. By being on the losing side in this war, they lost all their possessions, including, in 1917, Jerusalem itself.

Sir Richard Torkington (1517)

All that is known of Sir Richard was that he was an English priest who made a pilgrimage to Jerusalem in 1517, accompanied at certain points of his journey by two other pilgrims, Robert Crosse, a pewterer from London, and Sir Thomas Toppe, a priest from the west of England. His account, which includes a mileage chart and a list of relics to see en route, is rather matter-of-fact but is significant nevertheless because it marks the end of an era.

The Reformation and secular pilgrimages

Sir Richard and his party were among the last devotional English pilgrims of the Middle Ages. The Protestant Reformation was at hand. It rejected pilgrimages because of the abuses associated with indulgences, saints and relics. As liberal currents of Reformation thought spread across Western Europe, they began to demystify Christian pilgrimage and to set the stage for the appearance of the secular pilgrim. It is worth mentioning here some of the milestones along this road during the first half of the sixteenth century.

By coincidence, it was in 1517—the same year as Sir Richard's pilgrimage—that the German monk Martin Luther posted his revolutionary Ninety-five Theses on the door of the Castle Church at Wittenberg, where he was a pastor and a professor. Among other things, Luther heatedly denounced indulgences as an affront to the doctrine of God's free gift of grace. He insisted that the Pope had no authority over purgatory (the Church claimed that indulgences reduced the time a soul had to spend in punishment there) and that worship of the saints lacked any Biblical foundation. Luther's bottom line was that only the Bible was authoritative: justification (salvation) was to be won by faith alone, not by pilgrimages or other "good works."

In another revolutionary act, King Henry VIII, infuriated by Pope Clement VII's refusal to grant him a divorce, broke with Rome in 1534 and set up his own church with himself as the supreme head. Other important developments occurred two years later. In 1536 the Protestant reformer John Calvin published his *Institutes of Religion*. This treatise—in which, as mentioned earlier, Calvin dismissed pilgrimage simply as a form of "counterfeit worship"—put a solid theological foundation under Protestantism.

Moreover, in 1536 the Augsburg Confession[498] was translated into English, making it accessible to the Anglicans and Methodists of England, who used it in drawing up their own Articles of Religion. Not surprisingly, the reformers who drafted the Augsburg Confession took a negative view of pilgrimages, too, denouncing them as "childless and useless works" unworthy of serious attention.

Seeing "all of Arabia"

The Muslims of Palestine were not very helpful to Sir Richard's party, putting it "in great fear which were too long to write."[499] He found little to admire in Jaffa, where "now there standeth never an house but only two towers and certain caves under the ground."[500] But he was quite taken by Jerusalem itself. "This city of

Jerusalem," he tells us, "is situated in an attractive and eminent place, for it stands in such a position that no matter which direction a man approaches it from, he must go uphill. From the city a man may see all of Arabia.... I never saw such a city that had more pleasing views."[501]

Suleiman the Magnificent (1520)

Under the benevolent rule of Sultan Suleiman the Magnificent (1520–1566), Jerusalem flourished. The city's walls had been in ruins but between 1536 and 1541 they were entirely rebuilt. More than two miles long and up to 40 feet high, they are still standing today. Suleiman restored the sacred center of the Haram, especially the Dome of the Rock, and even waived his claim to the entrance fee paid by pilgrims there, in order to finance a year-long reading of the Koran at the site.[502]

Suleiman also caused a low wall to be built parallel to the Western Wall, separating it from the adjacent Maghribi Quarter where North African Muslims lived. After he issued a *firman* (official edict) that gave Jews the right to pray at the Western Wall, it soon became the focal point of Jewish religious life in the Holy City. It has remained so ever since.

Under Suleiman, Christians and Jews were considered as falling within the framework of Islamic law. They were treated as *ahl al-dhimma* (protected minorities). As such they were free to pursue their own religious interests, provided that they paid the appropriate taxes. These taxes included a poll-tax, pilgrims' fees, tolls of check-points on major roads, fees for visits to the Holy Sepulcher, and port fees in Jaffa. So many Christian pilgrims came to Jerusalem in the early days of Ottoman rule that revenues from the Holy Sepulcher tripled between 1525 and 1553.[503]

David Reubeni (1523)

David Reubeni was a charismatic Jewish imposter who claimed to be the prince of a mythical Jewish state in Arabia. By offering to lead a non-existent Jewish army against the Turks in Palestine and thus recover the Holy Land for the Jews, he initially won the support of both Pope Clement VII and King John of Portugal.

Reubeni had visited Jerusalem in 1523. In a long, unfinished manuscript probably written by his secretary, Solomon Cohen, he claimed that he was warmly received there. "I entered the house of the Holy of Holies," he asserted, "and when, I came to the sanctuary all the Ishmaelite guardians came to bow before me and to kiss my feet, and said to me, 'Enter, Oh blessed of the Lord, our lord, the son of our lord.'"[504]

Reubeni wanted to stay there all night to pray but the guards forced him to leave. He therefore prayed and fasted outside the sanctuary. When the guards returned in the morning, Reubeni paid them enough so that he was permitted to spend five weeks within the sanctuary itself. He tells us when he knew it was time for him to leave Jerusalem. This was the first day of the pilgrim festival of *Shavuot*, when the crescent on top of the cupola of the sanctuary, which had always faced westward, suddenly, of its own accord, turned toward the east.

Such an unexplained event greatly alarmed the Muslims. The next day they sent workmen to turn the crescent to face the west but the next day it was pointing east again. This time it could not be moved. Reubeni says that he knew this was the sign for him to leave because "our elders had already told me, 'When thou seest this sign, go to Rome.'" So, after visiting the Mount of Olives and Mount Zion, he asked a fellow Jew, "Make me a model [more likely, a map] showing Venice,

Rome, and Portugal ... I am going there for a good cause, but it is a secret which I cannot reveal, and I want thee to advise me how I should go."[505] As soon as he got the model he left Jerusalem for Europe.

However, despite the backing of Pope Clement and King John, Reubeni and a Jewish messianic colleague, Solomon Molcho, both failed to persuade the Holy Roman Emperor Charles V to arm the Jews. Instead, Charles V had both men imprisoned and handed them over to the Inquisition. Molcho was burned at the stake in 1532; Reubeni, sent to a Spanish jail, died a few years later, probably by poisoning.

Greffin Affagart (1533)

By the early decades of the sixteenth century a pilgrim needed a great deal of imagination to be able to visualize the holy sites of Jerusalem in their original, simple form. They were by then buried under such a heavy accretion of religious monuments that pilgrims had to rely entirely on their guides to tell them what had happened at each stop. A pious French traveler, Greffin Affagart, made a pilgrimage in 1533–1534 and reported to his readers that

> One needs a purse full of faith and belief, because [the guide] points out to us: there Jesus was born, there he was crucified, there he was buried. There is no one there anymore! One sees nothing but several churches and, in other places, only ruined walls. For those who do not wish to believe what the guides tell them, it is hardly worth the trouble to go there.[506]

Nasir al-Din (c. 1550)

In the mid-sixteenth century Nasir al-Din, a Muslim scholar, wrote a book

that included two chapters comprising a guide for Muslims pilgrims to Jerusalem. He drew on the body of Islamic writings known as the "merits" or "praises" of Jerusalem. He also used the pilgrimage handbook produced by Ibn al-Murajja in the eleventh century. Nasir al-Din went beyond these sources, however, by listing many additional Islamic holy places in the Old City.

Although it is not clear to modern scholars whether these new places date from before or after the Ottoman conquest of 1517, Ibn al-Din gives a total of more than 50 major and minor sites on or close to the Haram. It seems likely that his chapters were influenced by some of the Christian guidebooks written about the Holy Land. The Muslim pilgrim, for example, is strictly enjoined not to kiss "The Tongue of the Rock"—a marble pillar supporting the edge of the Holy Rock—because such an intimate physical act is a "disgraceful [i.e., a Christian] innovation."[507]

Antoine Regnaut (1573)

This French pilgrim was in Jerusalem from 1549 to 1550. Borrowing liberally from other earlier writers, he distilled his experiences into a guidebook, not published until 1573, entitled *Discours du voyage d'outremer au sainct Sépulcre de Jérusalem, et autres lieux de la terre Saincte* (*Discourse on the voyage overseas to the Holy Sepulcher of Jerusalem and to other sites in the Holy Land*). Regnaut put forward a clear, practical 11-point *Instruction au voyage* with the aim of keeping the Jerusalem pilgrim out of needless trouble. Lightly edited, this is what he recommended[508]:

1. Ensure that your motivation is holy, not self-serving.

2. Arrange your affairs at home and make out your will, so that if you die en route your inheritors will not have undue problems.

3. Take two purses, one full of patience, the other full of money, namely, 200 golden Venetian ducats. You will need 150 ducats for the journey and 50 for emergencies.

4. Make sure you arrive in Venice in good time to board the pilgrim galley. Before embarking, be sure to buy a fur robe for the return journey, when it will be cold. You will also need other kinds of clothing; a mattress in lieu of a bed; a long chest which can be locked; two barrels, one for wine, the other for water; cheeses, sausages, beef tongues and other delicacies. Once underway, do not leave the boat for anything in the world.

5. Try to stow your belongings amidships and near a doorway, where the air circulates more freely. This is especially important if you are prone to sea-sickness. This is where you will sleep, too.

6. Before sailing, negotiate a contract with the captain. Pay 60 ducats for passage and board. If you do not go on a galley but take a merchant ship instead, you should pay two ecus a month, not including food. Five ecus a month gets you a seat at the captain's table, while for three ecus you can sit at the cook's table. Pay the extra cost if you possibly can.

7. Buy eggs, chickens, preserves and fruit each time you stop at port. You will need the extra food when the captain and crew are too busy during storms to cook.

8. Dress poorly, so as to avoid having to pay endless tips.

9. Once in the Holy Land, carry your bedding with you. *Never leave the caravan*, and never argue with the locals: this is very dangerous.

10. Your money should be gold—in venetian sequins; for change carry smaller coins as well.

11. Before leaving home, get letters of permission to travel from your bishop and a safe-conduct from the king. Before leaving Jerusalem, get a certificate from the Pope's commissary saying you have been there.

Loys Barlourdet (1601) and Henri de Castela (1604)

Two guidebooks in French appeared at the beginning of the seventeenth century. These were Loys Barlourdet's 1601 *Guide des chemins pour le voyage de Hierusalem, et autres villes et lieux de la Terre Sainte* (*Guidebook for routes to Jerusalem, and other cities and places of the Holy Land*), and Henri de Castela's 1604 *Guide et adresse pour ceux qui veulent faire le S. [Saint] voyage de Hierusalem* (*Guide and information for those who want to make the Holy voyage to Jerusalem*).[509] Both men were French priests.

By the time these books appeared, the Protestant Reformation had been undermining the credibility of pilgrimages. As a result, neither Barlourdet nor de Castela could take it for granted that their readers would consider pilgrimage to be a meritorious activity. First, these authors had to establish their own credentials, which they did by asserting that, as priests, they had been empowered by God to define and explain the Jerusalem pilgrimage.

Next, both writers actually *had to argue the case* for *pilgrimage*, to the extent that, as one modern scholar puts it, "the guide-book itself becomes a part of polemic."[510] Finally, the authors clearly had their own doubts about the value of pilgrimage as it was then being practiced. They deplored, for example, the tendency of many returned pilgrims to rattle on only about themselves, rather than talking about the sacred places they had visited and the elevating spiritual experiences they had there.

Evliye Chelebi (1648–1650)

Chelebi, a Turkish gentleman, visited Jerusalem in 1648–1650, just before the Ottoman Empire began the slow but inexorable decline that did not come to an end until its successor, Turkey, was defeated in World War I.[511]

Palestine was a prosperous province, Chelebi reports, due largely to the Muslim and Christian pilgrimages. With a force of 500 soldiers at his disposal, the *pasha* of Jerusalem (*pasha* was the highest official title of honor in the Ottoman Empire) was able to charge for protective services. He was the commandant of the annual caravan that escorted Mecca-bound pilgrims between Damascus and Jerusalem. For this service he was paid 40,000 piasters a year. Moreover, at Easter the door of the Holy Sepulcher would not be opened to Christian pilgrims until both the *pasha* and the *mulla* (chief justice) of Jerusalem had arrived there. The priest in charge of the ceremonies then had to collect, from each of the 5,000 to 10,000 pilgrims gathered there, 10 to 15 piasters. The priest then gave 20,000 each piasters to the *pasha* and the *mullah*. This was, Chelebi assures us, "a considerable sum."

We learn from Chelebi that "the fief-holders [local Muslim lords] convey the pilgrims to Hebron and to the birthplace of Jesus at Bethlehem and to the Nebi Musa [the burial site of Moses], as the roads are insecure from the Arab rebels [*bedouin*]."[512] Although Chelebi gives no figures here, it is certain that the fief-holders, too, had to be paid for their escort duties: for one thing, they had to buy off the *bedouin* to prevent any attacks.

Muslim pilgrimage, for its part, had a trickle-down effect on Jerusalem's economy as well. Chelebi gives a detailed list of holy "stations" to be visited on the Haram, which was a beehive of activity. The Aqsa Mosque, one of the Muslim pilgrims' main destinations, employed no fewer than 800 people. This included prayer leaders, preachers, muezzins (men who call the faithful to prayer), reciters of litanies, readers, guards and assorted employees. Along the northern and western sides of the Haram, Chelebi saw that

> On all sides of the Shrine of the Holy Rock are rooms belonging to forty law schools. In each of them live pious people considered to be wonder-working dervishes. [A dervish, or Sufi, was a member of a Muslim mystic fraternity.] Some of them break their fast only once a week, while others have not tasted meat for forty or fifty years. Such are these pious souls who lead here a mystical life, while they at the same time are well versed in worldly knowledge and sciences.[513]

Thomas Fuller (1650)

One of the earliest semi-scientific studies of the Holy Land was published in London in 1650. This was Dr. Thomas Fuller's *A Pisgah-sight of Palestine and the Confines thereof with a Historie of the Old and New Testament acted thereon.* The phrase "Pisgah-sight" evokes the Biblical passage in which God commands Moses to ascend Mount Pisgah; from the summit, Moses is granted the sight of the Promised Land.[514] But because on an earlier occasion Moses had disobeyed God, he was not permitted to enter the Holy Land himself. "Pisgah-sight" is thus an archaic, evocative term that refers to a coming together of the human and the divine at the crowning point of a man's life.[515]

Fuller says that his book is an ecclesiastical history and that his goal is to give the reader a true understanding of the Bible. Relying entirely on the Bible and on his own vivid imagination, he describes, at great length and with many maps and illustrations, Palestine's geography, mineral resources and flora and fauna. He also discusses the settlements, farming methods and cultural patterns of ancient times. Although from a substantive point of view *A Pisgah-sight of Palestine* offers little of value for the modern reader, it is important historically because it helped lay the intellectual groundwork for later studies of the Holy Land in which science, not the Bible or the author's imagination, would play the leading role.

Al-Qashashi (d. 1660)

One of Chelebi's contemporaries was a Muslim traditionalist named al-Qashashi, who died in 1660. Al-Qashashi did not share Chelebi's cosmopolitan broad-mindedness. He complained that the seething crowds around the Haram were a scandalous threat to public morals:

> On Friday [the day for attending the mosque] the men and women mingle without a partition between them.... Some of the women unveil their faces [displaying] their beauty, their ornaments, and their perfumes. What temptation is stronger than this? By God, they were sitting cheek to jowl among the men as if they were closely related or members of the same household.... In fact, some of the merchants sat among the women with their goods.... May God kill all of those who are pleased by this great abomination.... In addition, on the festival day of Arafa the men and women gather together with intermingling from afternoon until evening. In addition, on the Eighth of Shawwal, the men and women gather together. During the days called "The Days of the Pilgrims" men and women gather together with much mingling occurring.... These days are the wedding feast of Satan. It is [a] festival of immorality and terror.[516]

Al-Qashashi objected so strongly to this mixing of the sexes because in traditional Islamic societies personal honor was (and still is today) a man's most important possession. A man's honor is inextricably bound up with the chastity of the women of his family. In comparison with men, women are held to be weaker and more subject to temptation. For this reason, the rules of traditional Muslim social behavior are extremely rigid: unless bound by close ties of kinship, the sexes must always be separated.[517]

An unnamed English pilgrim (1684)

In his *Pilgrim's Progress*, John Bunyan struck a responsive chord in many Christian hearts by focusing on Jerusalem. An unnamed English pilgrim, writing in 1684, the same year that Part II of Bunyan's work was published, had this to say about himself:

> And having heard by some means or other in times past, very much discourse of the beauty and the pleasant situation of that City; of the sweet temper of the inhabitants, and the many goodly things that were to be seen and enjoyed there; he was instantly prepossessed with a strong desire to remove his feet thither. When he did eat or drink *Jerusalem* would still be in his mouth, when he was in Company, *Jerusalem* stole his heart from him; Nay, in his very sleep it would [not] stay away, but he was wont to dream fine things of *Jerusalem*.[518]

Henry Maundrell (1697)

Chaplain of the British Levant Company in Aleppo (Syria), Maundrell spent about two months in the Holy City and later recorded his experiences in *A Journey from Aleppo to Jerusalem at Easter A.D. 1697*. This remained a popular guidebook for a long time because it was objective, well-written and displayed a nice sense of humor. By 1749 it had been translated into other European languages; seven editions had been published. Parts of the book continued to be used in travel accounts even in the nineteenth century. A basic reason for its popularity was that it reflected the new interest in traveling for pleasure and for cross-cultural experiences, rather than journeying simply as a ghostly pilgrim.

A Journey from Aleppo to Jerusalem appealed to the growing number of readers who had been caught up in Renaissance humanism. This new system of thought was a program of education and a method of intellectual inquiry that flourished in northern Italy during the fourteenth century. It later spread throughout much of Western Europe. Renaissance humanism challenged Christian orthodoxy on four levels:

• It encouraged scholars to pursue classical and secular studies, not just Christian studies.
• Humanistic philology called into question the authenticity of some of the most important Christian texts.
• Humanism strongly encouraged intellectual individualism. This seriously undermined the "received" quality of Christian beliefs, i.e., beliefs that were to be accepted unquestionably simply because they had been handed down through the hierarchical structure of the Church.
• Finally, humanism also stressed the need for religious reform, i.e., eliminating all the medieval accretions and procedural complexities that had been placed by the Church between the individual and God.[519]

Maundrell claimed that the purpose of his journey was simply pilgrimage. In fact, however, he was part of the new spirit of scientific inquiry that was sweeping across Western Europe. As a result, he devoted his time in the Holy Land not to worship but to copying ancient inscriptions, studying ruins and tracing old cisterns and aqueducts.[520] He was able to see Jerusalem with dispassionate eyes and to report on the seamier sides of life there.

After visiting the Church of the Holy Sepulcher, for example, he was struck by its "unholy wars":

But that which has always been the great prize contended for by the several sects is the command and appropriation of the holy sepulcher: a privilege contested with so much unchristian fury and animosity, that in disputing which party should go into it to celebrate their mass, they have sometimes proceeded to blows even at the very door of the sepulcher; mingling their own blood with that of their sacrifices. An evidence of which fury the father guardian showed us in a great scar upon his arm, which he told us was the mark of a wound given him by a sturdy Greek priest in one of these unholy wars.[521]

Maundrell offers us some snapshots of the Jerusalem pilgrimage, recording local customs ranging from tattoos to the Holy Fire, and sharing with us his droll sense of humor. He says of tattoos:

The next morning nothing extraordinary passed; which gave many of the pilgrims leisure to have their arms marked with the usual ensigns of Jerusalem. The artists, who undertake this operation, do it in this manner: they have stamps of wood of any figure you desire, which they first print off upon your arm with powder of charcoal; then taking two very fine needles tied close together, and dipping them often, like a pen, in certain ink, compounded, as I was informed, of gunpowder and ox-gall, they make with them small punc-tures all along the lines of the figure which they have printed; and washing the part in wine, conclude the work. The punctures they make with great quickness and dexterity, and with scarce any smart, seldom piercing so deep as to draw blood.[522]

His comments on the Holy Fire are scathing:

Those that got the fire applied it imme-diately to their beards, faces and bo-soms, pretending that it would not burn them like an earthly flame; but I plainly saw, none of them could endure this experiment long enough to make good that pretension…. The Latins take great pains to expose this ceremony as a most shameful imposture, and a scan-dal to the Christian religion; perhaps out of envy that others should be mas-ters of so gainful a business; but the Greeks and Armenians pin their faith upon it, and make their pilgrimages chiefly upon this motive; and 'tis the deplorable unhappiness of their priests, that having acted the cheat for so long already, they are forced now to stand for it, for fear of endangering the apos-tasy of their people.[523]

Together with about 2,000 other pil-grims "of every nation and sex," on Easter Monday Maundrell made a side trip to the River Jordan. He tells us, tongue in cheek, that

No sooner were we arrived at the river, and dismounted … but we were alarmed by some troops of Arabs [bedouin] ap-pearing on the other side, and firing at us; but at too great a distance to do any execution. This intervening disturbance hindered the friars from performing their service prescribed for this place; and seemed to put them in a terrible

fear of their lives, beyond what ap-peared in the rest of the company; though considering the sordidness of their present condition, and the extra-ordinary rewards, which they boast to be their due in the world to come, one would think in reason, they of all men should have the least cause to discover so great a fear of death, and so much fondness of a life like theirs.[524]

Sufi pilgrimages (1600s–1700s)

Sufism is a set of mystical Islamic be-liefs and practices designed to bring about direct personal experience with the divine. During the seventeenth and eighteenth centuries, many members of Sufi *tariqahs* ("brotherhoods") made the pilgrimage to Jerusalem, where they stayed in hostels as-sociated with Sufi theological institu-tions.[525] Special rituals, highlighted by rig-orous fasting and meditation, were held at the Dome of the Rock, the site of Muham-mad's ascension to heaven. Lengthy prayer sessions known as *dhikrs* ("recollections") induced a state of religious ecstasy in the Sufis, permitting them a foretaste of the delights the soul was thought to experi-ence when at death it escaped from the body and mounted heavenward.

Nathaniel Crouch (1719)

Writing under the pseudonym of Robert Burton, Crouch was an English pil-grim who produced several works about the Holy Land. He visited Jerusalem him-self in 1719 and commented on the diver-sity of its population. "Jerusalem is in-habited by some Christians (who make a great benefit of shewing the Sepulchre of Christ)," he writes, "and of Late Years also by Moors, Arabians, Greeks, Latines, Turks, Jews; nay, I may say, with the Peo-ple of all Nations."[526]

Crouch himself, however, had a miserable time in the Holy Land. He was arrested and jailed in Jerusalem. Later, in Egypt, he was captured by *bedouin* and had to pay them off to regain his freedom. For these reasons he ends one of his works, *A Strange and True Account of the Late Travels of Two English Pilgrims,* with a statement remarkable for its candor:

> Being wounded and well beaten [by the *bedouin*] we at last got to the gates of [Alexandria], but so late that they were shut, and we were forced to lie all night upon the hard stones. In the morning I got aboard my ship, after fifty days absence, and ended *my tiresome pilgrimage to Jerusalem.*[527]

Richard Pococke (1745)

The most learned work of the eighteenth century which dealt with the Holy Land was written by Richard Pococke, a scholar and clergyman who later became the bishop of Meath (Ireland). Pococke's three-part *Description of the East, and Some other Countries* appeared in 1743–1745. Published in two massive, expensive, leather-bound folio volumes which are still a joy to handle, the *Description* immediately became famous. It was quickly translated into French, German and Dutch.

The second of the two volumes dealt with Syria and Palestine. Pococke decided to retrace the likely path of the Jews' exodus from Egypt and gave his readers a careful eyewitness account of what he found.[528] Noticing every landmark and every change in vegetation, he enlivened his text with an extensive range of maps and illustrations of mosques and sepulchers. Upon reaching Jerusalem, he accepted nothing on faith, but studied each local tradition to see if it accorded with

known facts and whether it was probable or not.

Because of his knowledge and objectivity, Pococke can be regarded as the most accomplished of the early secular pilgrims. He was a conscientious recorder who took pains to give his readers an accurate account of what they might expect to find as pilgrims in Jerusalem:

> I shall give an account of how European pilgrims are received in [the Latin convent]. When they first arrive at the gate of Jerusalem, they send to the Latin convent, and the interpreter of the monks comes and conducts them to the monastery, where there is a building appropriated to the European pilgrims, and it is the office [duty] of one of the lay-brothers to take care of them, [and] they may also hire a servant for the better attendance; the lay-brother takes care that they are served with whatever they want, and always goes out with them.... The European pilgrims dine and sup in the refectory with the monks, where some of them read all the time in books of devotion; they are well served with three or four plates and have excellent white-wine of their own making.[529]

Like other European visitors, Pococke had a low opinion of the Holy Fire but he presents his views in a judicious and even understated manner. "It is said," he informs us, "that the Greeks think themselves obliged to carry on this affair, in order to bring pilgrims to Jerusalem; for the people set so great a value on this fire, that it is thought they would not otherwise come, which might ruin the Greeks, who live by this concourse of pilgrims."[530]

Frederick Hasselquist (1749–1752)

Trained as a botanist and medical doctor in his native Sweden, Hasselquist traveled to warmer climates to improve his health. He was avowedly a secular pilgrim. When a Christian official who was in charge of pilgrims in the Holy Land asked him "whether he had come to visit the holy places out of devotion," Hasselquist tells us, "I answered without ambiguity, No."[531]

In Jerusalem he found that both Jewish and Christian pilgrimages were continuing, much to the profit of the Turks:

> The greater part of the Jews are poor, as they have no opportunity for trafficking; for without it they cannot thrive in any part of the world. They have no other income here than what they can get from the Pilgrims of their own nation, who come from far and wide from all places to pay their respects to the seat of their forefathers. Their Rabbi has large revenues from his brethren throughout the world, of which the Turks draw the greater part; for Jews as well as Christians must constantly bring offerings to their altars [i.e., to the Turkish officials] if they would kiss their holy places in peace.[532]

Richard Tyron (1776)

An employee of the British Levant Company's headquarters in Aleppo, Richard Tyron paid a visit to Palestine and wrote a low-key, matter-of-fact account of his journey, entitled *Travels from Aleppo to the City of Jerusalem; and Through the most remarkable Parts of the Holy Land in 1776*. He does not say much about Jerusalem's former glories or future prospects, noting only that the decrepit condition of the Holy Land proved that somehow it "is now under a curse."[533]

As an avowed Protestant, Tyron had no inclinations toward experiencing religious ecstasy at the sight of Jerusalem's holy places. About the only thing that moved Tyron to a show of enthusiasm was the remarkable stamina of their aged guide, Father Tamafo. As Tyron puts it,

> Having seen all that was remarkable in these parts, we made for the convent, having got a great deal of credit with Father Tamafo, that we should be such zealous pilgrims, as to walk from five in the morning till mid-day; but to encourage us [he] would still go foremost, and told us always there was some place more worth our seeing than any before; and though he was old, and the weather hot, yet at the going up of a hill, he would run, that he might be foremost and give all the good words that could be, to encourage us Protestants, who never hoped or thought that we merited any thing by it; but at length we came to the convent again well weary, every one retiring to his lodgings.[534]

Constantin-François Volney (1783)

Volney was a French aristocrat, historian and philosopher whose works epitomized the rationalist historical and political currents of the eighteenth century. In Paris he was a friend of Benjamin Franklin, then the American envoy to France. Volney's most influential work, *Les Ruines, ou méditations sur les révolutions des empires* (*The Ruins, or meditations on the revolutions of empires*), appeared in 1791 and popularized religious skepticism.

Interested from a young age in history and ancient languages, Volney first traveled in Egypt and Syria, recording his impressions in a frank two-volume account entitled *Travels through Syria and Egypt, in the years 1783–1784, and 1785*. He tells his readers that "It is well known that at all times the devout curiosity of visiting the *holy places* had conducted Christians of every country to Jerusalem" and that there was "even a time when the ministers of religion taught it was indispensably necessary to salvation, and this pious zeal, pervading all over Europe, gave rise to the Crusades."[535]

Since then, he found, the zeal of Western Christians for pilgrimages had cooled considerably. The number of such pilgrims was reduced to a handful of Italian, Spanish and German monks. The Eastern Christians—or "Orientals," as he called them—were a different matter:

Faithful to the spirit of past times, they continue to consider the journey to Jerusalem as a work of the greatest merit. They are even scandalized at the relaxation of the Franks in this respect, and say, they have all become heretics or infidels. Their priests and monks, who find their advantage in this fervor, do not cease to promote it. The Greeks, especially, declare that *the pilgrimage ensures plenary indulgence, not only for the past, for even for the future; and that it absolves not only from murder, incest, and pederasty; but even from the neglect of fasting and the non-observance of festivals, which are far more heinous offenses.*[536]

Although Volney clearly considered these claims to be unwarranted and excessive, he could see that they produced results:

Such great encouragements are not without their effect; and every year a crowd of pilgrims, of both sexes and all ages, set out from the Morea, the Archipelago, Constantinople, Anatolia, Armenia, Egypt, and Syria, to the number of whom in 1784, amounted to two thousand. The monks, who find by their registers, that formerly ten or twelve thousand annually made this pilgrimage, never cease exclaiming that religion rapidly decays, and that the zeal of the faithful is nearly extinguished.[537]

Volney, however, thought that lack of money, not a falling-off of religious zeal,

was the real reason for the declining number of pilgrims. Even the most moderate pilgrimage was expensive, he found, never costing less than 4,000 livres, which he said was the equivalent of 166 pounds, a considerable sum at the time. When generous offerings were also made during the course of a pilgrimage, the total could easily rise to 50,000 or 60,000 livres (about 2,500 pounds).[538]

Most of the pilgrims arrived at Jaffa in November and went directly to Jerusalem, where they remained until after Easter, "lodged confusedly, by whole families, in the cells of the convents of their respective communions."[539] On Palm Sunday they made a mass exodus to purify themselves in the River Jordan. Volney was not very pleased by what he saw:

The reader must consult particular relations of this pilgrimage, to form an idea of the tumultuous march of this fanatic multitude into the plain of Jericho; the indecent and superstitious zeal with which they throw themselves, men, women, and children, naked into the Jordan; the fatigue they undergo before they reach the borders of the Dead Sea; the melancholy inspired by the sight of the gloomy rocks of that country, the most savage in nature....[540]

Once back in the Holy City, the pilgrims looked forward eagerly to witnessing the miracle of the Holy Fire, which, they believed, "*descends from heaven on the holy Saturday, brought by an angel.*"[541] Volney, however, injected the rationalist comment that "The Orientals still believe in this miracle, though the Franks acknowledge that the priests retire into the Sacristy, and effect what is done by very natural means." [542]

Far from experiencing religious ecstasies as a result of his visit, the levelheaded Volney focused on economic and social issues instead. He calculated, for example, that in a typical year the Christian pilgrimage, highlighted by the journey to the River Jordan, generated an income for the Ottoman governor amounting to 15,000 Turkish sequins, or 112,500 pounds. Only about half of this sum, however, went for the governor's own use. The other half he had to use to pay the expenses of the Turkish soldiers taking the pilgrims to the river and the passage rights demanded by the *bedouin*.[543]

Volney ended his account of Jerusalem on a pragmatic note. He commented that once Easter was over, each Christian traveler returned to his own country, proud of being able to use—like Muslims who had made the *hajj*—the honorable title of *Pilgrim*. Volney adds that Christian pilgrims even liked to style themselves *Mokudsi* ("the holy ones"), an honorific they said was derived from *al-Quds* or *al-Kuds* (The Holy), Jerusalem's name in Arabic. Volney also noticed that many Christian pilgrims were inclined to put on airs once they got back home, bragging about having been to the Holy City. This arrogance very much annoyed their stay-at-home colleagues. Thus Volney warns us in closing: "So much devotion does not, however, except these pilgrims from the proverbial censure thrown upon the *Hadjes* [the Muslim pilgrims to Mecca]; since the Christians say likewise: *beware of the pilgrims of Jerusalem*.[544]

François-Auguste-René de Chateaubriand (1805)

Author, diplomat, traveler and foremost literary figure in France during the early nineteenth century, Chateaubriand made a pilgrimage to Jerusalem in 1805–1806. His ambitions were secular and entirely self-centered. "J'allais chercher des images: violà tout [I went to gather impressions: that's all]," he boasted, and candidly admits that in the hundreds of pages of his *Itinéraire de Paris à Jérusalem, et de Jérusalem à Paris* (1810–1811), "je parle éternellement de moi [I speak eternally about myself]."[545] This unchecked egoism led him to boast that he was "the last Frenchman who left his country to travel in the Holy Land with the ideas, the goals, and the sentiments of a pilgrim of former times."[546]

The real legacy of Chateaubriand's pilgrimage, however, was the contribution it made to Orientalism, a venerable academic tradition which is now perhaps better known, especially to Americans, as Middle East area studies. According to Edward Said, a noted Palestinian-American literary critic (b. 1935 in Jerusalem), Chateaubriand's *Itinéraire* contained

> the first significant mention of an idea that will acquire an almost unbearable, next to mindless authority in European writing: *the theme of Europe teaching the Orient the meaning of liberty*, which is an ideal that Chateaubriand and everyone after him believed that Orientals, especially Muslims, knew nothing about.[547]

The notion that, left to their own devices, the Muslims of the Holy Land were entirely incapable of "progressing"—i.e., by developing democratic institutions on their own—helped set the stage for the Balfour Declaration of 1917 and British hegemony over Palestine, both of which are discussed below.

Ulrich Jasper Seetzen (1806)

Seetzen was a German scholar who went to the Middle East on behalf of the Goethe Museum to study, map and record the region. He is remembered today for having discovered, in 1806, the ruins of the Roman provincial city of Jerash, located about 30 miles north of Amman (Jordan). But Seetzen's comments about the economy of Jerusalem, which he visited that same year, are of interest, too.

The Holy City was at that time very much of an economic backwater. The only way for Christians there to make a living was to manufacture religious souvenirs and sell them to pilgrims in the city or export them to Western Europe. The result was the scene Seetzen describes in front of the Church of the Holy Sepulcher:

> The small square in front of the entrance to the Church of the Holy Sepulcher is continuously used as a small market for a variety of souvenirs which the pilgrims take back with them to their homeland. There they give them to their families and friends who regard them as valuable and cherished presents since everything that comes from Jerusalem is believed to be holy and that possession of them confers a blessing.[548]

The Muslims, too, were dependent on the Christian tourist trade: one of the few ways for Ottoman authorities to make money was to tax these souvenirs, most of which were manufactured in Bethlehem. They included rosaries of all kinds, some of them made from the bones of camels and water buffalo; crucifixes of wood, mother of pearl and other materials; models of the Holy Sepulcher, made of wood and inlaid with mother of pearl; glass articles (bead necklaces, bracelets, rings, mouthpieces of pipes, cups, porcelain); and, among the most expensive items, images of the Virgin Mary or of the saints, carved on sheets of flattened rhinoceros horn from Ethiopia.

Some of these trinkets were sold in Jerusalem itself; the rest were stored in a warehouse inside the Franciscan convent of Saint Savior's and then exported to agents in Italy, Spain and Portugal. Though modest in scale, this trade seems to have

been reasonably profitable. Seetzen probably overstated the case but says that

> on their sale in those parts depends the well-being of all the presently existing Latin convents in the Holy Land. Perhaps there are no articles in the world traded so profitably as these and one has to concede that this convent carries on the world's most lucrative trade. The Christian inhabitants of Bethlehem are the only ones who make them ... and so it can be said that it is the industry of the people of Bethlehem that supports all the convents in the Holy Land throughout the Levant.[549]

W. F. Sieber (1818)

Another secular pilgrim was the German physician and naturalist W. F. Sieber, who spent six weeks in Jerusalem in 1818 and who produced the first map of the city based on accurate topographic measurements and trigonometric calculations.[550] To do this, Sieber measured 200 different locations in Holy City. His map was a precursor of modern survey-based maps and was recognized at the time as a masterpiece. As soon as it was published it was warmly praised by geographers and scholars alike.

Alphonse de Lamartine (1833)

Lamartine, a French poet and statesman, was one of the key figures in the Romantic movement in French literature. He chronicled his 1833 visit to the Holy Land, Syria and Lebanon in *Voyages en Orient*, which was published two years later.

Using theatrical imagery, he described this pilgrimage as "the grand act" of his inner life. He then went on to sketch out what was in fact an imaginary Orient. "This Arab land," he solemnly assures the credulous reader, "is the land of prodigies; everything spouts there, and every credulous or fanatical man can become a prophet there in his turn."[551] The goal of his own pilgrimage is the Holy Sepulcher. Only after he finally reaches it does he somehow feel ready to return to his literary and political life in France.

Like Chateaubriand, Lamartine believed in the inevitability—indeed, the *necessity*—of Western hegemony in the Middle East. He describes the Muslim lands there simply as "nations without territory, *patrie* [homeland], rights, laws or security ... waiting anxiously for the shelter" which only European powers can provide.[552]

David Roberts (1839)

Born in Edinburgh in 1796, David Roberts began his artistic career as a house-painter and decorator. The turning point in his life came in 1838, when he set off for Egypt and the Holy Land as a painter-pilgrim to record the monuments and people there.[553]

He had long wanted to visit Palestine. Reaching the port of Jaffa in the spring of 1839, in one of his first pictures he depicted Polish Jews, wearing their traditional black broad-brimmed hats, who were making their way to Jerusalem. Later, as he crossed the plain of Sharon en route to Jerusalem, he joyously noted in his diary:

> Since childhood I have not felt such a perfect enjoyment of the beauties of nature; and this exhilaration of spirits can only, I think, be felt by those who have passed through the [Egyptian] desert to this beautiful country. The ground seems carpeted with wild flowers and the country, independent of its great

In his paintings, Roberts carefully edited out most of the dirt, confusion and clutter of daily life in the Middle East, leaving only dramatic scenes remarkable for their purity and simplicity of line. This is entitled *The Mosque of Omar, Shewing the Ancient Site of the Temple.* (Trustees of the British Museum.)

interest, is the most lovely I have ever beheld. The plain is studded with small villages with here and there groups of palms. The mountains of Judea bound the view and beyond this is the great city [Jerusalem].[554]

Since it was Easter, the Holy City was crowded with pilgrims. In the Armenian convent alone there were more than 1,000 visitors. Despite the huge crowds, Roberts managed to finish a number of admirable paintings of Jerusalem. Under the dead hand of late Ottoman rule, however, the Holy City had become choked with garbage. Roberts confided to his diary that "surely there cannot be any city more wretched.... On comparing the ponderous stones still remaining of the great temple with the superbundant [*sic*] rubbish heaped over them I have often laid down my pencil in despair."[555]

As the first painter-pilgrim, Roberts enjoyed an enormous success. His *Sketches of the Holy Land and Syria*, published in 1850 after his return to England, won him lasting fame and are frequently reproduced today. A British art magazine assured its readers in 1858 that "The fruits of this expedition are too well known to require pointing out—'Roberts' Holy Land' has a world-wide reputation; nothing of a similar character has ever been produced that can bear comparison with it."[556]

This verdict still stands today. One of his best lithographs, entitled *The Mosque of Omar, Shewing the Ancient Site of the Temple*, is set at al-Aqsa Mosque, not far from the Dome of the Rock. It depicts a group of Greek Christians praying, Muslim-style, in the direction of the Holy Sepulcher. The ruins of the ancient Jewish temple can be seen in the background.

Lady Francis Egerton (1840)

Lady Francis' account of her visit to Jerusalem, entitled *Journal of a Tour in the Holy Land, in May and June, 1840*, was written as a private diary. It was published in 1841 only to generate revenue for a charity, the Ladies Hibernian Female School Society. This book is an excellent example of how pilgrimage and tourism can overlap.

Lady Francis was a devout Christian, although as an upper class English Protestant she found it essential to suppress any public display of emotion:

We are arrived at Jerusalem! I certainly never expected to find myself here, and the anxious desire of my heart is fulfilled. I am *very* thankful.... The Mount of Olives, which I have so longed to see! The sight of it, and the city where that was transacted which has procured us salvation and felicity hereafter ... had a strange effect on me, which I shall never forget. Had I been alone, I should have cried; but one must not give way to these emotions in public....[557]

Her religious feelings, however, did not prevent her from appreciating and carefully recording the most colorful aspects of her journey:

We left Ramla at eleven o'clock. We met multitudes of pilgrims on their way from Jerusalem, where they had been attending the ceremonies of the holy week; Armenians, Georgians, etc., such as we had already seen in Jaffa, strange, picturesque-looking people, men, women, and children; their horses piled up with beds, bags, pipes, and goods of all descriptions and their riders perched upon the top of all, enveloped in cloaks, hoods, boots, and strange jackets, looking like monuments of rags.[558]

Lady Francis, however, was not one to let the picturesque dull her rationalist senses. She was quite appalled by what she had heard about the ceremony of the Holy Fire:

> We are come too late for the Easter ceremonies here. I am glad of it. They present a most disgraceful scene of violence, superstition, fraud, and schism. On Easter-even, the church of the Holy Sepulchre is crowded with Christians of the Greek and Latin churches, fighting for the holy fire, which the Greek priests have pretended to cause to issue, as from heaven, from two apertures in the sepulchre; and the confusion, and squabbling, and screaming, and struggling who shall first light his taper by this holy fire, is most disgraceful and disgusting.[559]

Edward Robinson (1841)

Professor of Biblical Literature at the Union Theological Seminary in New York City, Robinson left the United States in 1837 to explore Palestine and Syria. In 1841 he published *Biblical Researches in Palestine, Mount Sinai, and Arabia Petraea*, a work which won him academic fame and established his reputation as the father of biblical archeology and geography. Robinson's book became the definitive account and was used by most English and American travelers and Protestant biblical students.[560]

A careful and conscientious scholar, Robinson wanted to educate his readers. "My one great objective," he says,

> was the city itself: its topographical and historical relations, its site, its hills, its dales, its remains of antiquity, the traces of its ancient population; in short, everything connected with it that could have a bearing on the illustration of the Scriptures.[561]

Despite his commitment to objectivity, Robinson was also able to convey to readers his own enthusiasm for his subject:

> The feelings of a Christian traveller on approaching Jerusalem can better be conceived than described. Mine were strongly excited.... From the earliest childhood I had read of and studied the localities of this sacred spot; now I beheld them with my own eyes; and they all seemed familiar to me, like the realization of a former dream. I seemed to be again among cherished scenes of childhood, long unvisited, indeed, but distinctly recollected. At length "our feet stand within thy gates, O Jerusalem!"[562]

One reason for Robinson's success was that he took pains to base his work not only on personal exploration but also on a high degree of skepticism. Although he was a Christian himself, he refused to accept hearsay accounts of the Holy Land. He emphasized instead that "*all ecclesiastical tradition respecting the ancient places in and around Jerusalem* IS OF NO VALUE, *except so far as it is supported by circumstances known to us from the Scriptures, or from other contemporary testimony.*"[563] This kind of skepticism would prove to be the hallmark of other secular travelers, many of whom would downplay or reject the Scriptures themselves.

W. H. Bartlett (1842)

Bartlett was a British secular pilgrim who visited Jerusalem in the summer of 1842 in order to write a "clear, connected and accurate" guidebook to the Holy City. He accomplished this in 1843, when *Walks About the City and Environs of Jerusalem* was published. He followed it up with another book, *A Pilgrimage through the Holy Land*, in 1851.

Unlike ghostly pilgrims, Bartlett has little to say about Christianity *per se* but a great deal to say about the logistics of visiting the holy sites. We can see how far we have come from devotional pilgrimages by noting how he introduces Jerusalem to the reader:

If the traveller can forget that he is treading on the grave of a people from which his religion has sprung, on the dust of her kings, prophets, and holy men, there is certainly no city in the world that he would rather leave than Jerusalem. Nothing can be more void of interest than her gloomy, half-ruinous streets and poverty stricken bazaars, which, except at the period of the pilgrimage at Easter, present no signs of life or study of character to the observer.[564]

Even the most celebrated sites fail to impress him:

The center of attraction to the devoted but ignorant multitude is, of course, the Church of the Sepulchre; and marshalled by their respective religious guides, they rush with frantic eagerness to its portal, and in this excited state visit the many stations invented or imagined in credulous ages. The whole scene of Christ's crucifixion and entombment are before the eye with such vividness, that even Protestants who come to scoff, have hardly been able to resist the contagious effect of sympathy.[565]

The Mount of Calvary left a poor impression, too. It is "almost entirely disfigured by marble and decorations." Its "contrivances"—spurious holes for crosses and a fissure allegedly produced by an earthquake when Christ died—"tend both to produce disgust, and to weaken our faith in the locality."[566] Mount Sion, where David once ruled, presents a desolate pic-

ture as well: "a flock of goats, with a solitary shepherd, or at long intervals an Arab woman, slowly mounting the steep ascent, alone relieve the melancholy vacancy of a scene, which in general is as silent as the grave."[567]

He manages to praise the Armenian convent ("the only building in Jerusalem that presents any considerable appearance of comfort") but pours scorn on the Jewish Quarter. "If the traveller have [*sic*] the courage to inhale the infected air of its close alleys, reeking with putrid filth," he tells us, "he will soon hasten out of them with the deepest impression of the misery and social degradation of their unhappy occupants."[568]

Bartlett did, however, pay a warm tribute to the Jews' unflagging devotion to the Temple and to their confidence it would rise again:

The Jews of Jerusalem have obtained permission to assemble [on the Mount of Olives] to lament over the desolation of their people, and to implore the restoration of the scene of their former glory, changing in mournful melody, not unmingled with a dawn of hope:

"Lord, build—Lord, build—
Build Thy house speedily.
In haste! In haste! Even in our days
Build Thy house speedily."[569]

Eliot Warburton (1844)

In 1844 this English pilgrim wrote a guidebook which appeared in 17 editions over more than 40 years and which awoke in British readers "a sort of *patriotism for Palestine*"—a memorable phrase we will meet again in the pages to come.[570] Warburton's popular book, entitled *The Crescent and the Cross; of Romance and Realities of Eastern Travel*, echoed the convictions of many British pilgrims that their own country was destined to help "liberate" Palestine from Turkish rule. This conviction had a practical aspect, too: it was widely believed that England should "boldly assert" its right-of-way through Palestine and Egypt to its empire in India.[571]

Imperialism aside, *The Crescent and the Cross* contained much information of use to prospective pilgrims. The author's enthusiasm for his subject is infectious. Quoting unnamed "pilgrim-authorities," Warburton tells us the faithful believe "the pardons of the Holy Land begin at Jaffa" and that "he who walks six paces into Palestine shall never lose his soul."[572] He then goes on explain the unique quality of the Holy City itself:

> A residence in Jerusalem, for a solitary pilgrim like myself, is one of the strangest experiences of life. Apart from the associations by which it is hallowed, it is unlike any other city on earth. Its population consists, as it were, not of its own people, but rather resembles the inmates of some great carvanserai, accidentally huddled together, denizens of distant places, professors of various creeds, each hating and fearing each other as an alien and a stranger.[573]

Warburton reported that 20,000 Christians visited Jerusalem every spring and that "many shiploads of Moslems, transported in steamers at the Sultan's expense, also arrive annually at Jaffa, on their route to the Holy Land."[574] For many Jews, however, going to Jerusalem was a one-way trip. "The Jew performs no pilgrimage;" Warburton tells us, "if he visits the Holy City, it is in hope of dying there, and laying his bones in the Valley of Jehoshaphat."[575] Shiploads of Jewish skeletons were disembarked at Jaffa and from there were transported to Jerusalem for burial.

Jerusalem was not a rich city at the time of Warburton's visit. Only about 12,000 people lived there. Since there was little commerce to support them, the Jews, Latins and Greeks depended almost entirely on alms and on the pilgrim trade. There was a distinct undercurrent of hostility in Jerusalem:

> At one corner of the city you meet the scowl of some malignant Jew, who considers your [Christian] presence a profanation to his Holy City, and at another you encounter a fanatical Moslem, cursing the unhallowed foot that approaches the precincts of Omar's Mosque. Each sectary [believer] of the Cross or Crescent ... regards his heretic neighbour with pious horror, intermingled with contempt.[576]

Despite the city's shortcomings, however, Warburton gave it high marks for romance and local color. He was especially captivated by the annual pilgrimage to the River Jordan at Easter. We can easily imagine that his readers, living under the damp gray skies of England, were enthralled, too. Warburton writes:

> It is an imposing sight to witness that long array of pilgrims winding through the gloomy Passes of the Judean hills, with the brilliant sunshine flashing on the bristling spears of the Bedouin, and the gorgeous trappings of the Albanian cavalry; the long necks of the camels peering high over the mass, and the eager, huddling movement of the timorous crowd. Woe to the poor pilgrim who lags behind, or is overtaken at nightfall on the outskirt [*sic*] of the camp! They are vigilantly beset by the children of Ishmael, who consider the privilege of robbing as being theirs by divine right.[577]

Conrad Schick (1846)

A major figure in the study of Jerusalem's architecture and archeology, Dr. Conrad Schick was a German architect who brought to the Holy Land some of the building ideas of nineteenth century Europe. He initially came to Jerusalem a Protestant missionary in 1846 but during the course of the next 50 years he ended up planning many buildings and neighborhoods in the city, blending old and new and introducing new techniques of design and construction. For example, he helped design the Mea Shearim quarter outside the walls of the Old City as a continuous block of settlement where each set of houses was built around a communal courtyard. Mea Shearim is now the home of many ultra–Orthodox Jews.

In addition, Schick worked closely with the Palestine Exploration Fund (described below), discovering in 1867 the "Garden Tomb," a first-century tomb very similar to the biblical description of the tomb in which Christ was buried. He later served as a city engineer in the Turkish-administered part of Jerusalem. He even built a scale model of the Temple Mount and the Dome of the Rock. He sold this for 800 gold pieces, a considerable sum in those days—enough to encourage him to plan a beautiful home for himself and his family. When it was finished, he called this dwelling Tabor House, a name drawn from Psalm 89:12: "The north and the south Thou has created them; Tabor and Hermon shall rejoice in Thy name."[578] Tabor House is now the site of the Swedish Theological Seminary.

Schick's letters, plans, reports and the collection of photographs he sent back to Europe constitute one of the most significant archives at the Palestine Exploration Fund's office in London. He did not take photographs himself but instead collected and sent off pictures which illustrated some point or event that he considered significant. Today these documents are consulted by geographers, architects, archeologists and historians alike.

The Crimean War and the opening of the Haram (1855)

Named for the Crimean peninsula in the Ukraine where much of the fighting took place, the Crimean War (1853–1856) pitted Britain, France and the Ottoman Turks against the Russians. This conflict has such a tangled diplomatic history that we can touch on it only briefly here.[579] Basically the war came about because of conflicting ambitions of the great powers in the Middle East, e.g., Russia's aim of controlling Constantinople. What is most remarkable, however, is that the war itself was actually sparked by a trivial religious incident in Jerusalem.

In 1847 a fracas broke out between the Greek and Latin priests who held services at the Church of the Nativity.[580] These clergymen traded violent accusations about a missing religious ornament known as "the silver star." Blood was shed during this fight. Three years later, in 1850, Prince Louis Napoleon, recently elected President of France, decided to reassert and enforce certain traditional rights regarding the custody and administration of the holy places in Jerusalem. These rights, originally granted to French Catholics in the Middle East in 1535, had been restated in 1673 and enlarged in agreements known as the Capitulations of 1740. Since then, the Orthodox Christian community had undermined the rights of the French Catholics by taking possession of the keys to the north and south gates of the Church of the Holy Sepulchre and of the grotto of the Holy Manger in Jerusalem.[581]

In 1853 Czar Nicholas I of Russia demanded the right to intervene in order to protect Orthodox shrines and Orthodox pilgrims in Jerusalem. Toward this end he moved troops into the Turkish Balkans (Romania). However, counting on British support, the Turks refused to yield to Russian demands. The British were prepared to confront the Russians because they feared that their own access to the Middle East and India would be jeopardized if the Russians held the Balkans. The French, for their part, cast themselves in the role of protectors of the Catholics. The upshot of this mutual intractability was that war was declared in 1854.

The British and French fleets landed troops on the Crimean peninsula at the Russian naval base of Sevastopol. There was heavy fighting at Balaklava (which Tennyson immortalized in his poem "The Charge of the Light Brigade") and at Inkerman. A British nurse, Florence Nightingale, won lasting fame for her efforts to help the large number of sick and wounded. The British and French captured Sevastopol in 1855 and the Russians were defeated. The Crimean War was formally brought to an end by a treaty signed in Paris in 1856.

The Crimean War had a positive effect on pilgrimages to Jerusalem. As a sign of their good intentions, in 1855 the Ottoman Turks had opened the Haram itself to non–Muslim pilgrims for the first time in hundreds of years. The earliest Western visitors to the Haram were the duke and duchess of Brabant (Belgium). They were followed a few months later by the famous British philanthropist Sir Moses Montefiore, who had made the first of his seven pilgrimages to Jerusalem in 1827 and would make the last in 1875 at the age of 91. In 1855, while reading Psalm 121 ("I will lift up my eyes to the hills...."), Sir Moses had himself carried up to the Haram in a sedan chair—to prevent his feet from inadvertently profaning any spot holy to the Jews.

Moses Hess (1862)

A German journalist and socialist, Moses Hess was an early spokesman for what would come to be called Zionism. After experiencing anti–Semitism himself, he wrote *Rom und Jerusalem, die letzte Nationalitätsfrage* (*Rome and Jerusalem: A Study in Jewish Nationalism*). Hess never visited Jerusalem himself and his book was not widely read at the time of its publication in 1862. It did, however, make a strong impact on later Zionist leaders, such as Theodor Herzl, who came to share two of Hess' basic conclusions.

The first of these was that until the Jews had a country of their own they would always be a homeless people and would never be fully accepted by other nationalities. The second conclusion was that with the help of the major European powers, who could either purchase or colonize the Holy Land, the Jews could free Jerusalem from the Ottoman yoke and establish their own socialist society in Palestine.[582]

In his book, Hess cited what he claimed was "an old legend" to make his point. According to this tale, a knight left Europe to take part in the First Crusade. A friend of his—a pious rabbi—remained at home, immersed in the study of the Talmud. Months later, after the knight returned home again, he appeared suddenly at midnight in the rabbi's study. The rabbi was still absorbed in the Talmud. The knight said to him:

> God's greetings to you, dear old friend. I have returned from the Holy Land and bring you from there a pledge of our friendship. What I gained by my sword, you are striving to obtain with our spirit. Our ways lead to the same goal.[583]

So saying, the knight handed the rabbi a withered rose from Jericho. The rabbi took the rose thankfully and moistened it with his tears. Immediately, the rose began to bloom again in its full glory and splendor. The rabbi said to the knight:

Do not wonder, my friend, that the withered rose bloomed again in my hands. The rose possesses the same characteristics as our people: it comes to life again at the touch of the warm breath of love, in spite of its having been torn from its own soil and left to wither in foreign lands. So will Israel bloom again in youthful splendor; and the spark, at present smoldering under the ashes, will burst once more into a bright flame.[584]

Albert, Prince of Wales (1862)

In December 1861, Prince Albert, Queen Victoria's consort, died in Windsor Castle of typhoid fever, plunging the Queen into lifelong mourning. It is said that one of Albert's last wishes was that his eldest son—Albert, Prince of Wales—should visit the Holy Land and other parts of the Middle East. Since the 21-year-old Albert was not the well-behaved, prim-and-proper gentleman his father wanted him to be, the Queen agreed that a pilgrimage to Jerusalem and other travels in the region might help mature him. Moreover, it would be good for him to get away from the grief surrounding the royal family after his father's death. The trip was accordingly arranged in 1862.

Lest young Albert fail to grasp the historical and religious significance of what he was about to see, he was accompanied on his travels by the Dean of Westminster, Arthur Penrhyn Stanley, the foremost British scholar on the Holy Land. Stanley's guidebook, *Sinai and Palestine*, first published in 1856 and revised after the 1862 visit, would become the indispensable companion of all British travelers up

to the eve of World War I.[585] To record the trip for posterity, a photographer, Francis Bedford, came along, too, and produced an album of 182 plates showing the mid-nineteenth century layout of Jerusalem.[586]

Thanks to these careful preparations, Albert's visit to Jerusalem was a success. The prince enjoyed himself there and even had a Jerusalem Cross tattooed on his arm. (Taken from the armorial trappings of the feudal Kingdom of Jerusalem, a Jerusalem Cross is a large cross flanked on all four sides by smaller crosses.) Albert gave a royal stamp of approval to the Jerusalem pilgrimage and thereby encouraged many middle-class British travelers to come to the Holy Land later on.

Charles Wilson (1865)

The first archeological excavations in Jerusalem were conducted by the French scholar Félicien de Saulcy, who in 1860 unearthed royal tombs north of the Old City.[587] His discoveries occurred at a time when a growing number of Europeans believed that a new, peaceful, "scientific crusade" to modernize the Holy City would hasten the fall of the decrepit Ottoman Turks and bring Palestine permanently under Western control. As opening gun of this campaign, in 1865 the British decided to undertake an Ordnance Survey of Jerusalem.

Captain Charles Wilson of the Royal Engineers was chosen to lead this expedition. One of its goals was to improve the water supply of Jerusalem, which was then severely polluted. In the course of his work, Wilson produced a fine map of the city and its immediate environs. This was the first map of any part of the Holy Land that used contour lines to show topography. His map of Jerusalem was so good, in fact, that it has been hailed as "the first perfectly accurate map, even in the eyes of

The Ottoman Turks let Jerusalem slip into decay during the nineteenth century but took good care of their own officials. Now one of the landmarks of Jerusalem, the American Colony Hotel was built in 1860 as the palace of a Pasha, an official who bore the highest title of honor in the Ottoman Empire. This dining room still reflects the elegance of a long-gone era. (Photograph courtesy Garo Nalbandian.)

modern cartography."[588] For secular pilgrims arriving in the Holy Land, this new map effectively displaced medieval notions of sacred geography, which had traditionally been based on theology rather than on topography.

Wilson was not only a good map-

This Jerusalem cross is built into a wall of the Old City. (Photograph by the author.)

maker but also a good publicist. His discovery of what came to be called "Wilson's Arch," located in the subterranean cisterns of the Haram, led directly to the foundation of the Palestine Exploration Fund. In 1866 he carried out further reconnaissance and survey work in Palestine, paying particular attention to the archeology and ancient synagogues of the region. The next year he volunteered to take part in the Ordnance Survey of Sinai, during which he retraced the Exodus route the Israelites may have taken when they fled from Egypt.

Wilson also studied the prehistoric and Byzantine archeology of the area. He edited a huge four-volume opus, *Picturesque Palestine* (1880), which was aimed at the general reader. It was highlighted by many illustrations and by numerous articles contributed by illustrious people.

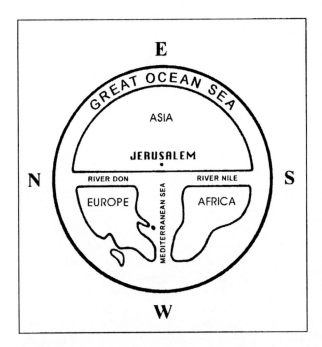

E

GREAT OCEAN SEA

ASIA

JERUSALEM

N   RIVER DON   RIVER NILE   S

EUROPE   MEDITERRANEAN SEA   AFRICA

W

Medieval "T in O" maps of the world reflected a sacred geography, not a physical geography. The map shown here is oriented toward the east, i.e., toward Asia, the direction in which Jerusalem lies from Western Europe. The Holy City itself is the center of the map. The Don and the Nile rivers form the top of the "T," while the Mediterranean forms its base. The lands of the earth are encompassed within the "O" formed by the "Great Ocean Sea," the ultimate destination of all the running waters of the world. (Eklectica Graphic Design.)

From 1886 to 1894, Wilson was Director-General of the Ordnance Survey. Throughout his long career he stayed in close touch with the Palestine Exploration Fund, serving as its Chairman from 1901 to 1906.

The Palestine Exploration Fund (1865)

The British "patriotism for Palestine," first articulated by Warburton, found its fullest expression in the Palestine Exploration Fund (PEF), which was set up in London in 1865. The Fund made its mark by consistently taking a scientific, non-political, non-religious approach

to the Holy Land. Between 1865 and 1914 the Fund was on the cutting edge of secular pilgrimages to Jerusalem. The reasons are not far to seek. The Fund is still active today. According to the Fund's website,

> The purpose of the PEF was (and is) to promote research into the archeology and history, manners and customs and culture, topography, geology and natural resources of Palestine and the Levant. The PEF now has a history rich in association with many of the outstanding names of Levantine exploration.... The PEF was central to the development of archeology in the region, undertaking ambitious and well-chosen projects that significantly enhanced the knowledge of those working in the area. However, its subject-base has never been limited to archeology alone, but includes natural history, anthropology, history and geography.[589]

By 1865 the British "patriotism for Palestine" was so strong that it almost seemed as though the Holy Land actually *belonged* to the British. Speaking figuratively, the first president of the Fund, the Archbishop of York, told the members of the Fund at the inaugural ceremony that

> The country of Palestine belongs to you and to me; it is essentially ours. It is the land from which news came of our Redemption. It is the land we turn to as the foundation of all our hopes. It is the land to which we look with as true a patriotism as we do this dear old England.[590]

Thanks to its impressive list of achievements, the Fund became one of the most important organizations during the formative years of archeology in the Holy Land. It conducted excavations in Jerusalem in 1867–1870 and at Tell el-Hesi (the word "tell" comes from the Arabic *tall*, meaning a mound or a hill) in southern Palestine in 1890–1893.

These projects are still important to scholars because they produced the primary data for Jerusalem which all subsequent excavations below ground have used. At Tell el-Hesi they established the first chronological framework through which artifacts could be organized meaningfully. Moreover, the Fund was also responsible for the first accurate geographical survey of the whole of Palestine west of the River Jordan—the ground-breaking *Survey of Western Palestine*, published between 1881 and 1884. Today the Fund publishes an academic journal, the *Palestine Exploration Quarterly*. It also presents lectures on a wide range of projects, funds several research projects in the Middle East and produces a monograph series.

Charles Warren (1867)

One of the great names of Holy Land archeology is that of Charles Warren (1840–1927), a captain in the Royal Engineers. Between 1867 and 1870 he carried out explorations in Palestine that formed the basis for scholarly knowledge of the topography of ancient Jerusalem and the archeology of the Temple Mount. This was the first major expedition of the Palestine Exploration Fund. It aroused in Britain such interest that large sums were collected by public subscription to carry out a later Survey of Western Palestine.

The Ottoman Turks would not let Warren desecrate the Haram by digging into it. He therefore rented land around the southern edge of the structure and proceeded to sink deep shafts and lateral underground passages which brought him to the base of the Haram's walls. One reason the British public was so interested in Warren's work was that he wrote very well. Here is how he describes a dig near the Haram:

> Our progress through these passages had been rapid, but unhappily the hammer-blows, resounding through the hollow walls in so unwanted a manner, alarmed the modern representative of the old High Priest. Infuriate [*sic*] with anger, the fine old sheikh would listen to no reasoning; but repairing to the south-east angle of the old Temple enclosure, mounted its battlements and summoned the Sheikh of Siloam to stand forth and answer for his misdeeds. With full turban and long flowing robes, edges tipped with fur, the old man stood, on the edge of the steep masonry, stamping his feet with rage and bellowing imprecations.[591]

Warren and his chief assistant, Sergeant Henry Birtles, ran great risks when investigating the ancient watercourses under the north side of the Haram. At one point, the two men decided to follow a very narrow, smooth-sided passage cut deep into the rock. Warren tells us that in it "the sewage was five to six feet deep, so that if we had fallen into it there was no chance of escaping with our lives."[592]

Our intrepid explorers were not deterred, however, and managed to find three old doors. Warren said that "The sewage was not water, and it was not mud; it was just in such a state that a door would not float, but if left for a minute or two would not sink very deep."[593] By gingerly walking on these doors (pulling the rearmost door from the slime and putting it down in front of them as they progressed), Warren and Birtles began to penetrate the sewer. Warren remembered that

We laid the first door on the sewage, then one in front of it, taking care to keep ourselves each on a door; then taking up the hinder of the three doors it was passed to the front, and so we moved on…. Everything had now become so slippery with sewage that we had to exercise the greatest caution in lowering the doors and ourselves down, lest an unlucky false step might cause a header into the murky liquid—a fall which might have been fatal—and what honor would there be in dying like a rat in a pool of sewage?[594]

Fortunately, there were no false steps. The men made their way 60 feet into the sewer, at which point further progress was blocked by a dam designed to retain sewage flowing in from another part of the Haram.

Mark Twain (1867)

Embarking on a famous literary pilgrimage, the American novelist and humorist Mark Twain sailed from New York in 1867 aboard the steamship *Quaker City*. He chronicled his trip to Europe and the Holy Land in *The Innocents Abroad* (1869), one of the most celebrated travel books ever written by an American. Twain's ability to cast even the logistics of travel in a humorous light still makes good reading. Here, for example, is an account of what his fellow passengers did when their ship neared the Holy Land:

Such a burrowing into the hold for trunks that had lain buried there for weeks, yes, for months; such a hurrying to and from above decks and below; such a riotous system of packing and unpacking; such a littering up of the cabins with shirts and skirts … such a cleaning and loading of revolvers and examining of bowie knives … then such a poring over ancient maps; such a

reading up of Bibles and Palestine travels … and morning, noon, and night, such mass meetings in cabins, such speech-making, such sage suggestions, such worrying and quarrelling, and such a general raising of the very mischief was never seen in the ship before![595]

When, however, after a long trip from Lebanon on horseback Twain and the other pilgrims finally reached Jerusalem, they were quite disappointed. "So small!" Twain remarks, "Why, it was no larger than an American village of four thousand inhabitants…. A fast walker could go outside the walls of Jerusalem and walk entirely around the city in an hour. I do not know how else to make one understand how small it is." [596]

Twain was struck by the number of Christian sects in the Holy City, listing them as the Greeks, Latins, Armenians, Syrians, Copts, Abyssinians, Greeks Catholics and a handful of Protestants. He also took note of the great diversity of the population. "It seems to me," he tells us, "that all the races and colors and tongues of the earth must be represented among the fourteen thousand souls that dwell in Jerusalem."[597] Like most other pilgrims who visited the Holy Land during the long twilight of the Ottoman Empire, Twain was appalled by the squalor he found there:

Rags, wretchedness, poverty, and dirt, those signs and symbols that indicate the presence of Muslim rule more surely than the crescent flag itself, abound. Lepers, cripples, the blind, and the idiotic assail you on every hand, and they know but one work of but one language apparently—the eternal "baksheesh" [a request for alms]. To see the numbers of maimed, malformed, and diseased humanity that throng the holy places and obstructed the gates, one might suppose that the ancient days had come again, and that the angel of the Lord was expected to descend at any moment to stir the waters of Bethesda. Jerusalem is mournful and dreary and lifeless. I would not desire to live here.[598]

Most of the holy sites did not make a favorable impression on Twain, either. He noted that the Stone of Unction, on which Jesus' body was believed to have been laid in preparation for burial, had to be hidden under a marble slab because "pilgrims were much given to chipping off pieces of it to carry home."[599] To his eye, the Holy Sepulcher itself was "scandalized by trumpery, gewgaws, and tawdry ornamentation," while the monks there, incessantly "flitting about in the gloom" with their candles, made "the dim of the church more dismal than there is any necessity it should be, even though it is a tomb."[600]

Muslim holy places did not escape Twain's gentle criticism, either. Citing the Islamic belief that the Rock had tried to follow the Prophet Muhammad when he ascended to heaven but that the angel Gabriel had restrained it, Twain jokes, "Very few people have a grip like Gabriel—the prints of his monstrous fingers, two inches deep, are to be seen in that rock today."[601]

Two sites did, however, meet with Twain's approval because there was no doubt of their authenticity. The first was the Western Wall:

At that portion of the ancient wall of Solomon's Temple, which is called the Jew's Place of Wailing, and where the Hebrews assemble every Friday to kiss the venerated stones and weep over the fallen greatness of Zion, anyone can see a part of the unquestioned and undisputed Temple of Solomon.[602]

The second site was the lower level of the Aqsa Mosque, which attracted him for the same reason:

Down in the hollow ground, underneath the olives and the orange trees that flourish in the court of the great mosque, is a wilderness of pillars—remains of the ancient temple; they supported it…. It is pleasant to know that we are disappointed, in that we never dreamed we might see portions of the actual Temple of Solomon and yet experience no shadow of suspicion that they were a monkish humbug and a fraud.[603]

Mark Twain was nothing if not good-natured. This is how he sums up his pilgrimage to Jerusalem:

Our experiences in Europe have taught us that in time this fatigue will be forgotten; the heat will be forgotten; the thirst, the tiresome volubility of the guide, the persecutions of the beggars—and then, all that will be left will be pleasant memories of Jerusalem, memories we shall call up with increasing interest as the years go by, memories which someday will become all beautiful when the last annoyance that encumbers them shall have faded out of our minds, never to return…. We are satisfied. We can wait. Our reward will come. To us Jerusalem and today's experiences will be an enchanted memory a year hence—a memory which money could not buy from us.[604]

Thomas Cook (1869)[605]

Founder of the worldwide travel agency Thomas Cook and Son, Cook left school at the age of 10 and later became a Baptist missionary. He first showed his talent as a travel agent by persuading a British railroad to run a special train between Leicester and Loughborough for a temperance meeting. Then he conducted "Grand Tours" from Leicester to France for the Paris Exhibition of 1855.

In the spring of 1869 Cook laid the

A Thomas Cook party in the Holy Land in 1903. The British firm of Thomas Cook prided itself in being able to provide a full range of services to travelers. Its Jerusalem office bore a large sign which read: "Thos. Cook & Son have the largest staff of dragomans [interpreters and guides] and muleteers. Also are sole proprietors of the best landaus [elegant carriages], carriages, camp equipments, saddlery, etc., in Palestine & Syria." (Thomas Cook Archives.)

foundation of subsequent trips to Egypt and the Holy Land when he took more than 30 travelers up the Nile by steamer and then escorted a party of roughly twice that size through Palestine. He returned to the Middle East later that year, accompanied by a small party of friends, to attend the opening of the Suez Canal. This great waterway made travel to India quicker, safer and more comfortable. The nascent travel business boomed. At Alexandria, India-bound steamers had to moor for a week to take on more coal and provisions. Cook promptly seized the opportunity to offer trips to the Holy Land during this necessary delay.

Tourists and pilgrims believed that Cook and his colleagues could be trusted to give them the facts about what they were seeing. In 1876, for example, the well-thumbed guidebook known as *Cook's Handbook* had this to say about the Via Dolorosa ("The Way of Sorrows"), the route Christ allegedly followed while carrying the cross:

No one can traverse its curious zigzags and look at its "holy places" with indifference, as it is sacred with the tears of many generations of pilgrims, who, according to their faith, strove to follow in the footsteps of the Lord. As a mere hard and dry matter of fact, however, there is no historical evidence whatever for the street was not even known until the fourteenth century.[606]

By the end of the nineteenth century, Thomas Cook and Son had arranged travel to Palestine for about 12,000 people. Thus his firm's contribution to the reemergence of the Protestant pilgrimage was considerable.[607]

Claude Reignier Conder (1872)

In 1872 Lieutenant Conder was appointed head of the Palestine Exploration Fund's Survey of Western Palestine. "The main object of the Survey of Palestine," he wrote,

> may be said to have been to collect materials in illustration of the Bible. Few stronger confirmations of the historic and authentic character of the Sacred Volume can be imagined than that furnished by a comparison of the Land and the Book, which shows clearly that they tally in every respect.[608]

The Survey's objectives were threefold: Biblical topography, archeology and "the study of the people." Conder had mixed feelings about the Holy City itself. From one point of view, it was quite disappointing:

> Jerusalem is a very ugly city. It is badly built of mean stone houses perched on the slope of the watershed, and seems in constant danger of sliding into the Kedron Valley ... the city as a whole is not beautiful; its flat-roofed houses and dirty lanes are neither pleasing nor healthy, and the surrounding chalk hills are barren and shapeless....[609]

At the same time, Conder found, the city exerted a compelling attraction:

> To the antiquary, nevertheless, Jerusalem is the most fascinating place in Palestine, and the longer one lives within its walls, the greater becomes one's interest in the "Jerusalem question." The present town stands on mounds of rubbish which average thirty feet in depth, and reach in places one

hundred feet above the rock. Nor is this a matter for astonishment when we remember how often the city has been razed to the ground.[610]

Conder was present at the ceremony of the Holy Fire. Like most Western observers, he had nothing good to say about it:

> Every educated Greek knows it to be a shameful imposition; but the ignorant Syrians and the fanatical Russian peasants still believe the fire to descend from heaven. The clergy dare not enlighten them, and that crafty diplomacy which encourages pilgrimages to Jerusalem by government aid, fosters the superstition which is the main inducement for the Russian pilgrims to visit the Holy City.[611]

Conder returned to England in 1875 after having surveyed 4,700 square miles of Palestine. The remaining 1,300 square miles of the Survey were finished by his colleague and friend, Lieutenant Horatio Kitchener. In 1881–1882, however, Conder was back in the field on behalf of the Palestine Exploration Fund. He discovered a lost city in Syria, began to survey the lands east of the River Jordan, learned Arabic and studied the ancient languages of Altaic and Hittite as well. Conder remained on the Executive Committee of the Palestine Exploration Fund until his death in 1910.

Ignaz Goldhizer (1873)

Acclaimed as the founder of the modern Islamic studies in the West, the Jewish scholar Ignaz Goldhizer spent the years 1873 and 1874 on an intensive study tour of the Near East. Like many other pilgrims, he had mixed views about the Holy City. On the one hand, he was struck with a tremor of "sacred awe" as the walls of the

Old City and the buildings on the Temple Mount came into view. "In that moment," he tells us,

> when I saw Zion the first time in my life with my own eyes, there awoke in me something entirely different from the deep contempt with which I relate to Pharisaism.[612] I did not think of the priests and Levites who carried on their absurd formalism in the high and mighty butcher's stall of Jerusalem.... I thought of the calumniated, persecuted prophetism of the Hebrew past, of the prophetism of the future, of the new Jerusalem, that "liberated" and rebuilt by spirit and thought, will become the place of pilgrimage of all those who, with a free mind, erect a new Zion for the Jehova [God] of freedom that embraces the whole of mankind.[613]

On the other hand, however, Goldhizer found that the contemporary inhabitants of the Holy City, Jews and Christians alike, left much to be desired. They were "disgusting people," "idlers," "religious swindlers," he says—to the extent he was forced to conclude, "If one wants to be sobered up in matters of religion, let him but come to Jerusalem."[614]

One of Goldhizer's scholarly accomplishments was to study the authenticity of the *hadith*. As mentioned earlier, the *hadith* are the collected traditions about the *sunna*, the specific actions and sayings of Muhammad. Muslims accord the *hadith* nearly the same reverence as they do the Koran itself. The *hadith* also form a basis for Islamic law (*shari'a*). For these reasons it is important for the faithful to be able to distinguish an authentic *hadith* from a large number of pious fabrications.

According to Goldhizer, 'Abd al-Malik, the Umayyad caliph who built the Dome of the Rock, fabricated a *hadith* himself. At that time, Syria was part of 'Abd al-Malik's empire. He wanted to stop the pilgrimages to Mecca because he was worried that one of his rivals there would force Syrian pilgrims to pay him (the rival) homage. Goldhizer argued it was for this reason that 'Abd al-Malik decreed that when Muslim pilgrims made the obligatory circumambulation in Jerusalem, it was just as valid there as in Mecca itself.

Goldhizer also claimed that a theologian in 'Abd al-Malik's court was ordered to find a persuasive theological justification for this new politically motivated reform. The theological dutifully made up—and sourced to Muhammad—the famous *hadith* cited earlier:

> The saddles of the camels shall not be fastened [for setting out on pilgrimage] except for three mosques: the Haram mosque [in Mecca], my mosque [in Medina], and al-Aqsa Mosque [in Jerusalem].[615]

Although Goldhizer and other Western scholars mounted a strong intellectual challenge to the authenticity of some of the *hadith*, their views were rejected by Islamic traditionalists. In the eyes of these religious conservatives, all the sayings, sermons, utterances, actions and deeds of Muhammad were divinely inspired. As a result, they are to be accepted on faith, not judged by reason alone.

William Flinders Petrie (1890)

This British scholar single-handedly established Middle Eastern archeology as a scientific discipline. As a boy, Petrie was thought by his parents to be too frail to attend school, so he was educated at home instead. Possessed of a very high degree of curiosity, he began studying coins and weights on his own. Later, with his father's help, he learned surveying and then rebuilt surveying instruments to make them more accurate. His only formal education was a university correspondence course in mathematics.

Petrie traveled to Egypt in 1880 to survey the pyramids of Giza and would spend most of his career as an archeologist in Egypt. One of his most celebrated discoveries, however, occurred when he only spent six weeks in Palestine in 1890 and excavated the mound known as Tell el-Hesi. At this site, located on the coastal plain about 30 miles south of Jerusalem, Petrie found that the mound was composed of a stratified sequence of small, successively superimposed "cities."

This was a sound conclusion because in ancient times, houses in the Middle East were usually made of piled-up mud, lumps of clay pressed together or sun-dried bricks. These structures were cheap and easy to build but they were not very durable. When rains weakened them or when wars destroyed them, they were simply knocked down and leveled off. New houses were then built on the ruins of the old. For this reason, tells are stratified: a lower layer can be presumed to be older than the layer immediately on top of it.

Petrie discovered that the "cities" in Tell el-Hesi could be accurately dated by studying the potsherds (fragments of pottery) found in each layer and then comparing them with other potsherds found in similar excavations in Egypt. The excavations at Tell el-Hesi constituted the second stratigraphic survey in archeological history (the first was conducted at Troy by Heinrich Schleimann, beginning in 1871). It was Petrie's work, however, that laid the foundations for all later archeological expeditions in the Middle East.

Petrie spent the next 37 years in Egypt but returned to Palestine again at the end of his career. He worked there from 1927 to 1938, studying the frontier sites between Egypt and the Holy Land. He went back to Tell el-Hesi and, remarkably, found the ruins of 10 additional "cities" there. This

distinguished archeologist died in Jerusalem in 1942 at the age of 89.

Frederick H. Bliss (1890)

Son of the Reverend Daniel Bliss, founder of the American University of Beirut, Frederick Bliss conducted independent research in Syria between 1888 and 1890. In 1890 the Palestine Exploration Fund invited him to continue the work begun by Petrie at Tell el-Hesi. After being trained briefly in Egypt by Petrie, Bliss went to Palestine. At Tell el-Hesi he used Petrie's ceramic sequence and his concept of successive "cities" to establish not only the archeology of that site but also the sequential framework for Levantine archeology as a whole.

At Tell el-Hesi Bliss found a cuneiform tablet that was similar to those found at the ancient site of Tell el-Amarna in Egypt.[616] This suggested that that the history of the Holy Land *predated* Biblical accounts. In Jerusalem itself Bliss unearthed other complexities when he dug into the Ophel hill, which extends south from the Temple Mount. This was where David had built his fortified city. Although the ruins of ancient buildings found in the strata there defied easy dating, it was clear that people had continuously lived on the hill from the pre–Biblical Bronze Age to the Byzantine period. These findings would prove unsettling to Christian traditionalists who wanted to accept the Bible as the ultimate authority on the history of the Holy Land.

Following his successes at Tell el-Hesi, Bliss went to Jerusalem and continued the work of the Palestine Exploration Fund there between 1894 and 1897. In 1900, however, he was dismissed from his prestigious position as the Fund's Explorer on the grounds of ill health. The real reason, though, was that Bliss' time-consuming, meticulous methods did not produce the kind of dramatic "finds" which would help the Fund raise money for its programs. Later, another distinguished archeologist would acknowledge that firing Bliss had been a mistake and a serious setback to Levantine archeology.

After leaving the Fund, Bliss taught at the Union Theological Seminary in New York City in 1903. His lectures there were published in 1906 under the title *The Development of Palestine Exploration*, a book that was to become a key work of scholarship in biblical studies and biblical archeology.

Elizabeth Butler (1891)

Lady Elizabeth Butler was an artist who visited the Holy Land in the spring of 1891 together with her husband, Major General Butler, who was commandant of the British forces in Alexandria. Because of his exalted rank, they received first-class treatment in Palestine, both from Turkish officials and from religious leaders. Lady Butler wrote a lively account of the trip for her mother, which was subsequently published under the title of *Letters from the Holy Land*.

In it, we can see that her interests were more artistic than devotional. For example, as her ship approaches Jaffa, she is enraptured by the sight:

At sunrise this morning the throbbing of the screw [the propeller of the ship] suddenly ceased, and as I went to the port-hole of our cabin I beheld the lovely coast of the Land of Christ, about a mile distant, with the exquisite town of Jaffa, typically Eastern, grouped on a rock by the sea, and appearing above huge, heaving waves, whose grey-blue tones were mixed with rosy reflections from the clouds.[617]

She continues in this artistic vein after she leaves the ship and makes her way to a German inn in Jaffa:

We noticed the air getting richer with the scent of orange-flowers, and soon we passed into the region of the orange-orchards. The trees were creamy white with dense blossom, and the ripe fruit was dotted about in masses of white.... I made my first sketch—the first, I trust, of a series I marked down before leaving Alexandria. It was of Jaffa, seen over the orange trees from the inn garden, and charming it was to sit there in the cool shade, with birds singing overhead as never one hears them in Egypt.... The Mediterranean appeared to my right, and overhead sailed great pearly clouds in the vibrating blue of the fresh spring sky. I must say I felt very happy at the reality of my presence on the soil of Palestine.[618]

With her eye for the colorful, Lady Butler was more smitten by the approaches to the Church of the Holy Sepulcher than by the building itself. "We reached the Church though stone lanes of indescribable picturesqueness, teeming with the life of the East," she tells us,

and there I saw the Jerusalem Jews I had so often read of—extraordinary figures in long coats and round hats, a ringlet falling in front of each ear, while the rest of the head is shaved. They looked white and unhealthy, many of them red-eyed and all more or less bent, even the youths. No greater contrast could be seen between these poor creatures and the Arabs who jostle them in the crowded alleys, and who are such upstanding athletic men, with clear brown skins, clean-cut features, and heads turbaned majestically. They stride along with a spring in every step.[619]

With her eyes "dazzled with all that colour" and by the spring sunlight, she entered the Church of the Holy Sepulcher but did not experience any surge of spirituality there. Instead, she was struck by "the long stretch of twilight church" that separated Calvary from the Sepulcher (her guidebooks had belittled this distance). She was also moved to see "a slab of stone worn into hollows by the lips of countless pilgrims" at the Sepulcher itself. Perhaps feeling guilty about her secular reactions to the most sacred spot of Christendom, she apologized to her mother and to her other readers. Despite her facility with words, she admitted, "I have made many attempts to tell you my thoughts and feelings during these bewildering moments of my first visit, but I find it is impossible, and you can understand why."[620]

On a side-trip to Bethlehem, Lady Butler encountered a group of about 20 Russian pilgrims who had come to worship at the Field of the Shepherds. These were poor men who were wearing fur coats and high leather boots despite the heat of the day. Through an interpreter, one of them told Lady Butler that he had walked all the way from the city of Tobolsk in northwestern Russia. His journey to the Holy Land had taken two years. This fact impressed her deeply:

> I think we English are too apt to suppose that because devotion is demonstrative it is not deep. Great pedestrians as we are, how many Englishmen would walk two years to visit this sheepfold? That two years' test borne by the Russian peasant must have gone very deep.... I saw these rough peasants throwing themselves heart and soul into their adoration of God, and I thought of Mary Magdalene and *her* prostrations and tears.[621]

Matilde Serao (1892)

This devout Italian woman visited the Holy Land in 1892 and described her trip in a book entitled *Nel Paese di Gesù* (*In the Country of Jesus*). One of the most popular books ever written about the Jerusalem pilgrimage, it reappeared in more than 30 editions within a year of its publication in 1897. The probable reason for its success was that it struck a responsive chord among the faithful. In an increasingly secular age, they must have welcomed an old-fashioned devotional pilgrimage that focused on God alone, not the traveler's personal interests.

Serao set the quasi-mystical tone of her work in the introduction to the book:

> I have endeavoured, in my journey through Palestine, humbly and honestly to seek out the soul of the Blessed Land where Christ dwelt and where His voice was heard. I found it in the clear skies of Samaria, in the tiny violet and yellow flowers that bloom where once stood the home of Martha and Mary, and by that fountain at Nazareth where the Virgin Mother bathed her gentle hands.... I have sought to chronicle my impressions of the Holy Land even as I felt them whilst still vibrating with the intense emotions I experienced, as I trod the paths He and passed along and visited the scenes hallowed by His Life and Passion.[622]

Despite her flights of religious fancy, Serao was also a level-headed commentator on the logistics of travel in the Holy Land. By the time of her visit, a single-track narrow-gauge railroad connected Jaffa and Jerusalem, supplementing the paved road built in 1867. She found the train trip most unpleasant. The train was expensive, uncomfortable and did not leave on time. It had to stop for water and then had to jolt along at top speed to make up lost time. It was so slow going uphill that in 1901 E. A. Reynolds-Ball, a British pilgrim, could report:

It requires only an ordinary amount of activity to jump out and pick the flowers along the line, and rejoin the train as it laboriously pants up the steep ascent—a feat I myself have performed occasionally.[623]

Moreover, Serao said,

It is simply intolerable and, indeed, quite horrible, to find oneself in a railway carriage full of fat, smoking, somnolent Turks, seated in their favourite attitude, with a shoeless foot in one hand. No Turk will keep his shoes on a moment longer than he can help![624]

In the final pages of her book Serao extended a warm, heartfelt invitation to all prospective pilgrims. "What I ardently desire," she said, "is this:"

that some of my readers, after perusing these pages and having gathered information of a practical character as to its ways and means of reaching Palestine, will be prompted to follow my example and undertake the holy pilgrimage ... a visit to the country of Jesus has an incomparable fascination and poetical charm all its own, the memory of which can never be obliterated. May I therefore, hope that ... I may have the joy of feeling that at least a few readers of my work will be inspired by its pages to see the cradle lands of Jesus. Indeed, if I cause but one solitary pilgrim to visit the Holy Land I shall feel that I have not written my book in vain.[625]

Theodor Herzl (1896)

An Austrian journalist, Herzl was the chief founder of Zionism. He was a figure straight out of the Old Testament: tall, charismatic, brilliant, an able organizer and a persuasive speaker. His long black beard made him look like a prophet.

In one of his early attempts to establish a Jewish homeland, Herzl interviewed French baron Maurice de Hirsch, one of the richest men of his time. The baron wanted to resettle Russian and Romanian Jews not in Palestine but in South America. Herzl came to the interview carrying 22 pages of notes; perhaps understandably, the baron refused to hear him out. But Herzl did not give up. In 1896 he published a famous pamphlet, *Der Judenstaat (The Jewish State)*. Its first sentence was: "The idea which I have developed in this pamphlet is a very old one: it is the restoration of the Jewish state."[626]

In 1897 he convened an international meeting in Basel (Switzerland), which set up a program to achieve a homeland for the Jewish people. Herzl was also elected president of the newly formed Zionist Organization. In 1898 he went to Palestine on a political pilgrimage to study its possibilities for a Jewish state. He did not like Jerusalem itself, noting in his diary that

Shouts, smells, tawdry colours, people in rags crowding the narrow, airless streets, beggars, cripples, starveling children, screaming women, bellowing shopkeepers. The once royal city had sunk to the lowest depths.... "When I remember thee in the days to come, O Jerusalem," it will not be with delight. The musty deposits of two thousand years of inhumanity, intolerance, and foulness lie in your reeking alleys.... If Jerusalem is ever ours, and if I were still able to do anything about it, I would begin by cleaning up it."[627]

Herzl wanted to get the help of the German Kaiser William II in arranging a Jewish land company in Palestine. The Kaiser, who was then making a what an official British account described as a "fantastic political pilgrimage"[628] of his own to the Holy Land (see below), was not responsive. Herzl later tried to persuade the Ottoman government to grant autonomy to Palestine, but Sultan Abd al-Hamid rejected this idea. "I cannot give away any part of it [the Ottoman empire]," he said, "... I will not agree to vivisection."[629] The British, however, proved to be more sympathetic and in 1903 offered the Zionists 6,000 square miles of uninhabited highlands in what was loosely called "Uganda."

This offer led to a bitter debate within the Zionist movement, which eventually voted to hold out for an independent state in the ancient homeland of the Jews—*Eretz Yisra'el*—"the Land of Israel," i.e., Palestine itself. But in 1904, in the midst of this controversy, Herzl himself, worn down by his exertions and suffering from heart disease, died at the age of 44. He was buried in Vienna. His remains were removed to Jerusalem in 1949, the year after Israel became an independent state, and are now entombed on Mt. Herzl, a hill to the west of the city.

Kaiser Wilhelm II (1898)

The Kaiser's pilgrimage to Jerusalem in 1898 may have been stimulated by a family tradition: his father, then Crown Prince Frederick of Prussia, had visited the Holy City in 1869. The ostensible reasons for Wilhelm II's own visit were to dedicate the new Lutheran Church of the Redeemer and to open the Augusta Victoria Hospice for pilgrims. Political considerations, however, played a much bigger role.

When he ascended the throne in 1880, Germany was becoming a powerful nation. Wilhelm II wanted to extend Germany's influence in the Turkish empire. Much like Russian, French and British leaders, he, too, quickly fell prey to what Barbara Tuchman aptly called "the Eastern disease."[630] This virulent illness centered on the fantasy that untold wealth and power could be had in the Middle East simply for the taking.

In Wilhelm II's case, the symptom of the disease was his desire to build a railroad running from Berlin to Baghdad. In that era, railroad concessions were often used as the advance guard of imperialism and colonization. Because the Ottoman Sultan Abdul Hamid wanted to increase his own influence in the Middle East, he welcomed the German initiative. As a symbolic gift, he even presented Wilhelm II with some land in Jerusalem.[631]

Soon the new Deutsche Palästina Bank became the headquarters for extensive German commercial and consular activities in the Middle East. Seeing no harm in tilting toward the Germans, who (unlike the British) did not seem to have any imperial ambitions, the Sultan began to loosen his ties with London. More and more he sided with Berlin, e.g., by giving Germany the concession to build the new rail line. Although at the time this was not an irrational act, it turned out to be a great mistake. The Sultan's pro–German slant ultimately put the Ottoman Empire on the losing side in World War I and resulted in its total destruction.

Wilhelm II's visit to Jerusalem in 1898 began with a demonstration of the extent of his political aspirations: a special entrance had to be cut through the Jaffa Gate so that he and his entourage could enter the Holy City on horseback, in proper imperial style. He later met with Theodor Herzl, first riding up to a Zionist colony, where he reached down from the saddle and shook Herzl's hand. The Kaiser told him that Palestine had a future but that "it needs water, plenty of water," shook hands again and then rode away.[632] Subsequently, Herzl had a longer meeting with him in Jerusalem but the Kaiser did not want to raise Zionist proposals with the Sultan, so nothing came of the meeting. Disappointed, Herzl turned his attention to winning British support for Zionism.

The Tomb of Absalom lies in the Valley of Jehoshaphat on the western slope of the Mount of Olives. Part of a Jewish burial complex belonging to a wealthy family, it dates from the latter half of the first century BCE. In the photograph, the first rider is a Palestinian sheikh. Prince Adelbert, wearing a white naval hat, is behind him to the left. He is accompanied by a Turkish employee of the German Consul and is followed by other young German officers. (Reproduced by permission of the Palestine Exploration Fund, London.)

Prince Adelbert (c. 1900)

The Kaiser counted his pilgrimage to Jerusalem as a success. In about 1900 he sent his second son, Prince Adelbert, there, too. This was a convenient visit for the young prince because he was then a cadet on a German training ship. His ship called at Jaffa and Adelbert made a two-day political-military pilgrimage to Jerusalem. Among the sites he visited was a collection of Hellenistic monuments then known (erroneously, as it later turned out) as the Tomb of the Kings.

Ada Goodrich-Freer (1900)

This British lady lived in Jerusalem for two years, beginning in 1900, and was struck by several things. One was the large number of Jewish inhabitants. More and more Jews had been coming to Jerusalem from Europe, motivated either by a religious–Zionist zeal to settle in the Holy Land or by a desire to escape poverty and persecution in Tsarist Russia. Freer was surprised to find that

Out of about 60,000 inhabitants some 40,000 are Jews; a large part of the trade is in their hands; not only have they overflowed in all directions from their own quarter within the walls, but they have established themselves in various colonies, amounting to some half-dozen villages all within a mile or so from the city gates.[633]

Still, the plight of the Jews was not an enviable one. Freer said that the Jerusalem Jew always remained

an immigrant, a foreigner, more distinctly so perhaps than even in London or New York. He is rigorously excluded from even the courtyard of the Holy Sepulchre…. From the Temple area, now entirely in the hands of the Moslems, he voluntarily excludes himself, lest, it is said, he should accidentally profane the Holy of Holies…. It is in the well known Wailing Place that one realizes that the Jew is a homeless exile…. On the ninth day of the month of Ab [Av]… then above all it is, in the words of their own litany, that "for the palaces laid waste, for the Temple destroyed, for the walls laid low, for the glory which has gone, for the great ones perished," they "sit solitary and weep."[634]

Another matter that caught her eye was the extent of German influence in Jerusalem. This had increased markedly since the visit of Kaiser Wilhelm II two years before. She noted that

Trade, agriculture and commerce in Jerusalem are never more flourishing than in the hands of the Germans. The suburb known as the German Colony is an admirable example of cleanliness and order. It is, to all practical purposes, a picturesque German village, having its own church, public hall, band, drill-hall, schools, farm, gardens, and of course Bier Halle. Three immense orphanages, a large general hospital and a children's hospital, main-

tained by the Germans, are the only Protestant institutions of the kind upon any scale of magnitude.[635]

Freer also commented on the babble of tongues heard in the Holy City. Jerusalem Jews and Armenians, she reported, were "in constant communication with India and receive large numbers of pilgrims and merchants, so that one often hears various languages of India in walking through the streets of Jerusalem."[636] These Indians were either Muslims visiting the Haram or were Christian followers of the Apostle Thomas, who had lived on the Malabar Coast of southwestern India.

Montague Brownslow Parker (1911)

The Dominican archeologist Père Louis-Hughes Vincent completed the work begun by Frederick Bliss in 1890 and proved that the earliest city of Jerusalem had been located on the Ophel hill rather than on Mount Zion. Although Père Vincent was an accomplished and honorable scholar, he made a grave mistake in 1911 when he agreed to help Montague Parker, a young British aristocrat with no training in archeology, dig for buried treasure underneath the Haram.

Père Vincent was motivated not by hope of gain but by fear Parker would damage the site unless he had the benefit of expert advice. Parker himself was sure the treasures of the Second Temple, e.g., the Ark of the Covenant, lay hidden under the Haram. He bribed his way into this holy place and began chipping away at the sacred rock with a pickax. There are two accounts of what happened next.

One story is that the noise awoke a Muslim attendant, who sounded the alarm. A better and more likely story is that Parker had paid off only the senior members of the Muslim family with hereditary responsibility for watching the Haram. No money had trickled down to the junior members, however, and one of them took revenge by telling the Ottoman government about Parker's plans.

In any case, when news of the attempted excavations spread throughout the Holy City, both Muslims and Jews were scandalized. Riots broke out and lasted for days. Estelle Blyth, daughter of the Anglican Bishop, tells us in a well-written account that Parker's foray took placed during the Muslim festival of Nebi Musa, which marked the death of Moses. That year, this celebration happened to coincide with Easter. As a result, she says,

> Jerusalem was filled to the brim with excitable pilgrims and strangers belonging to various creeds, whose physical resistance in many cases had been undermined by the long and rigid fasts which preceded the festivals, and who were therefore as dry tinder and ready to blaze up at the slightest suggestion. Into this inflammable mass of humanity fell as a bombshell the report that the English excavators had broken into an old underworld passage, leading from under the Rock in the Mosque to the Golden Gate.[637]

The Jews were especially upset. Freer tells us why:

> It must be remembered that the Jews had been wounded in their tenderest religious feelings, equally with the Moslems. Every Eastern Jew believes that somewhere under the great expanse of the Mosque enclosure, upon which their wonderful Temple once blazed forth its glory to the world, are hidden the Sacred Vessels and the Ark, and that if a Jew should tread upon the spot under which these are hidden he would instantly be struck dead.[638]

As a result of this debacle, Parker had to flee from the Holy Land. Because he was being watched, he had to work out an escape plan. He hit upon the ruse of inviting Muslim officials to meet with him on a friend's yacht in Jaffa. He told them, however, that first he had to go out to the yacht himself to make sure everything was in order. As soon as he was aboard, the yacht set sail and departed. Later on, when Parker tried to come back to Jerusalem to continue his excavations, the Ottoman government refused to let him land at Jaffa.

Stephen Graham (1912)

In the early years of the twentieth century, Russian pilgrims constituted the largest single group of visitors. In 1904, for example, as many as 10,000 to 14,000 Russian Orthodox Christians came from Black Sea ports to Jaffa. They then took the train to Jerusalem, where they lodged in large Russian hospices set up in the Holy Land to cater to them. These pilgrims, most of whom were simple folk, were not embarrassed to express their religious emotions publicly. They remained the most fervent supporters of the ceremony of the Holy Fire.

In the spring of 1912, Stephen Graham, a Russian-speaking Scotsman who accompanied a group of Russian Orthodox pilgrims, recorded that after the Holy Fire appeared and candles were lit from it,

> On our faces and our clothes hot wax kept dropping, and now and then the flames singed our ears. "Never mind," said one pilgrim to me, "the sacred fire cannot hurt any one for the first half-hour after it has come." Exalted Easterners took whole sheaves of lighted candles and plunged them into their bosoms to extinguish them; many willfully applied the flames to their bare

flesh and cried out in joy and ecstasy. Hundreds of pilgrims produced their black death-caps filled with sweet scented cotton-wool, and then extinguished the candles in them ... the crowd ... was to all appearance mad with ecstasy as if under the spell or some extraordinary drug or charm. The people shouted, yelled, sang, danced, fought, with such diversity of manner and object, and in such a variety of dress and language, that the calm onlooker thought of the tale full of sound and fury told by an idiot and signifying nothing.[639]

The Russians revered the Holy City not only in life but in death, too. Graham was amazed to see

the extent to which the pilgrims sought in Jerusalem tokens for the clothing of their dead bodies, and how much their thoughts were centered on death and the final resurrection morning. They sanctified crosses at the grave, little ones to wear round their necks in the tomb, and larger ones to lie on their breasts; they brought their death-shrouds and cross-embroidered caps to dip them in Jordan; they took Jerusalem earth to put in their coffins, and even had their arms tattooed with the word Jerusalem, and with pictures of the Virgin; so that they might lie so marked in the grave, and indeed that they might rise again, so marked, to show it in heaven. By these things they felt they obtained a sort of sanctity.[640]

World War I brings pilgrimage to a halt

The "war to end all wars" broke out in 1914. It involved most of the nations of Europe, as well as Russia, the United States, the Middle East and other regions. Turkey sided with the Germans against the British and the French. Jerusalem itself became the headquarters of a Turkish army. Amid the unprecedented slaughter, carnage and upheavals of the war, pilgrimage to the Holy Land ground to a temporary halt. In the next chapter we shall see how in 1917 the Jerusalem pilgrimage may have played a subtle, indirect role in the eventual establishment of the state of Israel in 1948.

X

Pilgrimages During the British Mandate and Under the Israelis (1917–2001)

During World War I the British government pledged its support, in a document known as the Balfour Declaration (November 1917), for the establishment in Palestine of a "national home for the Jewish people." In December 1917 Jerusalem surrendered to British forces led by General Allenby. The defeat of Turkey marked the end of four centuries of Ottoman control over Palestine and the beginning of more than 30 years of British rule. After capturing Jerusalem, the British first governed it through a British Military Administration. Between 1920 and 1948 they supervised it under a Mandate from the League of Nations. Zionism, a nineteenth century political movement calling for an independent Jewish state in Palestine, gathered strength and adherents in this era.

Tensions between Arabs and Jews led to bloody riots in 1920, 1921, 1929 and 1936–1939. After the end of World War II in 1945, Britain turned over the problem of Palestine to the fledgling United Nations. The Jews accepted but the Arabs rejected a UN plan for the partition of the country. As a result, the state of Israel was established unilaterally in 1948, a move that

sparked the first Arab-Israel war (1948–1949). The Israelis won this war but the Holy City itself was divided into two parts: East Jerusalem (controlled by the Jordanians) and West Jerusalem (controlled by the Israelis). During the Six Day War (1967) the Israelis captured East Jerusalem and reunified the city.

Subsequent Arab-Israeli conflicts have been victories for Israel but have been inconclusive because they failed to result in a lasting peace between Arabs and Jews. As shown by the clashes that erupted at the Temple Mount in September 2000, Jerusalem remains a dangerous flashpoint. Although more than half a century has elapsed since the first Arab-Israeli war, the final status of Jerusalem remains unresolved. Both Israelis and Palestinians continue to claim it as their rightful capital. It is unlikely that either side will make major concessions on this issue.

Arthur James Balfour (1917)

Just over a month before General Allenby captured Jerusalem, British Prime Minister Lloyd George ordered his Foreign

Secretary, Arthur James Balfour, to write a letter to Lord Rothschild, Vice-President of the Zionist Federation in Britain. This letter outlined a new and momentous British policy—one which ultimately led to an independent Israel and which made Jerusalem the flashpoint it is today. This is the text of the letter:[641]

> November 2nd, 1917
>
> Dear Lord Rothschild,
>
> I have much pleasure in conveying to you, on behalf of His Majesty's Government, the following declaration of sympathy with Jewish Zionist aspirations which has been submitted to, and approved by, the Cabinet.
>
> "His Majesty's Government views with favour the establishment in Palestine of a national home for the Jewish people, and will use their best endeavours to facilitate the achievement of this object, it being clearly understood that nothing shall be done to prejudice the civil and religious rights of existing non–Jewish communities in Palestine, or the rights and political status enjoyed by Jews in any other country."
>
> I should be grateful if you would bring this declaration to the knowledge of the Zionist Federation.
>
> Yours sincerely,
>
> Arthur James Balfour

Because there was a fundamental contradiction in this policy, it was doomed to failure. By a "national home for the Jewish people" both Balfour and Prime Minister Lloyd George clearly meant a Jewish state, not merely a Jewish enclave within Palestine.[642] The Muslims believed, however, that in the process of establishing a Jewish state the Jews would trample on the economic, civil and religious rights of the indigenous Arabs. Indeed, sparked by the virulent anti–Semitism preached by a Muslim religious leader, Haj Amin al-Husseini, race riots would break out in Jerusa-

lem in 1920, 1921 and 1929. Moreover, a full-scale Arab revolt against Britain's rule would erupt in 1936–1938.

Balfour himself recognized the contradiction in his policy but for reasons that are still unclear (see Appendix VI) he decided to side with the Zionists. In a famous statement, he said:

> The Four Great Powers are committed to Zionism. And Zionism, be it right or wrong, good or bad, is rooted in age-long traditions, in present needs, in future hopes, of far profounder import than the desires and prejudices of the 700,000 Arabs who now inhabit that ancient land. In my opinion, that is right. What I have never understood is how it [this policy] can be harmonized....[643]

Remarkably, Balfour almost seemed proud of the contradiction. He admitted publicly that "so far as Palestine is concerned, the Powers had made no statement of fact that is not admittedly wrong, and no declaration of policy which, at least in the letter, they have not always intended to violate."[644]

The Jerusalem Pilgrimage and the Balfour Declaration

What was the relationship, if any, between the Jerusalem pilgrimage and the Balfour Declaration? To try to answer this question we must first look at the revival of English Evangelicalism in Britain early in the nineteenth century and especially at the rise of what was called "Gentile Zionism"—the advocacy, by Christians, of the Zionist goal of a Jewish homeland in Palestine.

By the beginning of the nineteenth century, the Evangelical Revival had begun to displace some of the skepticism of the previous century. Christian piety was back in fashion by the time Victoria became queen in 1838. For our purposes here, the most important Evangelical teaching was that the Jews were the key to the Second Coming of Christ.[645] In fact, Evangelicals believed that without them there could be no Second Coming at all because the prophetic chain of events would be broken.

For the faithful, this line of reasoning was clear and unassailable. The Bible had prophesied that the Jews would be converted to Christianity and would return to their homeland in Palestine. After—and only *after*—this had been accomplished would the stage be set for the Second Coming. It followed, then, that to hasten the Second Coming the faithful had to work hard on two fronts: to convert the Jews and to get them back to Palestine.

The first part of this ambitious program was tackled by a number of British missionary enterprises, most notably the London Society for Promoting Christianity among the Jews, which was founded in 1808. Known informally as the London Jews' Society, this was a bully pulpit from which Evangelical leaders could press at the same time for the conversion of the Jews and for the establishment of a Christian Israel in Palestine. The most prominent of these leaders was the great industrial and social reformer Lord Anthony Ashley-Cooper, later the seventh Earl of Shaftesbury. He was instrumental in, among other things, securing Parliamentary approval for new and more humane regulations affecting factory workers, miners, impoverished tenants and the mentally ill.

Because of his strong evangelical beliefs, Shaftesbury was exceptionally interested in the status of the Jews. The word "Jerusalem" was engraved on the gold ring he always wore. Thanks to his academic studies and his extensive interviews with Jews, Shaftesbury came to consider himself an expert on contemporary Jewish cul-

ture. By 1838 his investigations led him to conclude that most of the Jews in Europe very much wanted to immigrate to Palestine. If Britain became the Jews' political and military protector in the Middle East, he reasoned, this immigration could actually begin. When it did, the Second Coming would be near at hand.[646]

The bad news for Shaftesbury and other Evangelicals was that their efforts to convert the Jews proved to be a singular failure. Although within five years the London Jews' Society had attracted a glittering list of patrons and more than 2,000 subscribers, the Jews themselves had no interest in becoming Christians. In 1839, after 30 years of missionary work, there were only 207 Jewish converts in the whole of London, an average of six or seven a year. In Baghdad, where 10,000 Jews lived, three missionaries made only two converts. There were no converts at all in Smyrna, with a Jewish population of 1,500, and the mission there had to be closed.[647]

The Evangelicals were heartened, however, by some good news. The second part of the program was apparently more achievable. In 1840 the British Foreign Secretary, Lord Palmerston, wrote to his Ambassador in Constantinople: "There exists at the present time among the Jews dispersed over Europe, a strong notion that the time is approaching when their nation is to return to Palestine...."[648] Only six days after this letter was written, the influential *Times* of London reported that a plan "to plant the Jewish people in the land of their fathers" was under "serious political consideration" in London.[649] Although large-scale Jewish immigration to Palestine did not begin until the early 1880s, we can see that 40 years earlier both the British government and the leading British newspaper had already been won over to the cause of Gentile Zionism.

There is no way to quantify the effects of the Jerusalem pilgrimage on Gentile

Zionism, on the Balfour Declaration or, ultimately, on the emergence of the independent state of Israel. Any comments on this process must necessarily be speculative. It is clear, however, that one reason why Gentile Zionism was so widespread in Britain was that it could draw on the deep well of British affection for Palestine. The ultimate source of this pro–Palestine sentiment was the constant exposure of generations of British people to the Bible.

Biblical passages were read at every church service. They played a major role in all the religious services marking the cycle of life: birth (christenings), adulthood (marriages) and death (funerals). The Bible was studied and read aloud at home. It provided a nearly unlimited range of topics for artists to depict. Scriptural themes and sayings, especially from the King James Bible, embedded themselves in the daily language of work and play.

Leopold Amery, one of the British civil servants responsible for the Balfour Declaration, wrote that, apart from the United States, "Bible reading and Bible thinking England was the only country where the desire of the Jews to return to their ancient homeland has always been regarded as a natural aspiration which ought not be denied."[650] Shortly after the Balfour Declaration appeared, the British Zionist Federation organized a celebration to toast this new British policy. Commenting approvingly, the *Times* of London said that the outstanding features of the celebration were "the Old Testament spirit which pervaded it and the feeling that … the approaching fulfillment of ancient prophecy was being celebrated with faith and favour."[651]

For Gentile Zionists, the earthly Jerusalem was the precursor of the heavenly Jerusalem. It seems possible that the Jerusalem pilgrimage was one of the subterranean springs replenishing that deep well

of British enthusiasm for the Holy Land. This thesis cannot be proven but circumstantial evidence points to its validity.

To begin with, we must remember that the Anglo-Saxons had been traveling to Jerusalem since the time of St. Willibald (720–726). For every person who actually made the pilgrimage, there must have been many other English men and women who wanted to do so but who for financial, physical or family reasons were obliged to stay at home. Even those who did not want to be pilgrims themselves were certainly familiar with this undertaking. As Chaucer testifies, in the Middle Ages pilgrimage was a popular and enjoyable activity for all classes of society.

We have also noted that that in the seventeenth century Bunyan's *Pilgrim's Progress* rivaled the Bible in popularity. For the English as well as for other Christians, Jerusalem was always the sacred center *par excellence*. Devotional pilgrimages seldom flagged. The well-publicized secular pilgrimages of the eighteenth and nineteenth centuries helped keep the Holy City in the public eye. The English "patriotism for Palestine," first mentioned, as we have seen, in Warburton's guidebook, *The Cross and the Crescent* (1844), continued long after the book itself went out of print 40 years later. Biblical archeology and the Palestine Exploration Fund continued to play important roles in calling attention to Palestine.

What influence did the Jerusalem pilgrimage have on Balfour himself? It is difficult to say. He was a skeptic, not a religious zealot like Shaftesbury, but he had been steeped in the Bible from childhood. As an adult he, too, remained deeply interested in Judaism. He believed that "Christian religion and civilization owes to Judaism an immeasurable dept, shamefully ill repaid."[652] The Holy City was part of that debt. Balfour himself did not visit Jerusalem until 1925, when he made a secular pilgrimage to open the new Hebrew University there.

During this ceremony, this aristocratic, brilliant, aloof man who was "imperturbable in any fracas"[653] had a very strong emotional reaction. An observer said that Balfour was "profoundly moved, [with] tears running down his face."[654] This was remarkable because at the same time he was convinced, intellectually, that his decision to come to Jerusalem had been a great mistake.

The visit sparked Arab demonstrations and a one-day strike. Balfour's companion and biographer was his niece, Mrs. Blanche E. C. Dugdale. She wrote that her uncle's visit to Palestine had been "an awful mistake—and it was driven home to him many times during his stay—and two or three times my diary records him saying, 'I suppose I ought not to have come.'"[655] All that is clear now is that Balfour's own pilgrimage to the Holy City aroused strong and conflicting feelings within his breast. Perhaps like the Balfour Declaration itself, he, too, was in the grip of a basic contradiction.

General Sir Edmund Allenby (1917)

Allenby, the last great British leader of mounted cavalry, led the Palestine campaign in World War I. He won a decisive victory over the Turks at Gaza in November 1917 and his army was pushing into Palestine when the Balfour Declaration was issued. The Turks abandoned Jerusalem and Allenby was able to enter it unopposed in December 1917.

Capturing the Holy City was one thing, but holding onto it legally was another matter. Sir Mark Sykes, one of the most famous of Britain's Middle East experts, offered this prescient advice to his government:

We should so order our policy that, without in any way showing any desire to annex Palestine or to establish a Protectorate over it, when the time comes to choose a mandatory power for its control, by the consensus of opinion and desire of its inhabitants we shall be the most likely candidate.[656]

Sykes' line of reasoning appealed to British sensibilities. London would not be adding Palestine to the long list of its imperial acquisitions. Instead, it would simply be administering the land on behalf of its ancient and rightful owners—that is to say, the Jews. Thus there was no need for remorse or any feelings of guilt: the British would rule the Holy Land as disinterested trustees, not as conquerors.

It may seem strange now to think of Allenby's capture of Jerusalem as a military pilgrimage but this is in some ways what it was. A key point here is that Allenby gave careful thought to how he himself should enter Jerusalem. He decided to dismount so he could show due respect for the Holy City by entering it on foot. The antithesis of such reverence, of course, was the imperious attitude shown by Kaiser Wilhelm II in 1898, who, as we have seen, had a breach cut into the city wall at the Jaffa Gate so he and his followers could enter Jerusalem on horseback.

Moreover, taking pains to demonstrate his peaceful intentions as a pilgrim, Allenby made his way on foot to the Citadel of Jerusalem, one of the highest points of the Old City. He chose this impressive structure—known in Crusader times as the Tower of David and now housing the Museum of the History of Jerusalem—to publicly assure the inhabitants of "Jerusalem the Blessed" that he would protect the holy places and would safeguard the religious freedom of Jews, Christians and Muslims alike. To the assembled citizens of Jerusalem, he read out a statement which said in part:

since your city is regarded with affection by three of the great religions of mankind, and its soil has been consecrated by the prayers and pilgrimage of devout people of these three religions for many centuries, therefore do I make it known unto you that every sacred building, monument, holy spot, shrine, traditional site, endowment, pious bequest, or customary place of prayer will be maintained and protected according to the existing customs and beliefs of those to whose faith they are sacred.[657]

No military flags were flown during this ceremony and religious sensitivities were scrupulously respected. Muslim troops from the British army in India were assigned to protect the Muslim holy places, while Christian soldiers guarded the Christian sanctuaries.

The British capture of Jerusalem was so widely hailed in Europe that church bells rang in Rome and London. Both Jews and Arabs were pleased. The Jews were elated, seeing in the defeat of the Turks the first step toward the national home promised them by the Balfour Declaration. The Arabs, for their part, discovered that in Arabic the name Allenby was written much like *al-Nabi*, the word for "prophet." They remembered an old prediction: "When the waters of the Nile flow into Palestine, then shall the prophet (*al-Nabi*) from the west, drive the Turks from Palestine."[658]

William Foxwell Albright (1920)

Pilgrims began to return to the Holy Land after the end of World War I in 1918. Many more would have come, according to British High Commissioner Sir Herbert Samuel, if Palestine had not been so impoverished. He reported that

The population had been much depleted; much cultivated land was left untilled; the stocks of cattle and horses had fallen to a low ebb; the woodlands, always scanty, had almost disappeared; orange groves had been ruined by lack of irrigation; commerce had long been at a standstill.[659]

One of the most famous of the secular pilgrims who did arrive was William Foxwell Albright, a brilliant scholar and natural linguist who knew Spanish, French, German, Latin, Greek, Akkadian and Hebrew and who could read ancient Egyptian hieroglyphs. An extremely ambitious and highly prolific archeologist, he published over 1,100 articles and books during the course of a productive life. It was, in short, the most influential Orientalist of the 50-year period beginning in 1920.

Albright came to Jerusalem that year as director of the American School of Oriental Research. He founded the prestigious *Bulletin of the American Schools of Oriental Research* and was its editor for 38 years—from 1930 until 1968, three years before his death. Since 1970 the American School of Oriental Research has been known as the W. F. Albright Institute of Archaeological Research. Today its Fellows are secular pilgrims from many different universities who study a wide range of scholarly topics. Recent examples of their work are listed in Appendix VII.

Albright himself was convinced of the fundamental historicity of the Bible. This led to the establishment of what came to be known as Albrightian School of biblical archeology, which saw archeological exploration as the best way to evaluate the physical and historical reality of biblical narratives. His greatest ability, however, was to set his own archeological discoveries within the context of the ancient Middle East as a whole. Albright adopted and applied to Levantine archeology the "3 age system," which used the Stone Age, the Bronze Age and the Iron Age to establish a meaningful chronological sequence. His influence was so pervasive that this terminology became widely used by other scholars.

Philip Graves (1922)

The Mandate period had its calm periods as well as its upheavals. In 1922 a British traveler, Philip Graves, commented on the colorful, excited and well-ordered procession of men who were taking part in Muslim celebrations at Nebi Musa. Graves watched them as they passed into Jerusalem through the Jaffa Gate:

> As they entered the old city, the enthusiasm of the crowds reached its highest intensity. Men with the set blank stare of extreme excitement danced round and round, bareheaded, their long locks flying wildly as they revolved…. Last came the green banner of Hebron surrounded by a guard of ten wiry swordsmen. Proudly they walked with their flag, till they came to where the narrow Street of David plunges down into the labyrinth of the old city. For the last time they whirled their bright blades above their heads and disappeared into the shadows of the streets.[660]

Haj Amin al-Husseini (1923)

Haj Amin (the honorific "Haj" showed he had made the pilgrimage to Mecca) became Mufti of Jerusalem[661] in 1921 and head of the Supreme Muslim Council the next year. He worked hard and successfully to raise the status of Jerusalem in the esteem of the Muslim world. His chief accomplishment was the restoration of al-Aqsa Mosque and the Dome of the Rock.

In 1923 Haj Amin sent a delegation to India to raise money for this joint project and followed up the next year with fund-raising ventures in Saudi Arabia,

Kuwait and Bahrain. Donors were responsive and work went ahead as planned. Thanks to the generosity of Arab and Indian rulers, the tattered façade of the Mosque was restored and the Dome was plated with gold. The restoration project was a great success and furthered Haj Amin's own political ambitions as well. Yehoshua Porath, a Jewish historian, agreed that the restoration was "of immense significance":

> It enhanced the value and importance of the two Jerusalem mosques, both in the eyes of the Muslims in Palestine itself and also in the eyes of Muslims in other countries. The fund-raising drive throughout the Muslim world attracted international attention, which became focussed in turn on Jerusalem and the rest of Palestine. This fitted in well with Haj Amin's efforts to achieve recognition as a Muslim personage of world standing.[662]

Haj Amin did achieve a measure of recognition but perhaps of a negative kind. Fearing that increased Jewish immigration to Palestine would reduce Arab influence there, he engineered bloody riots against Jewish settlement in 1929 and 1936. During World War II he tried, but failed, to mobilize Muslim support for Germany. Haj Amin's ambitions were dealt a final setback when the Israelis defeated the Arab armies in 1948.

Jerusalem is partitioned (1949)

Within a few hours after Israel declared its independence in 1948, it was attacked by armies from five Arab states—Lebanon, Syria, Iraq, Jordan[663] and Egypt. An armistice agreement, signed between Israel and Jordan in April 1949, divided Jerusalem along the cease-fire line that existed in November 1948. The result was that East Jerusalem, i.e., the Old City, was controlled by the Jordanians, while West Jerusalem was controlled by the Israelis. These sectors were divided by a "Green Line," which also demarcated two demilitarized zones and several no-man's-lands to prevent the warring parties from having physical contact with each other.

Such a drastic partition of the Holy City could not fail to have an impact on pilgrimages. Although Jordan promised in the armistice agreement that Israeli Jews would have free access to the Western Wall, in practice this did not happen. During the 19 years of Jordanian rule of East Jerusalem, no Israelis were permitted to visit this holy site.[664] The Jordanians did allow Christians and Muslims from all over the world to visit shrines in East Jerusalem. They would not, however, accord this same privilege to the tens of thousands of Muslims who were living in Israel. Ironically, it was therefore a Muslim government in Jordan that prevented Muslims in Israel from visiting the Dome of the Rock and al-Aqsa Mosque on the Haram.

Mary Clawson (1953)

Mary Clawson was a Californian who went to Jerusalem in 1953 when her husband was employed by the Israelis to give them advice on agricultural economics. Her letters to family and friends back in the United States give us a good snapshot of her secular pilgrimage during the early days of Israel's independence.[665]

The Israelis and Arabs were technically still at war and visiting the Old City required a permit. Tensions ran high. When Mrs. Clawson and her husband entered East Jerusalem through the Mandelbaum Gate, she noticed a sign posted by the American Consulate at the border crossing. It read:

In crossing the lines from the Jewish-held section of Jerusalem to the Arab-held, you are advised to be as closed-mouth as possible and as non-committal as possible about what you've been doing in Israel. Also carry with you as few souvenirs of obvious Israeli origin as convenient. The Arab authorities do not appreciate any evidence of pro–Israel sympathy on your part.[666]

She told her correspondents that going through the Mandelbaum Gate was an experience that took one back at least 2,000 years in time. The Old City was picturesque, she said, but she was struck by its poverty, which was in sharp contrast to the relative prosperity of the Israeli-held sector of the city. In the Old City, she said,

Many children are barefooted and in rags, men bowed in two under huge loads, people begging everywhere. And there is also the Eastern servility in hopes of getting a little money. In Israel any shoeshine man, or garbage collector, or what have you, figures he is every bit as good as you, if not a little better, and lets you know it, too…. But in the Old city, people bow to the ground in politeness, which I assume is far too often false…. Once we got inside the walls, I kept thinking, "Our feet are standing within thy gates, O Jerusalem." But though I was rejoicing at being within the gates, I also rejoiced that we lived outside them in Israel.[667]

Dame Kathleen Mary Kenyon (1961–1967)

No one person is associated more than anyone else with the excavation of Jerusalem, but Dame Kenyon would have to be on any list. This distinguished British archeologist began her career as a photographer on a pioneering excavation in Zimbabwe in 1929. She then worked in England,

Samaria, Libya and Jordan. The excavations she undertook at Jericho between 1952 and 1958 made her famous because she made ground-breaking discoveries there about the Neolithic cultures of the Levant.

From 1951 to 1966 Dame Kenyon served as director of the British School of Archeology in Jerusalem and between 1961 and 1967 she excavated in Jerusalem itself. This latter project did not result in any stunning finds but permitted her to put into mature practice the archeological skills she had honed over the years. These were described in her last book, *Digging Up Jerusalem* (1974).

Sacred centers and the Six Day War (1967)

At the beginning of the Six Day War, the Israelis intercepted a telephone call from President Nasser of Egypt to King Hussein of Jordan.[668] Nasser asked the king to order Jordanian forces to attack Israel in order to divert the Israelis from the Sinai Front, where the Egyptians would be fighting. The king was not eager to take on the Israelis, who were much stronger militarily, but he nevertheless gave the order to attack. After heavy fighting, his troops were driven out of East Jerusalem. The two sectors of the Holy City were reunited under Jewish control. The victorious Israelis thus regained Judaism's most holy places—the Temple Mount and the Western Wall.

The importance of the Wall as a sacred center for the Jews cannot be overemphasized. A foreign correspondent reported that as soon as they got to the Wall, "Tough Israeli troops covered with dust wept like small children at the sight"; an Israeli general was deeply moved as "the restrained weeping became sobs, full-throated, an uncontrolled emotional out-

burst."[669] Another Jewish commander, Yitzhak Rabin, who would later become Prime Minister and would be assassinated by a Jewish extremist in 1995, remembered that the Israeli soldiers

> were struggling to reach the Wall and touch it. We stood among a tangle of battle-weary men who were unable to believe their eyes or restrain their emotions. Their eyes were moist with tears, their speech incoherent. The overwhelming desire was to cling to the Wall, to hold on to that great moment as long as possible.[670]

One of the first things the Israelis did after their victory was to knock down the Maghribi (Moroccan) Quarter, which was located to the west of the Wall and which included a passageway in front of the Wall itself. The 619 inhabitants of this historic neighborhood were given only three hours to evacuate their homes, which were then bulldozed to make a huge space in front of the Wall for Jewish pilgrims. The *Jerusalem Post* commented with evident satisfaction that

> When the general public is admitted to the area sometime later this week they will find that the slum buildings which had cluttered the place for more than a century have been razed. There is now a large square before the Wall, which rises in its splendour before the visitor, the moment he turns right from the path leading in from the Dung Gate.[671]

This demolition took place during the Jewish pilgrim festival of *Shavuot*. For the first time in 19 years, Jews were able to visit their sacred centers. An estimated 200,000 Jews, not only West Jerusalemites but Jews from other parts of Israel as well, made a long-delayed pilgrimage to the Wall. The *Jerusalem Post* paid tribute to this event:

For centuries the Wall has been a place of pilgrimage to Jews, the religious first of all, but the non-religious as well. In the years of the British Mandate, people not only went to pray there, but annual pilgrimages, without any organisation or appeal, mobolised practically every Jew whose feet would carry him there and back. The tradition was renewed yesterday [14 June 1967] with an enthusiasm and fervour and in such numbers as must have astonished even those who were aware that these great blocks of stone that are said to date back to the Temple, recipients of the fervent prayers of so many generations, have a national symbolism quite unmatched in Jewish life, which has dealt so largely in abstractions.... *[U]nder no circumstances, whatever the pressures may be, will the citizens of Israel allow anyone to cut them off again from the Wall that stands at the centre of their city and is the essence and reason for its existence.*[672]

Pilgrimages since the 1967 war

The Israeli reunification of Jerusalem in 1967 had significant impacts on Jewish, Christian and Muslim pilgrimages alike. Secular pilgrims have been less affected, although they have profited from easier access to the holy places.

Jewish pilgrims

After the war, not only Israeli Jews but also Jews from many other countries could pray at the Western Wall. Since 1967, a status quo has evolved in Jerusalem. It leaves the Western Wall to the Jews, even though the wall itself is Muslim property and is administered by a Muslim charitable endowment, the Waqf. The Temple Mount is reserved for the Muslims, although a ruling by the Israeli High Court of Justice allows small numbers of Jews, under police escort, to pray on the Temple Mount. But as the right-wing Israeli politician Ariel Sharon found in September 2000, exercising this option may set off a riot. Other organized Jewish religious activity on the Temple Mount is prohibited on public safety grounds.[673]

Israel's capture of the Temple Mount in 1967 raised a number of difficult religious and political issues for the Chief Rabbinate. The fundamental question was whether the Israelis should build a new Temple or should try instead to incorporate the existing Temple Mount into existing religious ceremonies. This issue has never been resolved to the satisfaction of all the parties concerned. There seem to be three schools of thought.[674]

Some are in favor of building a new Temple immediately. Indeed, they have already crafted religious artifacts which could be used there. Others, however, insist that the Temple is destined to be built only by the Messiah himself; until he comes there is nothing for men to do but wait and pray. The third school of thought holds that Jews should be allowed to enter only those parts of the Temple Mount where it is clear that the Temple was *not* located.

Proponents of this third school believe that the site of the Temple must remain off-limits to Jews because the *Shekhina* (the Divine Presence) still resides there. To enter this area in a state of ritual uncleanliness would be to risk death by heavenly decree (*kareth*). This raises two problems, however. The first is that according to the Torah, ritual purification requires the ashes of an unblemished red heifer.[675] No flawless red heifer is considered to have been born in the Holy Land since the Romans destroyed the Second Temple in 70. Thus ritual purification is no longer possible. The second problem is that the precise site of the Temple remains a matter of rabbinical dispute. There is only agreement that the Temple was *not* situated in the northern or southern parts of the Temple Mount.

Since the 1967 war the Western Wall has been easily accessible. Many observant Jews living abroad now come to Jerusalem for one or more of the three great pilgrim festivals—*Pesah*, *Shavuot* and *Sukkot*. Understandably, they also use these visits to see friends and do some sightseeing, but as an American rabbi puts it, "Most Jews visit Israel as pilgrims, not as tourists." [676]

Christian pilgrims

Christian pilgrimages flourished after the Six Day War. It is estimated, in fact, that more Christian visitors have come to the Holy Land since this war than at any other time in history.[677] The scale of this peaceful Christian invasion can be seen from the following example, only one of the many which could be cited.

In about 1988 the Greek Orthodox Patriarch of Jerusalem gave permission for removal of some stone slabs in the Church of the Holy Sepulcher that covered part of the limestone rock which was held to be the site of Christ's crucifixion.[678] These slabs, located in the Chapel of Adam (underneath Calvary), had been laid there during restoration work after a fire in 1808. Once they were removed, this section of the rock would be visible to all the faithful. However, the magnitude of Christian pilgrims visiting this site—nearly 6,000 people every day—was so great it was clear that the rock had to be protected by some kind of covering. Otherwise, with so many people wanting to kiss it, touch it or stand on it, it would soon be worn away.

A technical difficulty was that any new covering had to be transparent, so the rock itself could be seen, but yet strong enough to bear the weight of several priests, who would stand on it during Good Friday ceremonies. The final solution was to install over the rock a special covering made of very strong Swiss glass.

Muslim pilgrims

If the Six Day War benefited Jewish and Christian pilgrims, the reverse has been true for Muslim pilgrims. According to the U.S. Department of State,

> Palestinians residing outside of the Jerusalem municipal boundary are required to obtain a permit to enter the city, even to visit a holy site; the permits are often denied and Israeli security personnel also sometimes deny permit holders access to Jerusalem. Israel has instituted these permit requirements to address its security concerns.[679]

What this means in less bureaucratic language is that ever since the 1967 war, Muslim pilgrimage to Jerusalem has come to a virtual standstill. The Israeli government's public posture is that Israel welcomes "any" religious pilgrims to Jerusalem, *subject to security restrictions.* This is a very broad and flexible definition, however. It is of course the Israelis who evaluate the security situation, so they have the final say in deciding which pilgrims are welcome.

As a practical matter, Palestinians living outside Jerusalem have had great trouble getting into the Old City for any purpose, including worship on the Haram. Moreover, many Arab countries are technically still at war with Israel and will not permit their citizens to go there. The upshot appears to be that about the only Muslim pilgrims coming to Jerusalem since 1967 are small numbers from Indonesia or from other countries which are not still at war with Israel.

Donald Nicholl (1981–1985)

The Tantur Ecumenical Institute for Theological Studies is located on the southern edge of Jerusalem. ("Tantur" is Arabic for "hilltop.") The Institute opened in 1971 and has been led by both Protestant and Roman Catholic rectors. One of the Protestant rectors was Donald Nicholl, a deeply religious British medieval and modern historian who served at Tantur from 1981 to 1985. This was such a challenging experience for him that he referred to it as "a pilgrim's journey" and used this phrase as the subtitle of his book about his rectorship, *The Testing of Hearts* (1989).

For the devotional pilgrims of the past, it may not have been easy to reconcile the dream of the heavenly Jerusalem with the reality of the earthly Jerusalem. What Nicholl discovered during his earliest days in office was that the gap between what he referred to as the "dreamland Tantur" and the "actual Tantur" had generated a good deal of frustration and criticism among the academic pilgrims within the Institute itself. "Sadly, and not for the first time in Christian history," Nicholl wrote, "it is precisely the act by which it is hoped to create the perfect community that seems to have precipitated the most division here at Tantur."[680]

Nicholl devoted himself to healing these divisions and trying to formulate a Christian response to Jerusalem's intractable political, religious and social conflicts. Writing only a few days before his death in 1997, he summed up what he had learned as a pilgrim-historian:

> the only way to end violence and injustice and ignorance … is by *grace*, attracting others through freely giving oneself to all. The attraction of goodness is the only way to draw others out of the world of injustice, violence, conflict and unhappiness. Not by forcing others, but drawing them gracefully

into communion with oneself and all creation.[681]

Pope John Paul II's pilgrimage (2000)

The first Pope to come to Israel was Paul VI, who made a low-key stop there in 1964. His pilgrimage was not designed to be an ecumenical triumph. Pope Paul VI was in the Holy Land for only 12 hours, never publicly uttered the word "Israel," refused to meet with the senior rabbi of Jerusalem, and made it clear that his visit did not mean that the Vatican was officially recognizing Israel. The contrast with Pope John Paul II's pilgrimage 36 years later is striking.

Before he became Pope, John Paul had made a personal pilgrimage to Jerusalem in 1963. In 2000, following a precedent first established by the Jews in the time of Moses and later approved for Christians by Pope Boniface VIII in 1300, John Paul proclaimed that the year 2000 would be a *Jubilee*, that is, a holy year dedicated to God. In so doing, he stressed the importance of pilgrimage, which he said

> evokes the believer's personal journey in the footsteps of the Redeemer. It is an exercise of practical asceticism, of repentance for human weakness, of constant vigilance over one's own frailty, of interior preparation for a change of heart.[682]

Although he described his papal visit of 21–26 March 2000 as a personal spiritual pilgrimage, it could not fail to have strong political overtones as well. For himself, he sought spiritual enrichment but for the three world faiths, he sought reconciliation and peacemaking.[683] His trip did not result in any bold new initiatives but this was not its purpose. As Father Remi

Left: Pope John Paul II prays at the Western Wall. (Servizio Fotografico de "L'O.R.") *Right:* Pious Jews write prayers on small pieces of paper and stuff them into crevices between the massive stones of the Western Wall. These prayer notes are later removed and buried in a Jewish cemetery to make room for others. (Photograph by the author.)

Hoeckman, the Pope's spokesman for Catholic-Jewish relations, put it,

> The Holy See does not want to interfere, but ... we want to reach a point at which the Holy Land can set an example for the rest of humankind, which it's definitely not doing right now. If ... in spite of a painful past we can speak with one voice, it is a sign for humankind to rediscover bonds among human beings.[684]

The most moving event in the Pope's pilgrimage came when prayed at the Western Wall. There, like countless Jewish pilgrims, he inserted a prayer-letter in a crack. His letter read:

> God of our fathers,
> You chose Abraham and his descendants to bring your Name to the Na-

tions: we are deeply saddened by the behavior of those who in the course of history have caused these children of yours to suffer, and asking your forgiveness we wish to commit ourselves to genuine brotherhood with the people of the Covenant.
> Jerusalem, 26 March 2000.
> Signed: John Paul II[685]

Johanna van Fessem (2001)

Given the pull that Jerusalem has exerted on men and women for three millennia, it is not surprising that arduous ghostly pilgrimages are still being made in our own time. Johanna van Fessem is a good example. This 52-year-old Dutch woman left her home in the Netherlands on 2 April 2000 and walked, by herself,

In April 2000, Johanna van Fessem left her home in The Hague and began walking toward Jerusalem. Her departure is shown here. (Photograph courtesy Peter den Haring.)

most of the way to Jerusalem, where she arrived on 5 March 2001.[686] Her story is well worth hearing, especially in her own words. Before setting off on her journey, she wrote:

> I am [now] free to start realizing a dream, which has grown in me for 13 years after visiting Israel for the first time in 1987. I am very interested in the peace process in the Middle East. It has been close to my heart ever since I realized the spiritual and political importance of Jerusalem. This is what I wanted to do: to walk this distance like the medieval pilgrims, with a special intention. I wanted to pray and meditate for the peace of Jerusalem, for political peace in the Middle East, which will be part of God's peace. I was originally a Roman Catholic but now travel beyond the borders of traditional belief. I studied Talmud for eight years, which was an enduring influence in my life and opened my mind and heart to the value

of Jewish views on life, people and God. I worked for four years [in the Netherlands] with Islamic women in a language project and learned more about Muslim values. This made me aware of the spiritual importance of all three religions for this one holy city, Jerusalem. In addition, I am greatly interested in practicing new forms of spirituality, such as meditation/prayer, especially in connection with body consciousness. This has for me a connection with living planet Earth from which our bodies are made. That is why I want to honor the planet by walking, a non-polluting way of travelling, and I want to honor women by travelling alone.[687]

Asked what she had learned from her pilgrimage, she replied with a lucidity which seems to capture the essence of the Jerusalem pilgrimage:

> This long walk has deepened my awareness of human dignity. I have met with

a lot of respect on my way, often from people who did not understand why I did such a strange thing. I have met with hospitality and interest. No harm has come to me during this long way to Jerusalem. I was allowed to experience love and to love myself. I hope this process will go on. More and more I have the feeling that the something that is called God, or Source, or whatever name you will give it, comes stronger into my life and I feel the longing of surrendering to it completely, to accept life more and more as it is, without conditions. It is an act of love and trust and gratitude on my part, a present to The Present One.[688]

XI

A Summing-Up: *"Unity in Diversity" and the Symbolism of the Journey*

We have now looked at more than 165 contemporary accounts of the Jerusalem pilgrimage. Paradoxically, despite the fact that each pilgrimage is unique, there is still a good deal of *sameness* about them. For unless they die en route or become too ill to travel, most pilgrims follow the same pattern. They weigh the pros and cons of going on pilgrimage. Having decided to proceed, they prepare for the journey. They leave home, family and friends behind them, not knowing whether they will ever see them again. They travel to a sacred center, often a long distance away and requiring a good deal of stamina to reach. They worship at the holy sites there. Then they return home again, renewed in spirit and, possibly, with the ability to see their old lives with newly opened eyes.

This much is explicit and perhaps nothing more can usefully be added here. But if at this point we are willing to leave purely factual accounts behind us and step out, somewhat gingerly, onto the thin ice of speculation, there may in fact be something more to be said. For what is *implicit* is that over the last 3,000 years the Jerusalem pilgrims have been bound together by two different factors. The first can be called

"unity in diversity." The second is the symbolism of the journey itself. Both concepts require a word of explanation.

"Unity in diversity"

This phrase happens to be the motto of Indonesia, a country whose 212,000,000 citizens belong to 300 different ethnic groups, speak 250 local dialects and are scattered across more than 13,000 islands. The diversity apparent in the Jerusalem pilgrimage is, in its own way, equally dramatic. As this book has tried to show, very large numbers of people have made their way to the Holy City over the last three millennia. They have come from many different countries for many different reasons and have spoken many different languages. Clearly, a great deal of diversity is on display here.

Granted that, what about unity? It seems clear that despite their enormous diversity, the Jerusalem pilgrims do in fact have one thing in common: they have all come to the Holy City on a quest of some sort. The objects of their quests may be as diverse as the pilgrims themselves. As was noted in the introduction to this book, there are many and frequently overlapping reasons for pilgrimages: to seek spiritual perfection, to ask for supernatural help in some enterprise, to express devotion, to perform an act of penance, to give thanks, to search for secular knowledge or simply to have a good time. There is, however, one common denominator implicit in all this—*the quest for something greater, or at least more fulfilling, than the routine of one's daily life.* It is this quest which, in the end, unites all the Jerusalem pilgrims.

The symbolism of the journey

Pilgrims have usually found that, as the Rev. Craig Eder, an American veteran of several pilgrimages puts it, "There is a huge benefit for a group of people to grow in spirit as they share both a physical and spiritual journey."[689] The tour guides interviewed in the Old City in April 2001 confirmed that Jerusalem pilgrims still come in groups. Travel by air is a cramped, isolating experience which is unlikely to result in any spiritual enlightenment, but even these pilgrims will have the opportunity to "grow in spirit" once they get to Jerusalem.

Air travel is only a recent phenomenon, however, and does not detract from the historic importance of the overland or sea journey itself. If anything, it has made travel too boring and too easy. In his poem "Journey of the Magi," T. S. Eliot evokes the inherent and, as the medieval preacher Jacques de Vitry said, the necessary difficulty of any ghostly journey to the Holy Land.[690]

The three Magi may have had to travel in winter to get to Bethlehem in time for the birth of Jesus, but few if any of the real Jerusalem pilgrims ever made their way voluntarily through deep snow. Like Chaucer's merry band, most Western pilgrims set out by choice in the spring, often in April. Nevertheless, Eliot's poem is relevant because it calls attention to the central role played by the journey itself. Many other modern writers have focused on this subject. Among them are John Steinbeck (1902–1968), Thomas Merton (1915–1968) and Victor Turner (1920–1983).

Many cultures have independently expressed their own belief in the importance of the journey. "To travel hopefully," proclaimed the Scottish writer Robert Louis Stevenson (1850–1894), "is a better thing than to arrive." Zen Buddhists assure us that "the journey is more important than the destination." Perhaps one could go even further and say that, for some pilgrims at least, *the journey is the destination.* This was what the American novelist John Steinbeck must have had in mind when he wrote "The Leader of the People," one of the stories in *The Red Pony* (1937).

The protagonist in this story is an old man who had led a wagon train across the western United States. Steinbeck has him say: "It wasn't getting here [California] that mattered, it was movement and westering. We carried life out here and set it down."[691] For this wagon-master, the journey had in fact become the destination.

One of the most distinguished Roman Catholic writers of the twentieth century, Thomas Merton, believed that pilgrimage was a sacred journey which had two equally important aspects—the *outer* and the *inner.* For him, the outer pilgrimage, i.e., the physical act of setting out from home, was "the symbolic acting out of an inner journey." While it was possible to have an outer geographical pilgrimage without an inner spiritual journey, it was, he thought, "best to have both."[692]

Merton drew these ideas from the lives of the ancient Celtic monks in Ireland. Not only had they practiced both the outer geographic pilgrimage and the inner spiritual journey, but they had also gone far beyond these constraints. Their ideal was not simply to make a journey and then return to the security of the monastic community when they were finished.[693] Instead, these hardy monks believed that to follow Christ meant they were called on to continue the sacred journey by passing much or all of the rest of their lives in solitude as hermits.

Merton caught the spirit of this Celtic eremitism in a poem that carried the symbolism of the pilgrimage journey to its farthest extreme. He believed that we are all exiles, living in solitude, and listening for the first faint warnings of Christ's second coming.[694]

Other insights into the journey were provided by the British anthropologist Victor Turner. In *Image and Pilgrims in Christian Culture: Anthropological Perspectives* (1978), co-authored with his wife Edith, he argued that

> *The point of it all is to get out, go forth, to a far holy place approved by all.* In societies with few economic opportunities for movement away from limited circles of friends, neighbors, and local authorities, all rooted alike in the soil, the only journey possible for those not merchants, peddlers, minstrels, jugglers, tumblers, wandering friars, or outlaws, or their modern equivalents, is a holy journey, a pilgrimage or a crusade.[695]

The Turners asserted that when pilgrims set off on a sacred journey, they leave behind them all the familiar demands and constraints of the social structure at home.[696] As a result, they enter into a world of "antistructure," that is, a world in which conventional behavior and expectations no longer apply, or at least do not apply with the same force. By traveling long distances with their co-religionists, by meeting other men and women from different walks of life along the way, and by worshiping together at holy sites, pilgrims can have such a positive communal experience that they enter into what the Turners called a state of "communitas."

Characterized by warmth, friendship, cooperation, consensus and sharing, this idyllic state may be more important and more enjoyable than reaching the destination. A pilgrim's fond memories of "communitas" might well last longer than memories of the often-tawdry realities of the holy places themselves. A number of objections to the Turners' theories have been raised, however, so they cannot be accepted without some qualification.

For example, when asked about *communitas*, Hindu pilgrims give very different explanations for the power of pilgrimages. They cite instead the redeeming qualities of holy places, the presence there of holy persons and the spiritual benefits of performing religious ceremonies.[697] It is obvious, moreover, that pilgrimage sites such as the Temple Mount can encourage not only peaceful "communitas" but intense political and social conflict as well.

Summing up the Jerusalem pilgrimage

Most if not all pilgrims have probably experienced, to varying degrees and perhaps only unconsciously, the twin themes of "unity in diversity" and the importance of the journey. Beyond this, it is difficult to generalize. All that is clear from a historical point of view is that this great adventure has meant different things to different people—to Jews, to Christians, to Muslims and to secular pilgrims. There have been many different understandings *within* these communities, too.

Nevertheless, rushing in where angels fear to tread, a summing-up will be attempted here. Perhaps the best formulation is a minimalist one:

Whatever people have come to Jerusalem to find, they have been likely to find, whether it is holiness and forgiveness at a sacred center or simply the chance to see new places and meet new people. True, some pilgrims have been disillusioned. The Old City is still crowded and dirty. In the past, local officials were rapacious. The Holy Fire was a sham. The bedouin *could be dangerous. The holy sites were tawdry and commercialized. There have been riots, civil wars, regional wars and world wars.*

Nevertheless, despite its shortcomings, Jerusalem has remained a city unique in all the world. The vast majority of pilgrims have found their journey deeply fulfilling. It has confirmed them in their own beliefs. The reports they have carried back home have encouraged other pilgrims to follow in their footsteps—a process which will almost certainly continue for centuries to come.

Selected Chronology

c. 3200 BCE	First traces of human habitation in Jerusalem
c. 1850–1810 BCE	Earliest mention of Jerusalem
c. 1250 BCE	Exodus of the Jews from Egypt
c. 1225 BCE	Jews settle in Israel
c. 1020 BCE	Saul becomes the first Israelite king
c. 1000 BCE	David conquers Jerusalem
957 BCE	Solomon finishes building the First Temple
c. 922 BCE	Divided monarchy begins as the Holy Land splits into two kingdoms, Israel and Judah; before the end of this period (c. 586 BCE) the independently verifiable history of Israel begins, too, thanks to corroborating Assyrian and Babylonian sources
722/721 BCE	Sargon II, king of Assyria, destroys the Kingdom of Israel
701 BCE	Sennacherib, king of Assyria, invades Kingdom of Judah
c. 640–609 BCE	During his reign, Josiah abolishes all sanctuaries other than the First Temple
604, 597 and 587/586 BCE	Babylonians loot the First Temple twice (in 604 and 597 BCE) and then destroy it completely (in 587/586 BCE); Jewish leaders and skilled workers are exiled to Babylon, where they remain for between 48 and 70 years
538/537 BCE	After defeating the Babylonians, Cyrus the Great gives the Jews permission to return to Jerusalem to rebuild the Temple
516/515 BCE	Israelites complete work on the Second Temple
333/332 BCE	Thanks to the conquests of Alexander the Great, Jerusalem becomes part of the wider Hellenistic world
c. 301 BCE	After the death of Alexander, Jerusalem becomes a possession of the Ptolomy Dynasty
198 BCE	Seleucid dynasty comes to power.
167 BCE	Antiochus IV Epiphanes desecrates the Second Temple by setting up an altar to Zeus and sacrificing a pig on it
168–164 BCE	Hasmonean revolt: Judas Maccabee recaptures Jerusalem and Jews reconsecrate the Second Temple
c. 150 BCE	Aristeas, a Hellenistic Jew, is impressed by the strength and ability shown by Temple priests when conducting sacrifices
63 BCE	Romans conquer Jerusalem: Pompey desecrates the Second Temple by daring to enter the Holy of Holies

19/20 BCE	Herod the Great decides to build a new Temple with a huge platform (the Temple Mount) surrounding it
c. 7–4 BCE	Birth of Jesus
26 CE	Work on the Herodian Temple Mount is completed; Jerusalem becomes a great metropolis of the Hellenistic world
c. 29–30	Jesus makes the annual pilgrimage to Jerusalem for *Pesah* (Passover) and is crucified there
40	Philo of Alexandria reports on the "countless multitudes" of Jewish pilgrims in Jerusalem
66	First Jewish revolt against Roman rule
c. 67	Death of St. Paul
70	Led by Titus, the Romans capture Jerusalem, destroy the Herodian Temple and disperse the Jews
100	Death of the Jewish soldier and historian Flavius Josephus
130	Roman emperor Hadrian decides to replace Jerusalem, which lay in ruins, with a new city known as Aelia Capitolina
132	Hadrian outlaws key Jewish practices, sparking the Second Jewish revolt against Roman rule, led by Simon Bar Koseba
135	Romans recapture Jerusalem
170	First recorded Christian pilgrimage to Jerusalem is made by Melito, bishop of Sardis
230–235	Biblical scholar Origen teaches in Palestine, stressing the importance of spiritual rather than earthly pilgrimages
313	Emperor Constantine decrees that Christianity will be one of the official religions of the Roman empire
324	Constantine brings Palestine into the Eastern Roman Empire
325	Constantine's mother, Queen Helena, makes a pilgrimage to Jerusalem where she discovers the True Cross
333	Bordeaux Pilgrim leaves first detailed itinerary of a pilgrimage to Jerusalem
334–336	Constantine builds the Church of the Holy Sepulcher
340	Death of the Biblical scholar Eusebius, who helped bridge the theological gap between the heavenly and the earthly Jerusalems
379	Two Western pilgrims—Rufinus and Melania—set up the first pilgrim hostel in Jerusalem
c. 380	Gregory of Nyssa criticizes pilgrimages to Jerusalem
384	Biblical translator St. Jerome and his friend Paula, a Roman noblewoman, begin an extensive pilgrimage to Palestine and Egypt
c. 386	Egeria, a Spanish nun, records her extended tour of the Holy Land
389	Jerome and Paula open their own pilgrim hostel in Jerusalem
c. 412	Hoping to escape controversy, the English monk Pelagius moves to Jerusalem but runs into problems there, too
413–426	In *The City of God*, St. Augustine divides humanity into those who yearn for the heavenly city (Jerusalem) and those who are enamored of the earthly city (Babylon)
c. 414	Bishop Eucherius describes Jerusalem

438	Empress Eudokia makes a pilgrimage to Jerusalem and is caught up in the Bar Sauma revolt
529	Samaritan Revolt
c. 530	*Breviarius* guidebook
c. 530	*On the Topography of the Holy Land* is written by the Western pilgrim Theodosius
c. 570	Piacenza Pilgrim leaves us the most vivid description of the Jerusalem pilgrimage before the First Crusade
c. 571	Birth of Muhammad
614	Persian army captures Jerusalem, slaughters its inhabitants and destroys Christian churches
630	Heraclius, emperor of Byzantium, conquers Jerusalem
632	Death of Muhammad
638	Muslim Caliph 'Umar I conquers Jerusalem
c. 660	First Muslim pilgrimages to Jerusalem
c. 680	Arculf, a French bishop, spends nine months in the Holy Land and later, in Scotland, dictates an account to the Venerable Bede
685	Umayyad Dynasty is in power
691	Caliph 'Abd al-Malik completes the Dome of the Rock
715	Al-Aqsa Mosque is completed
720–726	Travels of St. Willibald, the first English pilgrim to visit the Holy Land
mid–8th century	Abbasid Dynasty is in power
c. 800	A briefing paper, *Memorandum on the Houses and God and Monasteries in the Holy City*, is written for Charlemagne
c. 800	The monk Einhard travels with Charlemagne and records the emperor's dealings with Caliph al-Harun
c. 826–859	Experiences of anonymous Muslim holy women
867	First mention of the Holy Fire
903	Persian geographer Ibn al-Faiq is greatly impressed by the Haram
909	Benedictine abbey of Cluny is founded; it will become a key organizing center for the Jerusalem pilgrimage
c. 913	Ibn 'Abd Rabbih, a Spanish Muslim scholar, reports that an entrance to Paradise is located under the Dome of the Rock
c. 969	Fatimid Dynasty is in power
985	Muslim geographer al-Muqaddasi notes there are many Christian pilgrims and residents in Jerusalem
c. 1000	Millennial year brings large numbers of Christian pilgrims to Jerusalem
1006	Pilgrimage of the Russian abbot Daniel
1009	The mad caliph al-Hakim destroys the Church of the Holy Sepulcher and the tomb of Christ
1026	Pilgrimage of French abbot Richard of St. Vannes leads to a dramatic reaffirmation of his own faith

1040	A great sinner, Fulk III Nerra, makes a penitential pilgrimage
1044	Cluniac monk Rodolfus Glaber finishes *The Five Books of the Histories*, chronicling the "innumerable number of people from the whole world" who are going on the Jerusalem pilgrimage
First half of 11th century	Ibn al-Murajja writes the first step-by-step guidebook for Muslim pilgrims
c. 1047	In the *Book of Travels*, Persian pilgrim Naser-e Khosraw reports on his experiences in Jerusalem
1047	Pilgrimage of the Persian traveler Abu Mu'in Nasir
1053	English nobleman Earl Sweyn is forced to undertake a penitential pilgrimage
1059	Israel ben Sahlun, a scribe, admits that he has settled in Jerusalem to escape his debtors
1064/1065	Ingulphus, an Englishman, chronicles the great German pilgrimage
1073	Seljuq Turks capture Jerusalem; subsequent political instability results in the diversion or closing of pilgrimage routes, thus setting the stage for the First Crusade
1077	Pro-Fatimid groups in Jerusalem rebel against Turkish rule
1095	Abu Hamid al-Ghazali, greatest of Muslim scholars, goes to Jerusalem
1095	Pope Urban II preaches the First Crusade
c. 1096	Peter the Hermit and the People's Crusade
1098	Muslims (Fatimids) retake Jerusalem
1099	First Crusaders conquer Jerusalem and slaughter its inhabitants
1099	Pilgrimage of the English merchant Saewulf
1101	Fulcher de Chartres, French chaplain and chronicler of First Crusade, reports on the Holy Fire
1103	Scandinavian pilgrimages to the Holy Land
c. 1110	Pilgrimage of the Norwegian prince Sigurd
1113	Founding of the Knights Hospitaler
1128	Official founding of the Knights Templar
c. 1140	Remarkable experience of the Syrian gentleman Usama ibn Munqidh
1141	Death of the Jewish poet Judah ha-Levi
1145	Second Crusade
1149	Church of the Holy Sepulcher as it exists today is consecrated
1151	Pilgrimage of Jarl (Earl) Rognvald of Orkney
1160	Spanish rabbi Benjamin of Tudela begins his travels to the East
c. 1170	Pilgrimage of the German priest John of Würzburg
c. 1171	German pilgrim Theoderic reports on the Holy Fire
1173	Visit of the Arab traveler 'Ali al-Hawari
1174	Travels of German rabbi Petachia of Ratisbon
1180	Travels of Rabbi Jacob ha Cohen
1187	Saladin, founder of Ayubbid Dynasty, conquers Jerusalem

1187	Third Crusade
1192	Canon Richard of London visits Jerusalem
1198	Establishment of the Teutonic Knights
1198	Fourth Crusade
1207	Herbert of Patsley
1212	Children's Crusade
1215	Fifth Crusade
1217	Pilgrimage of Magister Thietmar
c. 1217	Construction of Castle Pilgrim
1217	Pilgrimage of Jewish poet Yehuda al-Harizi
1228	Sixth Crusade
1229	Peace treaty returns Jerusalem to Crusader control
1244	Khwarizmian Turks sack Jerusalem
1244	Seventh Crusade
1247	Al-Malik al-Salih Ayyub of Egypt conquers Jerusalem
1250	Bahri Mamluk dynasty comes to power
1259	Death of the medieval chronicler Matthew Paris
1263	Mamluk sultan Baybars sets up two new Islamic sanctuaries near Jerusalem
1267	Pilgrimage of Spanish rabbi Moses ben Nachman (Nachmanides)
1270	Eighth Crusade
c. 1280	Pilgrimage of German Dominican monk Burchard of Mount Sion
1291	Arab scholar Abu I-Fida describes the Muslims' conquest of Acre, the last Crusader stronghold in the Holy Land
1303/1304	Knights Templar are falsely charged with blasphemies and homosexuality
1328	Death of the Muslim traditionalist Ibn Taymiyya, who warned against religious excesses in Jerusalem
1334	William of Boldensele, a German monk, is sent on a penitential pilgrimage to Jerusalem and ordered to write a report
1334	Visit of the Spanish traveler and Kabbalist Isaac ben Joseph ibn Chelo
1335	Ibn Battuta, greatest medieval traveler of the Arab world, visits Jerusalem
1346	Pilgrimage of the Franciscan friar Niccolo of Poggibonsi
1346	Visit of Ludolph of Sudheim
1351–1353	Black Death (bubonic plague) kills many people in Jerusalem
1386–1387	Geoffrey Chaucer begins *The Canterbury Tales*
1382	Burji Mamluks come to power
1406	Richard Alkerton, an English pilgrim, describes pilgrim equipment
1412	A counterfeit pilgrim, William Blakeney, is sentenced to the pillory with a whetstone hung from his neck
1419	Nompar de Caumont brings home lavish presents from Jerusalem for his wife and friends

1420	An anonymous French pilgrim reports on how the friars in Jerusalem carefully maintain national and social distinctions between pilgrims
1421	Emmanuel Piloti calls for a new Crusade to recapture Jerusalem
1432	Bertrandon de la Broquière tells how to arrange a *bedouin* escort for crossing the Sinai desert
1434	En route to Jerusalem, Elijah of Ferrara loses two sons and one grandson to the plague
c. 1440	Death of English mystic and pilgrim Margery Kempe
1458	William Wey may have been commissioned by King Henry VI to write a guidebook to the Holy Land
1461	Louis de Rochechouart says that the *bedouin* "live like wild beasts"
1480	German Dominican monk Felix Fabri makes his first pilgrimage to Jerusalem; four years later, he will write the best single account of medieval Christian pilgrimages
1481	Rabbi Meshullam ben R. Menahem of Volterra warns prospective pilgrims about the *bedouin*, who hide in sand up to their necks, waiting for the best time to attack
1486	Bernhard von Breydenbach produces the first printed map of the Holy Land based on contemporary eyewitness accounts
1486	Another anonymous French pilgrim complains about the wretched food and poor accommodations in the Holy Land
1487	Pilgrimage of Obadiah ben Abraham Yare Bertinoro, a scholarly Italian rabbi
1494	An elderly Italian priest, Canon Pietro Casola, visits Jerusalem
1496	Arab historian Mujir al-Din puts Jerusalem on a par with Mecca and Medina
1506	Pilgrimage of Sir Richard Guildford, privy councilor to Henry VII
1517	Travels of English priest Sir Richard Torkington
1517	Sultan Selim I conquers Jerusalem, beginning 400 years of rule by the Ottoman Turks
1520	Suleiman the Magnificent comes to power; he will build Jerusalem's walls, restore the Haram and give Jews the right to pray at the Western Wall
1523	Adventures of David Reubeni, a charismatic Jewish imposter
1533	Greffin Affagart, a pious French pilgrim, is disillusioned by what he finds in Jerusalem
1536	Death of Dutch scholar Desiderius Erasmus, who laid the foundations for modern historical-critical studies of the Holy Land
c. 1550	Nasir al-Din writes a guide for Muslim pilgrims to Jerusalem
1559	Protestant reformer John Calvin derides pilgrimage as "counterfeit worship"
1600s–1700s	Sufi pilgrimages to Jerusalem
1630	Governor William Bradford describes the English Puritans who settled in Plymouth, Massachusetts, as "pilgrimes," i.e., exiles
1648–1650	Evliye Chelebi, a Turkish gentleman, visits Jerusalem
1650	Thomas Fuller conducts a semi-scientific study of the Holy Land

1655–1658	English poet John Milton dismisses pilgrims as misguided people
1660	Muslim traditionalist al-Qashashi is shocked by mixing of the sexes at the holy sites
1678–1684	John Bunyan's *The Pilgrim's Progress*
1684	An unnamed English pilgrim says that "Jerusalem stole his heart from him"
1697	Visit of Henry Maundrell, Chaplain of the British Levant Company
1719	Nathaniel Crouch makes a "tiresome pilgrimage"
1757	Ottoman edict known as the Status Quo agreements spells out the respective rights of Christian denominations at the Church of the Holy Sepulcher
1799	Napoleon tries to conquer Palestine but fails
1831	Ibrahim Pasha of Egypt conquers Jerusalem and introduces far-reaching reforms
1838	The rise of Gentile Zionism: Lord Shaftesbury concludes that most Jews in Europe want to immigrate to Palestine
1839	David Roberts, the Scottish painter-pilgrim, visits the Holy Land
Late 1830s	Steam begins to replace sail in the Mediterranean, making travel to Palestine safer and more popular
1839	Turks recapture Jerusalem
1853–1856	Crimean War
1855	Haram is opened up to non–Muslim pilgrims for the first time in hundreds of years
1862	Moses Hess publishes *Rome and Jerusalem*, a pioneering study of Zionism
1862	Albert, Prince of Wales, visits Jerusalem
1865	British set up the Palestine Exploration Fund to promote secular studies of the Holy Land
1865	Charles Wilson directs the British Ordnance Survey of Jerusalem
1867	Excavations by archeologist Charles Warren
1867	Mark Twain visits Jerusalem to gather material for *The Innocents Abroad*
1867	A paved road links Jaffa and Jerusalem, making pilgrimage easier and safer
1869	Thomas Cook brings tourists to the Holy Land
1872	Claude Reignier Conder directs the Survey of Western Palestine
1873	Ignaz Goldhizer begins to create the academic discipline of modern Arab-Islamic studies
1890	William Flinders Petrie begins to establish Middle East archeology as a scientific discipline
1890	Archeologist Frederick H. Bliss discovers layers of "cities" at Tell el-Hesi
1891	British artist Elizabeth Butler visits Jerusalem
c. 1891	A single-track narrow-gauge railway links Jerusalem and Jaffa
1892	Marie Serao, a devout Italian pilgrim and writer, visits the Holy Land to gather material for what will be a best-selling guidebook, *In the Country of Jesus.*
1898	Founder of Zionism Theodor Herzl visits Jerusalem

1898	Kaiser Wilhelm II makes a political pilgrimage to the Holy City
c. 1900	Prince Adelbert, the Kaiser's second son, visits Jerusalem
1900	A perceptive observer and writer, Ada Goodrich-Freer spends two years in Jerusalem
1911	Montague Brownslow Parker provokes riots by digging for buried treasure under the Temple Mount
1912	Stephen Graham accompanies Russian pilgrims to Jerusalem
1914	The last group of Russian pilgrims before the Russian Revolution celebrate the appearance of the Holy Fire in Jerusalem
1914–1918	World War I brings a temporary halt to pilgrimages
1917 (November)	Arthur James Balfour signs the Balfour Declaration, putting Britain on record as calling for "a national home for the Jewish people" in Palestine
1917 (December)	British General Sir Edmund Allenby enters Jerusalem as a military pilgrim during World War I
1920–1948	British Mandate period, marked by bloody confrontations between Arabs, Jews and British in 1920, 1921, 1929 and 1936–1939
1920	William Foxwell Albright goes to Jerusalem to become head of the American School of Oriental Research
1922	British traveler Philip Graves visits the Holy City
1923	In addition to his positive achievements (restoring the Aqsa Mosque and Dome of Rock), Haj Amin al-Husseini preaches a violent anti–Semitism that sparks riots
1927	Islamic Museum, located on the western side of Al-Aqsa Mosque and housed in two venerable buildings (one Ayyubid, the other Crusader) is established
1948	State of Israel is founded, precipitating the first Arab-Israeli war
1949	Israel wins the war; an armistice divides Jerusalem into East Jerusalem (administered by Jordan) and West Jerusalem (administered by Israel)
1950	Israel proclaims Jerusalem as its capital but most countries keep their embassies in Tel Aviv because they believe the final status of Jerusalem must be determined by negotiations
1953	Mary Clawson, an American visitor, reports on life in Jerusalem in the early days of Israel's independence
1961–1967	The famous British archeologist Dame Kathleen Mary Kenyon conducts excavations in Jerusalem
1967	Israelis capture East Jerusalem during the Six Day War and reunite the city
1981–1985	Pilgrim-historian Donald Nicholl serves as rector of the Tantur Ecumenical Institute in Jerusalem
2000 (March)	Pilgrimage of Pope John Paul II
2000 (September)	Visit of right wing Israeli politician Ariel Sharon to the Temple Mount sparks a Palestinian *intifada* (uprising)
2001	Dutch pilgrim Johanna van Fessem arrives in Jerusalem after walking most of the way from the Netherlands
2002	Final political status of Jerusalem still remains undetermined: both Israelis and Palestinians continue to claim it as their rightful capital

Appendix I:
Selected List of Accounts Cited, in Chronological Order

David (c. 1000 BCE)
Aristeas (second century BCE)
Herod (19 BCE)
Jesus Christ (c. 29 CE)
Philo of Alexandria (40)
St. Paul (c. 67)
Flavius Josephus (70)
Melito (170)
Origen (230)
Constantine (325)
Bordeaux Pilgrim (333)
Eusebius (before 340)
Melania and Rufinus (379)
Gregory of Nyssa (c. 380)
Egeria (c. 381)
Jerome and Paula (385)
Pelagius (c. 412)
Augustine (413)
Eucherius (414)
Eudokia (438)
Breviarius (c. 530)
Theodosius (c. 530)
Piacenza Pilgrim (c. 570)
Muhammad (before 632)
'Umar (638)
Arculf (c. 680)
Willibald (723)
Charlemagne (c. 800)
Darani (c. 826)
Ibn Daud (ninth century)

Ibn al-Faqih (903)
Ibn 'Abd Rabbih (c. 913)
Al-Muqaddesi (985)
Abbot Daniel (1006)
Richard of St. Vannes (c. 1026)
Fulk III Nerra (1040)
Glaber (1044)
Abu Mu'in Nasir (1047)
Ibn al-Murajja (first half of eleventh century)
Naser-e Khosraw (1047)
Earl Sweyn (1053)
Israel ben Sahlun (1059)
Ingulphus (1064/1065)
Urban II (1095)
Peter the Hermit (c. 1096)
Abu Hamid al-Ghazali (c. 1096)
Guibert of Nogent (c. 1096)
Arnulf (1099)
Raymond of Aguiles (1099)
Sigurd (after 1099)
Fulcher de Chartres (1101)
Saewulf (1101)
Usama ibn Munqidh (c. 1140)
Judah ha-Levi (1140)
Rognvald of Orkney (1151)
Benjamin of Tudela (1160)
John of Würtzburg (c. 1170)
Theodoric (c. 1171)

'Ali al-Hawari (1173)
Petachia of Ratisbon (1175)
Jacob ha Cohen (c. 1180)
Saladin (1187)
Richard of London (c. 1192)
Richard I (before 1199)
Herbert of Patsy (1207)
Samuel ben Samson (1210)
Gottfried von Strassburg (c. 1210)
Thietmar (1217)
Yehuda al-Harizi (1217)
Ibn al-Athir (before 1233)
Jacob, the "messenger" (1238)
Jacques de Vitry (1239)
Matthew Paris (before 1259)
Baybars (1263)
Moses ben Nachman (1267)
Burchard of Mount Sion (1280)
Abu I-Fida (1291)
William of Boldensele (1334)
Isaac ben Joseph ibn Chelo (1334)
Ibn Battuta (1335)
Niccolo of Poggibonsi (1346)
Ludolph of Sudheim (1346)
John Mandeville (1356)
Pietro Azario (14th century)
Walter Hilton (14th century)
Geoffrey Chaucer (1386)

Richard Alkerton (1406)
William Thorpe (1407)
William Blakeney (1412)
Nompar de Caumont (1419)
Anonymous French pilgrim
    (1420)
Emmanuel Piloti (1420)
Bertrandon de la Broquière
    (1432)
Elijah of Ferrara (1434)
Margery Kempe (before 1440)
William Wey (1458)
Louis de Rochechouart (1461)
Felix Fabri (1480)
Meshullam ben R. Menahem
    (1481)
Bernhard von Breydenbach
    (1486)
Anonymous French pilgrim
    (1486)
Obadiah ben Abraham Yare
    Bertinoro (1487)
Pietro Casola (1494)
Mujir al-Din (1496)
Richard Guildford (1506)
Richard Torkington (1517)
Suleiman the Magnificent
    (1520)
David Reubeni (1523)
Greffin Affagart (1533)
Nasir al-Din (c. 1550)
Antoine Regnaut (1573)
Loys Barlourdet (1601)

Henry de Castela (1604)
William Bradford (1630)
Evliye Chelebi (1648)
Thomas Fuller (1650)
Al-Qashashi (before 1660)
John Bunyan (1678)
An unnamed English pilgrim
    (1684)
Henry Maundrell (1697)
Nathaniel Crouch (1719)
Richard Pococke (1745)
Frederick Hasselquist (1749)
Richard Tyron (1776)
Constantin-François Volney
    (1783)
François-Auguste-René de
    Chateaubriand (1805)
Ulrich Jasper Seetzen (1806)
W. F. Sieber (1818)
Alphonse de Lamartine
    (1833)
David Roberts (1839)
Lady Francis Egerton (1840)
Edward Robinson (1841)
W. H. Bartlett (1842)
Eliot Warburton (1844)
Conrad Schick (1846)
Moses Hess (1862)
Albert, Prince of Wales (1862)
Charles Wilson (1865)
Palestine Exploration Fund
    (1865)
Charles Warren (1867)

Mark Twain (1867)
Thomas Cook (1869)
Claude Reignier Conder
    (1872)
Ignaz Goldhizer (1873)
William Flinders Petrie
    (1890)
Frederick H. Bliss (1890)
Elizabeth Butler (1891)
Matilde Serao (1892)
Theodor Herzl (1896)
Kaiser Wilhelm II (1898)
Prince Adelbert (c. 1900)
Ada Goodrich-Freer (1900)
Montague Brownslow Parker
    (1911)
Estelle Blythe (1911)
Stephen Graham (1912)
Arthur James Balfour (1917)
Edmund Allenby (1917)
William Foxwell Albright
    (1920)
Philip Graves (1922)
Amin al-Husseini (1923)
Mary Clawson (1953)
Kathleen Mary Kenyon
    (1961)
Mircea Eliade (1974)
Donald Nicholl (1981)
John Paul II (2000)
Johanna van Fessem (2001)

Appendix II.
The Destruction of the Herodian Temple: An Account by Flavius Josephus, 70 CE

Flavius Josephus, whose original name was Joseph Ben Matthias, was born into a Jewish priestly family in 37/38 CE. He was precocious as a youth, claiming that when he was only 14 years old, Jewish priests were asking for his opinions on points of Jewish law. He later became a politician, soldier, orator, historian and a traitor as well: a man who abandoned the Jewish rebels under his command and defected to the Roman side. Despite his personal shortcomings, however, Josephus was a gifted writer and an on-the-spot observer of the destruction of Jerusalem by the Romans in 70.

Four of his works have come down to us. The best known are *The Jewish War* (75/79 CE) and *Antiquities of the Jews* (93/94 CE). The following six excerpts are taken from G. A. Williamson's edited translation of *The Jewish War*, which Williamson entitled *The Destruction of the Jews* (1971).

The first two excerpts describe what Josephus calls "the Sanctuary," i.e., the central shrine, of the Herodian Temple.

The inmost chamber [of the Sanctuary] measured 30 feet and was similarly separated by a curtain from the outer part. Nothing at all was kept in it; it was unap-

proachable, inviolable, and invisible to all, and was called the Holy of Holies [Williamson, p. 282].

Viewed from without, the Sanctuary had everything that could amaze either mind or eyes. Overlaid all round with stout plates of gold, in the first rays of the sun it reflected so fierce a blaze of fire that those who endeavoured to look at it were forced to turn away as if they had looked straight into the sun. To strangers as they approached it seemed in the distance like a mountain covered with snow; for any part not covered with gold was dazzling white [Williamson, p. 283].

The next four excerpts chronicle the final destruction of the Sanctuary by the Romans under the leadership of Titus Caesar:

Then one of the [Roman] soldiers, without waiting for orders and without a qualm for the terrible consequence of his action but urged on by some unseen force, snatched up a blazing piece of wood and climbing on another soldier's back hurled the brand through a golden aperture giving access to the north side of the chambers built round the Sanctuary. As the flames shot into the air the Jews sent up a cry that matched the calamity and dashed to the resect, with no thought now of saving their lives or husbanding their strength; for that which hitherto they had guarded so devotedly was disappearing before their eyes [Williamson, p. 214].

Round the Altar the heap of corpses grew higher and higher, while down the Sanctuary steps poured a river of blood and the bodies of those killed at the top slithered down to the bottom. The soldiers were like men possessed and there was no holding them, nor was there any arguing with the fire [Williamson, p. 215].

Most of them [the Roman soldiers] again were spurred on by the expectation of loot, being convinced that the interior was bursting with money and seeing that everything outside was of gold. But they were forestalled by one of those who had gone in. He, when [Titus] Caesar dashed out to restrain his men, pushed a fire-brand into the hinges of the gate [leading to the Holy of Holies]. Then from within a flame suddenly shot up, Caesar and his staff withdrew, and those outside were free to set what fires they liked [Williamson, p. 215].

While the Sanctuary was burning, looting went on right and left and all [the Jews] who were caught were put to the sword. There was no pity for age, no regard for rank; every class was held in the iron embrace of war, whether they defended themselves or cried for mercy.... Yet more terrible than the din were the sights that met the eye. The Temple Hill [Temple Mount], enveloped in flames from top to bottom, appeared to be boiling up from its very roots; yet the sea of flame was nothing to the ocean of blood, or the companies of killers to the army of killed; nowhere could the ground be seen between the corpses, and the soldiers climbed over heaps of bodies as they chased the fugitives [Williamson, p. 216].

Appendix III: The Travels of St. Willibald, 720–726

This appendix is drawn primarily from John Wilkinson's *Jerusalem Pilgrims before the Crusades* (1977), pp. 11 and 125–132. Willibald's travels are of interest to us here not only because he was the first English pilgrim to visit the Holy Land but also because he dictated a detailed account of his adventures to a nun named Hugeburc, who wrote them down in about 780.

Willibald's travels began in 720, when he was only 20 years old. Together with his father and brother he sailed to France from Hamblehaven (near Southampton, England). They had an easy crossing of the Channel and camped on the River Seine near the city of Rouen. Continuing at a leisurely pace, they passed through Tortona and Lucca in northwestern Italy. Willibald's father died in Lucca but he and his brother pressed on toward Rome. His brother stayed there and later returned to England; Willibald, however, recruited two new companions and set out for Jerusalem by ship and by foot.

It was near Tartus (Syria) that he first ran into difficulties. By that time his party numbered seven people. Not knowing where these strangers had come from, the local villagers thought they were spies and promptly arrested them. Willibald and his companions were taken to an elder, "a rich old gentleman," who questioned them closely. Finally satisfied this group meant no harm, the old man told his fellow villagers: "Many times I have seen people coming here, fellow-tribesmen of theirs, from those parts of the world. They mean no harm. All they want to do is to fulfil their law."

Willibald's party then went to the palace to ask the governor for a permit to go to Jerusalem, but the governor, too, thought they were spies and had them arrested until the Caliph could be informed and could decide the case. A local businessman, however, took pity on them and fed and clothed them at his own expense. Moreover, a Spaniard who had a brother working in the Caliph's palace helped them as well. When they were finally brought to the palace, the Caliph was told by his staff: "These men have come from some western shore, where the sun goes down. We know of no land beyond theirs, nothing but water." The Caliph replied, "Why should we punish them? They have committed no crime against us. Give them their permit and let them go!"

Released forthwith, Willibald and his colleagues continued on to Jerusalem, arriving in 724. They visited all the holy sites in the region. Deeply moved, Willibald noted that inside the tomb of Jesus there was "a shelf on which the Lord's body [had been laid]. Fifteen golden bowls stand on the shelf. They are filled with oil, and burn day and night." Subsequently, while traveling around Palestine Willibald was stricken by an illness which blinded him for two months, but as soon as he returned to Jerusalem in 725 and again entered the Church of the Holy Sepulcher, "his eyes were opened and he recovered his sight."

Further travels repeatedly took Willibald to Lebanon and Syria and then back to Jerusalem again. Once, when crossing a great plain full of olive trees and escorted by an Ethiopian guide, he encountered a lion, "which opened its mouth and roared, and wanted to seize their limbs and eat them." But the Ethiopian told him, "Don't be afraid. Go straight on." Doing as he was told, Willibald was relieved when the lion moved off, giving another great roar "because he wanted to eat the limbs of the numerous people who had gone out picking olives."

Willibald was not only brave but resourceful as well. Before he left Jerusalem for the last time in 726, he bought some balsam—a valuable aromatic resin used to make medicines or incense—and poured it into a long, thin flagon. He slipped this flagon in a hollow cane, covered it with mineral oil to hide it and stoppered the cane. When his party came to the Lebanese border at Tyre, they were arrested and their baggage was searched carefully. Smuggling anything, even balsam, was a capital offense. The border guards opened the cane to see what was inside it but, smelling only the mineral oil, let the travelers pass unmolested.

Willibald never returned to the Holy Land or to England itself, but ended his days as a missionary bishop in Germany.

Appendix IV:
List of the Presents
Brought Home from Jerusalem
by Nompar de Caumont, 1420

Unlike most pilgrims to Jerusalem, Nompar was a wealthy man. The following account[698] shows that he was a generous man, too:

Here is a list of the precious objects which I [Nompar] bought in Jerusalem and carried home in a cypress chest.

First, an intricately embroidered red cloth, and a cloth of gold.

Then, fine pieces of woolen cloth, both black and white, as well as white striped cloth from India, and a piece of white silk.

A rosary made of white ivory.

Six rosaries made of nutmegs.

Four rosaries with beads made of semi-precious stones and crystal.

Four silk belts.

Gold thread as long as the Holy Sepulcher and as the church of Notre Dame.

Three purses made of silk and gold threads.

Two small cloths made of silk and gold threads, designed to cover the ciborium of Our Lord. [A ciborium is a goblet-shaped vessel for holding eucharistic bread.]

Then, thirty-three silver rings which have touched the Holy Sepulcher.

Twelve guilded silver crosses, one with semi-precious stones surrounded by silver; they have touched the Holy Sepulcher and the other holy relics.

A precious stone which reflects light from three sides, decorated with gold and with a pearl which has touched the Holy Sepulcher of Our Lord.

A precious stone, good for [soothing] the eyes.

Five *serpentines*, affording protection against snake venom; three yellow, one blue-green and white, and the last one entirely white. [A *serpentine* is a metamorphic rock with a dark green body highlighted by thin, snake-like veins of contrasting material.]

Then a big guilded cross which has touched the Holy Sepulcher.

Six rings made of scarlet semi-precious stone, which are good for stopping the flow of blood and which have touched the Holy Sepulcher.

Ten *serpentine* rings: five green and five identically multicolored, all of which have touched the Holy Sepulcher and the other holy relics.

Relics of the holy land of Jerusalem, coming from ... [here Nompar lists the sites where he got these items].

An intricately embroidered black purse, bordered with gold thread.

221

Two pairs of guilded spurs, one pair of which has touched the Holy Sepulcher.

Four *roses d'outre-mer* which have touched the Holy Sepulcher. [Literally, *roses d'outre-mer* means "roses from overseas"; the meaning here is unclear.]

Six pairs of gloves, white, made from soft leather.

A rosary made of gold, with a gold clasp, one ruby and eight pearls.

Five Turkish knives.

Fifteen rosaries made of cypress and aloe wood.

Six purses made of gold threads and silk.

Oiselets from Cyprus to perfume rooms. [*Oiselets* were small artificial birds filled with a perfumed powder.]

Three chests: one made of cypress and the other two painted; these chests contained the items listed here.

In addition, a small cypress chest in which I put four *écus de saint Georges*, bearing my coat of arms embroidered with silver thread and with silk. [In this context, *écus*, literally "shields," are small pieces of highly-decorated paper.]

Twelve Turkish knives.

Twenty-one silk purses.

A flask filled with water from the River Jordan and containing a palm-frond.

Fourteen silk purses sewn with gold thread.

I brought back these precious objects to give them to my wife and to the lords and ladies of my region.

Appendix V: Instructions for Christian Pilgrims, c. 1484

These are some of the 27 articles given to Christian pilgrims by the Franciscan Father Guardian, as reported by the monk Felix Fabri.[699]

Article 2: "No pilgrim ought to wander along about the holy places without a Saracen guide, because this is dangerous and unsafe...."

Article 3: "The pilgrim should beware of stepping over the sepulchers of the Saracens, because they are greatly vexed when this is done ... because they believe that our passing over them torments and disturbs the dead."

Article 4: "Should any pilgrim be struck by a Saracen, however unjustly, he must not return the blow, but must complain of him that struck him to the guardian or the dragoman [a Muslim interpreter and guide] ... who will see it right if they are able; if not, seeing that young men are sometimes insolent and stiff-necked, the pilgrims must bear it with patience for the glory of God and for their own greater merit."

Article 5: "Let the pilgrim beware of chipping off fragments from the Holy Sepulcher and from the buildings at other places and spoiling the hewn stones thereof, because this is forbidden under pain of excommunication."

Article 6: "Pilgrims of noble birth must not deface walls by drawing their coats-of-arms thereon or by writing their names or by fixing upon the walls papers on which their arms are painted, or by scratching columns and marble slabs or boring holes in them with iron tools to make marks of their having visited them; for such conduct gives great offense to the Saracens and they think those who have done so are fools."

Fabri tells us, however, that pilgrims did not heed this warning. "I knew one pilgrim," Fabri reports, "who always had a red stone in his purse, with which he used to write his name in every place, on every wall. This fool would sometimes go up to altars and mark the letters of his name at the top of the vacant margins of antiphonals, graduals, missals, and psalters [these were books used in church services], as though he were the author of the book.... He took especial pains to inscribe his name and arms in those places above all others which would be noticed by men passing in and out."[700]

Article 7: "The pilgrims must proceed to visit the holy places in an orderly manner, without disorder or disagreements, and one must not try to outrun another ... because the devotion of many is hindered thereby."

Article 8: "Pilgrims must beware of laughing together as they walk about Jerusalem to see the holy places, but they must be grave and devout, both on account of the holy places and of the example they afford to the infidels, and also lest the latter should suspect that we are laughing at them, which annoys them exceedingly. They are always suspicious about laughter and merriment among pilgrims."

Article 9: "Let the pilgrim beware above all of jesting with or laughing at the Saracen boys or men whom they meet, because however well meant this conduct may be, yet much mischief arises from it...."

Article 10: "Let the pilgrims beware of gazing upon any women whom they may meet, because all Saracens are exceedingly jealous, and the pilgrim may in ignorance run himself into danger through the fury of some jealous husband."

Article 11: "Should any woman beckon to a pilgrim or invite him by signs to enter a house, let him on no account do so, because the woman does this treacherously at the instigation of some in order that the Christian when he enters may be robbed or perhaps slain...."

Article 12: "Let every pilgrim beware of giving a Saracen wine when he asks for a drink ... because straightway after one single draught thereof he becomes mad, and the first man he attacks is the pilgrim who gave it to him."

Article 16: "No pilgrim may wear knives or anything else slung about him, lest they be torn from him and carried off, nor may he bear any arms whatsoever."

Article 17: "Should any pilgrim form a friendship with any Saracen, he must beware of trusting him too far, for they are treacherous; and he must especially beware of laying his hand on his beard in jest, or touching his turban ... for this thing is a disgrace among them and all jests are at once forgotten thereat, and they grow angry...."

Article 18: "Let every pilgrim carefully guard his own property, and never leave it lying about in any place where Saracens are,

otherwise it would straightway vanish, whatever it may be."

Article 19: "If any pilgrim has a bottle of wine and wishes to drink, let him hide his bottle and drink secretly if Saracens are present.... For, because the drinking of wine is forbidden to them, they envy us when they see us drink, and if they can, they molest those who drink."

Article 20: "Let no Christian have money dealings with a Saracen except in such sort that he knows he cannot be cheated; for they strive to cheat us.... And, above all, let the pilgrim beware of German Jews and be on his guard against them, for their whole object in life is to cheat us and rob us of our money. Let him also beware of Eastern Christians ... for they have no conscience, less even than the Jews and Saracens, and will cheat pilgrims if they can."

Article 21: "When pilgrims make covenants with Saracens, let them not dispute with them, nor swear at them, nor become angry with them; for they know [these] things are contrary to the Christian religion, and when they see anything of this sort they straightway cry out 'O thou bad Christian!' for all of them can say this in Italian or German...."

Article 22: "Let the pilgrim beware of entering mosques ... because if he be found therein, he will in no case escape unharmed, even should he escape with his life...."

Article 23: "Let the pilgrim especially beware of laughing to scorn Saracens who are praying or practicing the postures of their faith, because they cannot bear this at all. For they themselves refrain from molesting or laughing at us when we are at our prayers."

Article 25: "Pilgrims must not begrudge to pay money to save themselves from the many annoyances which beset them, but when money has to be paid they must give it straightway without grumbling."

Appendix VI:
Balfour and the Zionists

The diplomatic history of World War I and the Balfour Declaration of 1917 is too complex to discuss here in any detail. Excellent resources for the interested reader are David Fromkin's *A Peace to End all Peace* (2000) and Barbara Tuchman's *Bible and Sword* (1983). In essence, the British reached secret but conflicting understandings with France and Russia on how the spoils of the Ottoman Empire would be divided. The British also made conflicting promises to Arab leaders. What is not clear even today, however, is precisely why the British decided to back the Zionists by issuing the Balfour Declaration.

One explanation was that the Balfour Declaration was a reward to a Jewish chemistry instructor in Manchester, Dr. Chaim Weizmann, for his groundbreaking work in producing acetone, a key component of the high explosives urgently needed by the British during World War I. (Weizmann would later become the first president of Israel.) The "acetone theory," however, is simplistic and overlooks, among other things, the strategic importance of the Middle East as a major theater for the British during World War I.

The British civil servant Leopold Amery, for example, was a key player in the bureaucratic infighting that eventually produced the Balfour Declaration. Because the Holy Land was seen as an essential compo- nent of the overland route to British India, Amery was not alone in believing that German control of Palestine would be one of "the greatest dangers which can confront the British Empire in the future."[701] Indeed, Amery was convinced that Palestine was the vital missing link in what should be a continuous chain of pro–British states stretching from the Atlantic to the middle of the Pacific.[702]

He and like-minded British officials argued that Britain was obliged to play a permanent role in the Middle East. It should not withdraw from this region voluntarily, even after its League of Nations mandate had ended. These considerations suggest that far more than acetone was involved in the Balfour Declaration.

A different explanation was put forward by Prime Minister Lloyd George. In his memoirs, written in the 1930s, he claimed that the War Cabinet believed that a pro–Zionist declaration would encourage Jews in the Russia and the United States to support the Allied side in World War I. In retrospect, however, this thesis sidestepped two important facts.[703]

The first was that there were not very many Zionists in the world: only about one percent of the world's Jews were Zionists. In Britain itself, the prestigious committee which represented British Jews in all matters affecting Jews abroad was decidedly anti–

Zionist. In the United States, only about .4 percent of the Jews there (12,000 of 3,000,000) belonged to the Zionist Federation. Moreover, there is no evidence that winning the support of the Zionists would have resulted into widespread support among Diaspora Jews for Allied war aims.

The second fact was that this relative handful of Zionists had no political power, either in Russia or the United States. The British Ambassador in Petrograd reported to London that Russian Jews were only a weak, persecuted minority. In the United States, the vast majority of Jews—many of them recent immigrants—simply wanted to learn English and assimilate into American society. They lacked political power. Even if they had possessed it, they might well have failed to see the attraction of subsistence farming in hot, dry, distant Palestine.

What then, was, the underlying motivation of Lloyd George and Balfour in backing the Balfour Declaration? Nobody seems to know for sure but Barbara Tuchman's thesis merits attention. Their real motivation, she claimed, was "in large part a sentimental (that is, a Biblical) one."[704] Some confirmation of this view can be found in a letter written in 1920 by Lord Curzon, a senior British politician who was opposed to the Balfour Declaration. Of Lloyd George he said: "The Prime Minister clings to Palestine for its sentimental and traditional value, and talks about Jerusalem with almost the same enthusiasm as about his native hills [of Wales]."[705]

If this Tuchman-Curzon surmise is correct, perhaps we can understand why neither Lloyd George nor Balfour would be willing to admit publicly (or perhaps even to themselves) that it was their emotional attachment to the Holy Land, not any hard-headed balance of power considerations, which had committed Britain to the Balfour Declaration. The fundamental irrationality of this policy, i.e., the contradiction on which it was based, was arguably the result of this emotional commitment.

The failure of the Balfour Declaration can be summarized briefly. Few British officials in Palestine believed that the Balfour Declaration would work. The Arabs opposed any form of Zionism. The Zionists suspected (correctly, as it turned out) that the British would ultimately back away from their commitment to a Jewish state in Palestine. The upshot was that, after a long series of ethnic and anti–British riots before World War II, in 1947 the British decided to end their Palestine mandate and turn over to the newly born United Nations the insolvable problem of the Holy Land.

The UN, for its part, fared little better. It produced a plan to partition the country between Jews and Arabs. The Jews accepted the plan; the Arabs rejected it. Fighting between the two sides broke out immediately. The net result was the defeat of the Arabs and the establishment of the independent state of Israel in 1948. Arab-Israeli clashes since then are the continuing legacy of the Balfour Declaration.

Appendix VII:
Reports by Albright Fellows,
1990–2000

Between 1990 and 2000, the Fellows of the W. F. Albright Institute produced such a wide range of scholarly reports that it is worth listing them here. This information comes from W. F. Albright Institute, 1990–2000 Fellows Reports, pp. 7–21.

"Southern Jordan and the Negev in the Iron Age: Developing a New Model," by Piotr Bienkowski, Liverpool Museum Annual Professor

"The Upper Paleolithic Settlement of the Levant," by James L. Phillips, Annual Professor, University of Illinois at Chicago

"Southern Jordan and the Negev—Comparative Studies in Byzantine Urbanism and Ecclesiastical Architecture," by Abigniew T. Fiema, University of Helsinki, Finland

"Cult, Cache, or Commodity? Comparison of Intentional Artifact Deposits as Symbolic Practice During Late Prehistory in the Southern Levant," by Yorke M. Rowan, University of Georgia

"The Kathisma Church and the Origins of the Cult of the Virgin in Early Byzantine Palestine," by Stephen J. Shoemaker, University of Oregon

"Itureans and the Cult and Stelae of Har Sena'im," by Elaine A. Myers, University of Toronto

"Theatre in the Near East: A Study in the De-velopment of Form and Function in the Roman and Byzantine Periods," by Alexandra Retzleff, University of North Carolina at Chapel Hill

"Granulated Jewelry in the Bronze Age: Some Technical, Stylistic, and Social Considerations," by Thea A. Politis, University of Reading

"The Byzantine Remains from the Sepphoris Acropolis," by Melissa Aubin, Florida State University

"Understanding Variability of Upper Paleolithic Traditions in the Southern Levant," by Iman Nader Saca, University of Illinois at Chicago

"Fine Wares at Tell Keisan During the Persian and Hellenistic Periods: The Pattern of Importations," by Jolanta Mlynarczyk, Research Centre for Mediterranean Archaeology, Polish Academy of Sciences, Warsaw

"Two Persian Princesses: Pantheia and Rhodogoune," Tomasz Polanski, Jagiellonian University, Cracow, Poland

"Architectural Decoration in Roman Period Settlements on the Northern Shores of the Sea of Galilee," by Illona Skupinska-Løvset, University of Lodz, Poland

"The So-Called Pre-monetary Use of Silver in the Ancient Near East and the Silver Hoards from Tell el-'Ajjul," by Péter Vargyas, University of Pécs, Hungary.

Notes

Introduction

1. Historically, the line separating tourists from pilgrims has always been a fuzzy one. The reason is that on the same journey a traveler can be *both* a tourist and a pilgrim. A person who is merely admiring the sights or buying souvenirs can be considered a tourist. When that same person is worshiping at a sacred site, however, he or she is a pilgrim.

2. Associated Press, "Israel Seeking Tourism."

3. The following account is drawn from the Council on Foreign Relations, "Excerpts from the Text of the Mitchell Commission Report," pp. 2–3. Chaired by former U.S. Senate Majority Leader George J. Mitchell, the Mitchell Commission was a fact-finding committee set up at the conclusion of the failed Middle East Peace Summit at Sharm el-Sheikh, Egypt, on 17 October 2000. Its later mandate was not to determine guilt or innocence but to explore the reasons for the Israeli-Palestinian clashes of 2000–2001. As a result, the Commission was studiously even-handed. It pointed out that the Israelis did not understand "the humiliation and frustration that Palestinians must endure every day as a result of living with the continuing effects of [Israeli] occupation, sustained by the presence of Israeli military forces and settlements in their midst." The Palestinians, for their part, did not understand "the extent to which terrorism creates fear among the Israeli people and undermines their belief in the possibility of co-existence, or the determination of

the government of Israel to do whatever is necessary to protect its people." These two quotes are from p. 1 of the Report.

4. Assadi, "Bethlehem," p. 1.

5. Cited by Sontag, "Harsh Israeli Words."

6. The "right of return" is enshrined in Israeli law. It provides that Jews anywhere in the world have the right to return to and settle in Israel. The Palestinians have claimed the same right for the Muslims displaced by the Jews after the founding of Israel in 1948, an event the Palestinians refer to as the "day of catastrophe" (*Al-Naqba*). The year-long war that followed the birth of Israel created about 700,000 Palestinian refugees. Since then, that number has grown to about 4,000,000 people, who are living in camps in the West Bank, Gaza and in neighboring countries.

7. See, for example, Coleman, *Pilgrimage Past and Present*, p. 216: "A ... conventional goal for the secular pilgrim is the museum. Many museums (at least in the Anglo-Saxon world, for instance, the British Museum) are traditionally designed as if they were Greek temples, imbued with a classical rather than Christian sanctity, a holiness vested in the distant past."

8. See Conder, *Survey*, p. 2.

9. Cited by Fromkin, *Peace*, p. 313.

10. For the exploits of the Hellfire Club, see Connolly, *Dublin*, p. 64.

11. Gilbert, *Atlas*, p. 17.

12. See Orme, "Construction" and Jacobs, *Jerusalem*, p. 71.

Chapter I

13. The first clear case of pilgrimage to Jerusalem being imposed as a penance dates from the ninth century. Three Italian brothers killed a priest, who happened to be their uncle. Their bishops ordered them "to make iron chains and bind them tightly on their arms, and then make the circuit of the holy places in dust and ashes, until such time as God accepted their penance." The brothers spent three years complying with this directive. Cited by Wilkinson, *Jerusalem Pilgrims*, p. 43.

14. After Houseley, *Holy Land*, p. 5.

15. Birch, *Pilgrimage*, p. 4.

16. The Lollards were followers of the Oxford professor John Wycliffe (c. 1330–1384). They did not believe that men and women should not go on pilgrimages. The citation is from Thorpe, *Examination*, p. 3.

17. Augustine's concept of a heavenly Jerusalem proved to be very durable, lasting into the nineteenth century. The English artist and poet William Blake caught its spirit best in the Preface to his epic poem *Milton*, written between 1804 and 1808: "I will not cease from Mental Fight,/ Nor shall my sword sleep in my hand,/ Till we have built Jerusalem/ In England's green and pleasant land."

18. After Paula Fredriksen, "The Holy City in Christian Thought" in Rosovsky, *City*, pp. 74–92, cited p. 88.

19. See Fletcher, *Conversion*, p. 30.

20. Cited by Fletcher, *Conversion*, p. 31.

21. Cited by Encyclopædia Britannica Online, "Symbolism of the journey," pp. 1–2.

22. Sourced by the *Oxford English Dictionary* to Bradford's *History of Plymouth Colony 1620–47* but no page number is given. Bradford was drawing from Hebrews 11:13–14: "They [the Israelites] confessed that they were strangers and foreigners on the earth, for people who speak in this way make it clear that they are seeking a homeland ... they desire a better country, that is, a heavenly one."

23. *Pilgrim's Progress*, lines 207–210, cited by Johnson, Reading, p. 30.

24. The meaning of "Mount Zion" has varied over time. Geographically, this term was first applied to the southeastern extension of Jerusalem's eastern (Ophel) hill, which is where the ancient city of David was located. Later on, however, "Mount Zion" came to mean the southwestern spur of the Upper City of Jerusalem. This southwestern spur is now known as "Sion." In religious terms, "Zion" has long been equated with the heavenly Jerusalem. It also connotes the Jewish homeland and Jewish national aspirations; hence, "Zionism" as a Jewish political movement beginning in the late nineteenth century.

25. Cited by Christensen, *Inward Passage*, p. 89. See also Coleman and Elsner, *Pilgrimage Past and Present*, p. 78.

26. See Armstrong, *History of God*, p. 392.

27. After Armstrong, *History of God*, p. 393.

28. Tuchman, *Mirror*, p. xix.

29. Kempe, *Book*, p. 2.

30. There are numerous translations of Hilton's Ladder of Perfection. The one used here was cited by Encyclopædia Britannica Online, accessed 19 November 1999. The earliest English version of Hilton's *Ladder* that is held by the British Library is a 1659 reprint of the book as it was first published in 1494. This reprint uses the term "spiritual" rather than "ghostly" pilgrim. But since Hilton wrote in Latin, his translators have used "ghostly," "spiritual" or (later on) "true," as the English of their times dictated.

31. See "Pilgrimages," *New Catholic Encyclopedia* (1967), cited by Robinson, *Sacred Places*, pp. 34–35.

32. *Oedipus Tyrannus*, lines 800–813, cited by Joint Association, Athens, p. 71.

33. Pemberton, *Soulfaring*, p. 26.

34. The Kumbh Mela festival commemorates a mythical battle between demons and gods, during which an elixir of immortality was dropped into the Ganges.

35. See Sax, *Mountain Goddess*, pp. 23–13.

36. See Kelly and Roberts, *Kathmandu*, pp. 17–18.

37. The first documented Buddhist pilgrim was the Indian emperor Ashoka, who reigned from about 274–232 BCE and who left numerous edicts on pillars and rock faces attesting to his belief. The Rummindei Pillar in Lumbini, Nepal, for example, states that

"King [Ashoka], Beloved of the Gods, visited this place in person and worshipped here because the Buddha, the sage of the Sakyas, was born here." After Coleman, *Pilgrimage Past and Present*, pp. 170–173.

38. The temple of Phra Phutthabat is one of the sites where Buddha is believed to have left an imprint of his foot. The king's pilgrimage was recorded by Theodorus Jacobus van den Heuvel, a merchant of the Dutch East India Company. See Raben, *King's Trail*.

39. Rome attracts pilgrims because it has the tombs of St. Peter and St. Paul and is also the seat of the papacy. Santiago de Compostela is the supposed resting place of the bones of St. James the Greater, one of the twelve apostles. St. Iago means St. James in Spanish; Compostela means "field of stars," referring a trail called the "Path of the Milky Way" for pilgrims, which funneled pilgrims across the southwestern Pyrenees from France into Spain. The first of the apostles to suffer martyrdom, St. James was beheaded in Jerusalem. His remains, gathered together by his friends, were miraculously transported by boat to the Galician coast, where they were reburied on a hill called Libredón. See Dunn and Davidson, *Compostela*, pp. xxiii, xxvi.

40. Chaucer, *Canterbury Tales*, p. 3. This work has been so durable that when T. S. Eliot wrote his famous poem *The Waste Land* in 1922, highly literate readers immediately recognized that his opening lines reversed Chaucer's. Eliot wrote: "April is the cruelest month, breeding/Lilacs out of the dead land, mixing/Memory and desire, stirring/Dull roots with spring rain." See Eliot, *Poems*, p. 61.

41. Chaucer, *Canterbury Tales*, p. 4.

42. The Wife of Bath loved to go off on pilgrimages: "And thries had she been at Jerusalem;/She hadde passed many a straunge streem—/At Rome she hadde been, and at Bologne,/In Galice at Saint Jame, and at Cologne./She knoude muchel of wandrynge by the weye...." Chaucer, *Canterbury Tales*, p. 21.

43. Chaucer, *Canterbury Tales*, p. 204.

44. Chaucer, *Canterbury Tales*, p. 316.

45. Tuchman, *Bible*, pp. 40–41; emphasis added. The name "Palestine" has a long history. At first, this was the name given by Greek and Latin authors to the coastal region inhabited by the Philistines. Early in the Roman period, the region around Jerusalem was called "Palaestina." The Byzantines used "Palaestina Prima" to refer to the lands west of the River Jordan. After the Muslims came to power in 638, Palaestina Prima became "Filastin" in Arabic—hence our own term, "Palestine." See Kalidi, *Diaspora*, pp. 1–2.

46. See Peters, "Their Father's Business: Pilgrim Services in the Holy City" in his *Jerusalem and Mecca*, pp. 214–237.

47. Chaucer, *Canterbury Tales*, p. 334.

48. Cited by the *Oxford English Dictionary*, p. 282.

49. Robinson, *Sacred Places*, p. 2.

50. Eliade, *Myth*, pp. 17–18.

51. Joseph Dan, "Jerusalem in Jewish Spirituality," in Rosovsky, *City of the Great King*, p. 61.

52. T.S. Eliot, "Little Gidding," *Poems*, p. 197.

53. The Pastons were a prominent English family living in eastern Norfolk in the fifteenth century. Now preserved in the British Museum in London, their family letters constitute the largest surviving collection of English correspondence from this period. The John Paston referred to by Virginia Woolf (see below) was John I, who died in 1466.

54. Woolf, *Common Reader*, p. 3.

55. Robert L. Wilken, "Loving the Jerusalem Below: The Monks of Palestine" in Levine, *Jerusalem*, pp. 240–250, cited p. 242.

56. Coleman, *Pilgrimage Past and Present*, p. 80.

57. Cited by Wilkinson, *Egeria's Travels*, p. 21.

58. Pietro Azario, *Liber Gestorum in Lombardia, Rerum Italicarum Scriptores* cited by Webb, *Pilgrims and Pilgrimage*, p. 249.

Chapter II

59. Yahweh was only a minor god in the Canaanite pantheon but was adopted by the ancient Israelites as their major deity. In time the name of God came to be considered too

sacred to pronounce. So when in the early centuries CE, vowels were added to the ancient Hebrew text of the Bible, care was taken over the choice of the vowels that were added to the Tetragrammaton, as the consonants YHWH are called by linguists. To ensure that the Holy Name would not be pronounced, rather than inserting the vowels for YHWH, Jewish scholars inserted instead the vowels from the term *Adonai* ("My Lord"). This later gave rise to the mistranslation "Jehovah" in the King James version of the Bible.

60. Tubb, *Canaanites*, p. 17. Emphasis added.

61. The Israelites elaborated on but did not invent the concept of a Messiah, which had its roots in Mesopotamian culture.

62. After Shemaryahu Talmon, "The Significance of Jerusalem in Biblical Thought" in Kühnel, *Real and Ideal*, pp. 1–12, cited p. 1.

63. After Eliade, *Myth*, pp. 12–15.

64. Josephus, *Antiquities of the Jews*, vol. III, chapter 7, p. 7, cited by Eliade, *Cosmos*, pp. 77–78.

65. After Comay, *Temple*, p. 16. In Hebrew *Shekhina* means "Dwelling" or "Presence." Jewish tradition has it that the *Shekhina* was present in the Ark of the Covenant and in the First Temple, but not in the Second Temple. Since the *Shekhina* was divine, any description of it would be inadequate but a close approximation would be the blinding "glory of the Lord" referred to in Exodus 40:35.

66. See 1 Kings 8:9: "There was nothing in the ark except the two tablets of stone that Moses had placed there at Horeb, where the Lord made a covenant with the Israelites, when they came out of the land of Egypt."

67. See Cohen, "Temple Mount Question," pp. 4, 20.

68. Mishnah, *Kelim* 1.6–9, cited by Barker, *Gate of Heaven*, p. 25. The Day of Atonement was a day of communal worship for those who lived in or near Jerusalem; it was not a time of pilgrimage. See Sanders, *Judaism*, p. 141.

69. Our only source for the Exodus is the Bible. If the Israelites did in fact flee from forced labor in Egypt, this probably occurred toward the end of the Egyptian empire. They may have settled in the lands across the River

Jordan about one generation later, e.g., in about 1225 BCE. One of the great difficulties in establishing accurate dates here is that the Israelites were nomads. They did not have many worldly goods and those that they did have (tents, etc.) were highly perishable.

70. John 11:55, 57. 13:1.

71. Cited by Barber, *Pilgrimages*, p. 12.

72. Hoffman, *Guide*, p. 43.

73. See Luke 2:41–47.

74. John 11:55–57 tells us: "Now the Passover of the Jews was near, and many went up from the country to Jerusalem before the Passover to purify themselves. They [other Jewish pilgrims] were looking for Jesus and were asking one another as they stood in the Temple, 'What do you think? Surely he will not come to the festival, will he?' Now the chief priests and the Pharisees had given orders that anyone who knew where Jesus was should let them know, so that they might arrest him." After Jesus had been captured, Pontius Pilate, the Roman procurator of Judea, handed him over to the chief priests for crucifixion. As John 19:16–18 explains, "So they took Jesus; and carrying the cross by himself, he went out to what is called The Place of the Skull, which in Hebrew is called Golgotha. There they crucified him, and with him two others, one on either side, with Jesus between them." Pilate's decision to have Jesus killed was part of a pattern of violent misgovernment. Philo of Alexandria, who was Pilate's contemporary, said that Pilate's administration was notable for its "briberies, insults, robberies, outrages and wanton injuries, ceaseless executions of untried prisoners, and grievous cruelty." The Jewish historian Josephus reported that Pilate was dismissed from office because of his habit of executing large numbers of Jews. See Paula Fredriksen, "The Holy City in Christian Thought" in Rosovsky, *City*, pp. 74–92, cited in endnote 7, p. 480.

75. This doctrine was known as "chiliasm." Its name comes from the Greek word for "thousand" (*chilias*). It refers to the belief that one day Christ would return to rule on earth for 1,000 years before the heavenly Jerusalem came down from the heavens. After Wilken, *Holy*, p. 56.

76. As modified by new agreements over the years, the Status Quo now covers the

presence and rights of the Greek Orthodox, Roman Catholic, Armenian Orthodox, Assyrian, Greek Catholic, Coptic, Ethiopian Orthodox, Episcopal, and Lutheran Churches. See U.S. Department of State, 2000 *Annual Report on International Religious Freedom: The Occupied Territories*, p. 2.

77. For a short and elementary introduction to Islam, see Janin, *Saudi Arabia*, pp. 20–21, 71–81.

78. In early documents, *al-Quds* may have indicated chiefly, but not exclusively, the Temple Mount. Over time, however, it was understood as applying to the city as a whole. After Haggai Ben-Shammai, "Jerusalem in Early Medieval Jewish Bible Exegesis," pp. 447–464, in Levine, *Jerusalem*, p. 450.

79. After Angelika Neuwirth, "Jerusalem and the Genesis of Islamic Scripture," pp. 315–325, in Levine, *Jerusalem*, pp. 318–319.

80. See R. H. Zwi Werblowsky, "The Meaning of Jerusalem to Jews, Christians, and Muslims," pp. 7–21, in Ben-Arieh, *Jerusalem*, p. 9.

81. Kalidi, "Diaspora," p. 2.

82. After Khalidi, "Islam," p. 6.

83. After Angelika Neuwirth, "The Spiritual Meaning of Jerusalem in Islam" in Rosovsky, *City*, pp. 93–116, from pp. 113–114.

84. It is not clear whether Muhammad actually saw God. The "two bow-lengths" quote is from the Koran, Sura 53:9, cited by Khalidi, "Islam," p. 6.

85. This quote and some of the following discussion are from Angelika Neuwirth, "Jerusalem and the Genesis of Islamic Scripture," pp. 315–325, in Levine, *Jerusalem*, pp. 315–316. See also her article on "The Spiritual Meaning of Jerusalem in Islam" in Rosovsky, *City*, pp. 93–116.

86. Muslim tradition credits Muhammad himself with giving a religious value to Jerusalem: "There are those who say that, while in Mecca, he [Muhammad] would pray in the direction of Jerusalem, so that the Kaba was behind his back. There are, however, those who say that he simultaneously faced the Ka-ba and Jerusalem: he would thus turn toward both the qiblas [at the same time], with the Ka-ba between himself and Jerusalem." Cited by Moshe Gil, "The Jewish Com-

munity," pp. 163–200, in Prawer, *History*, p. 164. Probably because the Jews rejected Muhammad's teachings, he changed the direction of prayer from Jerusalem to Mecca in about 623. See Peters, *Jerusalem*, p. 182.

87. After El-Awaisi, "Jerusalem," pp. 12–20.

88. Cited by Tuchman, *Bible*, pp. 48–49.

89. Wilken, *Holy*, p. 112.

90. Milton, *Paradise Lost* 3:476–477, cited by Armstrong, *History*, p. 340.

91. "Levant" comes from the French *lever* ("to rise"), which in this context connotes the sun rising in the east. From the time of the Crusades to the end of World War II, "the Levant" was a synonym for Palestine, Lebanon and Syria. It is occasionally still used in this manner. The Palestine Exploration Fund, for example, deliberately uses "the Levant" it because it is a value-free term that does not threaten anyone's religious or political beliefs.

92. "Biblical archeology" is a term that can be defined in various ways. In its most extreme (American) form, it means the archeology of the Holy Land, using the Old Testament as the primary source of information and motivation for exploration. Biblical archeology tries to find, chiefly for religious reasons, tangible evidence for the places, peoples and events mentioned in biblical narratives.

93. After Nitza Rosovksy, "Nineteenth-Century Portraits Through Western Eyes" in Rosovsky, *City*, pp. 218–240, cited p. 219.

94. See Howe, *Revealing the Holy Land*, p. 9.

Chapter III

95. See Latin Patriarchate, *Welcome*, pp. 6–11.

96. The Talmud, Kiddushin 49:2, cited by Jacobs, *Jerusalem*, p. viii. The importance which the Talmud attaches to Jerusalem can be seen by these words, put into God's own mouth: " I will not enter the heavenly Jerusalem, until I have entered the earthly Jerusalem first." B. *Ta'anith* 5b, cited by R. J. Werblowsky, "The Meaning of Jerusalem to Jews, Christians, and Muslims," pp. 7–21 in Ben-

Arieh and Davis, *Jerusalem in the Mind of the West*, p. 17.

97. Cited by Peters, *Jerusalem*, p. 363.

98. Cited by Hockstader, "Jerusalem."

Chapter IV

99. This discussion of Jerusalem's early history follows Armstrong, *History*, pp. 1, 6–7, and Prag, *Jerusalem*, pp. 16–21.

100. "Execration Texts" refers to dishes and vases that were inscribed with the names of 19 of Egypt's enemies and were then broken in a rite of what is known as "sympathetic magic," i.e., a ceremony designed to assure a specific end—in this case, the downfall of Egypt's enemies.

101. Exodus 20:24–26.

102. It is conceivable that Jebusite temple in Jerusalem had been a site of local pilgrimage even before David's conquest of the city. Some scholars believe that Zadok, who became high priest in Solomon's temple, had been transferred by David from the Jebusite temple. This suggests that the Jebusite temple was an important institution; if so, it may have been a pilgrimage site as well. After H.J. Franken, "Jerusalem in the Bronze Age" in Asali, *Jerusalem*, pp. 11–41, cited p. 33.

103. 2 Samuel 5:6–10.

104. 1 Chronicles 11:6–7.

105. When David came to power, Jerusalem was only a modest city consisting of a citadel, a palace and houses for soldiers and bureaucrats. Its population was probably about 2,000 people living on some 15 acres. After Armstrong, *History*, p. 38.

106. Matthew 1:1–17.

107. Luke 1:32.

108. Acts 2:30–31.

109. See 1 Kings 5–7 and 2 Chronicles 2–8.

110. In its first sentence, the Old Testament describes this primordial world: "In the beginning, when God created the heavens and the earth, the earth was a formless void and darkness covered the face of the deep, while a wind from God swept over the face of the waters." Genesis 1:1–2.

111. See Rostovsky, *City*, p. 465, endnote 8.

112. Deuteronomy 16:16–17.

113. During the years between the Exodus of the Jews from Egypt (c. 1200 BCE) and David's conquest of Jerusalem (c. 1004 BCE), the independent tribes of the Israelites went to their local holy places, not to Jerusalem, to celebrate the three pilgrim festivals. These local sites included but were not limited to: Gilgal (northeast of Jerusalem) and Sichem, Silo, and Bethel (all north of Jerusalem). See Chélini, *Chemins*, pp. 27–33.

114. 2 Kings 23:19–20 tells us that "Josiah removed all the shrines of the high places that were in the towns of Samaria, which the kings of Israel had made, provoking the Lord to anger. He [Josiah] slaughtered on the altars all the priests of the high places who were there, and burned human bones on them."

115. After Auld, *Jerusalem I*, pp. 63–64.

116. See Lamentations 1–7.

117. According to 2 Kings 24:11 ff., "King Nebuchadnezzar of Babylon ... carried off all the treasures of the house of the Lord [the First Temple], and the treasures of the king's house; he cut to pieces all the vessels of gold in the Temple of the Lord, which King Solomon of Israel had made.... He carried away all Jerusalem, all the officials, all the warriors, ten thousand captives, all the artisans and the smiths; no one remained, except the poorest people of the land." Babylonian records show that this deportation occurred on 16 March 597 BCE; a second deportation occurred in 587 BCE when the Chaldeans captured the city and sent into exile all the remaining inhabitants except for the poorest people, who were left to grow crops and make wine.

118. Psalm 137:1–6. This psalm has inspired many poets and singers. One of the best modern versions is "Rivers of Babylon," a song by the Jamaican reggae group The Melodians. Recorded by Mango in 1973, this hit was used in the movie "The Harder They Fall."

119. Isaiah 62:1–2.

120. Jeremiah 41:5.

121. Ezra 3:10–13.

122. Midrash Tanhuma, Kedoshim 10, cited by Library, "Towards the Eternal Center," p. 6.

123. Cited by Dorothea R. French,

"Journeys to the Center of the Earth: Medieval and Renaissance Pilgrimages to Mount Calvary," pp. 45–76, in Sargent-Baur, *Journeys*, p. 52.

124. Ezekiel 5:5.

125. French, "Journeys to the Center," in Sargent-Bauer, *Journeys*, p. 52. The Christians carried on and elaborated the Jewish tradition of Jerusalem as the center of the earth. After his pilgrimage of c. 680, for example, the French bishop Arculf reported that "during the summer solstice at noon the light of the sun in mid heaven passes directly above this column [a column set up at the place where it was believed that the Cross had been placed on a dead man and brought him back to life], and shines down on all sides, which demonstrates that Jerusalem is the centre of the earth." See Wilkinson, *Jerusalem Pilgrims*, p. 99. Contemporary skeptics noted, however, that there were also other places on earth where the sun cast no shadow. In 1484, for example, the Dominican monk Felix Fabri wrote: "I do not see that the fact that the sun shines at mid-day so directly above men's heads that their bodies cast no shadow is true and certain proof that the spot where it does so is the middle of the earth for I have read in several books about many places where at certain times men's bodies cast no shadow...." See Palestine Pilgrims' Text Society, *Fabri*, p. 375.

126. Barber, *Pilgrimages*, p. 10.

127. Chélini, *Chemins*, pp. 46–47.

128. Jews who disobeyed Antiochus' edicts were put to death. If a woman circumcised her son, she was paraded around Jerusalem and then thrown, with her child, from the walls of the city into the valley below. It is said that one mother watched all seven of her sons die before being executed herself. Eliezar, a 90-year-old Jew, died rather than swallow a piece of pork. After Armstrong, *Jerusalem*, p. 114.

129. After Prag, *Jerusalem*, p 25.

130. Cited by Armstrong, *History*, p. 120.

Chapter V

131. See Martin Goodman, "The Pilgrimage Economy of Jerusalem in the Second Temple Period" in Levine, *Jerusalem*, pp. 69–76, cited by Goodman on pp. 74–75.

132. These measurements are taken from a drawing by E. P. Sanders, cited by Armstrong, *History*, p. 135.

133. Matthew 21:12 tells us that "Jesus entered the Temple and drove out all who were selling and buying in the Temple, and he overturned the tables of the money changers and the seats of those who sold doves. He said to them, 'It is written, *My house shall be called a house of prayer; but you are making it a den of robbers.*'"

134. After Sanders, *Judaism*, pp. 132–141.

135. Exodus 12:21–23.

136. See Deuteronomy 16:7. The reference to "the place that the Lord your God shall choose" is Jerusalem.

137. Deuteronomy 26:4–9.

138. Josephus, *War* 2.10–13, cited by Sanders, *Judaism*, p. 138.

139. Like many other ancient writers, Josephus greatly exaggerates numbers to make his point. He claims, for example, that in the incident described here between 20,000 to 30,000 Jews were killed. See Josephus, *War* 2.224–227, and *Antiquities* 20:112, both cited by Sanders, *Judaism*, p. 138.

140. Deuteronomy 26:1–2.

141. Josephus, *Antiquities* 17:221–268, *War* 2:42–44, cited by Sanders, *Judaism*, p. 139.

142. Taken from Leviticus 23:39–43.

143. Josephus, *Antiquities* 15:50, cited by Sanders, Judaism, p. 139.

144. Mishnah, *Sukkah* 5:4, cited by Sanders, *Judaism*, p. 139.

145. Josephus claims that 6,000 Jews were killed but this is surely an exaggeration. See Josephus, *Antiquities* 13:372f., cited by Sanders, *Judaism*, p. 140.

146. Josephus, *Destruction*, pp. 218–219.

147. Philo of Alexandria, "The Special Laws" in *Works*, I, Loeb Classical Library, London, 1929, p. 139, cited by Barber, *Pilgrimages*, p. 11.

148. After Armstrong, *History*, pp. 150–152.

149. Rubenstein, *Sukkot*, p. 1.

150. After Wilken, *Holy*, p. 37.

151. A "geniza"—"hiding place" in Hebrew—was a repository for sacred manuscripts and ritual objects. It was usually located in the attic or cellar of a synagogue. In 1896 a Jewish scholar found in the *geniza* of a synagogue in Cairo about 90,000 priceless manuscripts. This treasure-trove is now referred to as the Cairo Geniza.

152. Rending (tearing) one's garments was the approved way to express grief over the destruction of the Temple, but some Jewish writers also gave pilgrims practical advice about how to sew up the rents again so the clothes could still be used. The citation is from Robert A. Wilken, "Christian Pilgrimages to the Holy Land" in Rosovksy, *City*, pp. 117–135, cited p. 122.

153. Moshe Gil, "The Jewish Community" in Prawer, *History*, pp. 163–200, cited p. 174.

154. Like most ancient battle counts, these figures must be exaggerated but they do establish that a great slaughter occurred then.

155. Melito, "Paschal Sermon," cited by Armstrong, *History*, p. 171.

156. Cited by Hunt, *Holy Land Pilgrimage*, p. 81.

157. Ephesians 2:19–22.

158. Hebrews 12: 1, 22–24.

159. Origin, *An Exhortation to Martyrdom, Prayer and Selected Works*, cited by Robinson, *Sacred Places*, p. 133.

160. See Mayke de Jong, "Religion" in McKitterick, *Early Middle Ages*, pp. 131–164, cited p. 132.

161. After Prag, *Jerusalem*, pp. 182–183.

162. Cited by Sinclair, *Jerusalem*, p. 17.

163. A good source for the Bordeaux Pilgrim is John Wilkinson, *Egeria's Travels*, pp. 153–163, from which my account is taken. Wilkinson says that this intrepid pilgrim first traveled from Bordeaux to Constantinople through Arles, Aosta, Milan, Aquileia, Mitrowicz and Sofia. He crossed to Chalcedon, pressed on via Ankara and Mansucrinae to Tarsus, and then made his way through Antioch, Laodicea, Beirut, Sidon and Caesarea Palaestinae until finally reaching Jerusalem.

164. Wilkinson, *Jerusalem Pilgrims*, p. 19. When they were on well-marked roads in good weather conditions, pilgrims on foot could expect to make 20 to 25 miles per day.

165. Wilkinson, *Egeria's Travels*, p. 155.

166. Wilkinson, *Egeria's Travels*, pp. 156–157.

167. Wilkinson, *Egeria's Travels*, pp. 162–163.

168. Eusebius, *De vita Constantini* [The Life of Constantine], cited by Joshua Prawer, "Christian Attitudes towards Jerusalem in the Early Middle Ages," in Prawer, *History*, pp. 311–348, cited p. 317.

169. Rufinus and Jerome had sharp differences of opinion not only over the hostel but, more importantly, on doctrinal issues as well. In the early 390s these men became involved in a controversy over Origen's teachings, which were held by conservative theologians to be heretical. In about 397 Rufinus published a translation of Origen's "On First Principles" and in a preface he depicted Jerome as a follower of Origen. This infuriated Jerome; Rufinus' own orthodoxy was called into question and Rufinus had to write an apology to the Pope. See "Rufinus, Tyrannius" Encyclopædia Britannica Online, http://www.members.eb.com/bol/topic?eu=66044&sctn=1 (accessed 29 March 2000).

170. In fairness to Gregory, it should be noted that he did not reject pilgrimage to *local sites* but for both theological and political reasons he did not approve of the pilgrimage to Jerusalem. For details, see Brouria Bitton-Ashkelony, "The Attitude of Church Fathers toward Pilgrimage to Jerusalem in the Fourth and Fifth Centuries" in Levine, *Jerusalem*, pp. 188–203, cited p. 201.

171. Cited by Robinson, *Sacred Places*, p. 92.

172. Cited by Peters, *Jerusalem*, p. 153.

173. Cited by Coleman, *Pilgrimage Past and Present*, p. 80.

174. Cited by Armstrong, *History*, p. 202.

175. See Williams, *Pilgrimage*, p. 135.

176. See Robert L. Wilken, "Christian Pilgrimage to the Holy Land" in Rosovsky, *City*, pp. 117–135, cited p. 128.

177. Armstrong, *History*, p. 200.

178. Cited by Coleman, *Pilgrimage Past and Present*, p. 84.

179. Adapted from Peters, *Jerusalem*, pp. 148–149.

180. Cited by Coleman, *Pilgrimage Past and Present*, p. 87.

181. Wilkinson, *Jerusalem Pilgrims*, p. 2.

182. Cited by Coleman, *Pilgrimage Past and Present*, p. 82.

183. Cited by Peters, *Jerusalem*, p. 152.

184. Cited by Coleman, *Pilgrimage Past and Present*, p. 82.

185. Cited by Coleman, *Pilgrimage Past and Present*, p. 84. Emphasis added.

186. Cyril, *Catechetical Lectures* 13:22, cited by Armstrong, *History*, p. 191.

187. *Life of Peter the Iberian*, cited by Robert L. Wilken, "Christian Pilgrimage to the Holy Land" in Rosovsky, *City*, pp. 117–135, cited p. 497.

188. After Tuchman, *Bible*, p. 27.

189. Eucherius, *Letter to Faustus*, 1–7, cited by Peters, *Jerusalem*, pp. 153–154.

190. Runciman, *Crusades*, p. 40.

191. After Armstrong, *History*, pp. 205–208.

192. See Wilken, *Holy*, p. 181.

193. Cyril of Scythopolis, cited by Wilkinson, *Jerusalem Pilgrims*, p. 3.

194. Theologically, the quarrel over Monophysitism (a term derived from *mono physis*, "one nature") pitted two propositions against each other. The first was that in Christ the human and the divine natures were united indistinguishably into one nature. The second was that in him both natures coexisted separately, that is, in two natures. Politically, the quarrel pitted Constantinople, Alexandria, and Rome against each other for supremacy. These issues were partially resolved at the Council of Chalcedon in 451, when, thanks to Constantinople's support, the Orthodox proponents of the "two natures" doctrine carried the day. Many bishops and monks in the Middle East, however, continued to back Monophysitism to show their independence from Constantinople. The "one nature" school of thought continues to be represented in Jerusalem today by the churches run by Copts, Ethiopians, Armenians, and Syrian Jacobites.

195. After Coleman, *Pilgrimage Past and Present*, p. 85. The *Breviarius* has come down to us in two different versions, both of which derive from an original document which is now lost. See Wilkinson, *Jerusalem Pilgrims*, pp. 4–5.

196. After Peters, *Jerusalem*, p. 155.

197. Wilkinson, *Jerusalem Pilgrims*, p. 5.

198. Theodosius, *On the Topography of the Holy Land*, cited by Peters, *Jerusalem*, p. 157.

199. Wilkinson, *Jerusalem Pilgrims*, p. 6.

200. *Travels of the Piacenza Pilgrim*, cited by Coleman, *Pilgrimage Past and Present*, p. 85.

201. After Wilken, *Holy*, pp. 191–192.

202. See Brown, "Transformation" in Holmes, *Medieval Europe*, p. 29.

203. After Wilkinson, *Jerusalem Pilgrims*, pp. 8–9.

204. Wilkinson, *Jerusalem Pilgrims*, p. 9.

205. Wilkinson, *Jerusalem Pilgrims*, p. 8.

206. In Greek mythology, Lethe was the river whose waters caused those who drank it to forget the past.

207. Cited by Armstrong, *History*, pp. 215–216.

Chapter VI

208. The scholar was Henri Pirenne, professor of history at the University of Ghent in Belgium; cited by Hay, *Early Middle Ages*, p. 157.

209. The last three considerations are adapted from Armstrong, *History*, pp. 226–228.

210. Cited by Peters, *Jerusalem*, p. 433.

211. Cited by Wilkinson, *Jerusalem Pilgrims*, p. 9.

212. In 702/703 Bede compiled a work on the Holy Land. This won a wide contemporary readership but since he had never been to Palestine himself and since his book contained nothing original, it will not be discussed here. See Wilkinson, *Jerusalem Pilgrims*, p. 10.

213. See Bede, *History*, p. 301.

214. Cited by Gilbert, *Jerusalem*, p. 13.

215. Wilkinson, *Jerusalem Pilgrims*, p. 95.

216. Wilkinson, *Jerusalem Pilgrims*, p. 96.

217. After Mark Friedman, "Jewish Pilgrimage after the Destruction of the Second Temple" in Rosovsky, *City*, pp. 136–146, cited pp. 139–140.

218. Mark Friedman, "Jewish Pilgrimage after the Destruction of the Second Tem-

ple" in Rosovsky, *City*, pp. 136–146, cited p. 140.

219. Garaudy, "Dome," p. 1.

220. Prag, *Blue Guide: Jerusalem*, p. 117. The original dome, inspired by the dome on the Church of the Holy Sepulcher, was built of wood, which was first covered with lead and then guilded with gold. This dome was repaired or replaced many times.

221. After Prag, *Blue Guide: Jerusalem*, p. 129.

222. See Khosraw, *Travels*, p. 33.

223. After Prag, *Blue Guide: Jerusalem*, p. 120.

224. See Prag, *Blue Guide: Jerusalem*, pp. 129–139, for a thorough discussion of the history and the present layout of the Aqsa Mosque.

225. After Gil, *History*, p. 483. Details of the early Latin pilgrimages are from pp. 483–489.

226. Cited by Tuchman, *Bible*, p. 32.

227. These estimates, like almost all other medieval numeration, are exaggerated for effect. The figures come from Régnier-Bohler, *Croisades*, p. 920.

228. After F.E. Peters, "The Holy Places" in Rosovsky, *City*, pp. 37–59, cited p. 49.

229. Cited by Wilkinson, *Jerusalem Pilgrims*, p. 12.

230. Einhard, *Charlemagne*, p. 1.

231. Armstrong, *History*, p. 252.

232. Cited by McKitterick, *Early Middle Ages*, p. 245.

233. *Catholic Encyclopedia*, "Pilgrimages," p. 4.

234. After Runciman, *History*, pp. 43–44.

235. Founded in France in 909 by the Count of Aquitaine, the Abbey of Cluny first played a leading role in pilgrimages to Spain and then began to promote and organize pilgrimages to Jerusalem. Thanks in part to Cluny's efforts, during the eleventh century there was a great increase in the number of French pilgrims going to the Holy Land. See Runciman, *Crusades*, pp. 45–46. The exact extent of Cluny's direct involvement in the Jerusalem pilgrimage remains a matter of scholarly dispute. It is agreed, however, that in 1096 a French nobleman expressed his wish to join the First Crusade, which he described

as "this great and very large awakening of the Christian people to go to Jerusalem in order to fight for God against the pagans and the Saracens" and to finance his journey he mortgaged a piece of property to the Abbot of Cluny, receiving in return 2,000 French shillings and four mules. See Constable, *Cluny*, p. 180. Cluny itself was demolished after the French Revolution of 1789; all that remains today is its bell tower.

236. The following examples are from Gil, *History*, pp. 485–489.

237. Cited by Joshua Prawer, "Christian Attitudes towards Jerusalem in the Early Middle Ages" in Prawer, *History*, pp. 311–348, cited p. 335.

238. Cited by Touati, *Islam*, pp. 220–221.

239. After Kalidi, "Diaspora," p. 4.

240. Cited by Touati, *Islam*, p. 221.

241. After Jonathan M. Bloom, "Jerusalem in Medieval Islamic Literature" in Rosovsky, *City*, pp. 205–217, cited pp. 211–213.

242. Abdul Aziz Duri, "Jerusalem in the Early Islamic Period, 7th–11th Centuries AD" in Asali, *Jerusalem*, pp. 105–125, cited p. 118.

243. Jonathan M. Bloom, "Jerusalem in Medieval Islamic Literature" in Rosovsky, *City*, pp. 205–217, cited p. 211.

244. After Moshe Gil, "The Political History of Jerusalem during the Early Muslim Period" in Prawer, *History*, pp. 1–37, cited p. 24.

245. Caliph Hakim, who reigned from 996 to 1021, was one of the most colorful and eccentric Muslim leaders. Beginning in 1003, he turned against Christians and Jews because of their wealth and in 1009 ordered the governor of Jerusalem to "destroy, undermine, and remove all traces of the holy Church of the Resurrection." The governor did this so thoroughly that this church remained in a ruinous state until the Christians restored it in 1048. See Wilkinson, *Jerusalem Pilgrims*, p. 14. The destruction of these sacred centers had a great impact on both the lords and the people of northern France. They feared this event heralded the time when "the sun would assume the form of the moon"—an event that would mark the end of the world. See Petit Guide, *Moyen Age*, p. 3.

246. Palestine Pilgrims' Text Society, *Daniel*, pp. 75–76, 78.

247. After Muhammad Muslih, "Palestinian Images of Jerusalem" in Rosovsky, *City*, pp. 178–201, cited p. 179.

248. After Peters, *Jerusalem*, p. 374, and Angelika Neuwirth, "The Spiritual Meaning of Jerusalem in Islam" in Rosovsky, *City*, pp. 93–116, cited p. 107.

249. Isaac Hasson, "Muslim Literature in Praise of Jerusalem: Fada'il Bayt al-Maqdis" in Levine, *Cathedra*, vol. 1, pp. 168–189, cited p. 182.

250. After Armstrong, *History*, p. 262.

251. Cited by Webb, *Pilgrims*, p. 40.

252. Reuter, *Fulk Nerra's Pilgrimage*, p. 1.

253. After Glaber, *Histories*, p. 1. The Capetian dynasty of the "Kingdom of the Franks," which laid the foundations for modern France, began with the election of Hugh Capet in 987 and ended in 1328.

254. Cited by Birch, *Pilgrimage*, p. 173.

255. Glaber, *Histories*, p. 201, and Glaber, "Millennium," p. 4. The concept of the Antichrist has its roots in Iranian, Babylonian and Jewish eschatology. An early Christian view can be found in II Thessalonians 2:1–4, which tells the faithful that the last day "will not come unless the rebellion comes first and the lawless one [or "the man of sin"] is revealed, the one destined for destruction. He opposes and exalts himself … so that he takes his seat in the temple of God, declaring himself to be God."

256. This account and the two quotes in it come from Glaber, *Histories*, p. 201.

257. Glaber, *Histories*, p. 203.

258. Glaber, *Histories*, p. 203.

259. Glaber, *Histories*, p. 205.

260. After Elad, *Medieval Jerusalem*, pp. 65–66.

261. Elad, *Medieval Jerusalem*, pp. 63–64.

262. After citations by Le Strange, *Palestine*, pp. 87–88, and by Barber, *Pilgrimages*, p. 21.

263. Elad, *Medieval Jerusalem*, pp. 70–71.

264. Calculated from Elad, *Medieval Jerusalem*, p. xxiii.

265. Khosraw, *Travels*, p. 22.

266. Khosraw, *Travels*, pp. 22–23.

267. Touati, *Islam*, p. 212.

268. Khosraw, *Travels*, pp. 22, 32.

269. Khosraw, *Travels*, p. 24.

270. Khosraw, *Travels*, pp. 27, 28.

271. After Tuchman, *Bible*, pp. 34–36.

272. Tuchman, *Bible*, p. 36.

273. After Moshe Gil, "Aliya and Pilgrimage in the Early Arab Period (634–1009)" in Levine, *Cathedra*, pp. 163–173, cited pp. 166–167.

274. Moshe Gil, "Aliya and Pilgrimage in the Early Arab Period (634–1009) in Levine, *Cathedra*, pp. 163–173, cited p. 164.

275. Moshe Gil, "Aliya and Pilgrimage in the Early Arab Period (634–1009)" in Levine, *Cathedra*, cited p. 169.

276. Moshe Gil, "Aliya and Pilgrimage in the Early Arab Period (634–1009)" in Levine, *Cathedra*, pp. 163–173, cited p. 169.

277. Annalist, p. 1.

278. Hakluyt, *Voyages*, p. 43.

279. Annalist, p. 2.

280. These quotes are also from Annalist, p. 2.

281. Annalist, pp. 2–3.

282. Cited by Tuchman, *Bible*, pp. 33–34. According to one contemporary source (Guibert of Nogent), when Pope Urban II launched the First Crusade in 1095 he told his listeners that because the *bedouin* thought the pilgrims they captured had swallowed gold or silver, "they cut their bowels open with a sword and, spreading out the folds of the intestines, with frightful mutilation disclosed whatever nature held there in secret." Cited by *Medieval Sourcebook*, p. 10.

283. Cited by Webb, *Pilgrims*, p. 42.

284. Cited by Webb, *Pilgrims*, p. 43.

285. Jerusalem surrendered to the Seljuq Turks in 1073. Pro-Fatimid groups launched an unsuccessful revolt against Turkish rule four years later. This led to violent reprisals and widespread destruction by the Turks. As a result of such political instability, pilgrimage routes were diverted or closed entirely. A contemporary Muslim source claimed that what stimulated the First Crusade was that the Muslims living in coastal areas of Palestine prevented European and Byzantine pilgrims from getting to Jerusalem and massacred some of them in 1093. See Gil, *History*, p. 488.

286. Hakluyt, *Voyages*, p. 44.

287. Hakluyt, *Voyages*, p. 45.

Chapter VII

288. After Jean Subrenat, "Préface," in Régnier-Bohler, *Croissades*, pp. vii–xiii, cited p. ix.

289. Cited by *Catholic Encyclopedia*, "Pilgrimages," p. 13.

290. After Pernoud, *Hommes*, pp. 42–43.

291. For a balanced account of this debate, see the Appendix, "Byzantium and Jerusalem: The Motive and Objective of the First Crusade" in Erdmann, *Origin*, pp. 355–371. Erdmann admits that the consensus of modern research is that "the decisive appeals for help came from Jerusalem, not Byzantine; the crusading movement was set in motion by the cruelty of Turkish rule in Palestine and the harassment of Jerusalem pilgrims, not by the battles on the frontiers of the Byzantine Empire…" (p. 359). He adds, however, that the Pope's basic strategy was that "of wanting to go as far as Jerusalem, not in order to conquer this particular city but, more generally, in order to fight the Muslims wherever they were and liberate the Eastern [Byzantine] Christians" (p. 368). Erdmann therefore concludes that for the Pope, "assistance to Byzantium and to Jerusalem were not different things at all. Since he had in mind the totality of the Eastern church, he conceived of the two capitals in a both-and sense, not as an either-or" (p. 371).

292. Runciman, *Crusades*, p. 79.

293. After Runciman, *Crusades*, pp. 90–91.

294. Runciman, *Crusades*, p. 107.

295. Texts of the five versions of Urban's 1095 speech at the Council of Clermont can be found in the *Internet Medieval Source Book* (see bibliography).

296. Adapted from Pernoud, *Hommes*, pp. 39–41; Runciman, *Crusades*, pp. 107–108; and Goetz, *Middle Ages*, pp. 173, 179.

297. See "Robert the Monk" in *Medieval Sourcebook*, p. 5.

298. Cited by Goetz, *Middle Ages*, p. 179.

299. John France, "Patronage and the Appeal of the First Crusade" in Phillips, *First Crusade*, p. 6.

300. See Runciman, *Crusades*, p. 113.

301. Cited by Jones, *Crusades*, p. 28.

302. Runciman, *Crusades*, p. 124.

303. Runciman, *Crusades*, pp. 131–132.

304. See Merdrignac, *Moyen Age*, p. 62.

305. Calculated from Runciman, *Crusades*, p. 169.

306. After Riley-Smith, *Hospitallers*, p. 6.

307. Joshua Prawer, "Christian Attitudes towards Jerusalem in the Early Middle Ages" in Prawer, *History*, pp. 311–348, cited p. 345.

308. "Liquid fire," better known as "Greek fire," was first used against the Arabs at the siege of Constantinople in 673. Pumped over the walls of a city or thrown by catapults in breakable containers, this was a viscous (and vicious) liquid which burned so fiercely that covering it with sand was the only way to put it out. The original formula for Greek fire has been lost but it seems to have involved combustible metallic suspensions in a petroleum base.

309. Cited by Gabrieli, *Arab Historians*, p. 11.

310. Cited by Armstrong, *History*, p. 274.

311. Cited by Armstrong, *History*, p. 274.

312. *Histoire anonyme*, p. 4.

313. Cited by Armstrong, *History*, p. 275.

314. The First Crusade also left behind a number of what the French called *poulains* (literally "colts" but in this context "protégés"). These were the *petits* (the common folk) who initially followed the knights but who then settled permanently in the Holy Land rather than going back to Europe. Later Crusaders would criticize them for assimilating too thoroughly into Islamic culture and for getting along too well with the local Muslims. See Merdrignac, *Moyen Age*, p. 67.

315. Phillips, *Crusade*, p. 182.

316. Cited by the *International Herald Tribune* in a 3 November 2000 obituary on Sir Steven Runciman.

317. After Kalidi, *Diaspora*, Part 1, p. 4.

318. "Abstract of the Description of the Ceremony of the Descent of the Holy Light, by Fulcher de Chartres," cited by Palestine Pilgrims Text Society in Vol. IV, Appendix V, p. 108.

319. Gilbert, *Atlas*, p. 21.

320. Unless otherwise attributed, this account of Saewulf's pilgrimage comes from Wilkinson, *Jerusalem Pilgrimage*, pp. 94–116.

321. Wilkinson, *Jerusalem Pilgrimage*, p. 99.

322. Wilkinson, *Jerusalem Pilgrimage*, pp. 99–100.

323. Wilkinson, *Jerusalem Pilgrimage*, pp. 100–101.

324. Wilkinson, *Jerusalem Pilgrimage*, pp. 112–113.

325. After Wilkinson, *Jerusalem Pilgrimage*, pp. 5–6.

326. After Browner, *Viking*, pp. 1–8.

327. Cited by Browner, *Viking*, p. 7.

328. Birch, *Pilgrimage*, p. 177.

329. Birch, *Pilgrimage*, p. 177.

330. See Régnier-Bohler, *Croisades*, p. 557, and Nicholson, *Templars*, p. 2.

331. Theodoric, cited by Robinson, *Sacred Places*, p. 113.

332. St. Bernard founded the abbey of Clairvaux in 1115. This was part of the Cistercian monastic order, which followed a very strict interpretation of the Rule of St. Benedict, i.e., asceticism and manual labor.

333. For the Templars, homosexual behavior was a major violation of their rule of life, which denounced it as a crime "against nature and against the law of our Lord." On one occasion, three Templars "practised wicked sin and caressed each other in their chamber at night." They were summoned to the Templar castle at Acre, stripped of their uniforms and put in irons. One of them managed to escape and defected to the Muslim side; another tried to escape but died in the attempt; the third "remained in prison for a long time." Cited by Read, *Templars*, p. 213.

334. Cited by Gabrieli, *Arab Historians*, pp. 79–80.

335. Cited by Maalouf, *Arabes*, p. 145.

336. Cited by Gilbert, *Atlas*, p. 21.

337. Cited by Adler, *Jewish Travellers*, p. 37.

338. Gilbert, *Atlas*, p. 21.

339. Hess, *Rome and Jerusalem*, p. 170.

340. This analysis of ha-Levi's work is comes from Schweid, *Land of Israel*, pp. 55–60.

341. Schweid, *Land of Israel*, p. 59.

342. Richard, *Histoire*, p. 165.

343. Cited by Jones, *Crusade*, p. 114.

344. Cited by Jones, *Crusade*, pp. 111, 114.

345. Richard, *Histoire*, p. 172.

346. Gabrieli, *Arab Historians*, p. 59.

347. Unless otherwise attributed, this account is from Komroff, *Contemporaries*, pp. 253–277.

348. Komroff, *Contemporaries*, p. 273.

349. Komroff, *Contemporaries*, p. 274.

350. Komroff, *Contemporaries*, p. 276.

351. Komroff, *Contemporaries*, p. 276.

352. Komroff, *Contemporaries*, pp. 276–277.

353. Palestine Pilgrims' Text Society, *Description*, cited p. 69.

354. Dorothea R. French, "Journeys to the Center of the Earth" in Sargent-Bauer, *Journeys*, pp. 45–81, cited p. 67.

355. Palestine Pilgrims' Text Society, *Würzburg*, pp. 14–15.

356. Christian Information Office, *Holy Week*, pp. 83–82.

357. After Myriam Rosen-Ayalon, "Three Perspectives on Jerusalem: Jewish, Christian, and Muslim Pilgrims in the Twelfth Century" in Levine, *Jerusalem*, pp. 326–346.

358. Cited by Adler, *Jewish Travellers*, p. 90, and Régnier-Bohler, *Croisades*, p. 1342.

359. Cited by Adler, *Jewish Travellers*, p. 98.

360. Gabrieli, *Arab Historians*, p. 141.

361. Gabrieli, *Arab Historians*, p. 142.

362. Gabrieli, *Arab Historians*, p. 174.

363. Gabrieli, *Arab Historians*, pp. 174–175.

Chapter VIII

364. Gabrieli, *Arab Historians*, p. 226.

365. Cited by Peters, *Jerusalem*, pp. 360–361.

366. This citation and much of the information in this section comes from Nicholson, *Templars*, p. 3.

367. Cited by Robinson, *Sacred Places*, pp. 89–90.

368. After Hyams, "Appendix," p. 5.

369. Cited by Adler, *Jewish Travellers*, p. 103.

370. Cited by Adler, *Jewish Travellers*, p. 104.

371. *Tower of David*, p. 24.

372. Cited by Jones, Crusades, p. 64.

373. Régnier-Bohler, *Croisades*, pp. 931, 932.

374. After Peters, *Jerusalem*, pp. 362–363, and Régnier-Bohler, *Croisades*, p. 943.

375. Cited by Armstrong, *History*, p. 299.

376. Read, *Templars*, p. 197.

377. See, for example, the accounts in medieval French in Michelant, *Itinéraires*.

378. Mandeville, *Travels*, p. 58.

379. Al-Kamil, the sultan of Egypt, was willing to cede Jerusalem to the Crusaders because without walls the city was of no strategic use and because, facing a possible challenge from his brother (the sultan of Damascus) he did not want a war with the West. See Armstrong, *History*, p. 302.

380. Cited by Maalouf, *Arabes*, p. 248.

381. Cited by Maalouf, *Arabes*, p. 249.

382. Cited by Adler, *Jewish Travellers*, p. 115.

383. Not understanding that Islam was a new religion, medieval Christian scholars believed that the beginnings of Islam could be found in the Bible. They decided that the Arabs must be descended from Ishmael, the son of Abraham by his concubine Hagar. Genesis 16:12 tells that Ishmael was "a wild ass of a man, with his hand against everyone, and everyone's hand against him; and he shall live at odds with all his kin." This is the reason medieval Christian sources often referred to Muslims as "Ishmaelites." After Fletcher, *Conversion*, p. 305.

384. Cited by Adler, *Jewish Travellers*, pp. 118–119.

385. Medieval Sourcebook, *Tales*, p. 1.

386. After Birch, *Pilgrimage*, p. 4.

387. After Stopford, *Pilgrimage Explored*, p. 93.

388. Cited by Coulton, *Garner*, p. 198.

389. *Catholic Encyclopedia*, "Jerusalem," p. 1.

390. Al-Makrisi, *Account*, p. 3.

391. "Capture of Jerusalem," pp. 2, 3.

392. Vaughan, *Matthew Paris*, p. 128.

393. Vaughan, *Matthew Paris*, p. 129.

394. After Armstrong, *History*, p. 305.

395. Mark Friedman, "Jewish Pilgrimage after the Destruction of the Second Temple" in Rosovsky, *City*, pp. 136–146, cited p. 142.

396. Cited by Gilbert, *Atlas*, p. 23, and by Mark Friedman, "Jewish Pilgrimage after

the Destruction of the Second Temple" in Rosovsky, *City*, pp. 136–146, cited p. 146.

397. Cited by Coleman, *Pilgrimage*, p. 96.

398. There are various ways to date the eight "numbered" crusades. Some of the dates used here are from Merdrignac, *Moyen Age*, pp. 62–66, and Régnier-Bohler, *Croisade*, pp. xlvii–xlvix.

399. Cited by Coleman, *Pilgrimage Past and Present*, pp. 97–98, and by International Herald Tribune, 11–12 March 2000.

400. Coleman, *Pilgrimage Past and Present*, p. 98.

401. See Gabrieli, *Arab Historians*, pp. 323–350.

402. Gabrieli, *Arab Historians*, p. 346.

403. Cited by Régnier-Bohler, *Croisades*, p. 1016.

404. Cited by Régnier-Bohler, *Croisades*, p. 1016.

405. The citations are from Adler, *Jewish Travellers*, pp. 130, 131–132. Emphasis in original.

406. Cited by Adler, *Jewish Travellers*, p. 133.

407. After Peters, *Jerusalem*, p. 433.

408. Cited by Peters, *Jerusalem*, p. 438.

409. After Peters, *Jerusalem*, pp. 434–435, 438.

410. After Chareyron, *Pèlerins*, p. 105.

411. The examples which follow are taken from Régnier-Bohler, *Croisades*, pp. 1032–1056.

412. Mandeville, *Travels*, p. 184.

413. After Moseley, *Introduction*, Mandeville, *Travels*, p. 13.

414. Mandeville, *Travels*, pp. 43, 44, 45.

415. Mandeville, *Travels*, p. 72.

416. Mandeville, *Travels*, pp. 76, 77.

417. Medieval chronicles and legends identified Prester John (also known as Presbyter John or John the Elder) as a king-priest governing the lands east of Iran and Turkey. It was hoped that Prester John would help the West drive the Muslims from Jerusalem.

418. Cited by Robinson, *Sacred Places*, p. 73.

419. After Robinson, *Sacred Places*, pp. 55, 57.

420. After Simon, "In pilgers weys," p. 1.

421. Cited by Robinson, *Sacred Places*, p. 51.

422. "Punishment," p. 1.

423. "Punishment," p. 1.

424. After Régnier-Bohler, *Croisades*, pp. 1057–1123.

425. Other pilgrims, too, report being inducted into this order. In 1494 Canon Pietro Casola said he wrote letters for several men "testifying that they had been created knights at the Sepulchre, according to the form given me by the Superior, and he sealed the letters." See Newett, *Casola*, Internet, p. 22. Modern scholars, however, know of no statute formally authorizing a "knighthood of the Holy Sepulcher." See Régnier-Bohler, *Croisades*, p. 1083, note 1.

426. Cited by Régnier-Bohler, *Croisades*, p. 1083.

427. Cited by Régnier-Bohler, *Croisades*, p. 1089, 1091.

428. When Jerusalem was under Muslim control, many of the Christian holy places were converted to mosques. This meant, as Ogier d'Anglure, a French pilgrim of the Middle Ages, remarked, "there are many places for indulgences which pilgrims may not enter." He counted 32 of them, i.e., former Christian churches or ancient Jewish sites. See Chareyron, *Pèlerins*, p. 106.

429. After Chareyron, *Pèlerins*, p. 109.

430. After Régnier-Bohler, *Croisades*, pp. 1227–1231.

431. Piloti also wanted the new Crusaders to seize Alexandria. The citation is from Régnier-Bohler, *Croisades*, p. 1257.

432. Cited by Wright, *Early Travels*, pp. 283–284.

433. Cited by Wright, *Early Travels*, p. 286.

434. Cited by Peters, *Jerusalem*, p. 435.

435. Cited by Peters, *Jerusalem*, p. 436.

436. After Adler, *Jewish Travellers*, p. 151.

437. Cited by Adler, *Jewish Travellers*, p. 153.

438. Cited by Adler, *Jewish Travellers*, p. 155.

439. This pattern continues today. The "Jerusalem Syndrome" is a mental disorder unique to the Holy City. Those afflicted by it believe they are personages from the Bible, e.g., Jesus, Moses, one of the prophets, or the Virgin Mary. This disorder can lead to violence. In 1969, for example, a deranged Australian pilgrim tried to burn down the Aqsa Mosque to prepare the way for the Second Coming of Jesus.

440. Kempe, *Book*, p. 1.

441. Tuchman, *Bible*, p. 46.

442. Wey, *Itinerary*, pp. 1–3.

443. After Régnier-Bohler, *Croisades*, pp. 1124–1167.

444. Cited by Régnier-Bohler, *Croisades*, p. 1165.

445. Fabri's first (1480) visit was a disappointment. He complained that "We did not spend more than nine days in the Holy Land, and in that time we rushed around the usual Holy Places both by day and by night, and were hardly given any time to rest.... When we had hurriedly visited the Holy Places ... we were led out of the Holy City by the same road by which we had come, down to the sea where our galley waited." Cited by Coleman, *Pilgrimage Past and Present*, p. 206. But Fabri did not give up easily and wanted to try again. His second (1483) visit was an unqualified success.

446. See Palestine Pilgrims' Text Society, *Fabri*, pp. 280–540. Although this work is printed in two volumes, the volumes are bound together and the pages are numbered sequentially, so it is not essential to specify which volume is being cited.

447. The Venetian Republic made shipping available to the Crusaders of 1201–1204. Thereafter its increasing maritime capabilities encouraged more pilgrims to embark there for the Holy Land. Not only did Venice have sizeable naval and commercial fleets, but it also controlled a chain of ports on the mainland and on nearby islands—its share of the Byzantine Empire after this empire was dismembered by the Ottoman Turks in 1453. These ports helped ensure safe and reliable passages to Jaffa. By the fifteenth century a regular shipping service to the Holy Land had been established in Venice. Galleys sailed from Venice to Jaffa in spring or early summer, stopping at Cyprus, Rhodes, and Beirut en route, and made about five round trips to Jaffa each year. See Newett, *Casola's Pilgrimage*, p. 5, and Tuchman, *Bible*, pp. 44–45.

448. Palestine Pilgrims' Text Society, *Fabri*, p. 207.

449. After Palestine Pilgrims' Text Society, *Fabri*, p. 219.

450. Cited by Peters, *Jerusalem*, p. 431.

451. Cited by Peters, *Jerusalem*, p. 432.

452. After Peters, *Jerusalem*, pp. 427–431.

453. Peters, *Jerusalem*, p. 427.

454. Palestine Pilgrims' Text Society, *Fabri*, p. 280.

455. Palestine Pilgrims' Text Society, *Fabri*, pp. 343–344.

456. Palestine Pilgrims' Text Society, *Fabri*, pp. 283–284.

457. Palestine Pilgrims' Text Society, *Fabri*, pp. 382–383.

458. At the Temple of Apollo in Delphi, Greek pilgrims could contemplate a smooth rounded stone known as the *omphalos*, the navel of the world. Greek myth taught that Zeus had released two eagles, one from the west, the other from the east, and had ordered them to fly to the center of the world. They met at Delphi.

459. Cited by Dorothea R. French, "Journeys to the Center of the Earth: Medieval and Renaissance Pilgrimages to Mount Calvary" in Sargent-Baur, *Journeys*, pp. 45–81, cited p. 75.

460. Peters, *Jerusalem and Mecca*, pp. 221–222.

461. Cited by Robinson, *Sacred Places*, p. 87.

462. Cited by Peters, *Jerusalem*, pp. 433–434.

463. Cited by Adler, *Jewish Travellers*, p. 182.

464. Cited by Adler, *Jewish Travellers*, p. 194.

465. Cited by Adler, *Jewish Travellers*, p. 194.

466. Cited by Adler, *Jewish Travellers*, p. 196.

467. Osher, *Jerusalem 3000*, p. 2.

468. After Osher, *Jerusalem 3000*, p. 2.

469. Cited by Régnier-Bohler, *Croisades*, p. 1173.

470. Cited by Régnier-Bohler, *Croisades*, p. 1173.

471. Cited by Adler, *Jewish Travellers*, p. 235.

472. Cited by Adler, *Jewish Travellers*, pp. 238, 243.

473. The basic source for Casola's travels is M. Margaret Newett's 1907 translation, *Canon Pietro Casola's Pilgrimage to Jerusalem in the Year 1494*. Much of the Jerusalem portion of his travels, however, is also available on the Internet at http://www.uscolo.edu.history/seminar/casola/cas4.htm (accessed 11 October 2000). Citations from this website are given in the endnotes as "Newett, Casola, Internet, chapter …, p. …."

474. Newett, *Casola*, Internet, chapter X, p. 2.

475. Newett, *Casola*, Internet, chapter X, p. 2.

476. Newett, *Casola*, Internet, chapter X, p. 3.

477. Newett, *Casola*, Internet, chapter X, p. 3.

478. Newett, *Casola*, Internet, chapter X, p. 7.

479. Newett, *Casola*, Internet, chapter X, p. 7.

480. Newett, *Casola*, Internet, chapter XI, p. 12.

481. Newett, *Casola*, Internet, chapter XI, p. 13.

482. Newett, *Casola*, Internet, chapter XII, p. 14.

483. Newett, *Casola*, Internet, chapter XII, pp. 15, 16.

484. Newett, *Casola*, Internet, chapter XII, p. 16.

485. Newett, *Casola*, Internet, chapter XII, p. 18.

486. Newett, *Casola*, Internet, chapter X, p. 19.

487. Newett, *Casola*, Internet, chapter X, p. 20.

488. Newett, *Casola*, Internet, chapter XIII, p. 3.

489. Newett, *Casola*, Internet, chapter XIII, pp. 3–4.

490. Newett, *Casola*, Internet, chapter XIV, p. 13.

491. Cited by Peters, *Jerusalem*, p. 374. Emphasis in original.

492. See Jonathan M. Bloom, "Jerusalem in Medieval Islamic Literature" in Rosovsky, *City*, pp. 205–217, cited p. 217.

493. Cited by Peters, *Jerusalem*, pp. 376–377. Emphasis added.

494. Cited by Tuchman, *Bible*, p. 48.

495. Cited by Tuchman, *Bible*, p. 48.

496. After Ellis, *Pylgrymage*, pp. 43–45.

Chapter IX

497. Cited by Armstrong, *History*, p. 322.

498. The Augsburg Confession consisted of 28 articles that constitute the basic confession (statement of religious views) of the Lutheran churches. It was presented to Holy Roman Emperor Charles V at the Diet of Augsburg by seven Lutheran princes and two imperial free cities. Originally written in German and Latin, it was translated into English in 1536. See Encyclopædia Britannica Online, "Augsburg Confession."

499. Cited by Tuchman, *Bible*, p. 48.

500. Cited by Tuchman, *Bible*, p. 48.

501. Cited by Loftie, *Ye Oldest Diarie*, pp. 37–38. Loftie's text is hard to read, so I have put this quote into modern English.

502. Armstrong, *History*, p. 325.

503. K.J. Asali, "Jerusalem under the Ottomans, 1516–1831 AD" in Asali, *Jerusalem*, pp. 200–227b, cited p. 205.

504. Cited by Adler, *Jewish Travellers*, p. 263.

505. Cited by Adler, *Jewish Travellers*, pp. 265–266.

506. Cited by Chareyron, *Pèlerins*, p. 113.

507. After Elad, *Medieval Jerusalem*, pp. 167, 173.

508. Cited by Williams, *Pilgrimage*, p. 67.

509. After Williams, *Pilgrimage*, pp. 51, 55.

510. Williams, *Pilgrimage*, p. 55.

511. After Peters, *Jerusalem*, pp. 492–496.

512. Peters, *Jerusalem*, p. 493.

513. Peters, *Jerusalem*, p. 495.

514. Deuteronomy 34:1–4.

515. After Landow, "Pisgah Sight," p. 1.

516. Cited by Peters, *Jerusalem*, pp. 496–497.

517. In Saudi Arabia a woman could jeopardize her honor merely by talking to or sitting next to a man who was not related to her. Once lost, her honor could never, ever, be regained. See Janin, *Saudi Arabia*, pp. 65–66.

518. Cited by Gilbert, *Atlas*, p. 35.

519. After Encyclopædia Britannica Online, "Humanism," p. 1.

520. After Jerusalem Quarterly File, "Maundrell," p. 1; and Tuchman, *Bible*, p. 155.

521. Maundrell, *Journey*, pp. 94–95.

522. Maundrell, *Journey*, pp. 100–101. A later pilgrim, Constantin-François Volney, says that this was a painful and potentially dangerous operation. He had seen a pilgrim who had lost an arm as a result of the subsequent infection. See Volney, *Travels*, pp. 311–312.

523. Maundrell, *Journey*, p. 130.

524. Maundrell, *Journey* pp. 110–111.

525. After Kalidi, *Diaspora*, Part I, pp. 6–7.

526. Cited by Gilbert, *Atlas*, p. 35.

527. Burton, *Strange and True Account*, p. 116. Emphasis added.

528. Some of the following account is from Tuchman, *Bible*, pp. 156–157.

529. Pococke, *Description*, Vol. 2, p. 22.

530. Pococke, *Description*, Vol. 2, p. 29.

531. Hasselquist, *Voyages*, p. 117.

532. Hasselquist, *Voyages*, p. 124.

533. Tuchman, *Bible*, p. 155.

534. Tyron, *Travels*, pp. 21–22.

535. Volney, *Travels*, pp. 308.

536. Volney, *Travels*, pp. 308–309. Emphasis in original.

537. Volney, *Travels*, p. 309.

538. Volney, *Travels*, p. 309.

539. Volney, *Travels*, p. 309.

540. Volney, *Travels*, pp. 310–311.

541. Volney, *Travels*, p. 311. Emphasis in original.

542. Volney, *Travels*, p. 311.

543. Cited by Peters, *Travels*, p. 225.

544. Volney, *Travels*, p. 312. Emphasis in original.

545. Cited by Said, *Orientalism*, pp. 169, 171.

546. Cited by Said, *Orientalism*, p. 171.

547. Said, *Orientalism*, p. 172. Emphasis added.

548. Peters, *Jerusalem and Mecca*, p. 226.

549. Peters, *Jerusalem and Mecca*, p. 226.

550. After Milka Levy-Rubin and Rehav Rubin, "The Image of the Holy City in Maps and Mapping" in Rosovsky, *City*, pp. 352–379, especially pp. 376–378.

551. Cited by Said, *Orientalism*, p. 178.

552. Cited by Said, *Orientalism*, p. 179.

553. The phrase "painter pilgrim" is from Sim, *Roberts*, p. 182.

554. Cited by Sim, *Roberts*, p. 186.

555. Cited by Sim, *Roberts*, p. 191.

556. Cited in Roberts, *Holy Land*, pp. 5–6.

557. Egerton, *Journal*, pp. 15–16. Emphasis in original.

558. Egerton, *Journal*, p. 12.

559. Egerton, *Journal*, p. 19.

560. Moscrop, *Measuring Jerusalem*, p. 20.

561. Robinson, *Biblical*, p. 227.

562. Robinson, *Biblical*, p. 221.

563. Robinson, *Biblical*, p. 253. Emphasis in original.

564. Bartlett, *Walks*, cited by Gilbert, *Atlas*, p. 39.

565. Bartlett, *Walks*, cited by Gilbert, *Atlas*, p. 39.

566. Bartlett, *Walks*, cited by Gilbert, *Atlas*, p. 39.

567. Bartlett, *Walks*, cited by Gilbert, *Atlas*, p. 39.

568. Bartlett, *Walks*, cited by Gilbert, *Atlas*, p. 39.

569. Cited by Gilbert, *Jerusalem*, p. 31.

570. Cited by Tuchman, *Bible*, p. 212. Emphasis added.

571. Tuchman, *Bible*, p. 212.

572. Warburton, *Crescent*, p. 163. Jehoshaphat (c. 873–c. 849 BCE) was a king of Judah. The valley of Jehoshaphat lies south of the Haram, where it deepens to a shallow gorge with steep scarps on either side. It was used for burial in past ages.

573. Warburton, *Crescent*, p. 164.

574. Warburton, *Crescent*, p. 163.

575. Warburton, *Crescent*, p. 163.

576. Warburton, *Crescent*, p. 165.

577. Warburton, *Crescent*, p. 166.

578. Ministry of Foreign Affairs, "Focus," p. 1.

579. For a useful online summary of the Crimean War, see Rempel, "Crimean War," pp. 1–5.

580. After Armstrong, *History*, p. 355.

581. After Macfie, *Eastern Question*, p. 27.

582. Not all Jews were Zionists. Ultra-orthodox Jews believed that the return to the Jews to the Holy Land would come about only by divine intervention. Therefore they strongly opposed any human efforts, e.g., Zionism, to speed up this process. See Gilbert, *Jerusalem*, p. 57.

583. Hess, *Rome*, p. 147.

584. Hess, *Rome*, p. 148.

585. After Moscrop, *Measuring Jerusalem*, p. 46.

586. Moscrop, *Measuring Jerusalem*, p. 47.

587. See Bahat, "Jerusalem," for a detailed discussion of archeological exploration in Jerusalem since 1860s. This work is still useful even though later excavations have called his chronology into question.

588. Milka Levy-Rubin and Rehav Rubin, "The Image of the Holy City in Maps and Mapping" in Rosovsky, *City*, pp. 352–379, cited p. 378.

589. Palestine Exploration Fund website, "Introduction," p. 1.

590. Cited by Tuchman, *Bible*, p. 361.

591. Cited by Gilbert, *Atlas*, p. 45.

592. Cited by Kenyon, *Digging Up Jerusalem*, p. 16.

593. Cited by Kenyon, *Digging Up Jerusalem*, pp. 16–17.

594. Cited by Jacobson, "Search," p. 31, and Kenyon, *Digging Up Jerusalem*, p. 17.

595. Twain, *Innocents*, p. 319.

596. Twain, *Innocents*, pp. 414, 415.

597. Twain, *Innocents*, p. 416.

598. Twain, *Innocents*, pp. 416–417.

599. Twain, *Innocents*, p. 417.

600. Twain, *Innocents*, pp. 417, 418.

601. Twain, *Innocents*, p. 432.

602. Twain, *Innocents*, p. 433.

603. Twain, *Innocents*, p. 434.

604. Twain, *Innocents*, p. 437.

605. Part of this account comes from an e-mail of 5 December 2000 from Paul Smith, the Company Archivist of Thomas Cook.

606. Cited by Gilbert, *Jerusalem*, p. 51.

607. After John Davies, *Pilgrimage Yesterday and Today*, cited by Robinson, *Sacred Places*, p. 82.

608. Conder, *Tent Work*, p. xxi.

609. Conder, *Tent Work*, p. 311.

610. Conder, *Tent Work*, p. 312.

611. Conder, *Tent Work*, p. 345.

612. One of Judaism's many sects, the Pharisees are depicted in the New Testament as self-righteous hypocrites.

613. Cited by Netton, *Golden Roads*, pp. 130–131.

614. Cited by Netton, *Golden Roads*, pp. 131–132.

615. After VanDoodewaard, *Hadith*, pp. 5–6.

616. After Armstrong, *History*, p. 362.

617. Cited by Matthew, *Pilgrims*, p. 265.

618. Cited by Matthew, *Pilgrims*, pp. 267–268.

619. Cited by Matthew, *Pilgrims*, pp. 270–271.

620. Cited by Matthew, *Pilgrims*, p. 273.

621. Cited by Matthew, *Pilgrims*, p. 274. According to the New Testament, Mary Magdalene, one of Jesus' most fervent disciples, was the first person to see the resurrected Christ.

622. Serao, *Country of Jesus*, pp. 14–15.

623. Cited by Gilbert, *Atlas*, p. 49.

624. Cited by Matthew, *Pilgrimages*, p. 281.

625. Serao, *Country of Jesus*, pp. 235–236.

626. Herzl, *Jewish State*, p. 69.

627. Cited by Gilbert, *Jerusalem*, pp. 4, 55.

628. Cited by Gilbert, *Jerusalem*, p. 54.

629. Cited by Khaladi, *Diaspora*, Part 2, p. 2.

630. Tuchman, *Bible*, p. 269. I have relied heavily on her account of Ottoman-German relations, pp. 267–269.

631. Tuchman, *Bible*, p. 267.

632. Tuchman, *Bible*, p. 291.

633. Cited by Gilbert, *Jerusalem*, p. 8.

634. Cited by Gilbert, *Jerusalem*, p. 16.

635. Cited by Gilbert, *Jerusalem*, p. 8.

636. Cited by Gilbert, *Jerusalem*, p. 22.

637. Cited by Gilbert, *Jerusalem*, pp. 29–30.

638. Cited by Gilbert, *Jerusalem*, pp. 30–31.

639. Cited by Gilbert, *Jerusalem*, p. 35.

640. Cited by Gilbert, *Atlas*, p. 48.

Chapter X

641. Avalon Project, "Balfour Declaration," p. 1.

642. See Fromkin, *Peace*, p. 520.

643. The citation is taken in part from Armstrong, *History*, p. 374, and in part from The Zionist Century, "Balfour Declaration," p. 4.

644. Cited by Armstrong, *History*, p. 374.

645. After Tuchman, *Bible*, pp. 182–183.

646. After Polowetzky, *Jerusalem Recovered*, p. 9.

647. From Tuchman, *Bible*, 184.

648. Cited by Tuchman, *Bible*, p. 175.

649. Cited by Tuchman, *Bible*, p. 176.

650. Cited by Fromkin, *Peace*, p. 278.

651. Cited by Fromkin, *Peace*, p. 298.

652. Cited by Tuchman, *Bible*, p. 311.

653. After Tuchman, *Bible*, p. 311.

654. Michael C. Hudson, "The Transformation of Jerusalem, 1917–1987" in Asali, *Jerusalem*, pp. 249–283, cited p. 252.

655. Cited by Egremont, *Balfour*, p. 331.

656. Cited by Tuchman, *Bible*, p. 335.

657. Cited by Hoffman, *Guide*, p. 123.

658. Cited by Gilbert, *Jerusalem*, p. 56.

659. Samuel, "Interim Report," p. 1.

660. Graves, *Palestine*, pp. 96–97.

661. A Mufti is a senior Islamic authority who gives a formal legal opinion (known as a *fatwa*) in response to a question from a private citizen or from a judge. Issuing a *fatwa* is not a simple matter because it requires a detailed knowledge of Muhammud's life and sayings and of Islamic law. Haj Amin was later known as the Grand Mufti and became the most powerful Arab in Palestine.

662. Cited by Gilbert, *Jerusalem*, p. 107.

663. Until 1949 Jordan was known as Transjordan, but its present name is used here in the interest of simplicity.

664. Gilbert, *Jerusalem*, p. 241.

665. After Gilbert, *Jerusalem*, pp. 251–262.

666. Cited by Gilbert, *Jerusalem*, p. 259.

667. Cited by Gilbert, *Jerusalem*, pp. 255–256.

668. After Gilbert, *Jerusalem*, pp. 272–297.

669. Both citations are from Gilbert, *Jerusalem*, p. 285.

670. Cited by Gilbert, *Jerusalem*, p. 287.

671. Cited by Gilbert, *Jerusalem*, pp. 293–294.

672. Cited by Gilbert, *Jerusalem*, pp. 294–295. Emphasis added.

673. U.S. Department of State, *Country Reports on Human Rights Practices— 2000: Occupied Territories*, p. 4.

674. After Cohen, "Temple Mount Question," pp. 2–5.

675. After Yulish, *Ashes*, p. 1.

676. Hoffman, *Guide*, p. 30.

677. Kernohan, *Road*, p. 149.

678. After George P. Lavas, "The Rock of Calvary: Uncovering Christ's Crucifixion Site" in Kühnel, *Real and Ideal*, pp. 147–150.

679. Department of State, "Occupied Territories," p. 4.

680. Nicholl, *Testing*, p. 34.

681. Nicholl, *Testing*, pp. 265–266. Emphasis in original.

682. Cited by Latin Patriarchate, *Welcome*, p. 4.

683. After Biema, "A Pilgrim's Progress," pp. 1–6.

684. Cited by Biema, "A Pilgrim's Progress," p. 2.

685. Cited by Bard, "Pope John Paul II's Pilgrimage," pp. 2–3.

686. Since Johanna's website showed that she made the last leg of her pilgrimage by sea, I asked her to clarify what she had done. In an e-mail of 11 March 2001 (lightly edited), she said: "I walked [from the Netherlands] to Marmaris on the Turkish Mediterranean coast, then took a ferry to Rhodes. From there I wanted to take a boat to Haifa but since there were no tourists going to Israel because of the tense political situation, there were no boats, so I took an airplane from Rhodes to Tel Aviv. Bus from Tel Aviv to Haifa; started walking again from Haifa to Tiberias; back to Haifa by bus; walked along the beach from Haifa to Tel Aviv and from there to Jerusalem." A reasonable estimate is that on her pilgrimage she walked a total of about 3,000 miles.

687. Van Fessem, "Walk," pp. 1–2. This account has been lightly edited.

688. E-mails from van Fessem of 9 March and 10 April 2001.

Chapter XI

689. Private communication of 26 May 2000 from Rev. Craig Eder, a Protestant clergyman living in Washington, D.C.

690. Eliot, "Journey of the Magi," *Poems*, p. 103.

691. Steinbeck, *Pony*, p. 143. Emphasis added.

692. Cited by Pearson, *Celtic Monasticism*, p. 1.

693. See Mayke de Jong, "Religion" in McKitterick, *Early Middle Ages*, pp. 131–164, especially p. 136.

694. Cited by Pearson, *Celtic Monasticism*, p. 2.

695. Turner, *Image*, p. 7. Emphasis added.

696. Adapted from Coleman, *Pilgrimages*, p. 201.

697. After Sax, *Mountain Goddess*, pp. 12–13.

Appendices

698. Adapted from Régnier-Bohler, *Croisades*, pp. 1122–1123.

699. See Peters, *Jerusalem*, pp. 427–430.

700. Cited by Peters, *Jerusalem*, p. 444.

701. Cited by Fromkin, *Peace*, p. 277.

702. After Fromkin, *Peace*, pp. 277, 283.

703. This discussion is drawn from Fromkin, *Peace*, pp. 294, 296, 299.

704. Tuchman, *Bible*, p. 337.

705. Cited by Gilbert, *Jerusalem*, p. 86.

Selected Bibliography

Adler, Elkan Nathan (ed.). *Jewish Travellers in the Middle Ages: 19 Firsthand Accounts.* New York: Dover, 1987.

Andrews, Richard. *Blood on the Mountain: A History of the Temple Mount from the Ark to the Third Millennium.* London: Weidenfeld & Nicolson, 1999.

Annalist of Nieder-Altaich (trans. James Brundage), "The Great German Pilgrimage of 1064–65," *Internet Medieval Sourcebook.* www.fordham.edu/halsall/source/1064pilgrim. Accessed 12 June 2000.

Armstrong, Karen. *A History of God.* London: Mandarin, 1994.

_____. *A History of Jerusalem: One City, Three Faiths.* London: HarperCollins, 1997.

Asali, Kamil J. (ed.). *Jerusalem in History: 3,000 BC to the Present Day.* London: Kegan Paul, 1997.

Assadi, Mohammed. "Violence, Blockade Dash Christmas Joy in Bethlehem," Reuters story on http://dailynews.yahoo.com/h/nm/20001225/ts/mideast_christmas _dc_11.html, accessed 12 December 2000.

Associated Press, "Israel Seeking Tourism," *International Herald Tribune,* 7 March 2001.

Auld, Graeme, and Margreet Steiner. *Jerusalem I: From the Bronze Age to the Maccabees.* Cambridge: Lutterworth, 1996.

Avalon Project, "Balfour Declaration 1917." http://www.yale.edu.lawweb/avalon/balfour.htm. Accessed 7 July 2000.

Bahat, Dan. "Jerusalem" in *The Oxford Encyclopedia of Archaeology in the Near East,* pp. 224–38. Oxford: Oxford University Press, 1997.

Barber, Richard. *Pilgrimages.* Woodbridge, Suffolk: Boydell Press, 1991.

Bard, Mitchell. "Pope John Paul II's Pilgrimage to Israel." Jewish Student Online Research Center. http://www.us-israel.org/jsource/anti-semitism/jp.html. Accessed 19 November 2000.

Barker, Margaret. *The Gate of Heaven: The History and Symbolism of the Temple in Jerusalem.* London: SPCK, 1991.

Bede. *A History of the English Church and People* (Trans. Leo Sherley-Price). Penguin: Harmondsworth, 1972.

Ben-Arieh, Yehoshua, and Moshe Davis. *Jerusalem in the Mind of the Western World, 1800–1948.* Vol. V. Westport: Prager, 1997.

La Bible de Jérusalem. Paris: Éditions de Cerf, 1984.

Biema, David Van, Lisa Beyer and Greg Burke. "A Pilgrim's Progress." *Time South Pacific* magazine, 3 April 2000. http://www.britannica.com/bcom/magazine/article/0,5744,354948,00.html. Accessed 6 December 2000.

Birch, Debra J. *Pilgrimage to Rome in the Middle Ages: Continuity and Change.* Woodbridge: Boydell Press, 1998.

Brown, Thomas. "The Transformation of the Roman Mediterranean, 400–900" in Holmes, George. *The Oxford Illustrated*

History of the Middle Ages, pp. 1–61. Oxford: Oxford University Press, 2001.

Browner, Jessica A. "'Viking' Pilgrimage to the Holy Land." http://etext.lib.virginia .edu/journals/EH/EH34/browne34.html. Accessed 8 July 2000.

Burton, Robert. *A Strange and True Account of the Late Travels of Two English Pilgrims.* Bristol: Matthews, 1796.

"The Capture of Jerusalem." *Medieval Sourcebook.* http://www.fordham.edu.hal sall/source/1144falljlem.html. Accessed 20 August 2000.

Catholic Encyclopedia. "Jerusalem (After 1291)." http://www.newadvent.org/cathen/ 08364a.htm. Accessed 14 September 2000.

_____. "Pilgrimages." http://www.newadvent .org/cathen/12085a.htm. Accessed 14 September 2000.

Chareyron, Nicole. *Les Pèlerins de Jérusalem au Moyen Age: l'aventure du Saint Voyage d'après Journaux et Mémoires.* Paris: Imago, 2000.

Chaucer, Geoffrey. *The Canterbury Tales.* London: Penguin, 1996.

Chélini, Jean, and Henry Branthomme. *Les Chemins de Dieu: Histoire des pèlerinages chrétiens, des origines à nos jours.* Paris: Hachette, 1982.

Christensen, Bernhard. *The Inward Passage: An Introduction to Christian Spiritual Classics.* Minneapolis: Augsburg, 1996.

Christian Classics Ethereal Library. Appendix VIII, "Rabbinic Traditions about Elijah, the Forerunner of the Messiah." www.ccel.org/e/edersheim/lifetimes/htm/ APPENDICES.APPENDIXVIII. Accessed 22 February 2001.

Christian Education Office. *Holy Week and the Easter Feast* [2001]. Jerusalem: Christian Education Office, no date.

Cohen, Yoel. "The Political Role of the Israeli Chief Rabbinate in the Temple Mount Question" in *Jewish Political Studies Review*, vol. 11:12 (Spring 1999). http: //www.jcpa.org/jpsr/s99-yc.htm. Accessed 7 September 2000.

Coleman, Simon, and John Elsner. *Pilgrimage Past and Present: Sacred Travel and Sacred Space in the World Religions.* London: British Museum Press, 1995.

Comay, Joan. *The Temple of Jerusalem with a History of the Temple Mount.* London: Weidenfeld and Nicholson, 1975.

Conder, C. R. *Tent Work in Palestine: A Record of Discovery and Adventure.* 2 vols. London: Bentley, 1878.

_____, and H. H. Kitchener. *The Survey of Western Palestine: Memoirs of the Topography, Orography, Hydrography, and Archeology.* Vol. 1. London: Palestine Exploration Fund, 1881.

Connolly, Mark, Margaret Greenwood and Geoff Wallis. *Dublin.* London: Rough Guides, 2000.

Constable, Giles. *Cluny from the Tenth to the Twelfth Centuries.* Aldershot: Ashgate Variorum, 2000.

Coulton, G.G. (ed. and trans.). *A Medieval Garner: Human Documents from the Four Centuries Preceding the Reformation.* London: Constable, 1910.

Council on Foreign Relations. "Excerpts from the Text of the Mitchell Commission Report." 7 May 2001. http://www. cfr.org/p/pubs/MitchellComm_Report. html.

Demurger, Alain. *Brève Histoire des Ordres Religieux Militaires: Hospitaliers, Templiers, Teutoniques....* Gavaudun: Editions Fragile, 1997.

Dowman, Keith. *Power Places in Kathmandu: Hindu and Buddhist Holy Sites in the Sacred Valley of Nepal.* Rochester: Inner Traditions, 1995.

Duncan, Alistair. *The Noble Sanctuary: Portrait of a Holy Place in Arab Jerusalem.* London: Middle East Archive, 1972.

Dunn, Maryjane, and Linda Kay Davidson. *The Pilgrimage to Compostela in the Middle Ages: A Book of Essays.* New York: Garland, 1996.

Egerton, Lady Francis. *Journal of a Tour in the Holy Land, in May and June, 1840.* London: Harrison, 1841.

Egremont, Max. *Balfour: A Lie of Arthur James Balfour.* London: Collins, 1980.

Einhard. *The Life of Charlemagne.* http://

pages.prodigy.com/charlemagne/index.htm. Accessed 10 July 2000.

Elad, Amikam. *Medieval Jerusalem and Islamic Worship: Holy Places, Ceremonies, Pilgrimage.* Leiden: Brill, 1995.

El-Awaisi, Abd al–Fattah. *Jerusalem in Islamic History and Spirituality: The Significance of Jerusalem in Islam.* Dunblane: Islamic Research Academy, 1997.

_____. "The Significance of Jerusalem in Islam: An Islamic Perspective," *Journal of Islamic Jerusalem Studies* (Dunblane: 1998), vol. 1, no. 2, Summer 1998, pp. 47–71.

Eliade, Mircea. *Images and Symbols: Studies in Religious Symbolism* (trans. Philip Mairet). Princeton: Princeton University Press, 1991.

_____. *The Myth of the Eternal Return or, Cosmos and History* (trans. Willard R. Trask). New York: Princeton University Press and the Bollingen Foundation, 1974. (Republished by Garland in 1985.)

Eliot, T.S. *The Complete Poems and Plays of T S Eliot.* London: Book Club Associates, 1977.

Ellis, Henry (ed.). *Pylgrymage of Sir Richard Guyleford to the Holy Land, A.D. 1506.* London: Camden, Society, 1851.

Encyclopaedia Britannica Online. "Augsburg Confession." http://www.members.eb.com/bol/topic?eu=11374&sctn=1. Accessed 29 October 2000.

_____. "Humanism." http://www.members.eb.com/bol/topic?eu=109245&sctn=6. Accessed 30 October 2000.

_____. "Mysticism: Symbolism of the journey." http://www.members.eb.com.bol/topic?eu=117397&sctn=21. Accessed 19 November 1999.

Erdmann, Carl. *The Origin of the Idea of Crusade* (trans. Marshall W. Baldwin and Walter Goffart). Princeton: Princeton University Press, 1977.

Fletcher, Richard. *The Barbarian Conversion: From Paganism to Christianity.* Berkeley: University of California Press, 1999.

Foss, Michael. *People of the First Crusade.* New York: Arcade, 1997.

French, Dorothea B. "Journeys to the Center of the Earth: Medieval and Renaissance Pilgrimages to Mount Calvary" in Sargent-Baur, Barbara N. (ed.). *Journeys Toward God: Pilgrimage and Crusade.* Kalamazoo: Western Michigan University, 1992, pp. 45–81.

Fromkin, David. *A Peace to End All Peace: The Fall of the Ottoman Empire and the Creation of the Modern Middle East.* London: Phoenix, 2000.

Fuller, Thomas. *A Pisgah-sight of Palestine.* Aberdeen: King, 1869.

Gabrieli, Francesco. *Arab Historians of the Crusades* (trans. E. J. Costello). New York: Barnes and Noble, 1969.

Garaudy, Roger. "The Dome of the Rock." http://users.erols.com/ameen/domerock.htm. Accessed 18 February 2001.

Gil, Moshe. *A History of Palestine, 634–1099* (trans. Ethel Brodio). Cambridge: Cambridge University Press, 1992.

Gilbert, Martin. *Jerusalem: Illustrated History Atlas.* Third ed. London: Vallentine Mitchell, 1994.

_____. *Jerusalem in the Twentieth Century.* London: Pimlico, 1997

Glaber, Rodulfus. *The Five Books of the Histories.* John France (ed.). Oxford: Clarendon, 1989.

_____. "On the First Millennium." http://www.veling.nl/anne/templars/glaber-1000.html. Accessed 20 August 00.

Goetz, Hans-Werner (trans. Albert Wimmer). *Life in the Middle Ages: From the Seventh to the Thirteenth Century.* Notre Dame: University of Notre Dame Press, 1993.

Graves, Philip. *Palestine, the Land of Three Faiths.* London: Cape, 1923.

Hakluyt, Richard. *Voyages and Discoveries: The Principal Navigations, Voyages, Traffiques and Discoveries of the English Nation* (ed. Jack Beeching). Harmondsworth: Penguin, 1985.

Hasselquist, Frederick. *Voyages and Travels in the Levant; In the Years 1749, 50, 51, 52.* London: Davis, 1766.

Hay, Jeff (ed.). *The Early Middle Ages.* San Diego: Greenhaven, 2001.

Herzl, Theodor. *The Jewish State*. New York: Dover, 1988.

Hess, Moses. *The Revival of Israel: Rome and Jerusalem, the Last Nationalist Question*. Lincoln: University of Nebraska Press, 1995.

Histoire anonyme de la première croisade, 37–38, trad. Louis Bréhier, Paris, *Les Belles Lettres*, 1964. Cited by Histoire Géographie sur le Web, http://www.multimania.com/coll3/croisade.html. Accessed 13 August 2000.

Hockstader, Lee. "Jerusalem, City of Faith, Defies Rational Solution," *International Herald Tribune*, 21 July 2000.

Hoffman, Rabbi Lawrence A. *Israel, a Spiritual Travel Guide: A Companion for the Modern Jewish Pilgrim*. Woodstock: Jewish Lights, 1998.

The Holy Bible. New Revised Standard Edition. New York: Collins, 1989.

Horowitz, Dan, and Moshe Lissak. *Origins of the Israeli Policy: Palestine under the Mandate*. Chicago: University of Chicago Press, 1978.

Houseley, David, and Raymond Goodburn. *The Holy Land: Israel and Jordan—A Guide for Christian Visitors*. Woodbridge: Pilgrim Book Services, 1998.

Howe, Kathleen Stewart. *Revealing the Holy Land: The Photographic Explorations of Palestine*. Santa Barbara: Santa Barbara Museum of Art, 1997.

Hunt, E.D. *Holy Land Pilgrimage in the Later Roman Empire A.D. 312–460*. Oxford: Clarendon, 1982.

Hyams, Paul. "Appendix of Case Narratives." http:www.netserf.org/Features/Search/default.cfm. Accessed 25 March 2001.

International Herald Tribune. "Sir Steven Runciman, 97, Historian of the Crusades." 3 November 2000.

Jacobs, Daniel. *Jerusalem: Mini Rough Guide*. London: Rough Guides, 1999.

Jacobson, David M. "Search for the Holy Temple" in *Eretz: The Geographic Magazine from Israel*, no. 52, May–June 1997, pp. 26–34.

Janin, Hunt. *Cultures of the World: Saudi Arabia*. Singapore: Times Editions, 1992.

The Jerusalem Mosaic. http://jeru.huji.ac.il/eb1s.htm. Accessed December 19, 1999.

Jerusalem Quarterly File, "Maundrell in Jerusalem: Reflections on the Writing of an Early European Tourist." http://www.jqf-jerusalem.org/journal/2000/jqf9/classical.html. Accessed 28 October 2000.

Johnson, Barbara A. *Reading* Piers Plowman *and* The Pilgrim's Progress: *Reception and the Protestant Reader*. Carbondale: Southern Illinois University Press, 1992.

Joint Association of Classical Teachers' Greek course. *The World of Athens: An Introduction to Classical Athenian Culture*. Cambridge: Cambridge University Press, 1996.

Jones, Terry, and Alan Ereira. *Crusades*. London: BBC Books, 1994.

Josephus, Flavius. *The Destruction of the Jews* (trans. and ed. G.W. Williamson). London: Folio Society, 1971.

Kelly, Thomas L., and Patricia Roberts. *Kathmandu: City on the Edge of the World*. New York: Abbeville, 1989.

Kempe, Margery. *The Book of Margery Kempe*. http://www.luminarium.org/medlit/Kempe4.htm. Accessed 8 July 2000 (citing *The Norton Anthology of English Literature*, 6th Ed. Vol. 1. New York: Norton, 1993, no page number given).

Kenyon, Kathleen M. *Digging Up Jerusalem*. London: Benn, 1974.

Kernohan, R. D. *The Road to Zion: Travellers to Palestine and the Land of Israel*. Grand Rapids: Eerdmans, 1995.

Khalidi, Walid. "Before Their Diaspora." http://www.ojerusalem.com/previous/june/june_from2.html. Accessed 8 July 2000.

_____. *Islam, the West, and Jerusalem*. Washington, D.C.: Center for Contemporary Arab Studies, Georgetown University Press, 1996.

Khosraw, Naser-e (trans. W. M. Thackston, Jr.). *Book of Travels*. Albany: State University of New York Press, 1986.

Koester, James. "A Time of Renewal in the Holy Land," *Cowley*, Vol. 26, No. 1, Spring

2000, pp. 12–14. Cambridge: Society of Saint John the Evangelist.

Kölver, Bernhard. *Re-Building a Stupa: Architectural Drawings of the Svayambhunath.* Bonn: VGH Wissenschaftsverlag, 1992.

Komoroff, Manuel (ed.). *Contemporaries of Marco Polo, Consisting of the Travel Records to the Eastern Parts of the World … & The Oriental Travels of Rabbi Benjamin of Tudela (1160–1173).* New York: Boni & Liveright, 1928.

Kühnel, Bianca (ed.). *The Real and Ideal Jerusalem in Jewish, Christian and Islamic Art.* Jerusalem: Hebrew University, 1998.

Landow, George P. "The Pisgah Sight—Typological Image." http://www.thecore.nus.edu.sg/landow/victorian/type/pisgah.html. Accessed 27 October 2000.

Latin Patriarchate of Jerusalem. *Welcome to the Holy Land: Year of the Great Jubilee, Christmas Eve 1999–6 January 2001.* Jerusalem: Latin Patriarchate Printing Press, no date.

Le Strange, Guy. *Palestine under the Moslems: A description of Syria and the Holy Land from A.D. 650 to 1500.* London: published by Alexander P. Watt for the Committee of the Palestine Exploration Fund, 1890.

Levine, Lee I. (ed.). *Jerusalem: Its Sanctity and Centrality to Judaism, Christianity, and Islam.* New York: Continuum, 1999.

_____. *The Jerusalem Cathedra: Studies in the History, Archaeology, Geography and Ethnography of the Land of Israel.* 3 vols. Jerusalem: Izhak Ben-Zvi Institute, 1981–1983.

Library of the Theological Seminary of America. *Towards the Eternal Center.* New York, 1996.

Loftie, W. J. (ed.). *Ye Oldest Diarie of Englysshe Travell: Being the Hitherto Unpublished Narrative of the Pilgrimage of Sir Richard Torkyington to Jerusalem in 1517.* London: Leadenhalle, 1857.

Maalouf, Amin. *Les croisades vues par les Arabes.* Paris: J. C. Lattès, 1983.

Macfie, A. L. *The Eastern Question, 1774–1923.* London: Longman, 1989.

McKitterick, Rosamond (ed.). *The Early Middle Ages: Europe 400–1000.* Oxford: Oxford University Press, 2001.

Maier, Paul L. (trans. and ed.) *Josephus: The Essential Works.* Grand Rapids: Kregel, 1994.

Al-Makrisi. "Account of the Crusade of St. Louis." *Medieval Sourcebook.* www.fordham.edu/halsall/source/makrisi. Accessed 20 August 2000.

Mandeville, Sir John. *The Travels of Sir John Mandeville.* (trans. and ed. C.W.R.D. Moseley). London: Penguin, 1983.

Matthew, Antony. *Pilgrims to Jerusalem.* Sevenoaks: Fisher, 1999.

Maundrell, Henry. *A Journey from Aleppo to Jerusalem at Easter A.D. 1697.* Beirut: Khayats, 1963.

Mazar, Benjamin. *The Mountain of the Lord.* Garden City, N.Y.: Doubleday, 1975.

Medieval Sourcebook. "Tales of the Virgin." http://www.fordham.edu/halsall/source/tales-virgiin.html. Accessed 4 October 2000.

_____. "Urban II (1088–1099): Speech at Council of Clermont, 1095, Five versions of the Speech." http:/www.fordham.edu/halsall/source/urban2-5vers.html. Accessed 12 June 2000.

Merdrignac, Bernard, and Patrick Mérienne. *Le Moyen Age dans le monde.* Rennes: Éditions Ouest-France, 1999.

Michelant, Henri, and Gaston Raynaud. *Itinéraires à Jérusalem et Descriptions de la Terre Sainte.* Geneva: Fick, 1882.

Ministry of Foreign Affairs, "Focus on Jerusalem—Architecture in the late Ottoman Period," http://www.mfa.gov.il/mfa/go.asp?MFAH0et80. Accessed 19 December 2000.

Morris, Roderick Conway. "Keepers of the Shrines: A Visit to the Holy Land of Muslim and Christian," *International Herald Tribune,* 11–12 March 2000.

Moscrop, John James. *Measuring Jerusalem: The Palestine Exploration Fund and British Interests in the Holy Land.* London: Leicester University Press, 2000.

Netton, Ian Richard (ed.). *Golden Roads: Migration, Pilgrimage and Travel in Medi-*

aeval and Modern Islam. Richmond: Curzon, 1993.

Newett, M. Margaret (trans.). *Canon Pietro Casola's Pilgrimage to Jerusalem in the Year 1494*. Manchester: Manchester University Press, 1907.

Nicholl, Donald (ed. Adrian Hastings). *The Testing of Hearts: A Pilgrim's Journey*. London: Darton, Longman and Todd, 1998.

Nicholson, Helen. *Templars, Hospitallers and Teutonic Knights: Images of the Military Orders, 1128–1291*. Leicester: Leicester University Press, 1993.

Orme, William A. "Construction at 2,000-Year-Old Religious Site Unleashes a Tempest," *International Herald Tribune*, December 23, 1999.

_____. "For Ex-General, Another Battle Won," *International Herald Tribune*, February 7, 2001.

Osher Map Library. *Jerusalem 3000: Three Millennia of History*." http://www.usm.maine.edu/~maps/exhibit1/. Accessed 14 June 2000.

Painter, Sidney. *A History of the Middle Ages, 284–1500*. London: Macmillan, 1975.

Palestine Exploration Fund. *Frederick H. Bliss*. http://www.pef/org.uk/Pages/Bliss.htm. Accessed 14 October 2000.

_____. *Introduction*. http://www.pef.org.uk/Pages/into.htm. Accessed 14 October 2000.

Palestine Pilgrims' Text Society. *Description of the Land, by John of Würzburg (A.D. 1160–1170)* (trans. Aubrey Stewart). Vol. 5. London: Palestine Pilgrim's Text Society, 1890.

_____. *Felix Fabri (c. 1480–1483 A.D.)* (trans. Aubrey Stewart). 2 vols. London: Palestine Pilgrims' Text Society, 1892 and 1897.

_____. *The Hodoeporcion* [Guidebook] *of Saint Willibald (c. 754 A.D.)* (trans. Rev. Canon Brownlow). Vol. III. London: Palestine Pilgrims' Text Society, 1891.

_____. *The Pilgrimage of the Russian Abbot Daniel in the Holy Land, 1106–1107 A.D.* (ed. C.W. Wilson). Vol. IV. Palestine Pilgrims' Text Society, 1897.

Pearson, Paul M. "Celtic Monasticism as a Metaphor for Thomas Merton's Journey."

http://www.ucl.ac.uk/~ucylpmp/celtic.htm. Accessed 30 July 2000.

Pemberton, Cintra. *Soulfaring: Celtic Pilgrimage Then and Now*. Harrisburg: Morehouse, 1999.

Pernoud, Régine. *Les Hommes de la Croisade*. Paris: Fayard/Tallandier, revised ed. 1982.

Peters, F.E. *Jerusalem: The Holy City in the Eyes of Chroniclers, Visitors, Pilgrims, and Prophets from the Days of Abraham to the Beginnings of Modern Times*. Princeton: Princeton University Press, 1985.

_____. *Jerusalem and Mecca: The Typology of the Holy City in the Near East*. New York: New York University Press, 1986.

Petit Guide. *Le Moyen Age*. Vichy: Aedis, 1999.

Philips, Jonathan (ed.). *The First Crusade: Origins and Impact*. Manchester: Manchester University Press, 1997.

Pococke, Richard. *A Description of the East, and Some Other Countries*. 2 vols. London: Bowyer, 1743–145.

Polowetzky, Michael. *Jerusalem Recovered: Victorian Intellectuals and the Birth of Modern Zionism*. Westport: Prager, 1995.

Prag, Kay. *Blue Guide Jerusalem*. London: Black, 1989.

Prawer, Joshua, and Haggai Ben-Shammai (eds.). *The History of Jerusalem: The Early Muslim Period 638–1099*. Jerusalem: Yad Izhak Ben-Zvi, 1996.

Prescott, H. F. M. *Jerusalem Journey: Pilgrimage to the Holy Land in the Fifteenth Century*. London: Eyre & Spottiswoode, 1954.

"Punishment of the Pillory and Whetstone, for Pretending to Be a Hermit." *The Geoffrey Chaucer Page*. http://www.courses.fas.harvard.edu/~chaucer/special/varia/pilgrimage/falsepil.html. Accessed 30 July 2000.

Raben, Remco, and Dhiravat na Pombejra. *In the King's Trail: An 18th Century Dutch Journey to the Buddha's Footprint*. Bangkok: Royal Netherlands Embassy, 1997.

Read, Piers Paul. *The Templars*. London: Weidenfeld and Nicolson, 1999.

Regnaut, Anthoine. *Discours de voyage d'outre mer au Saincte Sépulcre de Ieru-*

salem [*sic*] *et autres lieux de la terre Saincte.* Lyon: no publisher given, 1573.

Régnier-Bohler, Danielle (ed.). *Croisades et Pèlerinages: Récits, Chroniques et Voyages en Terre Sainte, XIIe–XVIe Siècle.* Paris: Laffont, 1997.

Rempel, Gerhard. "The Crimean War: 1853–1856." http://mars.acnet.wnec.edu/~grempel/courses/russia/lectures/19crimeanwar.html. Accessed 5 November 2000.

Reuter, Timothy (trans.). *Fulk Nerra's Pilgrimage to Jerusalem.* http://humanities.uwe.ac.uk/corehistorians/papacy/document/doc_107a.htm. Accessed 30 July 2000.

Richard, Jean. *Histoire des Croisades.* Paris: Fayard, 1996.

Riley-Smith, Jonathan. *Hospitallers: The History of the Order of St John.* London: Hambledon Press, 1999.

"Robert the Monk," pp. 3–5 in *Medieval Sourcebook: Urban II (1088–1099): Speech at Council of Clermont, 1095, Five versions of the Speech.* http://www.fordham.edu/halsall/source/urban2-5vers.html. Accessed 12 June 2000.

Roberts, David. *The Holy Land.* London: Studio Editions, 1990.

Robinson, Edward. *Biblical Researches in Palestine and the Adjacent Regions: A Journal of Travels in the Years 1838 & 1852.* 3 vols. London: Murray, 1867.

Robinson, Martin. *Sacred Places, Pilgrim Paths: An Anthology of Pilgrimage.* London: Fount, 1998.

Rosenau, Helen. *Visions of the Temple: The Image of the Temple of Jerusalem in Judaism and Christianity.* London: Oresko, 1979.

Rosovsky, Nitza (ed.). *City of the Great King: Jerusalem from David to the Present.* Cambridge: Harvard University Press, 1996.

Rowley, H. H. *Worship in Ancient Israel: Its Forms and Meaning.* London: S.P.C.K., 1967.

Rubenstein, Jeffery L. *The History of Sukkot in the Second Temple and Rabbinical Periods.* Atlanta, Ga.: Scholar's Press, 1995.

Runciman, Steven. *A History of the Crusades: Vol. 1. The First Crusade and the Foun-*dation of the Kingdom of Jerusalem.* Harmondsworth: Penguin, 1951.

Said, Edward W. *Orientalism.* New York: Vintage, 1994.

Samuel, Sir Herbert. "An Interim Report on the Civil Administration of Palestine, During the Period 1st July, 1920–30th June, 1921." http://domino.un.org/UNISPAL.NSF/a.../349b02280a930813052565e90048edlc!OpenDocumen. Accessed 4 March 2001.

Sanders, E. P. *Judaism, Practice and Belief, 63 BCE–66 CE.* London: SCM Press, 1992.

Sanders, Ronald. *The High Walls of Jerusalem: A History of the Balfour Declaration and the Birth of the British Mandate for Palestine.* New York: Holt, Rinehart and Winston, 1983.

Sargent-Baur, Barbara N. (ed.). *Journeys toward God: Pilgrimage and Crusade.* Kalamazoo: Western Michigan University, 1992.

Sax, William S. *Mountain Goddess: Gender and Politics in a Himalayan Pilgrimage.* New York: Oxford University Press, 1991.

Schweid, Eliezer (trans. Deborah Greniman). *The Land of Israel: National Home or Land of Destiny.* Canterbury: Associated University Presses, 1985.

Scott, Jamie, and Paul Simpson-Housley. *Sacred Places and Profane Spaces: Essays in the Geographics of Judaism, Christianity, and Islam.* Westport, Conn.: Greenwood Press, 1991.

Serao, Matilde (trans. Richard Davey). *In the Country of Jesus.* London: Nelson, 1919.

Silberman, Neil Asher. *Digging for God and Country: Exploration, Archeology, and the Secret Struggle for the Holy Land, 1799–1917.* New York: Knopf, 1982.

Sim, Katharine. *David Roberts R.A., 1796–1864: A Biography.* London: Quartet, 1984.

Simon, Anne. "In pilgers weys: Medieval Pilgrimage Literature: The Problems of a Genre." http://www.laurentian.ca/www/engl/arachne/vol11/simon.htm. Accessed 15 September 2000.

Sinclair, Andrew. *Jerusalem: The Endless Crusade.* London: Century, 1996.

Sontag, Deborah. "Harsh Israeli Words for Nonvisiting Jews," *International Herald Tribune*, 12 June 2001.

Steinbeck, John. *The Red Pony*. New York: Covici-Friede, 1937.

Stopford H. (ed.). *Pilgrimage Explored*. York: York Medieval Press, 1999.

Thorpe, William. *The Examination of Master William Thorpe, Priest, of Heresy, Before Thomas Arundel, Archbishop of Canterbury, in the Year of Our Lord 1407*. http://www.courses.fas.harvard.edu/~chaucer/special/varia/pilgrimage/thorpe.html. Accessed 30 July 2000.

Touati, Houari. *Islam et voyage au Moyen Age*. Paris: Seuil, 2000.

The Tower of David Museum. Jerusalem: Tower of David Museum of the History of Jerusalem, 1992.

Tubb, Jonathan N. *Canaanites*. London: British Museum Press, 1998.

_____, and Rupert L. Chapman. *Archeology and the Bible*. London: British Museum Press, 1990.

Tuchman, Barbara W. *Bible and Sword: How the British Came to Palestine*. London: Macmillan, 1983.

_____. *A Distant Mirror: The Calamitous 14th Century*. New York: Ballantine, 1979.

Turner, Victor, and Edith Turner. *Image and Pilgrimage in Christian Culture: Anthropological Perspectives*. New York: Columbia University Press, 1978.

Twain, Mark. *The Innocents Abroad, or The New Pilgrims Progress*. New York: Penguin, 1966.

Tyron, Richard. *Travels from Aleppo to the City of Jerusalem; and Through the most remarkable Parts of the Holy Land in 1776*. Glasgow: no publisher given, 1790.

U.S. Department of State. *Country Reports on Human Rights Practices— 2000: Israel*. Released by the Bureau of Democracy, Human Rights, and Labor, February 2001. http://www.state.gov/g/drl/rls/hrrpt/2000/nea/index.cfm?docid=794.

_____. *Country Reports on Human Rights Practices— 2000: Occupied Territories*. Released by the Bureau of Democracy, Human Rights, and Labor, February 2001. http://www.state.gov/g/drl/rls/hrrpt/2000/nea/index.cfm?docid=882.

_____. *2000 Annual Report on International Religious Freedom: Israel*. Released by the Bureau of Democracy, Human Rights, and Labor, 5 September 2000. http://www.state.gov/www/global/human_rights/irf/irf_rpt/.

_____. *2000 Annual Report on International Religious Freedom: The Occupied Territories (Including Areas Subject to the Jurisdiction of the Palestinian Authority)*. Released by the Bureau of Democracy, Human Rights, and Labor, 5 September 2000. http://www.state.gov/www/global/human_rights/irf/irf_rpt/.

VanDoodewaard, William. *Hadith Authenticity: A Survey of Perspectives*, unpublished article, The University of Western Ontario, London (Canada), 1996. http://www.rim.org/muslim.hadith/htm. Accessed 9 November 2000.

Vaughan, Richard. *The Illustrated Chronicles of Matthew Paris: Observations of Thirteenth-Century Life*. Cambridge: Sutton, 1993.

Volney, C. F. *Travels through Syria and Egypt, in the Years 1783–1784, and in 1785*. 2 vols. London: Robinson, 1787.

Warburton, Eliot. *The Crescent and the Cross*. 14th ed. London: Ward, Lock, 1888.

Webb, Diana. *Pilgrims and Pilgrimage in the Medieval West*. London: Tauris, 1999.

Wey, William. *Itinerary for a Pilgrimage to Jerusalem*. Geoffrey Chaucer Page. http://www.icg.fas.harvard.edu/~chaucer/special/varia/pilgrimage/wm-wey.html. Accessed 30 July 2000.

Wigoder, Geoffrey. "Pilgrims' Progress in the Holy Land," *The Jerusalem Post*, Internet Edition, http://info.jpost.com/2000/Supplements/Millennium/pilgrims5.html. Accessed 15 June 2000.

Wilken, Robert L. *The Land Called Holy: Palestine in Christian History & Thought*. New Haven: Yale University Press, 1992.

Wilkinson, John. *Egeria's Travels to the Holy Land*. Revised ed. Jerusalem: Ariel, 1981.

_____. *Jerusalem Pilgrimage, 1099–1185*. London: Kakluyt, 1988.

_____. *Jerusalem Pilgrims Before the Crusades*. Warminster: Aris and Phillips, 1997.

Williams, Wes. *Pilgrimage and Narrative in the French Renaissance*. Oxford: Clarendon, 1998.

Wilson, Colonel C.W. (ed.). *Picturesque Palestine*. 4 vols. London: Virtue, 1880.

Woolf, Virginia. *The Common Reader: First Series*. London: Hogarth, 1984.

Wright, Thomas (ed.). *Early Travels in Palestine*. London: Bohn, 1848.

Yulish, Stephen M. "Ashes of the Red Heifer." http://www.direct.ca/trinity/ashes.html. Accessed 6 May 2001.

The Zionist Century. "The Balfour Declaration: A Watershed in the History of the Zionist Movement." http://www.jajz-ed.org.il/100/act/23/zion.html. Accessed 8 September 2000.

Index

'Abd al-Malik 72
Abu Hamid al-Ghazali 95
Abu I-Fida 121
Abu Mu'in Nasir 80–81
Acre 98, 107, 110, 111, 114, 115, 116, 117, 120, 121, 122, 131, 142, 148
Adelbert 183
Adomnan 70
Aelia Capitolina 50, 57
Affagart, Greffin 151
Albert, Prince of Wales 169
Albright, William Foxwell 192–193
'Ali al-Hawari 106–107
Aliya ("going up to") 82–83
Alkerton, Richard 127, 128
Allenby, Sir Edmund 5, 34, 187, 191–192, 192
Amin al-Husseini 193
Aqsa Mosque 1, 31, 33, 37, 69, 72, 73, 78, 81, 82, 93, 99, 101, 106, 108, 116, 143, 153, 163, 174, 177, 193, 194
Archeology 7
Arculf 70–71
Arnulf 93
Aristeas 49
Ark of the Covenant 21, 44, 45, 46, 72, 113, 146, 184, 185
Ashley-Cooper, Anthony (Lord Shaftsbury) 189–190
Astarte 43
Augustine, St. 10, 64
Atheism 11
Azario, Pietro 18

Baal 43
Balfour, Arthur James 187–188, 190–191
Balfour Declaration 34, 160, 187–188, 189, 191, 192

Bar Koseba, Simon 57
Bar Sauma 65
Barak, Ehud 1
Barbarossa, Holy Roman Emperor Frederick 110
Barlourdet, Loys 152
Bartlett, W.H. 164–165
Baybars I (Mamluk sultan) 119, 121
Bazaars 143
Bede, Venerable 70, 97
Bedouin 8, 69, 70, 84, 85, 99, 123, 127, 131, 134, 137, 148, 153, 156, 157, 160, 166, 205
Benjamin of Tudela 104–105
Bernard of Clairvaux, St. 100, 103
Bertinoro, Obidiah ben Abraham Yare 140–141
Blakeney, William 129
Bliss, Frederick H. 178–179, 184
Blyth, Estelle 185
Boniface, St. 18
Book of Arousing Souls 145
Bordeaux Pilgrim 59, 60–61
Bradford, William 10
Breviarius 66
Broquière, Bertrandon de la 131
Buddhist temples (*stupas*) 13
Bunyan, John 10, 11, 154, 190
Burchard of Mount Sion 115, 120–121
Butler, Elizabeth 179–180

Canterbury Tales 9, 14, 15
Casolla, Pietro 141–144
Castela, Henri de 152
Castle Pilgrim 115, 121
Caumont, Nompar de 129–130
Chanson de geste 74
Charlemagne 73–74
Chartres, Fulcher de 93

Chateaubriand, François-Auguste-René de 160, 162
Chaucer, Geoffrey 9, 14, 15, 16, 190, 203
Chelebi, Evliye 153
Chelo, Issac ben Joseph ibn 123
Children's Crusade 113–114
City of God 10
Clawson, Mary 194
Cluny 75, 88, 89
Cohen, Jacob ha 107
Conder, Claude Reignier 3, 176
Constantine the Great 50, 59, 60, 62, 66, 70, 71
Constantinople 62, 65, 70, 82, 84, 90, 91, 92, 99, 112, 126, 148, 159, 167, 189
Cook, Thomas 174–176
Council of Clermont (France) 89, 90
Council of Piacenza (Italy) 89
Crimean War 148, 167–168
Croisé (marked with the cross) 86
Crouch, Nathaniel 156–157
Crusade(s) 15, 67, 69, 83, 87, 88, 89–95, 99, 103–104, 107, 110–112, 113–114, 115–116, 117, 118, 120, 130–131, 159, 168
Crusader(s) 73, 74, 86, 89, 99, 100, 103, 104, 107, 108, 112, 114, 116, 118, 120, 121, 122, 131

Daniel 77
Darani 75–76
David, career of 44–45
Davidson Exhibition and Virtual Reconstruction Center 52
Diderot, Denis 11

Dome of the Rock 5, 31, 32, 33, 37, 69, 72, 73, 81, 82, 93, 106, 108, 116, 139, 146, 150, 156, 163, 167, 193, 194

Eastern Question 148
Eckehart, Meister 10
Egeria 59, 62–63
Egerton, Lady Francis 163–164
Eirik the Good 98
Eliade, Mircea 15–16
Eliot, T.S. 16
Elijah of Ferrara 132
Eucherius 65
Eudokia, Empress 65
Eusebius 59, 61

Fabri, Felix 70, 134–137
fada'il 145
First Guide 97
First Temple (Jerusalem) 21, 45–47
Five Pillars of Islam 28
Frederick II (Germany) 115–116
Fulcher de Chartres 93–94, 95
Fulk III Nerra 78–79
Fuller, Thomas 153

George, Lloyd 3
"Gentile Zionism" 188–190
Ghostly 9, 12, 15, 16, 18
Glaber, Rodolfus 74, 79, 80
Goodrich-Freer, Ada 183–184
Goldhizer, Ignaz 176–177
Graham, Stephen 185–186
Graves, Philip 193
Gregory of Nyssa 18, 61–62
Guibert of Nogent 90, 113
Guilford, Richard 145–146
Guillaume de Tyr (William of Tyre) 99

Ha Cohen, Rabbi Jonathan 113
Ha-Levi, Judah 102–103
Hanukkah ("Dedication") 48
Haram al-Sharif 1, 7, 31, 34, 37, 70, 72, 77, 78, 82, 109, 145, 148, 150, 151, 153, 154, 168, 170, 172, 173, 184, 185, 194, 197; *see also* Temple Mount
al-Harizi, Yehuda 41, 115
Al-Harun al-Rashid 73–74
Hasselquist, Frederick 157–158
Helena, visit to Jerusalem 59, 62, 70
Hellfire Club 5
Herbert of Patsley 112
Herod 50–51, 52, 54
Herodian Temple 21–22, 50–53, 56–57
Herzl, Theodor 181–182

Hess, Moses 34, 102, 168–169
Hilarion, St. 18
Hilton, Walter 12
Holy Fire 77, 80, 95, 106, 107, 127, 155, 156, 157, 159, 164, 176, 185, 205
Holy war, Christian concept of 88, 89
Holy Sepulcher, Church of the 25, 26, 26, 28, 37, 38, 50, 59, 63, 67, 69, 71, 77, 78, 79, 80, 85, 86, 89, 94, 95, 100, 104, 105, 106, 106, 108, 117, 123, 124, 127, 129, 130, 131, 133, 135, 136, 139, 140, 142, 143, 148, 150, 151, 153, 155, 156, 161, 162, 163, 164, 165, 167, 174, 179, 180, 184, 197

Ibn 'Abd Rabbih 76
Ibn al-Athir 93, 108
Ibn Battuta 123–124
Ibn Daud 71–72
Ibn al-Faqih 76
Ibn al-Muqaddesi 76–77
Ibn al-Murajja 81, 151
Ibn al-Qalanisi 104
Ibn Taymiyya 145
Ihram (state of ritual purity) 76
Imad ad-Din al-Isfahani 108
Ingulphus 84, 85
Intifada (Palestinian uprising) 1, 3
Israel (also Israeli and Israelis) 1, 3, 4, 41, 52, 54, 83, 102, 103, 107, 116, 182, 186, 187, 190, 194, 195, 197, 198, 200

Jacob, Rabbi 116
Jaffa 85, 96, 97, 98, 115, 131, 133, 134, 137, 139, 141, 142, 144, 145, 149, 150, 159, 162, 163, 166, 179, 180, 183, 185
Jaffa Gate 36, 38, 182, 191, 193
Jerome, St. 61, 63–64
Jerusalem (importance to Jews 19–24; importance to Christians 24–25; importance to Muslims 25, 28–32; importance to secular pilgrims 33–35) 1, 3, 5, 6, 7, 8, 9, 10, 11, 12, 15, 16, 17, 18, 19, 20, 24, 29, 30, 31, 34, 35, 41, 42–44, 45, 46, 47, 48, 50, 51, 53, 56, 58, 60, 61, 62, 64, 65, 66, 67, 68, 69, 70, 71, 73, 74, 75, 76, 77, 78, 79, 80, 81, 82, 83, 84, 85, 86, 87, 88, 89, 90, 91, 92, 93, 94, 95, 96, 97, 98, 99, 100, 101, 102, 103, 104, 105, 106, 107, 108, 109, 110, 111, 112, 113,

114, 115, 116, 118, 120, 121, 123, 124, 125, 126, 127, 128, 129, 130, 131, 132, 133, 134, 135, 136, 137, 139, 140, 141, 142, 143, 144, 145, 146, 147, 148, 149, 150, 151, 152, 153, 154, 155, 156, 157, 158, 159, 160, 161, 162, 163, 164, 165, 166, 167, 168, 169, 170, 171, 172, 173, 174, 175, 176, 177, 178, 179, 181, 182, 183, 184, 185, 186, 187, 188, 189, 190, 191, 192, 193, 194, 195, 196, 197, 198, 199, 200, 201, 202, 203, 204, 205
Jerusalem Cross 169, 170
Jeshua 55
Jesus Christ 24, 44–45, 50, 53, 58, 64, 66, 67, 71, 81, 104, 106, 107, 111, 122, 124, 124, 135, 136, 143, 153, 165, 167, 175, 179, 180, 181, 189, 197, 203, 204
Jihad ("holy struggle") 69, 107
John of Würzburg 99, 106
John Paul II 1, 198–199
Josephus, Flavius 7, 20–21, 50, 54, 55, 56

Kempe, Margery 12, 132
Kenyon, Kathleen Mary 194–195
Knights Hospitaler 86, 99, 100, 101, 104, 111, 118, 140, 142
Knights Templar 73, 86, 99–101, 104, 108, 111, 115, 118
Knytlinaga Saga 98

Lamartine, Alphonse de 161–162
Lethbaud 79–80
Ludolph of Sudheim 124–125

Mahabharata 13
Al-Makrisi 117–118
Mandeville, Sir John 125–127
mappe mundi (map of the world) 17
Maundrell, Henry 154–156
Maurice of Sully 9
Mecca 13, 15, 16, 24, 25, 28, 29, 30, 31, 72, 76, 77, 78, 80, 81, 101, 144, 145, 153, 160, 177, 193
Medina 28, 31, 72, 78, 82, 145, 177
Melania 61, 63
Melito 58
Meshullam, Rabbi 137, 139
Meslier, Jean 11
Milites Christi (Knights of Christ) 89

Muhammad 25, 28–31, 69, 72, 78, 81, 106, 144, 177
Mujir al-Din 144–145

Nachman, Moses ben (Nachmanides) 120
Naser-e Khosraw 81–82
Nasir al-Din 151
Nebi Musa 119, 153, 185, 193
Netanyahu, Benjamin 7
Niccolo of Poggibonsi 124
Nicholl, Donald 198
Night Journey (Isra'), Muhammad's 28–29, 72, 111

Olaf's Saga 98
Origen 58–59, 61
Orientalism 160
Ottobonian Guide 98

Painter-pilgrim 162–163
Palestine Exploration Fund 3, 34, 167, 170, 171–172, 176, 178, 179, 183, 190
Palestinian(s) 1, 3, 8
Paris, Matthew 86, 118–119
Parker, Montague Brownslow 184–185
Passover *see Pesah*
Paston(s) 16
Paul, St., legacy of 58, 61
Paula 63–64
Pelagius 64
Peregrinatio 10, 86
Pesah (Passover) 23, 24, 41, 46, 52, 53–54, 57, 197
Petachia of Ratisbon 107
Peter the Hermit 90–92, 113
Petrie, William Flinders 177–178
Philo of Alexandria 53, 55–56
Piacenza Pilgrim 67
Pilgrim(s) (see also painter-pilgrim and secular pilgrims) 1, 3, 5, 6, 7, 8, 9, 10, 11, 12, 13, 14, 15, 16, 20, 23, 33, 34, 41, 46, 47, 48, 49, 51, 53, 54, 55, 59, 60, 62, 63, 64, 65, 67, 71, 72, 73, 74, 75, 76, 77, 78, 79, 80, 81, 82, 83, 84, 85, 86, 87, 88, 89, 92, 94, 95, 96, 99, 100, 102, 103, 104, 105, 106, 107, 109, 111, 112, 114, 115, 116, 117, 119, 120, 121, 123, 124, 125, 126, 127, 128, 129, 130, 131, 132, 134, 135, 136, 137, 139, 140, 141, 142, 143, 144, 147, 150, 151, 152, 153, 154, 155, 157, 158, 158, 160, 161, 163, 165, 166, 168, 173, 174, 175, 175, 176, 177, 180, 181, 184,

185, 186, 191, 192, 195, 196, 197, 198, 200, 202, 203, 204, 205
Pilgrimage(s) 1, 3, 6, 8, 9, 10, 11, 13, 14, 15, 16, 18, 19, 23, 24, 28, 35, 42, 43, 46, 48, 51, 52, 55, 56, 58, 59, 61, 62, 63, 64, 65, 67, 70, 71, 72, 73, 74, 75, 76, 77, 78, 79, 80, 81, 82, 83, 84, 85, 86, 89, 90, 94, 98, 106, 108, 109, 110, 112, 113, 115, 117, 119, 120, 121, 123, 124, 125, 127, 129, 131, 133, 134, 139, 145, 146, 147, 148, 152, 153, 155, 156, 157, 158, 159, 160, 161, 162, 163, 164, 165, 166, 168, 169, 176, 177, 180, 181, 182, 186, 187, 188, 190, 191, 192, 193, 194, 195, 196, 197, 198, 199, 200, 202, 203, 204
Pilgrim festivals (*Pesah, Shavuot, Sukkot*) 41, 48, 53–54, 54–56, 57, 65, 71, 83, 116, 150, 195, 197
Pilgrimage in the Holy Land (Peregrinatio in terram sanctam) 139
Pilgrim's Progress 10–11, 190
Piloti, Emmanuel 130–131
Pococke, Richard 157

Qualiter 97
Al-Qashashi 154

Ramban Synagogue 120
Raymond of Aguilers 93–94
Regnaut, Antoine 151–152
Reubeni, David 150
Reuwich, Erhard 139
Richard of London 111
Richard of St. Vannes 78
Richard the Lion-hearted 110, 111, 112
"Right of return" 3
Roberts, David 34, 162–163
Robinson, Edward 34, 164
Robinson, Martin 16
Rochechouart, Louis de 133
Rufinus 61, 63

Sacred center(s) 9, 15–16, 20, 72, 100, 102, 105, 106, 136, 145, 195, 202, 205
Saewulf 95–97
Sahlun, Israel ben 83
Saladin 107–109, 110–111
Samson, Samuel ben 113
Scandinavians, pilgrimages of 98–99
Schick, Conrad 167

Second Temple (Jerusalem) 21, 47–49
Secular pilgrims and pilgrimages 3, 18, 36, 147, 148, 149, 155, 157, 158–160, 161, 164, 170, 171, 173, 181, 190–191, 192, 194, 196, 198, 204
Seetzen, Ulrich Jasper 160–161
Serao, Matilde 180–181
Shaftsbury, Lord *see* Ashley-Cooper, Anthony
Sharon, Ariel 1, 196
Shavuot 23, 46, 52, 54, 57, 150, 197
Sieber, W.F. 161
Sigurd 98
Sukkot 23, 46, 52, 54–55, 57, 65, 71, 83, 120, 195, 197
Suleiman 150
Sweyn, Earl 82

Tafurs 113
Tariqahs (Sufi brotherhoods) 156
Teiku ("unresolved," "let it stand") 41
Temple(s) (First, Second, and/or Herodian) 20, 21–23, 37, 42, 45, 46, 47–48, 49, 50–53, 54, 55, 56, 57, 58, 60, 65, 66, 71, 72, 94, 102, 102–103, 116, 163, 165, 174, 184, 185, 196, 197
Temple Mount 1, 33, 37, 38, 43, 45, 51–52, 53, 65, 66, 69, 72, 110, 115, 116, 120, 121, 139,143, 162, 167, 172, 177, 178, 184, 187, 195, 196, 197, 204; *see also* Haram al-Sharif
Teutonic Knights 111, 115, 116
Theodoric (Theoderich) 100, 106
Theodosius 66–67
Thietmar, Magister 114, 115
Thorpe, William 9–10
Torkington, Richard 149–150
The Travels of Sir John Mandeville 125–127
"Triple honorary name," Jerusalem's 30–31
Tristan und Isolde 128
Tubb, Jonathan 19
Tuchman, Barbara 11, 15, 82, 182
Twain, Mark 3, 173–174
Tyron, Richard 158

'Umar, Caliph 70, 71, 73, 108
Urban II 88, 89, 90, 92
United States 3
Usama ibn Munqidh 101–102

Van Fessem, Johanna 199–201
Vitry, Jacques de 116–117, 203
Volney, Constantin-François 158–160
Von Breydenbach, Bernhard 138, 139
Von Strassburg, Gottfried 128

Warburton, Eliot 165–166
Warren, Charles 172–173
Western (Wailing) Wall 1, 5, 22, 23, 37, 51, 65, 69, 72, 123, 137, 150, 174, 184, 195, 196, 197, 199
Wey, William 133
Wilhelm II 182, 184, 191
William of Boldensele 121, 123

Willibald, St. 73, 190
Wilson, Charles 169–171
Woolf, Virginia 16
Worde, Wynkn de 15

Zionism 102, 187, 188
Ziyara (pious visit or pious journey) 78, 145